*The Politics
and
Morality
of
Deviance*

SUNY Series in Deviance and Social Control
Ronald A. Farrell, Editor

THE POLITICS AND MORALITY OF

DEVIANCE

Moral Panics, Drug Abuse,
Deviant Science, and
Reversed Stigmatization

Nachman Ben-Yehuda

STATE UNIVERSITY OF NEW YORK PRESS

0253610

Published by
State University of New York Press, Albany

© 1990 State University of New York

For information, address State University of New York Press,
State University Plaza, Albany, NY 12246

Library of Congress Cataloging-in-Publication Data

Ben-Yehuda, Nachman.
    The politics and morality of deviance : moral panics, drug abuse,
deviant science, and reversed stigmatization / Nachman Ben-Yehuda.
        p.   cm. — (SUNY series in deviance and social control)
    Bibliography: p.
    Includes index.
    ISBN 0-7914-0122-7. — ISBN 0-7914-0123-5 (pbk.)
    1. Deviant behavior — Philosophy.   2. Power (Social sciences)
    3. Deviant behavior — Comparative method.   I. Title.   II. Series.
HM291.B3863   1990
302.5'42 — dc 19   89-4201
                                                                          CIP

10 9 8 7 6 5 4 3 2 1

To
Erich Goode
and
Victor Azarya

Contents

Acknowledgments   ix

Part One: General Theoretical Foundations

Chapter One: Theoretical Foundations: Deviance   3

Chapter Two: Theoretical Foundations:
                The Micro-Macro Link   15

Part Two: The Politics and Morality of Deviance: Theory

Chapter Three: Politics and Deviance   35

Chapter Four: Political Elements in Regular Deviance and
                Political Deviance   65

Part Three: The Politics and Morality of Deviance: Cases

Chapter Five: A May 1982 Drug Scare: Toward a New
                Sociological Synthesis of Moral Panics   97

Chapter Six: Drug Abuse Social Policy in Comparative
                Perspective: When Symbolic-Moral
                Universes Meet   135

Chapter Seven: Deviant Sciences: Early Radio Astronomy   181

Chapter Eight: The Politicization of Deviance: Resisting
                and Reversing Degradation, Stigmatization,
                and Deviantization   221

0253610

Part Four: Concluding Discussion

Chapter Nine: Concluding Discussion   253

Part Five: Notes and Bibliography

Notes   267

Bibliography   285

Index   333

Acknowledgments

Writing a book is a long process. I would first and foremost like to express my deepest gratitude to Etti, Tzach, and Guy, who were most loving, understanding, and patient during this process. My gratitude is also to our parents, Dina, Hanna, and Yehuda.

Menachem and Delila Amir, Gideon Aran, Zvi Ariel, Said Arjomand, Ivan Chase, Nils Christie, Erik Cohen, Stephen Cole, Gerald Cromer, Steve Dubin, Stanley Einstein, S. N. Eisenstadt, Ruth El-Roy, Kai Erikson, Yaron Ezrachi, Ken Feldman, Norman Goodman, Don Handelman, Ziv Hassid, Menachem Horowitz, Mike Inbar, James Inverarity, Einat Usant, Roberta Karant, Baruch Kimmerling, Pat Lauderdale, Rafael Mechoulam, Israel Nachshon, Dan Patinkin, Jim Rule, Adam Seligman, Michael Shalev, Boas Shamir, Vered Vinitzky-Seroussi, and Rachel Wasserfal all helped with good advice, information, and sometimes lengthy discussions of various ideas.

Gary Albrecht and Judith A. Levy provided most useful suggestions and comments for chapter five. Harvey Goldberg's constructive and essential comments on chapter eight are greatly appreciated. The late Joseph Ben-David's comments on the early work in radio astronomy were most helpful. Woodruff T. Sullivan and Grote Reber provided indispensable advice on radio astronomy.

Victor Azarya, Stanley Cohen, Moshe Lissak, Barry Schwartz and William Shaffir gave me some of the most valuable suggestions, ideas and constructive comments. My discussions with Erich Goode, his detailed and continuous suggestions and comments, valuable and generous help and support are gratefully, admirably, and deeply acknowledged. The amount of effort and constructive criticism that went into reading a long manuscript and commenting on it in fact keeps renewing my faith in my colleagues.

I am most thankful to the five anonymous readers whose comments on the original draft helped to improve the quality of the manuscript in numerous and constructive ways.

I am also very grateful for the competent technical assistance given to me by Ora Dill, Michal Falk, Sabina Honigwacks, Anna Ketof, and Nili Sobol. I am grateful to Advanced Communications in Jerusalem and, particularly, to Libby Lazewnik's endless patience and superb typing.

The former "Mercaz Letiud" in the Department of Sociology, Hebrew University, provided the necessary newspaper clips for chapter eight.

The funds to begin this research were provided by Keren Eshkol (research contract no. 0381037) and the research fund of the Faculty of Social Sciences, Hebrew University. I am particularly indebted to Nava Enosh, whose advice was most fruitful. The study was later funded by the Israeli Foundations Trustees, research contract no. 86–01–007. I am very grateful to both for their support. My gratitude is to the Department of Sociology at State University of New York, Stony Brook. This department provided all the necessary means that enabled and helped me to begin this study during one fruitful sabbatical. The firm, enthusiastic, and continuous support, sometimes during difficult times, of my colleagues at the Department of Sociology and Social Anthropology at Hebrew University most certainly gave me the strength to continue and finish the project.

I am very grateful to Rosalie M. Robertson, my most helpful and cordial editor from SUNY Press, for all her efforts and kindness, and to Sharon Lougheed and Dana Foote, production editors, for their most essential help. I am also very grateful to Professor Ronald Farrell, whose help and advice were most valuable.

The practical, emotional, and moral support given enthusiastically by Goggie and Al Blitstein, our most cherished and deeply loved second family, helped transform this project from the realm of the imagination into the realm of reality.

Part One

General
Theoretical
Foundations

Chapter One

Theoretical Foundations
Deviance

THE PUZZLE OF THIS BOOK

This book attempts to provide one interpretative answer for the intellectual and empirical puzzle regarding the sociological nature of the connections among politics, morality, and deviance.

The sociology of deviance has been accused of trivializing itself. *The Politics and Morality of Deviance* charts first a theoretical framework and then applies it to four different and specific case studies in an explicit and continuing attempt to drive the sociology of deviance into mainstream sociology. I argue that deviance should be analyzed as a relative phenomenon in different and changing cultures vis-à-vis change and stability in the boundaries of different symbolic-moral universes. Deviance is interpreted as the product of negotiations about the nature of morality *and* the use and legitimization of power. Mills's (1940) concept of *motivational accounting systems* is utilized throughout the text in order to illustrate how processes in the micro and macro levels of analysis can be integrated. Thus, the theoretical framework brings together, in an unconventional way, neofunctionalism, non-Marxist conflict approach, and symbolic interaction theory to create an integrated new analytical look on deviance.

I will argue that the legitimization of power should be thought of in terms of *a moral order* that in turn defines the societal boundaries of different symbolic-moral universes. *Problematic behavioral acts, which take place at the realm of the seams, where boundaries of different symbolic-moral universes meet and touch or which are directed from the periphery of a symbolic-moral universe toward its center and vice versa, and which involve challenges (use or abuse) of power and morality, would fall into the area of politics and deviance.*

I make a distinction between *political deviance*, which includes direct and explicit acts that either challenge the social order, or the abuse of power and morality by those in the centers, and *political elements in "regular" deviance*. The last category refers to exposing and

3

analyzing the elements of power and morality in so-called regular deviance.

The four different case studies are presented in four separate chapters. The first case is an analysis of the development of a moral panic that was focused on the issue of drug abuse. The second case compares drug abuse social policy in the United States and Israel. The third case details the development of early radio astronomy from a deviant knowledge claim to an orthodox science. The fourth case examines how, and why, in a particular case, a political figure was able to *totally* reverse a process of deviantization. In all the cases, the analysis is based on the confrontations and negotiations between different symbolic-moral universes and on the use and legitimization of power. The concept of motivational accounting systems is used in each case in order to bridge the micro-macro levels of analysis. Furthermore, each case is interpreted in such a way so as to provide the largest possible basis for generalizations within sociology in general and the sociology of deviance in particular.

The book is divided into nine chapters, organized in five parts. The first part includes chapters one and two and is focused on two topics. The first is a discussion of the analytical approach that is taken in this book regarding deviance. The second focus is on motivational accounting systems as a bridging mechanism between the micro and macro levels of analysis. The second part includes chapters three and four and analyzes the complex analytical relationships among deviance, morality, and power. The third part consists of four chapters that provide detailed analyses of the cases. Part four presents the concluding discussion, and part five the notes and bibliography.

INTRODUCTION: DEVIANCE[1]

Defining deviance has always been problematic. With the exception of the general statement that deviance is focused around the violation of norms, a satisfactory solution to the problem of definition has apparently not yet been found (e.g., see Lemert 1983; Rock 1985). Such a broad definition, however, only begs the question of what the specific nature of deviance is. In addition, there exists the dichotomy of deviance being approached by some as one facade of a defined social reality and by others as a sociologically constructed analytical concept. Furthermore, while for many scholars deviance has been identified as a legitimate sociological specialty, they still tend to place it on the margins of mainstream sociology. One must be reminded, however, that while the specific content of what actually constitutes "deviance" changes from one culture to another, as well as within one culture, deviance itself as a social and analytical category is a universal one (e.g., Schur 1979; Goode 1984a).

Since its inception, the sociology of deviance seems to have suffered from at least two major problems. The first is a theoretical chaos. This problem was raised originally in 1943 by C. Wright Mills and was again mentioned in 1981 by Piven and in 1984 by Scull. Terry and Steffensmeier (1988, 60) have recently pointed out that " . . . theorizing in contemporary deviance has stagnated." Thus, even today the sociology of deviance can be characterized as fragmented and theoretically chaotic.

The second major problem was also mentioned by C. Wright Mills in 1943 and was echoed by Scull in 1984. This is the fact that the sociology of deviance failed to consider total social structures and fell into a deep (yet interesting) trap of small-scale studies about various esoteric, sensational types of deviance, such as call girls, prostitution, the hit man, the con man, the check forger, the drug user, and the like. Rock (1973a) even claimed that the emphasis in the sociology of deviance on studying the phenomenon has given rise to a radical type of *phenomenalism* that views society as a collection of small units lacking an overall structure. Later, Rock (1974) also claimed that the sociology of deviance had created an artificial contradiction between *phenomenalism* (emphasizing the need for an accurate and reliable reconstruction of the social world as seen by those living in it) and *essentialism* (searching for the underlying properties of the social order).

Elsewhere (Ben-Yehuda 1985), I argued that the sociological study of deviance must consider total social structures and/or processes by examining deviance as a relative phenomenon and as part of larger social processes of change and stability in the realm of symbolic-moral universes (Berger and Luckmann 1966) and their boundaries. This approach is consistent with those envisaged by Piven (1981), Scull (1984), and Terry and Steffensmeier (1988) in maintaining that the study of deviance should be reframed (Goffman 1974) within general societal processes, in a dynamic historical and political perspective.

This conceptualization means that the sociological study of deviance need not be problematic or marginal, and could be used to explain major societal processes of stability and change. This book, however, goes beyond my 1985 formulation, first, by focusing not only on *morality* but also on the *political* sphere too; and second, by coherently integrating the micro-macro levels of analysis, using the concept of motivational accounting systems.

To achieve the above goals, I shall first explain how the concept of deviance can be interpreted within such mainstream sociological concepts as change and stability. Second, I shall explain how and why the concept of motivational accounting systems can be used to bridge the micro-macro levels of analysis. The *"theoretical foundations"* part will be dominated by these considerations.

DEVIANCE, CHANGE, AND STABILITY

Complex pluralistic societies are characterized by a multiplicity of centers, each one enveloped by a particular symbolic-moral universe that demarcates its moral boundaries. Reactions to deviance, in this context, would either help to redefine the moral boundaries of these symbolic-moral universes in a rigid way or help to introduce elements of flexibility and hence change. This conceptualization fits very well the more general theoretical orientation of viewing deviance as a relative phenomenon within the context of societal change and stability (a fuller discussion of this particular conceptualization will be presented in chapter three).

This analytical approach obviously reinforces the stand that deviance, as an empirical phenomenon and a theoretical concept, is an important sociological construct. Its importance lies with the fact that the social construction of deviance, and the way it is reacted to, may be utilized as key analytical concepts if we wish to better understand change and stability; the ways symbolic-moral universes meet, negotiate, and clash; and how the societal moral boundaries of these universes change or, conversely, remain rigid.

The concept of deviance that emerges from this book, and from my previous work (1985), is anchored in a specific theoretical framework that is focused on an *interpretative analysis* (e.g., see Orcutt 1983, 59–62; Geertz 1973; Walzer 1987). It implies that *deviance is a relative rhetorical device that is socially constructed*. Consequently, deviance may become an important concept in interpreting processes of change and stability.

A successful, and enforceable, social construction of a particular label of deviance depends on the ability of one, or more, groups to use (or generate) enough power so as to enforce *their* definition and version of morality on others. This process *always* involves delineating and emphasizing boundaries between different symbolic-moral universes. What this theoretical approach implies is that the process of negotiating the moral meaning of rhetorical devices is continuous and ongoing between deviants and the social environment in which they live and function. Deviance, in this analytical perspective, always results from negotiations about morality *and* the configuration of power relationships.

DEVIANCE AS A RELATIVE RHETORIC

The implication of the above theoretical stand is relativistic and negates the opposite absolutist or normative and narrower approach (e.g., see Hills 1980, 8–11; Douglas and Waksler 1982, 8–25; Orcutt 1975, 1983, 3–29; Thio 1988, 3–24; and a similar argument by Woolgar and Pawluch 1985).[2] In Thio's terms (1988, 15–21), the perspective presented here is modern. It emphasizes deviance as a (1) relative phenomenon; (2) subjective experience; and (3) voluntary act.

The "relativity" of deviance is easily illustrated in the following two examples. "In Pilgrim America of the 1600's, a wife who defied the wishes of her husband could be placed in the pillary on public display. Today, labeling the husband a 'male chauvinist pig' would be only one of several possible responses to a husband who treated his wife in any such manner" (Suchar 1978, 7). Conrad and Schneider (1980, 35) notice the "disease" called "drapetomania," which was discussed in 1851 by Samuel Cartwright, M.D., and which only affected slaves. Its major symptom was running away from the white masters' plantations.

While the relative conception of deviance seems almost self-evident, it has been attacked. Theoretical approaches that take the existence of deviance as nonproblematic (e.g., positivism) most certainly do not adopt the relative position. In 1975, Wellford attributed to the labeling approach the following stand: "no act is intrinsically criminal . . . [because] crime is a form of behaviour defined by the powerful to control the powerless . . . " (334; see also Pearce 1976). The concept of deviance presented in this book is much more complex than the above robust and simple attribution made almost thirteen years ago. Deviance, as presented here, is the result of a long process of negotiation. This process does mean that the powerless can resist deviantization.

While it is easy to see how such "soft" types of deviance as homosexuality, pornography, and marijuana use are relative, it is not so easy to see the relativity in such "hard" types of deviance as murder, theft, or burglary. I shall next show that even such "hard" deviances are relative.

The first example cited by Wellford (1975) as an illustration that deviance is *not* relative is that of murder. In order to demonstrate how even "homicide" is a relative rhetorical device, I shall broaden the basis of the interpretation (based on Ben-Yehuda, forthcoming).

Following the biblical command "Thou Shall Not Murder" may be interpreted to mean that taking another human being's life is a universal crime. It is not. The act of killing is treated differentially in different times and cultures (Nettler 1982). It is also treated differentially in the same culture. Hence, different types of accounts and rhetorical devices have been developed to make such an act "explainable" or "justifiable." These, in turn, depend on the interpretation of the circumstances.

The type of rhetorical device that will be used to describe the death of an actor depends, first of all, on whether we view that death as natural. A natural death would usually mean that the actor has finished what we may consider his/her natural life span and dies, without any intentional help from him/herself or another person. Such rhetorical devices as "deceased," "passed away," or simply "died" would be typically employed in this particular case.

When death is not being defined as "natural," other rhetorical devices are invoked. One very basic issue in this case is whether the potential victim agreed, or even willed and wished, to die. If the answer to this question is positive, then a small pool of rhetorical devices becomes available. For example, the rhetorical device called "suicide" and its variations (e.g., *hara-kiri*), "euthanasia" (with consent), and the like.

The other possibility is that the potential victim does not agree or wish to die. The act of taking the victim's life against his/her wish thus becomes a typically forceful and violent act.

Let us examine briefly some of the possible rhetorical devices that have been developed and employed to interpret acts of taking other peoples' lives against their will.

When a situation is defined by the rhetorical device called war, then taking other humans' lives is not only excusable; it is mandatory for so-called combat soldiers, even rewardable with some high-powered symbols. Hence, under normal combat circumstances, we do not say that a soldier murdered his enemy or vice versa. Wars, however, do have some rules, and some acts of taking other people's lives—even in a war situation—may in fact be regarded as murder (e.g., killing prisoners of war).

Such rhetorical devices as "self-defense," or "blood revenge" in some Middle Eastern societies (e.g., see Ginat 1984), as well as genocide or "lynching" and "assassinations," may also be used to justify and explain acts of taking other people's lives against their will, as well as such other ritualistic situations defined as vendettas, human sacrifices, and duels.

The famous rhetorical device called *homicide* may itself be classified into criminal and noncriminal. Each of these devices is further divided into finer distinctions. *Criminal homicide* is defined differently in different countries and states. Goode (1984a), for example, draws our attention to the legal accounts used in New York State for this particular rhetorical device: murder, voluntary manslaughter, involuntary manslaughter, and criminally negligent homicide. He also draws our attention to two forms of noncriminal homicide: *excusable* (i.e., in specified automobile accidents) and *justifiable* (i.e., a policeman shooting what may be defined as a fleeing felon; see, e.g., Scharf and Binder 1983). Furthermore, some people view abortion as homicide.

We can realize, therefore, that acts of taking other peoples' lives against their will get different labels as different rhetorical devices are utilized to describe them. Thus, Goode's (1984a, 221) conclusion that *"the taking of human life is tolerated under certain circumstances"* is clearly valid (see also Reid 1982, 214–19; Bonn 1984, 187–91; Barlow 1984, 135–47; Conklin 1986). Circumstances, however, are not just "given" and typically require definitions and interpretations. Hence, cultures provide a variety of rhetorical devices, vocabularies of motives and accounts (some of which are institutionalized in the law), aimed at defining differentially acts of taking other people's lives (for a review see Nettler 1982). Furthermore, murderers tend to develop their own vocabularies of motives for justifying murder (e.g., see Dietz 1983; Hepworth and Turner 1974; Levi 1981).

A similar intellectual exercise can be made with another "hard core" deviance called "theft." This time, I shall make the exercise very short. Reflecting various degrees of sensitivity regarding property, almost all social systems have rules forbidding the taking of property by force. However, many so-called guerrilla movements (which later came to power) not only allowed and encouraged but even sanctified operations such as theft, armed robbery, and burglary in order to secure the means for their activities. In the histories of these movements, such acts are justified and accounted for as acts against oppressors.

Deviance such as theft and swindling can be shown to be related to very basic assumptions concerning the sacredness of private property. Where private property does not exist, the meaning of theft will be very different. A contemporary and relevant example concerns fund-raising techniques among various "world-transforming" socio-religious movements (e.g., the "Moonies" or "Hare Krishna"). Bromley and Shupe (1980) show that fund raising becomes a central component of the individual member's role and a major focus of daily missionary activity. Fund raising becomes a sacred activity and is ideologically legitimized by being linked with the movement's goals, contributing to the salvation or spiritual improvement of all mankind. Many of the activities included in such fund raising, however, could be easily defined as deceptive, corrupt, and manipulative. These movements, therefore, have developed special vocabularies of motives that allow members to neutralize the negative implications of such practices. The Hare Krishna calls such practices "transcendental trickery," while the Moonies call it "heavenly deception" (Bromley and Shupe 1980, 231–33).

Deviance and moral boundaries.   Delineating moral boundaries between the "right" and "wrong," the "appropriate" and "inappropriate" is an important sociological process. Its importance lies with the fact that in this process power and morality are utilized to mark socially constructed differences between different groups of persons.

Traditional theories of deviance have usually emphasized the "negative" aspect of deviance or took it for granted. The view that deviance can be "positive," even in the sense of helping a process of societal change into being and change societal symbolic-moral boundaries as well, not to mention power, is less widespread (e.g., see Dodge 1985). This "positive" side of deviance was illuminated originally by Durkheim's statements on deviance, that is, that deviance can be "functional" in helping a societal reaction into being in a way that either reaffirms moral boundaries (1933:70–110) or changes them (1938:65–73). This viewpoint was further amplified by Erikson's work (1966), as well as by others.

Since Durkheim's original essays (1933, 1938) on the functionality of deviance, there have been numerous scholars who utilized this idea to illustrate that, in many cases, a functional way of coping with pressures exerted by the social order is to commence and/or maintain a deviant career. Thus, Cohen (1966, 6–11), Box (1981), Farrell and Swigert's review (1982 ch. 2) and Pfohl (1985 ch. 6) suggested several functions for deviance such as creating integration cohesion and solidarity; facilitating flexibility; being a safety valve for unhappy members of society; serving as a warning signal that something is wrong in society; helping to clarify latent from manifest functions; contributing to the clarification, maintenance, and modification of social rules. Harris (1977) even implied that deviance designations may help draw lines between the powerful and the powerless.[3]

Hence, one theoretical line of argument going from Durkheim through Erikson to more recent sociological formulations could be taken to suggest that societies "somehow" generate, or even manufacture, deviance "in order" to define moral boundaries. While interesting, this particular claim remained unrefined for decades of sociological work. One possible way to continue this claim is by making a distinction between the temporal and spatial dimensions of how moral boundaries are redefined. In the temporal dimension, we could redefine moral boundaries in the present or make what Schur (1971, 52–56) called a "retrospective interpretation," and reinterpret past events, thus causing a change in the cognitive images that social actors have of past boundaries. Rewriting histories in this way may certainly cause significant and profound changes in both collective and personal identities. In the spatial dimension, one could make a distinction between attempts to redefine intersocietal (or internal) boundaries and external moral boundaries, that is, between an inner societal differentiation process and an external process.

Another way of conceptualizing this problem was suggested by Lauderdale (1976). He indicated that society's moral boundaries fluctuate constantly, exposing different social actors, depending on time and place, to the label of "deviant" (see also Shapiro, Lauderdale, and Lauderdale 1985).

While many scholars followed the idea of reactions to deviance as attempts to enhance stability (e.g., Erikson 1966; Bergesen 1984; Pallone 1986), fewer followed the idea of deviance as producing change. Coser's (1962) and Douglas' (1977) works are clear exceptions. Coser pointed out that deviance may contribute to what he called "normative flexibility." Douglas, much more explicitly, suggests the term "creative deviance": "Deviance is the mutation that is generally destructive of society, but it is also the only major source of creative adaptations of rules to new life situations" (60). Thus, Douglas suggests that whole societies may change through deviance. More recently, Dodge (1985) argued that sociologists should in fact start to study "positive" deviance.

In my previous work (1985), I indeed examined how the social construction of deviance, and reactions to it, could be *interpreted* within an analytical framework that emphasized the approach taken in this subsection.

Conceptualizing deviance in this light makes it clear that, while "deviance" as an analytical and empirical category is universal, a universal *content* of deviance is nonexistent (see also Hagan 1977; Schur 1979, 1980; Conrad and Schneider 1980; and Turk 1979, to mention only a few). Deviance is essentially socially constructed and is therefore always culturally relative. In order to understand a specific type of deviance, we have to understand its context within the social system and, in particular, the system's value structure, or moral universes, *and* the specific configuration(s) of power relationships. Depending on the sociohistorical context, some forms of deviance could either create cohesion and rigidity or help reflect such a situation, while other forms of deviance could either create or reflect flexibility. Furthermore, the same type of deviance in certain circumstances could create rigidity while leading in other circumstances to flexibility.

The macro sociological assumption of this work takes for granted the existence of a number of symbolic-moral universes within one society. The negotiations *between* members of these universes, and *within* them, can assume the form of processes of stigmatization, deviantization, and criminalization.

Deviance thus viewed is no longer a peripheral phenomenon but rather a central element of any functioning social system. The analysis of social deviance hence becomes a crucial factor in our understanding of the social order itself.

Prima faci, it appears that processes aimed at changing or stabilizing the moral boundaries of symbolic-moral universes must involve negotiations about power, morality, status, and respectability. These concepts bring us unavoidably to politics. The possibility that deviance does not necessarily have to be evil and dangerous, or polluting and "dirty" (Douglas M. 1966; Scott 1972) is closely linked to politics and deviance. There, deviance may clearly, explicitly, and deliberately generate (or be part of) processes of social change, thus negating the idea that deviance necessarily and pointlessly flouts order. Thus, the application of politics—that is, of power and morality—to deviance may, on the one hand, illustrate vividly how deviance can be thought of as preserving a specific symbolic-moral universe through designating specific behavioral patterns as bad, evil, polluting, and dirty. On the other hand, the analysis of political deviance and of political elements in deviance may illustrate how deviance can be thought of as intimately associated with processes of change, closer to Coser's "normative flexibility" (1962) and Douglas' (1977) "creative deviance."

Politics and deviance; power and morality.   Entering the area of politics and deviance means that we have to develop new, or use existing, concepts and terminology. The concept of power is essential to this area because it basically helps us to understand who can deviantize whom.

The concept of power alone, however, is insufficient. Power must be legitimized, and moral universes (or morality) provide that legitimacy. In this perspective, we may view many different centers enveloped by corresponding symbolic-moral universes, which confront, conflict, and negotiate with one another. In these negotiations, power may be generated and moral boundaries negotiated. This conceptualization means that it is not always the case that the powerful would necessarily deviantize the powerless. The powerless may persuade inhabitants of other symbolic-moral universes in the "truth" of their cause, be engaged in power generation, and negotiate a settlement. Discussing politics and deviance necessitates therefore using concepts of power, moral universes and boundaries, moral entrepreneurs, moral crusaders, hierarchies of credibility, and accounts.

Having clarified my theoretical orientation toward the area of politics and deviance, I argue that this area should be divided into two distinct domains. One domain is *political deviance* proper; the other consists of analyzing *political elements in so-called regular deviance.*

Political deviance proper consists of three classes of deviant acts. One class consists of acts done by one person, or a group, that challenge the authority and legitimacy of those in power. These acts usually aim at transforming moral universes and changing moral boundaries. The second class consists of deviant acts by those who were invested with power and legitimacy. Those social actors are, supposedly, the guardians of symbolic-moral universes and their boundaries. Sometimes these guardians abuse their power and twist and mock their moral obligations, committing despised and harmful acts of deviance. Third class consists of clashes *between* symbolic-moral universes (or cultures).

The second domain included in *politics and deviance* involves the designation of particular behavioral patterns as "deviant." This process (Pfuhl 1986) contains some important, although often implicit, political elements—that is, elements of power and morality. Exposing these elements is not always an easy task. It can be claimed that the very attempt to define a particular behavioral pattern as "deviant" is inherently a political act. This attempt is based on using power to impress the view of a specific symbolic-moral universe upon other universes. Applying a process of deviantization does not, however, necessarily mean that the application would be successful and culminate in the actual identification of one person (or a group of persons) as deviant (e.g., see Ben-Yehuda 1987).

The micro-macro link. One axis of the theoretical framework is the emphasis on deviance, power, and morality in an historical dynamic context. The other axis emphasizes the micro-macro link.

A major problem in sociology has always focused around attempts to integrate the analysis of processes between the micro and macro levels (e.g., see Knorr-Cetina and Cicourel 1981; Collins 1986; Scheff 1986; Alexander, Giesen, Munch and Smelser 1987; Wiley 1988). Terry and Steffensmeier (1988, 61–62, 64) emphasized that this necessity exists in the sociology of deviance as well. In the second part of the *theoretical foundation*, I will argue that the concept of motivational accounting system can, and should, be thought of as a bridging mechanism for the micro-macro levels of analysis; what follows in the next chapter is the explanation.

CONCLUDING SUMMARY

The theoretical framework is focused along two complementary axes. The first axis, which was presented in this chapter, emphasizes that the analysis of deviance in this book will not be confined to phenomenalism. It seeks to continue the reframing of the study of social deviance within the more general sociological context of change and stability. It is focused on the moral boundaries of the different symbolic-moral universes of which society is constituted. Deviance is interpreted here as a relative, emergent, and socially constructed concept. Put in this fashion, the problem for the sociology of deviance becomes one of integrating its specific observations and interpretations within larger theoretical formulations in sociology, preferably within the context of politics and history. Developing this particular type of sociological discourse is an explicit goal of this book.

The second axis is focused on an attempt to link processes in the micro and macro levels of analysis and is presented in the next chapter.

Chapter Two

Theoretical Foundations
The Micro-Macro Link

MOTIVATIONAL ACCOUNTING SYSTEMS:
CONVERGENCE OF MICRO-MACRO LEVELS OF ANALYSIS

In order to bridge processes on the micro and macro levels of analysis, we shall, to some extent, have to break from the Durkheimian oriented view that was emphasized thus far.[1] With the exception of the concept of "anomie" and its possible interpretation as a dispersion of the individual's cognitive maps, Durkheimian terminology does not provide the concepts necessary to perform the synthesis.

The analysis of the maintenance or the change of moral boundaries must be supplemented by an analysis of vocabularies of motives and subjective meanings. This approach leads us directly to problems of social interaction, symbolic interaction, and motivational accounting systems because these are the mechanisms through which meaning is created, sustained, or changed. The social interaction between and among people is the unit to analyze if we are to understand how macro sociological considerations filter down to the personal level and vice versa.

SYMBOLIC INTERACTION

Social symbolic interactions are the loci where values, motivations, tensions, desires, and interests find expression; there, symbols are exchanged and negotiated. On the one hand, through symbolic interaction individual behavior is shaped and constrained continuously by social pressures; on the other hand, social processes are directed, influenced, and shaped by individual interpretations. Symbolic interaction poses a chronic problem for the understanding of such terms as "social reality" and "meaning." The fact that symbols may have many "meanings" and be subject to interpretations and reinterpretations requires the development of specialized research strategies and tools (e.g., Hewitt 1976; Meltzer, Petras, and Reynolds 1975; Karp and Yoels 1979; Blumer 1969; Manis and Meltzer 1972).

Briefly stated, symbolic interactionism interprets human existence and identity as a process of becoming. The identities of interactants are being constantly negotiated through exchanges of symbols within the framework of an interaction process. The interpretation, negotiation, and meaning of the symbols exchanged are considerably influenced by a number of independent elements including significant others (family, friends), primary relationships, social control agents (police, psychiatrists, judges), the social setting, prejudices, power, and interests.

Goffman (1959) indicated that each interaction situation is inherently tense and fluid because each participant seeks to unfold a specific self, maintain credibility, and, in short, establish a specific "definition of a situation." The dramaturgic analysis of daily symbolic interactions reinforce this viewpoint by conceptualizing social interaction as a theater (see Karp and Yoels 1979; Messinger 1962; Douglas and Waksler 1982). This tension is of crucial theoretical importance, for the fact that identities are negotiated means that the potential for change lies within each interaction. A simple social interaction will, on the one hand, reflect and maintain such macro level elements as existing norms, morality and values, patterns of deference, and social distance. On the other hand, within such situations, meaning is negotiated, conceivably giving rise to new, innovative deviant interpretations and definitions of situations that may diffuse to the macro level and thus cause change in that level. Thomas and Thomas' (1928, 571–75) famous dictum, "If men define situations as real, they are real in their consequences," shows that it is not important whether a particular situation is, in fact, real as long as the definition of the situation is real. In this sense, everyday rituals of symbolic interaction are the time and place both where continuity is maintained and where changes may occur. It is possible to analyze such interactions using Turner's (1977a, b) concept of "liminality." Every symbolic interaction may be thought of as a potential "rite of passage" where old traditions are reemphasized and where new forms of interaction are introduced. This formulation is further strengthened by the perception of the social order as a negotiated order. Order is negotiated not only on the micro level, as identities and selves are created and emerge, but also on the macro level of politics, economics, ideology, and the like. The two levels influence each other, and the negotiated character of the social order means that stability and change are integrated into such situations. Let us look into three examples.

In the early decades of this century, prohibition laws regarding the consumption of alcohol were enacted in the United States (Gusfield 1963; see Dingle 1980 for a comparative perspective) because various respected societal moral agents (Becker 1963) defined alcohol consumption as immoral. This moral definition filtered down into simple day-to-day language and interactions. When the gay movement militantly (Teal 1971; Kitzinger 1987) demanded that homosexuality and lesbianism not be defined as a psychopathic manifestation, the psychiatric profession yielded to the pressure[2] and changed its nomenclature. Likewise, for years the use of cannabis was portrayed in popular and scientific literature as a menace. In the last decades, however, the formal and informal pressure of the millions of people in the United States and Europe who used marijuana has forced moral agents to reevaluate their attitudes. Many states in the United States have decriminalized the use of marijuana, which was no longer considered a characteristic of lower class, uneducated, impoverished, minority groups. It has become the "thing to do" for many among the middle class, educated, and affluent. Thus, in the simple terms of day-to-day social-symbolic interactions, the "definition of the situation" regarding the use of marijuana has changed drastically. In these two cases, changes from the micro level changed the macro level.

Becker (1953) suggested that becoming a marijuana user encompasses the following three consecutive stages of learning: how to inhale the drug, how to recognize the drug's effects, and to define the drug's effects as pleasant. This is a learning process whereby an individual is being influenced by the social environment to become a marijuana user.

Becker describes a process that provides the novice user not only with technical knowledge but also with a value system. The very process of "becoming" gives the novice access to a particular symbolic-moral universe and provides him/her with a motivation to use marijuana. It helps him/her to define the effects of the drug as pleasant; it provides him/her with social acceptability, support, and security against societal stigmatizing processes; and last, but not least, the process of "becoming" provides the novice user with a vocabulary of motives by which he/she can justify, and meaningfully interpret, his/her experience in a way that increases the probability that he/she will use the drug again. This process is infused with values and needs from three directions: first, the group's symbolic-moral universe, which includes its needs, values, norms, and definition of social reality, is transmitted to the novice drug user. Second, the novice's needs, such as social approval, support, acceptability, and pleasure-sensation seeking, are being negotiated and met through his/her joining the group. Third, the more successful "pot" users are in recruiting others and the more users there are, the more pressure would then be applied upward to change macro antimarijuana values and norms.

The end-product of this process is that a novice drug user may "become" a regular user. In other words, the process of "becoming a marijuana user" provides the user with a motivational accounting system.

MOTIVATIONAL ACCOUNTING SYSTEMS

The credit for developing this concept must be given to C. Wright Mills. In 1940, he published a paper in which he argued that statements of motivation have a basic social character because they enable people to be integrated into social groups and provide the actors with directions for subsequent actions. These motivations reflect morality, and as such, a vocabulary of motives serves as a prime internal source of social control. Mills was aware of the fact that vocabularies of motives would differ from one group to another because these vocabularies reflect moral stands. Mills (1940) notes that:

A motive tends to be one which is to the actor and to the other members of a situation an unquestioned answer to questions concerning social and lingual conduct. . . . When an agent vocalizes or imputes motives, he is not trying to describe his experienced social action. He is not merely stating "reasons." He is influencing others — and himself. (P. 907)

The verbalized motive is not used as an index of something in the individual but as a basis of inference for a typical vocabulary of motives of a situated action. (P. 909)

Vocabularies of motives constitute a large reservoir of rhetorical devices, from which individual and explicit motivational accounting systems are constantly constructed. According to Mills, motives vary between small preindustrial villages, where only a small variety of motives exists, and industrial towns, where many (even conflicting) vocabularies of motives exist. Mills's distinction is consistent with the differences between simple and complex social systems, once we accept its translation to mean societies characterized by very few symbolic-moral universes versus those characterized by a multiplicity of such universes. The size, quality, and number of vocabularies of motives available in these two ideal polar types of social systems obviously differ significantly. This concept of "motivational accounting systems" was thus introduced into sociological literature but was, unfortunately, largely ignored.

THEORETICAL DEVELOPMENTS ASSOCIATED WITH THE IDEA OF MOTIVATIONAL ACCOUNTING SYSTEMS

Four theoretical developments can be linked to the idea of motivational accounting systems. The first is Lyman and Scott's (1970, 111–43) discussion of "Accounts," which they defined as:

"A linguistic device employed whenever an action is subjected to valuative inquiry. Such devices are a crucial element in the social order since they prevent conflicts from arising by verbally bridging the gap between action and expectations. Moreover, accounts are "situated" according to the statuses of the interactants and are standardized within cultures so that certain accounts are terminologically stabilized and routinely expected when activity falls outside the domain of expectations. . . . By an account . . . we refer to a statement made by a social actor to explain unanticipated or untoward behavior (p. 112).

Furthermore, they clearly state (p. 136) that: *Every account is a manifestation of the underlying negotiation of identities* (emphasis in original). Elsewhere, Scott and Lyman (1968a, b) point out that what makes one account more acceptable than another is the fact that it is consistent with the group's expectations, which in turn emerge from the group's definition of a situation.

The second development is focused on the theoretical and empirical studies called "attribution theories" (e.g., see Crittenden 1983; Hewstone 1984). These theories attempt to understand those factors within social interactions that come into play when the actors attempt to interpret their experiences, including their own actions and those of others. The study of the causal interpretations people make, so as to give sense to events in their environment, is of central importance in attribution theories. A major thesis of attribution is that the expectations, cognitions, and actions of people are based on their motivation and ability to control the causal environmental network. Thus, attributions of lacking responsibility are usually linked to such social behavior as drug abuse, prostitution, alcoholism, and mental illness.

Motivational accounting systems provide social actors with ready-made attributions, explaining events not only after they occur, but also giving cause to future behavior. When a call girl claims, for example, that she performs an important service for society, this motivational accounting system not only explains past behavior but also provides a rationale for future actions. Of related interest are the works by Snyder, Higgins, and Stucky (1983) and Potter and Wetherell (1987), which examine, from a psychological point of view, the issues of excusing, discourse, and accounting.

A third theoretical development relevant for the study of motivational accounting systems is Sykes and Matza's (1957) theory of delinquency, particularly the emphasis on techniques of neutralization.[3] Sykes and Matza found enough evidence to suggest that delinquents experienced a sense of guilt and admired law-abiding persons. However, these delinquents were simultaneously also impervious to demands for conformity. The researchers suggested, therefore, that delinquency, similar to criminality, was rationalized in the form of justifications that were accepted as valid by the delinquent but not by the legal system or society at large.

Sykes and Matza thus isolated five types of motivational accounting systems that were used by deviants and that could negate guilt,[4] give the delinquent a justification for his acts, and help him in future delinquent behavior: (1) denial of responsibility, where the delinquent defines himself as not responsible for his deviant actions; (2) denial of injury, where the delinquent feels that his behavior did not really cause harm despite the fact that it was against the law; (3) denial of the victim, where the delinquent insists that the injury was not wrong in light of the circumstances; (4) condemnation of the condemners, where the delinquent rejects his rejecters, claiming that they are hypocrites, deviants in disguise, etc.; (5) an appeal to higher loyalties, where the delinquent may see himself as caught up in a dilemma, the resolution of which is at the cost of violating the law.

The fourth comparison, a more complex one, is focused on so-called social control theories. According to these theories deviance is not caused but is made possible (Frazier 1976, 49). This book is strongly influenced by Durkheim's ideas, and in the area of social control theories, Durkheim also made some of the classic statements. In his work, particularly that on suicide, he specifically mentioned that when the hold of society (or groups within it) on the individual weakens deviance occurs. One page 209 of *Suicide* (1951), Durkheim states that: "Society cannot disintegrate without the individual simultaneously detaching himself from social life, without his own goals becoming preponderant over those of the community, in a word without his personality tending to surmount the collective personality. The more weakened the groups to which he belongs, the less he depends on them, the more he consequently depends only on himself and recognizes no other rules of conduct than what are found in his private interests. If we agree to call this state egoism . . . we may call egoistic the special type of suicide springing from excessive individualism." Thus, Durkheim implies a causal connection between social disorganization and personal deviance. States of anomie are another example of this causal relationship. On page 252, Durkheim (1951) pointed out that "when society is disturbed by some painful crisis or by beneficient but abrupt transitions, it is momentarily incapable of exercising . . . influence (on the individual); thence come the sudden rise in the curve of suicides."

In past years, a number of social control theories emerged. They all shared the assumption that deviance did not simply occur, but became possible due to an inability to prevent it. Control theories not only spell out when and where deviance becomes possible, but also specify the conditions under which no deviance will take place.

Most control theories use both concepts (external vs. internal control) and give specific content to each control sphere. However, the relative importance of each sphere varies (e.g., see Reiss 1951; Nye 1958; Reckless 1967; Hirschi 1969).

Let me use the example of Matza's most interesting control theory (1964; 1969) as an illustration for the relevance of control theory to motivational accounting systems. Matza claims that it is overly simplistic to assume that whenever control weakens deviance will follow almost automatically. In his view, one must identify those factors intervening between lack of control and deviance. Accordingly, he posited that "neutralization" and "subterranean convergence" explain how a rupture between social actors and society becomes possible. The first concept refers to the technique of violating conventional norms without rejecting them, through neutralization. The second concept refers to the mixing of elements from conventional culture with a deviant, or delinquent, subculture. The convergence occurs in a way in which conventional values actually lend support to deviance. In this way, conventional morality is neutralized; for example, a conventional justification may exempt social actors from responsibility, once they can claim to have been in a temporary state of insanity.

Both subterranean convergence and neutralization provide actors with motivational accounting systems to justify deviant behavior and annul guilt. As Matza rightly points out, these motivational accounting systems are derived from the morality that characterizes society as a whole. While these motivational accounting systems facilitate deviance, they certainly do not guarantee its occurrence. They enable actors to enter a situation of "drift," which "makes delinquency possible or permissible by temporarily removing the restraints that ordinarily control members of society, but of itself it supplies no irreversible commitment or compulsion that would suffice to thrust the person into the act" (1964, 181). Matza suggested that the missing element is 'will." However, "will" itself is activated by two other conditions: preparation, referring to the learning through experience that deviance can, and probably may, occur; and desperation. A drifter, therefore, eternally hovers between deviance and conformity.

On the one hand, control theories chart the macro motivational accounting systems sanctioning, or encouraging, particular behavioral patterns. These systems in fact delineate the boundaries of specific symbolic moral universes and provide control agents with the vocabularies of motives needed to justify their actions. On the other hand, control theories also chart the vocabularies of motives that deviants—on the micro level—use to justify their behavior. Thus, in Matza's (1964) analysis, and to a lesser degree in Hirschi's (1969), one can follow the motivational accounting systems that are employed within situations of interaction to map how the micro and macro levels of analysis are bridged. In this way, the role that motivational accounting systems play as mechanisms of social control becomes evident.

Finally, in 1971, Blum and McHugh examined the sociological status of motives. They pointed out that "motivation" has a strong sociological aspect and that a "motive is a sociological procedure for describing how organisms show themselves as persona" (p. 108). In 1983, three works were published. Wallis and Bruce and Bruce and Wallis published two papers where they argued that the study of accounts should take a central position in sociology.[5] In the same year, Gilbert and Abell edited a book containing the lectures given at the Surrey Conference on Sociological Theory and Method. This book contains about ten different papers on accounts, focusing on the possible methodologies to be used and what now seems to be an almost eternal problem—can (and should) one infer from accounts anything about the *real* intention of the actors? The different participants' papers show how intriguing, fascinating, and useful (however, also problematic) the use of motivational accounting systems can be. In this collection, Gilbert and Mulkay (pp. 8–34) suggest a specific methodology providing illustrations for accounts from the sociology of science.[6] This line of research was continued in Gilbert and Mulkay's 1984 book. There, they examine the ways scientists provide varying accounts for their actions and beliefs in different social situations. Of special interest is chapter four, where we can learn of the types of accounts, and the ways in which scientists construct accounts, to explain and justify errors and mistakes.

GENERALIZED MOTIVATIONAL ACCOUNTING SYSTEMS

One need not confine the concept of motivational accounts to the micro level only. We can conceptualize ideologies and values as forms of *generalized motivational accounts*. In this way, institutional justifications, which are generated by large organizations, could be thought of too in terms of motivational accounting systems (see also Douglas M. 1986). Institutions and control agents develop specialized (sometimes even peculiar) vocabularies of motives and consequently use motivational accounting systems in much the same way individuals do. In this way, these macro societal organizations are involved in reality construction, in justifying past and future actions, and in attempts to delineate and negotiate moral boundaries. The amounts of power and credibility that large organizations typically enjoy usually surpass the amounts held by individuals; institutions therefore are very influential. However, much like individuals, generalized motivational accounts are not accepted automatically. Despite the amounts of power and credibility that these organizations have, they *can* be challenged successfully. To illustrate this idea, I shall use the area of medicine and deviance.

The process of the medicalization of deviance (e.g., Conrad and Schneider 1980; Smith 1981) gives us a case of powerful and credible organizations attempting to apply their expertise to unconventional behavior.

Nye (1984) provides an illustration for using medical motivational accounting systems on a national level. He argues that French politicians, and the public, in the last half of the nineteenth century adopted scientific theories of the causes and treatment of French national decline, cultural crisis, and social deviance based on a medical vocabulary of motives.

Although in some cases using medically provided motivational accounting systems for deviant behavior is a positive step, in some other cases its abuse has mistakenly stigmatized healthy people as deviants. As Conrad and Schneider (1980, 222–23) emphasized, one of the dangers of medicalizing deviance and turning crime into "illness" is the resulting emergence of a therapeutic tyranny? The political elements in such a process are obvious.

The deviant's motivational accounting systems, if any, are interpreted as further symptoms indicating the seriousness of the condition. Although the decision to transform the identity of a "criminal" into one of a "sick" individual may superficially appear to be grounded in a scientific rational ethos, it is in nature a *political* decision. A regime that for various reasons feels uncomfortable to deviantize or criminalize an undesirable political opponent may send that opponent for "treatment." Well-known examples include countries that treat political dissidents as mentally ill: "with diagnoses such as 'paranoia with counter-revolutionary delusions' and 'manic reformism' and hospitalized [them] for their opposition to the political order" (Conrad and Schneider 1980, 75).

Social pathology, as any other pathology, can *only* be determined after establishing a definition of the nonpathological, or normal. Such forms of deviance as homosexuality, prostitution, leisure-time drug use, gambling, masturbation can be defined as "pathology" only because the opposite, "normal" condition, can be clearly defined.

> The danger of therapeutic tyranny lies in the fact that under a purely therapeutic approach to crime, health standards and regulations can become little more than tools for political coercion and oppression. For example, the Nazi leaders apparently believed it necessary to first define political opponents as mentally ill before ordering their extermination. (Conrad and Schneider 1980, 223)

Without a doubt, manufacturing medical motivational accounting systems to interpret what is defined as deviance shifts responsibility into the hands of a few experts, thus making medicine a central agent of social control. This statement is particularly valid in the case of mental illness and psychiatry. The widespread use of the powerful new psychoactive drugs (e.g., Valium) for daily functioning verifies

Chambers, Inciardi, and Siegel's theory (1975) of "chemical coping," or the chemical control of large populations. Thus, unhappiness, stress, and agony over unbearable life conditions can all be "treated" by using medical-pathological terms such as "depression" or "anxiety," to be treated by drugs such as Valium. Civil disobedience and riots can likewise be attributed to brain malfunctions.

Conrad and Schneider (1980, 251) noted that pathologization of evil, as illustrated in the cases of Hitler, "Son of Sam," Charles Manson, and Idi Amin has attributed unthinkable horrors to a few pathological personalities. Medical generalized motivational accounting systems, when used as explanations for deviant or destructive behavior, excuse humankind not only from individual responsibility but from collective responsibility as well.

MacAndrew (1969, 488–491) applied this idea to cases of social actors who drink excessively ("alcoholics") when he stated that:

> When an accounting is called for in situations such as this [excessive drinking], what is at issue is not an explanation, but a justification. The context of discourse is not that of a dispassionate inquiry, but of the assessment of one's blameworthiness. . . . In effect, then, in calling the chronic drunkard to account, that is, in asking him "why," a charge is being made against him and a defense is being called for. And because the drinker himself is typically incapable of providing "good reasons" in defense of his continued trouble-making . . . he is deemed properly deserving of censure and/or punishment. . . . In allowing the chronic drunkard this opportunity to justify himself, we are actually engaging in empty formality. What, after all, could a convincing justification possibly look like?

Finally, the concept of *motivational accounting systems* is also fully compatible with the Weberian concept of *elective affinities* (see Howe 1978). That is, motivational accounting systems constitute rhetorical devices that construct a Weberian *universe of meaning* "to which actors orient their actions . . . [O]rder is to be found in the elective affinities and words . . . It is this order in the universe of possible actions which makes [Weber's] social science possible . . . " (p. 382).

THE CRIME, AND ACCUSATIONS, OF WITCHCRAFT

The use of motivational accounting systems as a bridging

mechanism for the micro-macro levels can be colorfully illustrated, particularly in the area of magic and witchcraft as deviant belief systems.

Evans-Pritchard stated that witchcraft among the Azande (who were located in the 1920s in the Southern Sudan) is identified with a psychological substance over which the individual has little, if any, control: "Generally, a witch will protest his innocence of intention and his ignorance of the harm that he is doing to his neighbour. . . . He addresses the *mangu* in his stomach beseeching it to become inactive" (1929, 38). Likewise, in the sixteenth century, when some nuns were suspected of being witches, Teresa of Avila suggested to the Inquisition officials that the nuns were "comas enfermes" ("as if sick"), implying that they had no control over their behavior. Apparently, this particular motivational accounting system saved the nuns' lives (Sarbin 1969). In this respect, it is interesting to note that in the 1692 Salem witch-hunt, a witch who *confessed* was not executed. In these cases, the motivational accounting systems that "explained" witchcraft shifted responsibility from the conscious individual to external and uncontrollable elements.

The ideology of the European witch-craze of the fourteenth to seventeenth centuries (Ben-Yehuda 1980, 1985) gave the masses an easy-to-use generalized motivational accounting system for the confusion and agony with which they had to cope. Simply put, the ideology of the witch-craze, developed and supported by various officials of the Church, postulated that the world had become a battlefield between God and the devil. People could help the good powers win the battle against the devil by detecting and eliminating his human servants — the witches. This solution was embraced and accepted popularly and served as a generalized motivational accounting system to explain the misery people were experiencing.

Monter (1980, 33) notes that: "secular judges . . . remodeled popular beliefs in order to make them conform to official 'notions' of how witches ought to behave." The "official" demonology was well reflected in the witches' confessions. Due to the nature of the crime, it became obvious that a witch would not confess easily to having committed the terrible crime of conspiring with Satan against God. Consequently, a witch had to be tortured into confessing. Under torture, uniform loaded and leading questions, the suspected witches gave almost uniform confessions, usually confirming the witch-craze ideology. This should not really surprise us. However, some sources (e.g., Parrinder 1958; Hughes 1952) also report on cases where people *voluntarily* confessed to witchcraft and then were put to torture to make *sure* and verify that their confessions were not false. Trevor Roper (1967, 125–26) notes that: "For every victim whose story is evidently created or improved by torture, there are two or three who genuinely believe in its truth. . . . Again and again . . . we find witches confessing . . . without an evidence of torture. . . . It was this spontaneity, rather than the confessions themselves, which convinced rational men that the details were true." Thus, we can see how, despite the terrible consequences of a confession, people accepted the official demonology and freely admitted to an imaginary crime.

The vocabularies of motives that were used in the confessions *reflected* the official ideology (i.e., the generalized motivational accounting systems) regarding witchcraft. This ideology, coupled with contemporary social stress, provided in turn the *motivation* and the *accounts* for the confessions, as both constituted a positive feedback loop. Apparently, some of the people who freely confessed had a strange (and for us unintelligible) pleasure from the fear they generated as Satan's powerful servants. The general stress, the official ideology, and the degradation ceremonies (Garfinkel 1956) that the accused suffered, produced a cultural and social transformation that brought about the production of new identities—witches—which received the meaning, content, and motivation for their existence from the official demonological theories and, in turn, reinforced them. Thus, a true micro-macro level link was in operation

PREVIOUS WORKS ON DEVIANCE THAT USED THE CONCEPT OF ACCOUNTS

While C. Wright Mills published his original work in 1940, not very many works have since utilized this innovative concept, nor has a tradition of research using the concept emerged. It thus becomes important to examine the few works in deviance that did utilize the concept and how much support, or challenge, are found there for the theoretical formulations presented here concerning motivational accounting systems. In the following review, I shall confine myself only to those works that have some relevance and bear directly on motivational accounting systems and deviance.[8]

The use of motivational accounting systems in kleptomania and pyromania was found to help deviants to explain their behavior in terms that were popular, sanctioned, or current in a specific culture (Cressey 1962).

McCaghy (1968) found that persons convicted of sexual offenses against children tried to maintain an identity of being "normal" by either denying the act or by attributing the act to excessive consumption of alcohol. Bart (1968) compared the accounts used by two groups of females seeking help in one of two hospital departments: neurology and psychiatry. She found that the different motivational accounting systems used by the two groups were linked to the different social backgrounds from which these females came. Taylor and Walton (1971) examined the types of meanings and motives that industrial saboteurs use to explain and justify their sabotage.

It appears that the field of motivational accounting systems drew some sporadic attention from American sociologists, including some of its "classical" statements, until the early 1970s. From that time on, for reasons that are not at all clear, British sociologists began to be attracted to the field (e.g., see Taylor 1979), and some most significant contributions between the early 1970s and the mid 1980s were indeed made by British sociologists.

Taylor (1972) examined motivational accounting systems among sex offenders, explaining that: "as long as the desire can be described as an uncontrollable urge, it can be allowed to exist as an alien element in an otherwise rational system. The individual does not have to come to terms with it in the same way as he has to come to terms with his belief in democracy" (p. 30). In 1973, Auld investigated the accounts given by drug addicts about themselves, and how the printed media and various control agents gave accounts containing drug-abuse issues. Auld shows how "drugs" were used to explain many "crazy" behaviors. For example, when the 1970 Miss World Contest was interrupted by members of Women's Liberation, Bob Hope (who was the star guest) tried to "make sense" out of what to him seemed utter nonsense and commented that the interrupters "must be on some kinda dope" (p. 157). Likewise, the police explained murder as: "it looks like the act of a drug-crazed man" (p. 159).

Hepworth and Turner (1974) claimed that societal processes influenced a particular type of motivational accounting system—that of confession to murder. "The process of secularization which we referred to earlier as conditioning the nature of confession and enhancing men's awareness not only of a newly discovered personality structure but a different order or relationship to God through men, was accompanied by the emergence of murder as mass entertainment" (p. 43; see also their 1984 book). Clearly, this study links micro-macro societal process by illustrating how people's confessions to murders echoed larger societal processes.

In 1976, Taylor considered the stated and recorded motives of homosexuals outside the "institutional apparatus of criminalization" (p. 97), by focusing on the literary production of a group of British poets. In another 1976 study, Henry Stuart argues that: "the facilitation of criminal activity by drug addicts is, in part, made possible by the actors' use of language constructs, or accounts. These constructs protect persons from, and make them oblivious to, the possibility of State punishment and allows them to maintain a self conception of 'goodness' in the face of adverse moral judgment" (p. 91).

Ditton (1977) found that bread salesmen regularly "fiddle" small amounts of money from their customers. Although this practice was, simply put, stealing, the salesmen managed to sustain a definition of the act as merely "trifling." Ditton showed how these deviant salesmen were able to manipulate their vocabularies of motives in such a way that, despite an unpleasant objective reality, they could negate the guilt and escape responsibility, thus sustaining a positive construction of reality and of their identity and self-image. Ditton also showed that *alibis* were produced publicly and neutralized blame, while *aliases* were generated privately and neutralized feelings of shame.

In 1979, Hardiker and Webb examined the treatment ideology held by probation officers. In the terminology I suggested earlier, we could regard this ideology as a generalized motivational accounting system. They found that: "the structural context of probation work—utilitarian justice and casework treatment notions—creates more 'space' for offering a greater variety of explanations than has often been appreciated" (p. 1) and that the specific given-and-accepted account in each individual case depended on the circumstances of the case.

In 1981, Marshall's and Levi's works were published. Levi's work focused on how the novice hit man develops a system of motivational accounts that helps him reframe (in Goffman's [1974] sense of the term) his experiences and neutralizes guilt and shame. Smith and Preston's (1984) work on gamblers suggested that: "respondents were providing socially acceptable vocabularies of motives to defend self by neutralizing the social stigma attached to gambling and/or justifying one's monetary gains and losses" (p. 725).

Ben-Yehuda and Einstein (1984) examined the written accounts given by thirteen government offices and other major organizations in Israel. They were asked to "explain" the existence of the largest methadone maintenance program in Israel in the midst of the largest garbage dump in the country. Analyzing these accounts revealed a distinct and consistent pattern of "institutional violence" (Liazos 1972) against heroin addicts.

Finally, Boles and Myers (1988) described the accounts which were used in the unlawful practice of sending chain letters through the mail.

CONCLUDING SUMMARY

This chapter constitutes the second axis of the *Theoretical Foundation*. It argues that we should create an analytical integration of processes on the micro-macro levels of analysis through the concept and mechanisms of motivational accounting systems.

Accounting situations are primarily bargaining situations and are therefore fluid, constantly changing and giving rise to emergent identities. This means that they can be, potentially, a liminal ritual where macromoral boundaries of society can be routinely reaffirmed by virtue of the motivational accounting systems to be raised, rejected, or accepted.

Situational motivational accounting systems provide a link between the micro and macro sociological levels of analysis. This two-way link materializes within defined situations of symbolic interaction. On the one hand, macro sociological level elements, such as institutional values, morality and interests, infiltrate face-to-face interactions, influencing definitions of situations, participants' roles, and the interactions' outcomes. On the other hand, new orientations, values, meanings, and moralities that are being constantly generated and negotiated on the face-to-face interaction level can influence values, meanings, and orientations of a whole social system. Thus, the content and structure of motivational accounting systems are basically fluid, negotiated among various societal levels as well as within each level, resulting either in the reinforcement of stability or in change.

Accounting situations, therefore, are a potential source for projected innovation, deviance, and change, to be filtered upward and to help cause change in the moral boundaries of society. These situations also reflect changes in the macro level. Values, power, status, ideology, and interests all play crucial roles in accounting situations and, no doubt, influence the outcome of bargainings over the question of what type of motivational accounting systems can be used in a particular situation.

Viewed in this fashion, the question whether situational motivational accounting systems provide us with the *true* intent of the actors becomes a marginal, really unimportant, question. Any given motivational accounting system must be interpreted as a question "is this a good and acceptable explanation of...." Once accepted, rejected, and/or reacted to in other ways, the actors are free to invoke the use of particular vocabularies of motives and to remold their motivational accounting systems until this bargaining process is exhausted and then finished or stopped. The "truth" in, or validity of, any specific motivational accounting system is, therefore, limited and very specific to a culture, to a symbolic-moral universe, and to a specific social construction of a situation. To claim that these motivational accounting systems hold, perhaps, an objective or transcendental truth, regardless of how, where, when, and why they were manufactured and used, is, in my opinion, misleading and analytically fruitless. Furthermore, the study of motivational accounting systems cannot be isolated from actual behavioral patterns. Vocabularies of motives and motivational accounting systems constitute the essence of symbolic interactions and should not be separated from the context in which they are used. Thus, Fauconnier (1981) notes that: "Truth values are not external to individuals and the course of events ... they are ... *linked to the action and power of individuals* belonging to a rule-governed social system. The testimony of those who hold social power may be the *only observable clue* to the truth value of a proposition ... " (p. 183). "The truth expressed is accepted as *relative to context* rather than absolute" (p. 184).

The types of motivational accounting systems the individual chooses to use are not random inventions. They reflect the type of justification acceptable in a specific moral universe and culture and, therefore, also the way moral boundaries are changed or stabilized. Because morality is an important tool in symbolic interaction and in motivational accounting systems, the analytical break from Durkheim is not complete. Durkheim certainly considered morality and values as most important mechanisms in achieving social integration and control.

Part Two

The Politics and Morality of Deviance: Theory

Chapter Three

Politics and Deviance

INTRODUCTION

The area of politics and deviance has been somewhat chaotic and seems to be much less crystallized than other areas of deviance research. This part of the book is meant to acquaint the reader with the problems involved and suggests a solution.

I shall first describe the historical emergence of the sociological interest in politics and deviance. This part is crucial if we are to understand the field. Then, I shall delve into some definitional problems and suggest a new analytical solution for the problem of conceptualizing politics and deviance. The analysis will reveal that the area of politics and deviance should be thought of in terms of two broad divisions: first, there is *political deviance* itself; second, we have *political elements in what is usually considered as regular, nonpolitical deviance.*

THE DEVELOPMENT OF SOCIOLOGICAL AND CRIMINOLOGICAL INTEREST IN POLITICS AND DEVIANCE

Although Eve's crime implies that the origin of political deviance, in which authority is being challenged, lies back in biblical times, the fact remains that a *real* sociological interest in politics and deviance did not develop until the last decade. There are a few reasons for this.

Political deviance always entails some form of a conflict between two, or more, symbolic-moral universes: that of the challengers and that of those being challenged. Therefore, the history of political deviance is also, in an inverse fashion, the history of morality and the distribution of power. However, in the popular and older professional literature, political deviance was usually taken to mean challenges against the power and legitimacy of the rulers, not vice versa.

When according to Athenian law Socrates was defined as a criminal and condemned to die, his "crime" was so labeled out of a moral conviction that rejected freedom of thought. Athenian society, through the moral agents who defined its moral boundaries, used the generalized motivational accounting system—in the form of the law—to condemn and execute Socrates (and possibly a few others; see Stone 1988), who justified his activity using a very different motivational accounting system, which reflected a different symbolic-moral universe. In the culture in which Socrates lived, his persecutors had more legitimized power, so when the two symbolic-moral universes and opposing systems of vocabularies of motives collided, Socrates lost. In today's Western democratic societies, freedom of thought is hailed as a primary virtue. In other regimes, the individual who exercises freedom of thought, or challenges the "order," is liable to find him/herself imprisoned or committed to an insane asylum. Giordano Bruno died because he challenged the Ptolemaic worldview and the morality that supported it; Galileo as well suffered because of this worldview. Freud's theory, which revolutionized psychology and psychiatry and enriched other disciplines, was originally criticized heavily on moral grounds.

The question of who interprets whose behavior, why, where, and when is very crucial:

> Is, for example, the leader of loose-knit bands of hit-and-run killers of British soldiers a "homicidal maniac," a "crazed cult killer," or a "bandit"? Or is George Washington a revolutionary hero? Is Nat Turner, who executed Virginia slave owners and their families in 1830, in the same category? Is the Jewish terrorist in Palestine in 1948 distinguishable from the Palestinian terrorist in Israel in 1978? (Lauderdale 1980, 5)

The "political" nature of some of these past cases seems irrefutable (see also Cohen S. 1986a).

While societal reactions to assumed acts of drug abuse, prostitution, abortion, homosexuality, as well as rigid sanctions against those who challenged the Ptolemaic worldview were all employed to define the boundaries of symbolic-moral universes, to create rigidity and block change, there can be no doubt that both Socrates and Joan of Arc provide examples of "political deviants" who were severely punished for a deviancy that actually served as a turning point for change.

Joan of Arc, a peasant girl who believed she was acting under divine command, was instrumental in leading the French to a decisive victory and the subsequent coronation of Charles VII. Joan was later captured, put on trial, and convicted as an heretical "deviant." She was executed in 1431, and 489 years later, she was canonized by Pope Benedict XV. In 1920, the French government declared her festival, May 30, a national holiday (Schafer 1974, 50; Robbins 1959, 282–87). Obviously, the vocabularies of motives that were given by her prosecutors and the ones given to justify her canonization in 1920 vary greatly.

In February 1431, she was accused, among other things, of disobeying her parents, of claiming that she would go to paradise and had been responsible only to God and not to the Church (which the judges represented), and of wearing masculine dress. These accusations paved the way for her accusers to explain her behavior in a framework that put blame on Joan of Arc's shoulders. She was cast into an apologetic position and had to explain behavior she had been proud of. From her point of view, these accusations and her prophecies, visions, and voices justified her perception that she was experiencing signs of divine intervention and grace. Thus, two separate, contradictory sets of interpretative moral vocabularies of motives were applied to the same type of behavior, one in the form of formal accusations implying Joan of Arc's guilt and the other in the form of her own beliefs that what the Church interpreted as "deviant" were, in fact, signs of divine grace. Again, a clash of two opposing moral-symbolic universes.

The last illustration I shall bring in this context is a more modern one—that of the famous U.S. Nobel laureate chemist Linus Pauling (e.g., Goodstein 1984), who was awarded his first Nobel prize in chemistry in 1954. During the 1950s, Pauling campaigned very militantly and aggressively against nuclear bomb testing. In 1958, he brought to the United Nations a petition signed by thousands of scientists from different countries, requiring to put an end to tests with nuclear weapons. He based his campaign primarily on the genetic and biological damages these tests were causing. His actions were not taken lightly by contemporary political figures in the United States. He was interrogated by a subcommittee of the U.S. Senate and was prevented from attending international scientific meetings. At some point, he was not very far from being arrested. After the international treaty that put a ban on atmospheric nuclear testing was signed, Pauling received in 1962 a second Nobel award—one for peace, recognizing his endless efforts in this area. Societal reactions to Pauling's acts illustrate how contradictory interpretations may exist regarding one man's action, how respectability can be negotiated and created, and how something that was once defined as "deviant" may be redefined as heroism and appropriate later by differing and clashing symbolic-moral universes. This change signifies the fact that moral meanings were in fact negotiated and that moral boundaries did change. The vocabularies of motives that were employed by the different parties to this controversy in the 1950s and 1960s and now in the 1980s obviously reflect these changing concepts of morality.

The above illustrations indeed indicate that one can trace easily the concepts of politics and deviance from biblical times to the present. Any particular choice of cases would certainly reflect this. They also point to the fact that while the examples and cases for political deviance were available for anyone who would have wanted to interpret them, the interpretations were not made.

One historical development that facilitated the development of the area of politics and deviance was the development of pluralistic and complex cultures where the very definitions of what is, and what is not, deviance became problematic (e.g., see Douglas 1970a).

From the classical approach to positivism. Beginning with the so-called classical school in criminology in the eighteenth century and continuing with almost no interruptions until the 1960s, virtually no attention was paid to the element of *power* in deviance. That was true for the perspectives of "social pathology," "social disorganization" (and the "Chicago School"), "deviant behavior," and the positivist perspective in general.[1] While the *moral* nature of deviance was very clear to theoreticians who worked in these perspectives, the *political* nature of deviance simply escaped their attention. For them, the power element in deviance remained elusive and implicit. As Stanley Cohen (1986a) pointed out: "The faith of positivist criminology was that there was a 'thing' out there—crime—whose existence and pathological nature were self evident" (p. 468; see also Cohen, 1986b). These approaches accepted, to a very large extent, a nonproblematic and consensual interpretation of the social system, hence followed a nonproblematic definition of the "real" nature of deviance and crime.

The value-conflict approach of the 1930s (Rubington and Weinberg 1971, ch. 4; Davis 1975, ch. 6) helped bring into a clear and sharp focus the political nature of deviance and crime. However, the approach itself did not last for long and was overpowered by the tidal wave of positivism.

Developments in the 1960s and 1970s. The 1960s and 1970s witnessed the rise of a few approaches in the sociological study of deviance.

While they did not focus on politics and deviance exclusively, their methods, formulations, and interpretations, as well as their challenge to previous theoretical approaches, drew attention to various aspects of power and morality. These included the dramaturgical, existential, ethnomethodological, and phenomenological approaches to deviance (e.g., see for reviews Thio 1988; Goode 1984a; Douglas and Waksler 1982). The *most* influential approach, however, was the symbolic interactionist inspired *labeling approach* (e.g., see Becker 1963; Schur 1971; Goode 1978; Dotter and Roebuck 1988).

Becker (1963) defined the approach as:

Social groups create deviance by making rules whose infraction constitutes deviance, and by applying those rules to particular people and labeling them as outsiders. . . . Deviance is not a quality of the act a person commits but rather a consequence of the application by others of rules and sanctions to an "offender." The deviant is one to whom the label has successfully been applied: deviant behavior is behavior that people so label. (P. 9)

Erikson (1962) added that:

Deviance is not a property *inherent* in certain forms of behavior; it is a property *conferred upon* these forms by the audience which directly or indirectly witness them. Sociologically, then, the critical variable is the *social* audience . . . since it is the audience which eventually decides whether or not any given action or actions will become a visible case of deviation. (P. 308)

In this approach, a deviant was defined by the societal reaction to a presumed violation of expectations (Rubington and Weinberg 1971; 169).

The labeling approach argues that deviance is essentially relativistic and interactional, that it is the product of lengthy negotiations, and that it is less dependent on the acts of the deviant than on the acts of the respondents. This approach focused attention not only on the deviant's own reactions to the labels but also on the actions of social control agencies and actors who were themselves producing deviance through the creation of moral panics, laws, stigmatization, and labeling. Labeling theory thus shifted attention from the individual deviant to the environment and emphasized the conflictual nature of the labeling process.

The labeling approach's characterization of deviance introduced—quite explicitly—elements of power and morality into deviance research in a way similar to the older value conflict approach. If society creates the rules whose infraction constitutes deviance, and if deviance is not a property inherent in any particular behavioral pattern, but one that is a conferred property, then one must ask how and why rules are made and who holds the power to invoke the label "deviance." Once this conclusion is made, the road to politics and deviance is almost open.

An illustration of the labeling approach to the study of political deviance is Ingraham's (1979) work, where he stated explicitly that all those acts that officials consider political and criminal indeed constitute political crime. His approach totally disregarded the actual nature of the acts, power, morality, and motivational accounts given by those committing them.

All the above-mentioned approaches, with labeling at the front, emphasized the *problematic* nature of deviance and hence called much more explicit attention to the elements of power and morality.

Lauderdale and Inverarity (Lauderdale 1980, ch. 1) noted that, in addition to these developments, the approach to a political analysis of deviance was furthered in the 1960s and 1970s by studies of the relativity of deviance, the theoretical case studies of changes in definitions of deviance, and the antipsychiatry movement. Kooistra (1985) adds that, during these years:

> Alleged discriminatory prosecution of political dissidents by agents of the government, the investment of "ordinary" crime with symbolic political meaning, the politicization (and glorification) of criminals from minority groups, illegal governmental activities conducted for political advantage—ranging from violations of civil rights to breaches of international law in Viet Nam—political trials such as the trial of the "Chicago Eight," and some forms of mass dissident—ranging from urban riots to peaceful college demonstrations—were forms of behavior that begged for analysis and classifications. (P. 100)

Two other, more significant developments contributed, perhaps more than others, to the increased interest in politics and deviance: control theory and the revival of interest in conflict theories, especially as developed in British criminology in the 1970s.

Control theory.   Control theory, which has long been a part of the sociological study of deviance, did not seek direct answers to questions relating to the causes of deviance, but rather asked about the source(s) of conformity. Conceptualized within this perspective, deviance is not thought of as *caused* by "something," but is rather thought to be *made possible* because social systems (or specialized parts in them) fail to prevent its occurrence (Frazier 1976; Thio 1988; 43–50). Deviance, therefore, occurs when a society loses control over individual members, ergo Nettler's (1972) observation that while human beings "may be domestic animals . . . they need domestication" (p. 333). Durkheim's classical study on suicide and anomie also illustrated this point. Parsons (1951) summarized this issue by stating that the sociology of social control focuses on the analysis of the processes that tend to counteract deviance (assuming, of course, that "deviance" is nonproblematic; see also Gibbs 1985).

Social control theories assume the existence of two types of control mechanisms. First, there are the "inner mechanisms," which are thought to be somewhere within the individual, for example, ego, superego, and conscience. Second, we find the "external mechanisms," which are thought to be outside the individual, for example, parents, the law, police, and community. In some cases, the distinction is hazy, especially if one starts analyzing the "inner representation" of external events. For example, while "conscience" should be considered an inner mechanism, its development, formation, and crystallization are certainly due to "external" factors.[2]

Finally, in recent years, sociologists of deviance and criminologists have begun to focus attention on control theory on the macro levels—control and the state, control and politics (e.g., see Cohen and Scull 1983; Cohen 1985; Davis and Anderson 1983; Black 1984). In this way, whole social systems may be conceptualized as control organs. It is not entirely clear, however, whether these two different approaches to social control—the micro and the later macro—are compatible, and if so, in what way.[3]

Neither the control theories mentioned here nor the statement that control theories have traditionally focused on internal versus external factors should mislead us about the nature of control. Every ideology or religion provides various control mechanisms, some of which are external, while others are internalized through various processes of socialization. Norbeck (1961, ch. 10) pointed out that morality construction is an essential part of every religion and that these constructions, in the form of ethical codes, are translated into actual, micro level behavior of individual actors. Adherence to rules is often justified by a moral universe (or code of ethics) that was either inspired or dictated by a sacred deity. Religious (or cultic) moral universes are typically embedded in a specific and finite cosmic order, linked with awesome, transcendental, universal deities. Furthermore, all religions offer explanations for temporal occurrences. Adherents to religion are told that if one leads a pious life-style, supernatural rewards will ensue (e.g., eternal life in paradise). If, however, one goes astray, supernatural punishment will follow. Reinforcement of these ideas (about what is morally and socially acceptable and appropriate behavior) coupled with a complex system of divine rewards and punishments is a very effective form of social control. As Norbeck noted, a belief in supernatural forces can give credibility to various man-made laws. The confession in Christianity illustrates this point (e.g., see Hepworth and Turner 1984). However, not only religions exercise powerful control; such ideologies as Marxism or Maoism have similar powerful control mechanisms. Although the idea of social control on the micro level may help us link the micro-macro level motivational accounting systems, the idea of control on the macro level is linked easier to the idea of *generalized motivational accounting systems*.

Control is linked intimately not only to particular symbolic-moral universes, but to the use of power to enforce the moral dictates and boundaries of these symbolic-moral universes. Davis and Anderson (1983) state that: "social control is always, in the final analysis, experience of power. . . . The social control institutions are 'packages' of power techniques" (p. 318). It should not, therefore, surprise us to find that interest in control theories also raises interest in politics and deviance.[4] Control theory has explicit political overtones. Morality and power are understood in terms such as "internal control" and "external control," and control theory's basic assumption is that people must be politically controlled. Likewise, Davis' (1975, 192–224), chapter on social control, contrary to other texts in social deviance, is heavily influenced by a model of political conflict and interprets social control as part of a specific politico-economic perspective.

Conflict theory. The second significant development that aroused sociologists' interest in political factors in deviance were *non-Marxist and Marxist conflict theory*, in general, and the new British criminology in particular (for short reviews, see Pfohl 1985, ch. 10; Goode 1984a, 70–79).

The Marxist theory of deviance is actually a variant of the more general conflict theory. Modern conflict theories in deviance stem from the older value-conflict approach, and they may encompass the following theories: subcultural theories maintaining that subgroups promote values that oppose those of the surrounding society; labeling theories emphasizing the societal response to assumed acts of deviance; and group conflict theories stating that conflict leads to deviance from the activities of socially and economically dominant groups in society (Hagan 1977, 103–42). Marxist theories of deviance are included in the third category.

The Marxist approach genuinely tried to associate deviance directly with the elements of sociological analysis in general. Krisberg (1975), for example, defined privileges as: "the possession of that which is valued by a particular social group in a given historical period" (p. 20), and he further claimed that the societal privilege structure was closely linked to deviance because it determined who received various societal privileges and why. This analysis represents a stratification problem, directly related to the Marxist analysis of deviance, which claimed that crime is a by-product of an unjust and alienating structure of economic institutions, which in turn shape the social and political institutions. Thus, the structure of society as a whole is perceived as "criminogenic" (e.g., Schur 1969; Reasons 1974a; Galliher and McCartney 1977; Quinney and Wildeman 1977; Chambliss 1978; Greenberg 1981;Beirne and Quinney 1982. See also Alexander 1982).[5]

Stanley Cohen (1974) portrayed the complicated development of the fields of criminology and sociology of deviance in Britain, noting that:

the very categories of crime and deviance . . . are problematic in specifically political ways. That is, the field has something to do with control, power, legitimacy, ideology. Skolnik points to two cases: "it's becoming increasingly apparent to a whole generation of criminologists and sociologists, that it is increasingly difficult to distinguish between crime and political and moral dissent" . . . then, in connexion with drug legislation, if one asks questions such as how the political structure ever allowed laws like this to be passed, "as a criminologist or sociologist you necessarily come into the field of political science" . . . the problem is the structural and political *loci* of definitions of deviance. (P. 5)

In the early 1970s, a group of British criminologists developed a new Marxist criminology.[6] The most representative presentation of their ideas appears in *The New Criminology: For a Social Theory of Deviance* (1973), written by Ian Taylor, Paul Walton, and Jock Young and originally published by Routledge and Kegan Paul. This book, one of the finest critiques in the field of the sociology of deviance, clearly leaned toward Marxist conflict theory. The book was the first of an entire literature that emerged from the neo-Marxist British group of sociologists (see e.g., Carlen and Collison 1980; Cohen 1981).

American scholars, such as Quinney, Chambliss, as well as others (e.g., see Goode 1984a; 38–39), responded by developing their own brands of Marxist-oriented sociology of deviance. This criminology, often called "new" or "radical," paved the way for the political analysis of deviance and for the investigation of the political aspects of deviance. It is interesting to note the topics that were included in Taylor and Taylor's (1973) volume, *Politics and Deviance*: crime, corporations, and the American social order; social control in Cuba; housing; psychiatry and the university; hippies; among others. Clearly, the authors chose these problems in an attempt to show how various forms of behavior may be interpreted as deviant by using a political perspective.

These two developments—control theory and the new "radical" criminology—have during the last decade brought very forcefully the topic of politics and deviance into the halls of criminologists and sociologists of deviance.

Summary.   This part provided a brief review of the concept of politics and deviance within the sociological study of deviance.

The descriptive analysis given here explains both the late emergence of the field of politics and deviance and, in part, its chaotic nature. For a very long time, no approach in the sociological study of deviance analyzed explicitly the analytical combination of politics and deviance. The value-conflict approach (both of the 1930s and the 1970s) attempted this task, more successfully in the last decade, within a very particular theoretical framework. Politics and deviance have never received the same attention as traditional areas of deviance research, such as mental illness, drug abuse, sexual deviance, juvenile delinquency, and others.

CONCEPTUAL BACKGROUND:
POWER AND MORALITY

As can be inferred from the above, the relation between politics and deviance, and the definition of this area, has always been elusive (Kooistra 1985). Nettler (1972) even pointed out that "being political . . . generates its own pressures for fraud. To be political is to be entangled by the need to attain and maintain power, through the appeasement of conflicting interests, within the limitations of a real world. This entanglement stimulates lying—to oneself and to others. . . . Lying is a vocational hazard of the politician . . . " (pp. 181–182).

Problems of definition. Schafer (1974) suggested that political criminals are those who believe that their criminal actions will result in an improved social order. Ingraham (1979), in the spirit of the labeling approach, chose to define political crime as those acts that public officials regard as political and criminal, regardless of their real nature or the motivation of those who committed them.

Lauderdale's (1980, 3–12) work distinguished between two alternate approaches to the definition of political deviance. The first approach defines a specific deviant act as political according to the nature of the act itself. An act would be considered political deviance according to the magnitude of harm caused. Examples of deviance in this category are exploitation, sexism, racism, imperialism, profiteering, and consumer fraud (Lauderdale 1980, 6). This approach implies that the distinction between "political" and "nonpolitical" deviance lies in the consequences of the act (depending on the moral evaluation of the consequences), and may contradict the view that deviance is a relative phenomenon. Even in this approach, however, one has to answer such questions as "who defines what as sexism, racism, etc., and why." The ideological context of defining something as "political deviance" as based on the magnitude of harm done is of crucial importance— as well as the concepts of power and morality of those making the evaluation. Thus, I find the category of "universal" crime—as implied by this approach—extremely problematic.

Lauderdale's alternate definition of political deviance is according to the *intent* of the deviant. Minor (1975), who examined thoroughly this approach, noted that political deviance consisted of those forms of deviance and crime with political motivations, perpetrated by altruistic individuals: "Political crime is defined as legally proscribed acts . . . which are motivated by the desire to influence public policy or power relations through the commission of the crime, and which are characterized by concern for group or societal welfare over considerations of personal gain" (p. 395).

Minor's and Lauderdale's focus is on the deviant's motivational accounting system as a means of defining intent. Deviants who justify their actions on the basis of self-interest fall into the category of general, nonpolitical deviance. However, if the deviant acts are attributed to the interests of an oppressed group, the deviant is considered political. Thus, a spy motivated by ideals is somehow perceived as more respectable (and dangerous) than one working simply for a salary (e.g., see Hagan F. 1987). Robbing a bank for personal gain is considered a regular crime, while committing the same act for an underground movement is considered a political act. This distinction, however, may become easily confusing. For example, if someone steals food in the self-interest of not starving, is this a crime or is it political deviance? Another difficulty with focusing on intent is that the deviant's motivational accounting systems may not always reflect his/her original motivation. Frequently, a motivational accounting system is provided for the deviant by interested parties in order to impress particular audiences in the validity of particular constructions of reality, or of specified selves (e.g., make the deviant appear as insane, hero, repentant sinner, and the like). The determination of intent, therefore, depends on the situation and is socially negotiated and constructed. Patricia Hearst illustrated this problem.

When booked at the San Mateo County Jail, Patricia Hearst changed the motivational accounting systems that she used several times in rapid succession, fitting and addressing them to different symbolic-moral universes. She first

> defiantly listed her occupation as "urban guerrilla". In the course of the legal proceedings against her involving bank robbery, assault, and kidnaping, Patty Hearst came to accept an alternative psychiatric definition of her behavior as illness induced by traumatic episodes of solitary confinement and extreme anxiety. Ultimately her behavior was defined as criminal in nature and intent. . . . What makes this . . . particular episode unusual is the ease and rapidity with which a single actor moved from political to medical to criminal definitions of the same behavior. . . . (Inverarity 1980, 104)

Sagarin (1973, viii) states that violations of the law that are motivated by political aims—that is, by the intent of bringing about (or preventing) a change in the political system, in the distribution of political powers, or in the structure of political-governmental bodies —are political deviances.

Kooistra's (1985) work summarized critically what he saw as the three broad theoretical approaches to the definition of "political crime." The first "consists of codified legal categories that are presumed to describe *acts* which are political offenses by nature." (p. 101) The second "stresses the *motivation* of the offender as the key for determining whether a crime is political." (p. 101) The third "contends that the essence of political crime is the *social reaction* it elicits." (p. 101) The applicability of these three approaches to my approach is limited. To begin with, we have to ask ourselves about the nature of the relations between politics, crime and deviance. Let me start, therefore, by clarifying a possible conceptual problem: that of the distinction between political deviance and political crime. Generally speaking, *crime* is a sub-category of *deviance*. Crime implies that specific state made rules/laws were violated, and state pre-determined punishments are applied following apprehension and trial, Hence, there are various forms of deviance which are *criminalized* by the state. Because political crime is a sub-category of political deviance, and in order to keep the analytical level on the broadest level of generalization, I shall focus on the broader intersection of politics and deviance and not on the more limited political crime. Second, the relativistic position I take precludes the first of Kooistra's approaches. My approach would touch the second and third approaches.

The issues of power, threat, and legitimacy. Conrad and Schneider (1980) pointed out that the question of who defines who as "deviant" is determined by social power and "The power to . . . define and construct reality is linked intimately to the structure of power in a society at a given historical period . . . constructions of deviance are linked closely to the dominant social control institutions in . . . society" (p. 17). Thio (1988, chap. 4) takes a similar view, pointing out that the distribution of power in societies is intimately linked to deviance, especially regarding such issues as social consensus about what is right and what is wrong, and the type of deviance expected from both the powerful and the powerless.[7] Sykes (1978), Thio (1988), Box (1983), Haskell and Yablonski (1983), Bonn (1984), and Michalowski (1985) all state that political deviance involves, somehow, power and that political deviance always involves a struggle between the powerful and the powerless.

   Haskell and Yablonski (1983, 415) state that political deviance is usually committed either to affect changes in the political or social system or for the purpose of maintaining power (see also Turk 1982, 14). However, the perception that deviance in general and political deviance in particular is an arena wherein the "powerful" and "powerless" play a futile game is not new (Schafer 74, ch. 4). As early as 1898, Proal pointed out that power was an important factor in political deviance. Garofalo's well-known book, *Criminology*, first published in 1885, also viewed political crime in this context.

It seems that all crimes and deviance have a political nature because "social groups create deviance by making the rules whose infraction constitute deviance" (Becker 1963, 9). This approach, however, must consider the problem of *who* makes the rules and *why*. The concept of power, in itself, cannot possibly explain the issue sufficiently. After all, there are numerous cases of rules and laws *against* the powerful, and while societies can be characterized by conflict, there is also much consensus. It should not surprise us to find that political deviance and crimes may be committed by the powerless and the powerful. This view is consistent with Foucault's (1980): "Power can be analyzed as something which circulates. . . . It is never localized here or there. . . . Power is employed and exercised through a netlike organization" (p. 98). As we shall see in chapters five to eight, power is indeed dispersed and can be used and generated by different groups and individuals. Hence, power is a necessarily analytical element if we are to assess correctly the nature of deviance and politics. It is clear that power and conflict, in the broadest sense of the terms, help define who will deviantize whom.

In this sense, we can even state that deviants are those who simply do not have enough power to prevent others from defining them as such. Horowitz and Liebovitz (1968) stated that: "Deviance is a conflict between at least two parties: superordinates who make and enforce the rules, and subordinates whose behavior violates those rules" (p. 282). Lofland (1969) further strengthened this definition when he stated that deviance was: "The name of a conflict game in which individuals or loosely organized small groups with little power are strongly feared by a well organized, sizable minority, or majority, who have a large amount of power" (p. 14). Schur (1980) coined the term "deviantization process," referring to the process through which particular groups of people become deviantized, and stated that "stigma contests" are the major mechanism for such processes: "partisans in collective stigma contests are widely engaged in the manipulation of political symbols for the control of public opinion" (p. 135).

Scholars writing from the perspective that emphasizes the element of power in deviance and politics tend sometimes to add the "threat" potential. Turk (1979) noted that "deviations are whatever is felt, consciously or not, to be threatening" (p. 466). The "threat" potential implicit in deviance is a very interesting idea. If "deviance" is only a contest between the powerful and the powerless, then we must also ask who can be threatened and why? The real answer to this question is not who but what. Mizruchi (1983) noted that "dissident behavior may be perceived as a threat to the normative system of a society" (p. 11). Although Mizruchi's statement is in the right direction, he did not go far enough. Bonn (1984) rightly noted that in political crime "the symbolic meaning of the criminal act is more important than the act itself" because "it is the symbolic nature of their actions that constitutes a threat to society" (p. 358). Schur (1979) stated that deviance, politics, and social change should be thought of as one theoretical construct: "The concept of *perceived threat* provides a key link between the overall or basic boundary-maintaining function of deviance defining and the emergence of particular collective definitions of deviance within specific social contexts" (p. 24). Hence, Schur implied that a society actually "gets the deviance it deserves."

The reason that deviance and politics involve a threat potential, and that the symbolic nature of the political deviance is perceived to be of such importance, is precisely because the concept of power itself is insufficient to explain this phenomenon.

Max Weber (1947), made a distinction between legitimate power (which he referred to as "authority") and illegitimate power (which he referred to as "coercion"). In a very fundamental sense, power *has to be legitimized*. Attempts to use sheer naked power alone to stigmatize or deviantize would probably fail because in a negotiated social order the use of power must be explained and accepted. An acceptable, individual, collective, or generalized motivational accounting system must be invented and given in order to justify the act of using power. Therefore, a clever utilization of an accepted motivational accounting system can justify a political deviance by the powerless and help them gain, or generate, power and in this way help promote social change. The powerful, who might use power without providing acceptable motivational accounting systems, might lose some — or in the long run all — of their power. Rock (1973b) added that in complex societies "the coercive face of power is usually masked or partially replaced by a set of legitimations which exact a more or less willing compliance from the ruled" (p. 144).

On what grounds can power, or its use, be legitimized or accounted for? Weber's (1947, 324–92) classical work distinguished among three major types (or bases) of legitimation: charismatic, rational, or traditional. Here, I would like to go beyond these types. Let me suggest that the use of power is legitimized through the use of a complex system of symbols: morality (or ideology), which in itself may be delineated by a charismatic, rational, or traditional source. Morality can be thought of as the societal generalized motivational accounting system on the macro level that provides actors with rules and legitimizes the use of power. It can also justify resistance to those who are considered to be powerful by developing a countermorality. I shall next examine the sociological nature of morality and then locate the analytical place, meaning, and implication of morality within social systems.

The issue of morality. Deviance is linked intimately to what is perceived as conventional morality and serves as its mirror image. In this sense, it is true that all crimes and deviances have a political nature because socially upheld prohibitions always defend a specific value system or morality (Schafer 1974, 19). However, although the problem of understanding deviance in general, and politics and deviance in particular, is linked very closely with that of morality, very little has been written about the complex interaction between the two. Rock (1974) even claimed that the sociology of deviance has failed to study morality systematically and that if we are to understand deviance we must first understand the moral order.

Morality is an important sociological concept, its main function being to orient and direct social actions toward specified goals. Morality not only determines social goals but defines the legitimate ways to achieve them. Morality, in any society, is represented by a complicated structure of symbols that are communicated and establish the significance attached to various societal issues.

A value system, or morality, can be broadly defined as those ideals, mores, or criteria that shape normative behavior. Thus, the value of the sacredness of life would dictate the norm of "do not kill." Not all values, or morals, are of equal importance in the individual's cognitive map or within a particular culture. A hierarchy of morals is, therefore, usually established in which some values gain priority over others.[8]

Doing morality is the process through which an object or process is evaluated as good or evil. What is regarded as good or bad varies among societies and fluctuates over time within one society. In complex and pluralistic societies, morality is negotiated. Laws and punishments therefore reflect not only society's moral hierarchies but also the outcomes of complex negotiations about morality. Negotiating morality means that the moral boundaries of society are constantly fluctuating. According to Becker (1963, ch. 8), in certain periods and places, people arise who by virtue of their initiative, political power, influence, connections, access to decisionmakers, skillful use of publicity, and success in neutralizing opposition are successful in forcing their interests, ideologies, and values onto society as a whole (see also Hills 1980, 35–37). Becker called these people "moral entrepreneurs" or "moral crusaders," and he termed the process through which they help shape societal moral boundaries a "moral crusade." A successful moral crusade may create awareness to particular issues by providing appropriate vocabularies of motives that *explain* the situation and make it meaningful. Under the proper conditions, such a moral crusade may give rise to dynamics characteristic of "social problems" and help promote social change as well (e.g., homosexuality, prohibition, antidrug use, pro marijuana use, abortion, etc.; see, e.g., Kitsuse and Spector 1975; Spector and Kitsuse 1977; and chapter five).

The sociology of the law provides a most interesting illustration for the application of the concepts moral entrepreneur and moral crusade. The law symbolizes and reflects different moral ideas in society. As sociologists know all too well, the law reflects the final outcome of a long process of interaction and negotiation among different interest groups and does not necessarily embrace the legitimate needs of large sections of the population (e.g., Hagan 1985). Marijuana laws in the United States today demonstrate this problem.

> Marijuana has become the "new Prohibition" in contemporary American society, with upwards of 40 million persons having used this illicit drug, perhaps one third of them using it on a more or less regular basis. Effective enforcement of the law has become impossible. The use and sale of marijuana remain illegal, however, primarily because most of the older adult public are ideologically opposed to total decriminalization. Use of the drug is symbolically associated in much of the public mind with many kinds of activities, lifestyles, and moral and political beliefs that these dominant groups find repugnant (e.g., hedonism, sexual promiscuity, altered states of consciousness, radicalism, irreverence towards authority, and so on) (Hills 1980; 38).

Morality runs deeper than its "technical" or "definitional" aspects (e.g., see Astrachan 1985; Jayyusi 1984). First, Becker (1967) noted that societies have "hierarchies of credibility," which provide a stratification principle in the moral hierarchy. These hierarchies mean that specific members of society—by virtue of their social position— are perceived to be more credible than others. Second, Rock (1973b) pointed out that:

> In complex societies, the distribution of deviant phenomena is

closely linked to the distribution of power and life-chances. . . . A stratification system can also be viewed as a moral system: a major organization of beliefs about the rights, duties and moral properties of the members of a society. . . . A system of control based on authority rests, in part, on a recognition of the *moral* right of the authoritative to make decisions. . . . Thus, in a stable, but unequal society class position is often identified with moral position—the higher one's position in a stratification order, the greater is one's moral worth. (P. 47).

Rock's thesis established a clear relationship between moral status and social position. If a particular type of "deviant" occupies a lower social position, the probability of his/her being regarded as an actual deviant and thus acquiring a deviant identity increases. A change in the social position of the deviant could transform the moral meaning and the "threat" potential of the deviance. Thus, particular classes of actors in any society may be more susceptible to being charged with moral inferiority and deviance than other classes of actors (Duster 1970, 247). Two illustrations for this idea appear in this book. In the case of deviant sciences, we shall see that the probability of ideas being branded "deviant" increases in direct relation to the social status (within academia) of the scientists promoting them. In the second illustration, we shall see that the change in the type of population using illicit psychoactive substances was closely linked to changes in morality and, therefore, to changes in society's reaction toward these drug users. When drug use was restricted to the lower class, scant attention was paid to the problem, and societal response was principally through law enforcement. When, however, educated, middle-class youth started abusing drugs, the response changed to a therapeutic, rehabilitative, educational, and preventative one, and the emphasis on law enforcement diminished.

Religion, politics, medicine, the arts, and sciences are other areas that define morality through complex sets of symbols in the form of ethics and rituals. Morality thus renders a most important service to society through defining its boundaries.

One must realize that competing moral crusaders and moral panics, all reflecting a "collective search for identity" (Klapp 1969), can be widespread phenomena primarily in pluralistic, heterogenous societies where morality itself is subject to negotiations. Morality debates are usually carried out by moral agents, such as politicians, law enforcement agents, lawyers, psychiatrists, social workers, and media people. Complex societies are morally heterogeneous, and different sections of society present different moral universes.

Society's moral stratification has a few implications. Douglas (1971) noted that "Every . . . police force has a vice squad and narcotic squad, but no police force has a professional squad, a medical squad or a lawyer squad. Doctors, lawyers and other professionals . . . are allowed to police themselves, so that their criminal activities do not often become officially categorized as crimes, whereas the lower classes have their policing done for them by the police" (p. 92).[9]

Morality and value systems are important concepts for our understanding of the nature of deviance because the differential damages attributed to various deviant acts (e.g., drug abuse, prostitution, homosexuality) are peripheral to the main offense, which is a moral one. A moral challenge may be perceived as far more threatening than a physical threat. Durkheim's (1933) keen observation that "An act is criminal when it offends strong and defined states of the collective conscience. . . . When [a crime] is committed . . . it is the common conscience which is attacked" (pp. 70–110), corroborates this conclusion. If, in essence, crimes damage morality, then we have to ask *whose* morality? How powerful are the upholders of the offended moral system? And to what extent do they feel threatened?

Deviance, power and morality.   Understanding politics and deviance means that, in addition to understanding societal power negotiations and configurations, we have to examine how the use of that power is legitimized in the form of morality negotiations. These negotiations mean that actors exchange motivational accounting systems, aimed to construct specific social realities, either reinforcing existing moral boundaries of what is considered right and what wrong, or aiming to change these boundaries (e.g., Jayyusi 1984). Thus, Rock's (1973b) statement that political deviance "is deliberately organized to persuade, convert or force others in redefining important sectors of the world" (p. 100) becomes meaningful.

Diagram 1 may be useful to clarify the issue:

In brief, the diagram describes moral entrepreneurs who initiate moral crusades in order to persuade other social actors in the validity of the formers' symbolic-moral universe. These moral crusaders try to generate power and influence in order to restructure societal moral boundaries and consequently to redefine morality, values and conduct norms which in turn define the ideological and behavioral parameters of the social order. Deviance, and political deviance, are

Diagram 1

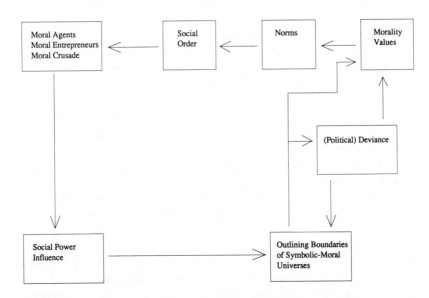

defined by existing moral boundaries, but they also challenge them. Regular deviance does that implicitly; political deviance does that explicitly. Political deviance is thus influenced by the process, but it also influences it. While political deviance is located on the right side of the chart, moral entrepreneurs *may* sometimes be considered as deviants, e.g., conscientious objectors, war resisters, Robin Hood types. It is the societal reaction to the challenge of (political) deviance which may be helpful in the process of redefining moral boundaries. Thus, when political deviance become formalized, it may itself start a cycle similar to the one described in the chart. Primarily, however, political deviance, constitutes an explicit challenge on moral boundaries. This is how we can conceptualize political deviance within the context of sociological processes of change and stability.

The flow through this chart may be easier to interpret in a simple social system but more complicated to follow in a pluralistic social order characterized by negotiated moral boundaries and a relatively high degree of cultural compartmentalization.

So far, I clarified the nature of morality in the context of power, politics, and deviance. The other issue I have to address now is that of locating the analytical place, meaning, and implication of morality within social systems.

The concept of a symbolic-moral universe has become very central to my analysis. Berger and Luckmann (1966) characterize symbolic universes as: "bodies of theoretical tradition that integrate different provinces of meaning and encompass the institutional order in a symbolic totality. . . . symbolic processes are processes of signification that refer to realities other than those of everyday experience. . . . the symbolic sphere relates to the most comprehensive level of legitimation" (p. 113). Furthermore, they suggest the concept of "universe maintenance," claiming that when two, or more, contradicting symbolic universes (i.e., moral sets) meet, a conflict is unavoidable: "heretical groups posit not only a theoretical threat to the symbolic universe, but a practical one to the institutional order legitimated by the symbolic universe in question" (p. 124; see also Scott 1972). In other words, a specific symbolic universe helps its inhabitants to better understand their reality, to make sense out of what might otherwise seem senseless. A symbolic universe therefore provides its inhabitants with the necessary motivational accounting systems (based on particular vocabularies of motives) that are utilized by the inhabitants to explain and justify their past and future behavior. In this sense, each elective center (Cohen, Ben-Yehuda, and Aviad 1987) offers its adherents a symbolic-moral universe and the derivative motivational accounting systems. The different motivational accounting systems expressed by inhabitants of different symbolic-moral universes would necessarily expose the symbolic differences between these groups.[10]

Viewed in this way, deviance and deviantization become central phenomena when two, or more, symbolic-moral universes meet, compete, negotiate, and clash. Each of these universes is vitally interested not only in its own survival but also in showing its moral superiority. Thus, each symbolic-moral universe is engaged in generating power and in attempting to widen the basis of its legitimacy—that is, these symbolic-moral universes are involved in moral, power, and stigma contests. The ability of different symbolic-moral universes to generate and use power, as well as their ability to legitimize their claims, will eventually determine who will deviantize whom, where, and when.

Where morality is continuously negotiated, moral boundaries are constantly fluctuating. Moral entrepreneurs, moral crusades, social power, and interest groups play a crucial role in such negotiations. The perceived threat of any particular real, imaginary, or assumed type of deviance is an important issue for basic boundary-maintaining or boundary-changing functions of deviance.

The analysis so far points out that every deviance has a political nature because, basically, power and morality determine who would deviantize whom (Schur 1980). However, the process of defining any particular behavioral pattern as "deviant," and persecuting those who adhere to it, is primarily based on negotiations. It is not always the case that the "powerful" get their way. Furthermore, laws sanctioning a specific behavioral pattern are not always enforced. For example, while, for many years, the law in Israel did not allow homosexual acts (even between consenting adults), the Israeli police did not enforce this law—unless there was a complaint. Clearly, a few groups (especially the religious parties), in Israel were able to mobilize enough power to persuade others that it was important—symbolically—to have this law. They were also acutely aware that, for other moral reasons, this law was not enforceable. Thus, the law existed, the symbolic message was there, but no real enforcement followed.

Another type of deviance happens when deviants distinctly threaten the moral legitimacy of those who have the power, or when those who have the power and are considered to represent negotiated, agreed-upon morality abuse the power and morality vested in them.

Thus, Spector and Kitsuse (1977) map the ways in which specific issues may be transformed into a "social problem" as a "claim making activity" (ch. 5) of different moral entrepreneurs. This is an interesting way to examine how social change may be introduced via societal reactions to real, imaginary, or assumed deviance.

Simple and complex societies: power, morality, and deviance. Durkheim (1973) was well aware of the problem concerning the moral structure of society (see also Wallwork 1972). Discussing Durkheim's (1933) conceptualization of morality inevitably brings us back to what he felt was the very core of society: the collective conscience, which he defined as follows: "The totality of beliefs and sentiments common to average citizens of the same society forms a determinate system which has its own life; one may call it the 'collective' or 'common conscience' . . . It is independent of the particular conditions in which individuals are placed" (pp. 79–80). Thus, the collective conscience is the essence that defines the moral boundaries of any social system, and it therefore is regarded as sacrosanct. Each individual's meaning of life is associated with his/her society's collective conscience. It follows that Shils's (1970) "center" is equivalent to the collective conscience: "The center . . . is . . . the realm of values and beliefs. . . . This central value system is the central zone of society" (p. 1). Durkheim's collective conscience and Shils's center also parallel Parsons' (1971) "societal community": "the salient foci of tension and conflict, and thus of creative innovation" (p. 121). Obviously, the closer one is to the moral center, the higher is the credibility, respectability, and decency attributed to that actor (Duster 1970).

In simple societies, the collective conscience (or center) appears quite specific, simple, and integrative. In complex societies, the existence and role of the collective conscience become problematic.[11] In such societies, a few competing and different centers exist; yet society still maintains some general form of integration. Support for this idea can also be found in Durkheim's discussion of the "non-contractual elements of contract" (Durkheim 1933: 111–115, 206–219). Despite the existence of different, or differentiated, collective consciences, there is still a symbolic-moral universe (or enough overlapping between the different symbolic-moral universes) that is shared by all members of society. Once this situation withers social disintegration is inevitable. This situation obviously facilitates both variety and organic solidarity.

In both simple and complex societies, the consciousness of likeness is a problematic issue. While relatively simple, integrated, and cohesive social systems are characterized by fewer competing symbolic-moral universes, and by greater stability, social change *does* occur. By the same token, while change appears to be a hallmark of modern, complex, and pluralistic social orders, such orders also exhibit elements of social stability. In both types of society, deviance plays a crucial role regarding social change and social stability.

In simpler social systems, the societal reaction triggered by deviance will typically strengthen rigidity and help define moral boundaries. Interpreting deviant acts will be less problematic there because moral statements are clearer. In more complex and pluralistic societies, general consensus and acceptance of moral statements are more difficult to achieve. The more abstract such statements are, the more problematic they become. Douglas (1970a) pointed out that, in a monolithic social order, the meaning of such terms as "loyalty" or "traitor" is clear, but in a pluralistic society, the meaning of these terms may become vague. Hence, the meaning and interpretation of morality and deviance there become problematic. The primary trait of such societies is change, with much effort invested to create feelings of likeness, common cause, and cultural heritage. While deviance in such societies can, and often does, help maintain stability, it also contributes much to processes of social change.

By definition, a more complex and pluralistic social system, based on negotiated agreements, is characterized by multiplicity of elective centers that are enveloped by symbolic-moral universes (see Ben- Yehuda 1985; Cohen and Ben-Yehuda 1987; Cohen, Ben-Yehuda and Aviad 1987). Many of these universes compete with one another for widespread legitimacy, resources, followers, and influence. These symbolic-moral universes present alternative value and belief systems and advocate life-styles. Each of these centers can be defined and is surrounded by its own, more-or-less identifiable, periphery.

Complex societies are considerably different than simple societies, especially regarding the number of centers and symbolic-moral universes available, their relative openness and overlappings. These societies possess few so-called geographically segregated cultural spheres and are described more accurately as having limited meaningful contacts and hence also limited access to specific reservoirs of empirical knowledge. The social meaning of deviance in such societies becomes essentially (Rock 1973a) and situationally problematic, both to members of society and to the sociologist. Criminal law in a complex society may therefore become increasingly relied upon as a formal mechanism of social control, integrating all those who live within its political jurisdiction (Hills 1980, 35).

TOWARD A NEW CONCEPTUALIZATION
OF POLITICS AND DEVIANCE

In order to say something meaningful about politics and deviance, I developed the concepts of power, legitimacy, center, symbolic-moral universes, and boundaries together. I argued that differrent societies allow the existence of a different number of competing centers, each of which is enveloped by a particular symbolic-moral universe, identifiable by its own moral boundaries and unique vocabulary of motives. The social groups that inhabit these universes possess different amounts and types of power (influence, political, monetary, etc.). These symbolic-moral universes may be in contact and competition for a variety of resources, and consequently, a conflict is unavoidable.

Furthermore, this picture can be hopelessly complicated because actors may consider themselves members of more than one symbolic-moral universe. Therefore, the characterization of this immensely complex system does not lie exclusively with the concept of "conflict," but with that of "consensus" as well. A rational and real outcome of this fact is that these centers and their enveloping moral universes keep negotiating both power and morality. They offer potentially new members, and old inhabitants, the possibility to recentralize, revitalize, and change the moral boundaries of their individual social worlds. Some of these universes are actively involved in competing for new members (i.e., many of the new religious movements; see, e.g., Ben-Yehuda 1985, ch. 3; Cohen, Ben-Yehuda, and Aviad 1987; Wilson 1981; Wallis 1984; Stark and Bainbridge 1985); others try to enforce *their* version of morality, or parts of it, on other symbolic-moral universes. Something all these different elective centers, with their enveloping symbolic-moral universes, strive for is widespread moral legitimacy.

Not all symbolic-moral universes enjoy the same amount of legitimacy. Clearly, the amount of legitimacy enjoyed by Moonies, Hare Krishna (Krishna Consciousness), Scientology, Transcendental Meditation (T.M.), Gay Liberation, and others varies significantly. Therefore, the various symbolic-moral universes may be stratified along the dimension of widespread popularity, legitimacy, and acceptance among the different symbolic-moral universes. Each symbolic-moral universe separately, however, also has its inner moral stratification. The closer one is to the center of that universe, the higher is one's position on the hierarchies of credibility and morality. Furthermore, the vocabularies of motives, and therefore the motivational accounting systems, that each symbolic-moral universe arms its inhabitants with—in Gouldner's (1970, 266–73) terms, the "language of morality," the integration of the micro-macro levels of analysis—are expressed in the particular color that each of these universes paints the particular symbolic interaction of its members.

This view fits very well into the conceptualization of deviance (and reactions to it) as a relative phenomenon within the context of change and stability. My characterization of politics and deviance is as follows:

Problematic behavioral acts, which take place at the realm of the seams, where boundaries of different symbolic-moral universes meet and touch or which are directed from the periphery of a symbolic-moral universe toward its center and vice versa, and which involve challenges (use or abuse) of power and morality, would fall into the area of politics and deviance.

Politics and deviance thus characterize particular interactions *between* different symbolic-moral universes as well as similar interactions *within* one symbolic-moral universe. Processes of shaming vilification, stigmatization, deviantization, and criminalization, and counterpro-

cesses, are the hallmarks of these interactions. This particular conceptualization of deviance is totally consistent with the relative conception of deviance presented in this book.

In some very shallow sense, this approach may resemble the
labeling approach to deviance and to Ingraham's (1979) approach
(which essentially defined political crime as that which public officials
define as such). This may be so because, one may ask, who decides
what is a "problematic behavioral act." This approach, however, is
much closer to Giddings (1898), who stated that "political crime" has
two meanings: "crimes against government . . . [and] crimes
perpetrated by governments" (pp. xvii–xviii). The approach presented
here, however, goes beyond these approaches and specifies the conditions and analytical locations where the likelihood of invoking the
label politics and deviance increases significantly.

Politics and deviance refer to behavioral patterns that are defined
as *deviant* by social actors in relevant and significant symbolic-moral
universes. This process of deviantization (Schur 1980) clearly involves
explicit issues of power and morality. Such deviant behavioral patterns may invoke processes of deviantization and criminalization, but
they need not necessarily have to do that. Much depends on the
specific moral negotiations about the interpretations of such acts. Furthermore, acts that challenge the power and/or morality of a specified
symbolic-moral universe are not the only ones to be included in the
category of politics and deviance. Similar acts involving power and
morality by inhabitants of the center should be included here as well.
These inhabitants, trusted with guarding prevailing morality in a
specified moral universe and trusted with legitimized power, may
abuse their privileges and commit acts of deviance under the
camouflage and protection of respectability and decency (e.g., see
Thio 1988; Michalowski 1985).

The concept of politics and deviance implies, first of all, that any
analysis in this area has to direct itself into the nature of *challenges*: of
power, legitimacy, and moral boundaries. These challenges are different in nature: some explicit and some implicit. The challenges in
regular deviance are implicit, and the challenges in political deviance
are more explicit. Challenges from the periphery are likely to be
accompanied by explicit attempts to gain as much publicity as possible. There the challenge must not only be made; they must also be
made public so that power may be generated and legitimacy gained.
In contradistinction, challenges from the center are not likely to be
accompanied by any attempts for publicity. On the contrary, challenges from the center subvert the respectability and camouflage

given by the center's structural position to basically abuse, bend, ignore, and/or violate the rights of the periphery to have a fair "game" in the social system. Although this is an obvious political challenge, the last thing the challengers want is publicity. One final note is that the challenges discussed here are not within the accepted "rules of the game," but are within the realm of deviance. We have to notice, however, that what is—and what is not—defined as deviance is in itself negotiable.

One illustration for this approach is the increase in the organization of various deviants into unique and different symbolic moral universes, developing their own vocabularies of motives, accounting systems, and boundaries, and attempting to generate some power, legitimacy, and influence. This development received a dramatic expression in recent years with the establishment of many self-help groups for a variety of deviants. Among these groups we find such organizations as therapeutic communities for drug addicts (e.g., Synanon, Gateway House, Phoenix House, Odyssey House, Daytop, First Genesis, and others), Alcoholics Anonymous, Parents Anonymous, Lesbian and Gay self-help groups, Fat Americans (e.g., see Goode and Preissler 1983), Overeaters Anonymous, and numerous others (e.g., Gartner and Riessman 1984).

While one might mistakenly infer that what is involved here are marginal actors that act in an unorthodox way, in reality this is not the case. These actors actually clash over major issues of power and morality. Although the actual patterns of behavior involved in processes of boundaries' negotiations may frequently be labeled as "deviant," the peripheral moral boundaries and the centers of symbolic-moral universes become very central in processes of social change and stability. Viewed in this way, processes of deviantization and stigma contests are thrown back into the mainstream of sociological theorization—well into the domain recommended by Piven (1981) and Scull (1984), that of politics and history.

A political deviant is likely to be characterized as irresponsible, unwilling to "play the game" by the old rules, stigmatized, and dishonored. In contradistinction, individuals who are parts of the central value system of symbolic-moral universes and of the ruling body not only are perceived to be respectable, but also are usually ranked high on the hierarchies of credibility and morality. In Douglas' (1970a, b; 1967) terms, a political deviant's interpretation of abstract meanings (i.e., more "objective") may be more valid than that of the official societal institutions; yet the situated meanings (i.e., more "subjective") are interpretated by the official moral agents so that a political deviant may be labeled a "pariah." However, the moral victory of one side in a value conflict situation is not always guaranteed, especially in a pluralistic society.

I would like, therefore, at this point to make a distinction between two divisions in the discussion about politics and deviance. *One* division consists of what are usually perceived as "nonpolitical" types of deviance. The *other* division consists of political deviance proper, which is further divided into three more categories. In the next chapter, we shall explore these two divisions in more depth.

CONCLUDING SUMMARY

In this chapter, I reviewed the historical development of the sociological interest in politics and deviance, and some of the problems involved in defining the nature of politics and deviance. The discussion culminated in a new suggestion for characterizing the area of politics and deviance.

The theoretical framework I suggest to use for analyzing politics and deviance is based on a few key analytical concepts. First is power. Power in itself is a necessary concept, but not a sufficient one. The use of power must be legitimized in terms of morality (or ideology). I view societies, particularly complex ones, as characterized by a multiplicity of competing and elective centers enveloped by symbolic-moral universes. Actors may choose a center, or a symbolic-moral universe, toward which they will gravitate and be committed. These centers have various degrees of power, and they obviously promote different moral standards. However, even in such a complex pluralistic society, cohesion does exist because actors share a loosely defined macro symbolic-moral universe (e.g., language, history, nationality, ethnicity, etc.). These competing centers and symbolic-moral universes, maintain their interaction in a social order that is morally negotiated. In this kaleidoscopic social arena treaties are negotiated, broken, and maintained as each of the competing groups attempts to use and generate power, to legitimize its own brand of morality, gain popularity and ascendancy. These moral negotiations necessarily mean that societal moral boundaries are always in flux and problematic because it is never clear to what extent they will remain the same or change. Politics and deviance are, therefore, almost natural topics to analyze within the analytical concepts of symbolic-moral universes, boundaries, change, and stability.

We characterized the area of politics and deviance as follows: problematic behavioral acts, which take place at the realm of the seams, where boundaries of different symbolic-moral universes meet and touch or which are directed from the periphery of a symbolic-moral universe toward its center and vice versa, and which involve challenges (use or abuse) of power and morality, would fall into the area of politics and deviance.

I argued that the area of politics and deviance should be divided into two separate divisions: political elements in so-called regular deviance and political deviance proper.

Chapter Four

Political Elements
In Regular Deviance and Political Deviance

The area of politics and deviance can be divided into two broad divisions. The *first* consists of political elements in regular deviance. The *second* consists of political deviance.

POLITICAL ELEMENTS
IN REGULAR DEVIANCE

Making power and morality explicit. The designation of particular behavioral patterns as deviant contains some important, although often implicit, political elements—that is, elements of power and morality.

The very act of defining a particular behavioral pattern as deviant is inherently political: it uses power to impose the view of one specific symbolic-moral universe upon other universes. Schur (1980) noted that "Deviance situations seem to arise when . . . people who are in a position to impose their judgements find other people's behaviour in one way or another 'unsettling' . . . " (P. 4). Schur called the process through which society reacts to particular behavioral acts as deviances a process of "deviantization," which obviously involves shaming (Braithwaite 1989), vilification, degradation ceremonies (Garfinkel 1950) and stigmatization processes (Goffman 1963). Schur emphasized that the process of deviantization was a key element in the social stratification order because it intervened in the process of resource allocation. Schur's analysis is significant because it links primary stratification processes to the process of deviantization. Thus, actors in societal centers who negotiate power and morality, attempting to define particular patterns of behavior as deviant (or non-deviant), are necessarily engaged in constructing the boundaries of symbolic-moral universes. These moral entrepreneurs seek constantly to manipulate political, as well as moral, symbols in order to mobilize support, generate power, and control public opinion.

Gusfield's (1963) work on the Temperance Movement's anti-liquor struggle illustrates this:

> What prohibition symbolized was the superior power and prestige of the old middle class in American society. The threat of decline in that position had made explicit actions of government necessary to defend it. Legislation did this in two ways. It demonstrated the power of the old middle classes by showing that they could mobilize sufficient political strength to bring it about, and it gave dominance to the character and style of old middle-class life in contrast to that of the lower urban and middle classes. The power of the Protestant, rural, native American was greater than that of the Eastern upper classes, the Catholic and Jewish immigrants, and the urbanized middle class. (Pp. 122-23)

What Gusfield's work implies is that a contemporary "problem" of what was perceived as excessive use of alcohol was *socially* constructed (for similar analyzes, see Beauchamp 1980; Wiener 1981).

Furthermore, Zurcher et al. (1971) showed that in two cases of antipornography campaigns, the moral crusaders emphasized a general life-style and sets of values instead of the specific steps they demanded in order to abolish pornography.

Parties to a potential moral-political conflict, and therefore to negotiations, are engaged in an effort to create or maintain a collective identity by defining the moral boundaries of the symbolic-moral universe of that collective. Hence, collective definitions of deviance always result in stigma contests and in deviantization processes. The creation of rules and penal punishments implies that the life-style, values, and morality of a specific social group gained ascendancy over those of other groups, many times at those other groups' expense (Gusfield 1963).

The process of creating, and maintaining, collective definitions of deviance (Davis and Stivers 1975) is characterized by *technical* as well as *symbolic* elements. Such processes involve interest groups that are identifiable by specific moralities and power and that may bring about the legislation of laws, exposing specific subpopulations to deviantization.

Generating power and gaining legitimacy by deviants.   In principle, the only way to neutralize the deviant stigma is to create a countermovement that would attempt to use, or generate, power and to redefine morality and create a new symbolic-moral universe. Thus, the collective search for identity is not monopolized by deviant-producing groups. It also involves deviants who may try to organize themselves and successfully generate enough power and public support for their version of morality and for their collective attempts to destigmatize themselves. Since deviantization processes have a moral-political base (although often obscure), the only means of reversal is a change in, or challenge to, that moral-political base. Political deviance is one of the few cases in which this reversal process can be achieved successfully (see chapter eight). "Normalizing" (Schur 1980, 150) deviance, therefore, cannot be carried out only on the micro level. A change in the perceptions about the nature of morality must either precede or accompany normalization of deviance.

Among the movements of deviants who have chosen this course of action, we can find the moral-political campaign by militant gay activists. This movement has been very successful in transforming the image of the homosexual from a dangerous, sick, and perverted pariah into a *human* image, demanding and receiving equality in various areas. We can find other examples in Sagarin's book (1969), where he recorded the formation of various self-help groups among deviants such as alcoholics, drug addicts, gamblers, illegitimate children, homosexuals, transvestites, transsexuals, fat people, dwarfs, convicts, former convicts, and former mental patients. While most of these groups were typically created in order to help their members cope with their deviations, the very act of organizing and trying to define a common symbolic-moral universe is in itself a political activity. Some more politically oriented groups have actually "come out of the closets" with direct political statements. For example, we find attempts by former mental patients to establish their bill of rights, and the creation of a professional group for prostitutes ("Coyote") demanding the removal of "prostitution from the criminal code and from any governmental control" (Schur 1979, 440–44). Thus, in an illuminating analysis, Dominelli (1986) explored the interaction between power and gender by examining prostitution and the efforts of prostitutes to organize collectively in the *Programme for the Reform of the Law on the Soliciting*, to decriminalize prostitution. Dominelli's main conclusion was that women deviants could become more powerful by organizing collectively, but they also failed to challenge existing social relationships and the distribution of power between men and women.

Furthermore, a "regular" deviant may try and use a "political" explanation to account for his/her deviance and then, hopefully, gain more respectability. The fact that behavioral acts that are called "deviant" may be given to different interpretations by occupants of different symbolic-moral universes necessarily contributes to the fact that deviance is a relative phenomenon. Consequently, a real and exhausting effort must often be made if one wants to expose the political element in regular deviance. An historical-dynamic (or a natural history) approach, as well as examining the motivational accounting systems used by deviants and nondeviants alike, is probably the best approach that could enable us to expose this political element. Chapter eight provides an analysis for this.

One immediate example can be found in laws concerning sexual behavior. These laws attempt to regulate the following four aspects: the degree of consent; the nature of the sexual partners: the nature of the sexual act; and the setting in which the act occurs (Wheeler 1960). The specific content of these laws stems from a particular symbolic-moral universe that provides the appropriate vocabulary of motives for conceptualizing sexual conduct.

Deviant phenomena, such as swinging, group sex, and prostitution, can be directly linked to the unique European marriage pattern that emerged from the fifteenth and sixteenth centuries (Hajnal 1965) and is still prevalent today. Much of what we call sexual deviance often provides alternative access to sexual services and gratification. As such, it challenges the very basic social norms regarding the control of the sexual act and the societal utilization of sex as a means to viable, long-term social and economic arrangements (e.g., marriage). For many years, in more rigid and cohesive social systems, various agents of moral and social control attempted either to generate or to use power in order to condemn and stifle acts of what they saw, from the particular perspective of their own symbolic-moral universe, as sexual deviance, trying to preserve intact society's moral boundaries. However, as these acts persisted on the micro level and as ideas concerning sexual behavior filtered from the micro to the macro level, it became exceedingly difficult to deviantize such sexual practices as homosexuality, oral sex, prostitution, premarital sex, and swinging. It is conceivable that the institution of marriage itself will be transformed and sexuality redefined. Under these circumstances, it is very likely that the meaning of sexual deviance will also change.

Therapy as a power contest.   To illustrate the previous discussion, we shall focus on an "innocent" area — therapy — and see how power and morality play a role in it. Therapy, we must remember, is a particularly prevalent and popular form of a societal reaction to a variety of deviant behaviors. Particular forms of treatment of deviants can be conceptualized as sophisticated control mechanisms. This conclusion is not widely accepted because many of the social actors who administer treatment do not usually see themselves as control agents. Treatment, especially for a social deviation, often offers patients interpretations for their behavior that neutralize any inherent political criticism. Therapists are not agents of social change; "rehabilitation" and "integration into society" of the deviants imply that patients' behavior must undergo various changes to reflect norms of mainstream society.

Rehabilitating deviants is not a simple matter, for it may involve social change (or, as Pinel demonstrated, it may need to occur within the context of a social revolution. See Hunter and Macalpine 1963: 602–620; Zilboorg and Henry 194: 319–341). When a specific morality prevails, rehabilitation of deviants may sometimes be successful only if the deviant's past is concealed from society (e.g., see Ben-Yehuda 1984; there are very few and rare exceptions for this need to conceal. One example is that of former addicts using their experience to help treat others). Some of the most interesting control therapies are those run by former deviants, such as Alcoholics Anonymous (Maxwell 1984) and Synanon (Yablonski 1963; Mitchell, Mitchell, and Ofshe, 1982). For such control mechanisms, treatment as we know and understand the term has a marginal role. Sooner or later, these agencies give rise to specific types of morality and vocabularies of motives with explicit assumptions (e.g., "alcoholism is sickness," "easy does it," "addicts are always addicts"), and treatment assumes a form of reeducation and resocialization. Lowinger (1977) even showed how rehabilitating Chinese drug addicts became part of the Chinese revolution. Therapeutic communities—whether for addicts, alcoholics, or the mentally ill—that lack an ideology (or a charismatic leader) eventually fail. Generally, the ideologies present in these forms of therapeutic control, particularly in the case of drug addicts, exaggerate conventional morality. Strong emphasis is placed on the work ethic, on proper eating habits, and on relations with others, while strong controls are put on both sex and aggression (for addicts, a strong control is also put on medications).

Treatment in general and psychotherapy in particular try "to relieve a person's distress and improve his functioning by helping him to correct errors and resolve conflicts in his attitudes about himself and others" (Frank 1961, 44). Psychotherapy as a symbolic-moral universe is supposed "to produce and maintain a degree of arousal optimal for learning, to foster hope, self-confidence, and trust, and to combat despair, insecurity, and suspicion" (Frank 1961; 233). Therapists, therefore, are engaged in reintegrating patients into the *existing* symbolic-moral universes, not in producing social revolutions. The therapeutic-professional generalized motivational accounting systems reflect this moral stand. Therapists are not taught to be agents of social change but to facilitate personal change so that deviants would be reintegrated into conformist society. Nineteenth-century American psychiatrists were even called "alienists" because their patients were considered mentally alien. The prominent treatment then was the famous "moral treatment" aimed at reintegrating mental patients into the community (see Caplan 1969).

Frank (1961), Norbeck (1961), Torrey (1972), and Levi-Strauss (1963, 193–94) state that similar situations and processes exist in non-complex, nonpluralistic cultures.

It is thus possible to view "treatment" as a particular form of a power contest and as a form of social control (e.g., see Horwitz 1984; Pallone 1986). In this contest, therapists use their professional power and prestige to try to bring back into the fold (i.e., into conformist, conventional morality society) social actors who deviated by providing them with acceptable motivational accounting systems (more on this later in this chapter, in the discussion of political deviance).

Summary.   The relationship between alleged acts of deviance and societal reactions to these acts is neither automatic nor simple. If the deviants or the group of deviants, mobilizes enough power to oppose the societal reaction, then the process of deviantization becomes a lengthy round of bargaining and negotiations. This process offers deviants the opportunity to avoid stigmas, to neutralize imputation of deviance, and even to change accepted definitions and conceptions of conventional morality, thereby normalizing deviance. In this process, different actors (or centers) with varying degrees of power, prestige, and credibility, representing different symbolic-moral universes, negotiate definitions of moral boundaries, that is, of deviance, its interpretation, and its consequences. A deviant, therefore, is the final product of lengthy negotiations about power and morality. Obviously, these processes rely on the type and nature of the motivational accounting systems that each side employs in order to gain ascendancy. For example, there are great differences between explaining/justifying the motivation for a particular deed as resulting from insanity or as resulting from a symbolic-moral ideology.

We should note that while specific forms of political deviance are easily identifiable, analyzing the political elements in what appears to be nonpolitical deviance is tricky. Changes in morality, and therefore in the moral boundaries of society, are linked intimately to changes in definitions of deviance. First, limited availability of resources underlies all social stratification, indirectly influencing forms of deviance (especially those that are property-related). Second, types of deviant behavior, and their prevalence, are closely associated with social class. For example, violent crimes, theft, and robbery often characterize the lower classes. The upper-middle class is usually characterized by more sophisticated forms of deviance, such as white-collar and professional crime or leisure-time drug use (see also Thornberry and Farnworth 1982). Third, the definition of what constitutes deviant behavior varies, not only among societies, but also within one society such definitions change over time. Finally, the questions of who defines whom as deviant, why, where, and when have proven to be of crucial importance.

The above four factors are all linked to political considerations of power and to definitions of the boundaries of symbolic-moral universes. These considerations reflect the image society has and projects of itself. Political elements are therefore involved in developing motivational accounting systems that define as deviant such specific behavioral patterns as prostitution, homosexuality, drug abuse, mental illness, and juvenile delinquency.

The cases discussed in chapters five, six, seven and to some extent eight focus on analyzing power and morality in what otherwise might seem to be "regular" deviance. The decision to do that was guided by the consideration that not much work was previously done on *this* particularly difficult aspect of politics and deviance.

POLITICAL DEVIANCE

Introduction

Roebuck and Weeber (1978) developed an elaborate and systematic exposé of political crime in the United States. They emphasized that defining political crime had been a difficult task and that any discussion should take into consideration crimes committed against the state (e.g., political bombing, assassination, bribery, tax evasion, draft evasion, conscientious objection, spying); those committed against society (e.g., false advertisements, medical fraud, environmental pollution, radioactive wastes, occupational hazards, unsafe machines); and crimes committed by the government (e.g., police corruption, governmental violations of basic human rights, arms sales, intervention in a foreign nation's internal affairs, police violence). Roebuck and Weeber's sophisticated approach characterized political crimes not only as those against the state, but also as those by the state against the citizens.

The analytical term "political deviance" (e.g., see Sagarin and Kelly 1986) applies to three categories of deviance. The first consists of symbolic acts that challenge the right of the rulers to rule. This challenge is aimed at the heart of the legitimacy of any moral universe's center. In this sense, political deviance aims to change symbolic-moral universes and their moral boundaries.[1] Being such, this category of political deviance constitutes the most dangerous form of deviance, at least from the point of view of the inhabitants of the symbolic-moral universe that is being challenged, and particularly of those inhabiting the center. A challenge coming from outside a particular symbolic-moral universe is easier to deal with, basically because it may be interpreted to represent a different and alien symbolic-moral universe. A challenge from the periphery, or from the center, to the center within the same symbolic-moral universe is usually perceived as far more threatening. After all, it is the center's moral right to rule and its moral hierarchy and legitimacy that are being challenged. The threat hidden in such a challenge is clearly one of a moral revolution.

The second category included in political deviance consists of deviant acts by inhabitants of the center itself; that is, by those who were invested with power and morality and who abused their power and twisted their moral obligations. This category includes deviant behavior by governments and by those who are perceived to carry and symbolize conventional morality. Deviances by these people, and by institutions, use existing moral and social boundaries to camouflage their deviant acts. They do not aim to change moral boundaries; on the contrary, they will usually oppose proposed changes in these boundaries. Thus, while giving other members of society the false impression that they do, in fact, guard existing moral boundaries, they nevertheless are sometimes involved in a variety of activities that are clearly deviant. While the first category has traditionally been identified as political deviance, the emergence of the second category as a target for sociological inquiry in the area of political deviance is much more recent.

The third category of political deviance is focused on moral and power contests between two, or more, separate symbolic-moral universes (or cultures). Such deviances as war crimes, crimes against humanity, (e.g., see Friedman 1983), assassinations, racism, and discrimination are included in this category (e.g., see the trials at Nuremberg [Luban 1987] and of Eichmann [Vaughan and Sjoberg 1970]). Virtually no attention will be paid in this book to this particular class of political deviance (see Ben-Yehuda, forthcoming).

Contrary to chapters five to eight, where specific cases of politics and deviance are analyzed, this chapter aims at a general review of political deviance. In this chapter, I shall touch, in a focused presentation, on topics that have appeared before in the context of political deviance, reinterpreted from the theoretical perspective of this book.

Challenging Symbolic-Moral Universes

The blatant message of those who aim to change the societal-moral boundaries by deviant acts is that a particular symbolic-moral universe has no right and legitimacy to exist as such and that those who rule have no right or legitimacy to monopolize legislation, use power, and enforce the law; the challengers typically provide alternative governmental policies and structures (e.g., Bergesen 1984), as well as alternative motivational accounting systems.

Ingraham and Tokoro (1969) stated that, until the time of the French Revolution, political crimes "were always viewed by the state as the gravest offenses and were normally requited with the most severe and barbaric punishments, since an attack against the holders of power was not seen as an assault on their personal prerogatives, nor as an attack against the interests of a privileged class, but as an attack of a foreign country" (p. 145). Ingraham and Tokoro hence emphasized that the original interpretation of political crime was taken to mean a crime against the state, either by foreign powers or by *all* criminal acts aimed at "some rearrangement of political power within the state" (p. 146). While the state regarded political crime as the worst form of crime, it paradoxically endowed those who were defined as political criminals with a respectability that "ordinary" criminals lacked altogether.

Unfortunately, the literature on political deviance is meager. Davis (1975, 148) noted that the general lack of specific and focused case studies centered on the category of political crimes suggested that the body of research itself was too limited. Most of the studies antedated the radical social movements of the late 1960s and early 1970s. Should such groups as Black Power, Red Power, the student subculture, draft resisters, feminists, gay liberationists, or ghetto revolutionaries be regarded as truly political deviants or just as social movements in a legitimate struggle for recognition within the existing rules of particular symbolic-moral universes? The conservative view, that political crime constitutes only a violation of law and not a political protest, misses the essence of the phenomena. Likewise, the idea that housing problems (and that citizens' invasion into what they perceive as an empty apartment) constitute merely a violation of the law, misses the same point (Bailey 1973).

Furthermore, the question of whether or not a particular action should be regarded as political deviance is misleading. A much better question is *to what extent* does a specific behavioral pattern constitute a political deviance, who defines it as such, and why. In other words, we have to analyze the amount of threat existing in various acts to the powers that prevail in specified symbolic-moral universes. The personalized, or generalized, motivational accounting systems used in this context provide good clues to deciphering and interpreting the act. The actual damage caused by a specific political act of deviance may be marginal, while the real victim is morality, or Durkheim's "collective conscience," (1933: 79–80) because a *symbolic* threat may constitute a much more powerful intimidation than an actual physical threat.

Schafer (1974) illustrated this point: "in distinguishing political criminals from heroes, one may be tempted to see a remarkable paradox: the former failed while the latter succeeded in representing an accepted value or cause within their social group" (p. 3). Reality, however, is much more complex than Schafer's analysis admits, for success and failure are relative concepts. Joan of Arc, Jesus Ché Guevara, Marx, and Lenin were considered as deviants by many of their contemporaries, only to be much later recognized as heroes. On the other hand, such "heroes" as Stalin and Hitler were later denounced as criminals. Socrates, Galileo, and Bruno represent another form of contemporary deviancy (or heresy) turned heroism. These illustrations highlight one of the clearest demarcation lines between a common criminal and a political deviant. The former would usually try to hide his/her acts; the latter would thrive on publicity. Since the political deviant aims his/her challenge at the center in his/her attempt to generate power, sympathy, and legitimacy and to change a symbolic universe, he/she is vitally interested that their motivational accounting systems would be diffused and received, debated and talked about, by as many people as possible (Coser 1962).

The distinction between a *political criminal* and a *political hero* brings forth the problem of social change and social stability. While political deviants may view themselves as important agents of change, their persecutors view them as criminals, or terrorists, and may try to use the formers' actions to strengthen their own position. For example, the motivational accounting systems used by political dissidents in the Soviet Union reveal that they envision themselves as agents of freedom and change, clearly inhabiting a different symbolic-moral universe than that of their persecutors. The response of the inhabitants at the center of the powerful Soviet symbolic-moral universe, however, aims at maintaining stability and rigidity. Hence, they react through trial, arrest, Siberian exile, or certification of political opponents as mentally ill to be locked up or "treated." The authorities then display publicly the unsuccessful (real or fabricated) political deviants in order to deter future deviants, much like in ancient times (e.g., the Roman Empire or the Inquisition).

Political deviance is probably the only type of deviance that can become a real asset in a political career. This can be seen by the actions of political figures and leaders who use their deviant past to advance a political career. For example, the late president of Egypt Anwar Sadat described extensively in his autobiography the time he spent in jail. Israel's former prime minister Menachem Begin exploited his persecution as a "terrorist" and "criminal" at the hands of the British (who occupied Palestine between, 1917 and 1948) as a respected and important part of his career.

Political criminals and political heroes — the problem of identifying the valid motivational accounting system. Using a political vocabulary of motives in order to develop what may be regarded as a respectable political motivational accounting system may be a course of action that is used by various deviants in order to justify their actions and to enjoy the prestige of heroism. I shall use two examples from research in drug rehabilitation to support the above claim. Covington (1984) illustrated how heroin addicts politicized their drug problem and thus gained an effective defense that minimized their self-rejection. Pallone (1986) also reported how Sunrise House (a drug rehabilitation program) tried to make its clients (drug addicts) politically aware and turn them into urban revolutionaries. According to Pallone, this type of rehabilitation was *very* successful. Federal authorities, however, replaced the management. In chapter eight, I will show the process and illustrate the motivational accounting systems that a particular deviant used in order successfully to reverse processes of stigmatization so that deviancy was transformed into a political asset.

Mills (1940) suggested that in order to determine whether a specific act of deviance occurred out of a political motivation we must analyze the deviant's own account. This solution, however, is only partial, for, in addition to reflecting a true political motivation, the deviant's motivational accounting system may also reflect other motives, such as social pressure, need to conform, need to feel like a hero, or a defensive "need" to transform criminal and deviant acts into political statements and consequently gain self-esteem.

In 1982, under the terms of the peace treaty with Egypt, Israel evacuated Yamit, a town built near the pre-1967 border between Israel and Egypt. The extreme right movement in Israel, including Gush Emunim,[2] and some local settlers staged a fierce and organized resistance against the evacuation, which culminated in a decision to physically destroy the town. The protesters engaged in fights with the Israeli soldiers sent to carry out the evacuation. There can be little question that many of the occurrences in Yamit were criminal; however, the context of the struggle enabled the authorities to define these acts as "political," hence avoiding getting involved in criminal prosecutions. Yet it appears that some of the local settlers staged the battle in Yamit for economic reasons, hoping that the government would raise its offer of compensation if the settlers agreed to evacuate the town peacefully. Thus, while some of the resisters in Yamit indeed had purely political motivations, others had economic or mixed motivations. Listening to the motivational accounting systems given by some of the settlers in public could give the impression that their resistance to evacuate Yamit had only a strong political motivation. Hearing some of these settlers' vocabularies of motives as they were given in private, not to the public, revealed a very different motivation (on the Yamit evacuation see Aran 1985; Cohen 1987).

Another example has to do with a chronic problem Israeli society faces regarding the relations and allocation of resources between the inhabitants of the secular and the orthodox Jewish symbolic-moral universes. Israel has traditionally had coalitional governments, representing a variety of symbolic-moral universes. This type of government is vulnerable to the demands of symbolic-moral universes representing small groups within the coalition. These groups may sometimes present demands that are unacceptable to the great majority of people in Israel. The small religious parties have traditionally and regularly made demands for state support of their interests. Sometimes these negotiations were accompanied by deviant acts, such as illegal demonstrations by the religious factions, aimed at getting more concessions from the government, all in the name of a mythical "national consensus." For example, the ancient City of David in Jerusalem was excavated under the supervision of the Department of Archaeology at the Hebrew University and with the appropriate license from the government. In September 1981, a group of fanatic and extreme Orthodox Jews organized violent demonstrations near the site of the excavations because, so they claimed, ancient wars took place there, making the site in fact a burial site. They demanded an immediate halt to the excavations, which they said desecrated this cemetery. Rather than treat the illegal demonstrations as a violation of the law and as a criminal act, the authorities chose to treat them as politically motivated, allowing the religious zealots to win more concessions. The various motivational accounting systems, therefore, given by the different parties to this conflict—the government, police, orthodox fanatics, scientists, political leaders—reflected the different interests these parties had, and their different symbolic-moral universes. In this case, moral arguments were mixed with political arguments in a confused debate about who should get how much. Likewise, in the next chapter, I shall analyze how in fact moral panics, using moral themes, can cloak economic and political interests.

A much more general illustration for this point is bank robbery or blackmail. Such crimes, when committed for personal economic reasons, are defined as regular, nonpolitical deviant acts. However, when the same behavioral acts are committed in order to finance a revolutionary movement, then a totally different motivational accounting system is provided, reflecting the fact that a different type of negotiation over the moral nature of the act takes place.

Thus, we should be cautious about accepting a deviant's own motivational accounting system alone. To solve the problem regarding the nature of the deviant's use of a particular vocabulary of motives, we can use one of three approaches. First, we may consider all crimes political in nature, and consequently, *all* the motivational accounting systems would be likewise defined as political. This approach, however, is insensitive and does not help us to understand or analyze different problems, policies, and theories in the field of deviance. Second, we may trust the deviant's own account. But as we saw, this solution is problematic because we do not always know whether the deviant really believes the claims he/she makes. Third, we may assume that the symbolic-moral universe in which the deviant acts occurred is the one that will have to cope with the vocabularies of motives given by the deviants, so that an analysis of the different and competing motivational accounting systems is called for, as well as an analysis of the process whereby these different symbolic-moral universes negotiate morality in a dynamic and historical analysis.

Schafer (1974) suggested that the solution lies in developing external social criteria for determining whether or not a particular deviant act is political. Schafer suggested the term "convictional criminal" to differentiate the political criminal from other types of criminals. A convictional criminal is one who appears to be: " . . . 'convinced' about the truth and justification of his own beliefs. . . . It is a settled belief, essentially a deep-seated consideration in the political criminal's conscience that makes him feel that he has a rendezvous with destiny. . . . By contrast . . . the conventional offender almost always acts to fulfill his ego or personal interest, and his acts often lack an overarching coherence. . . . The convictional criminal . . . has an altruistic-communal motivation rather than an egoistic drive" (pp. 145–47). Schafer proposed five major specific criteria for defining a political crime: no personal gain is involved; the deviant act occurs as part of a *collective* action; the crime is accompanied by considerable publicity; it usually challenges the legitimacy of the law; and although political crime does not usually deny the existence of law or morality, it nevertheless does appeal to "higher loyalties."

The following example will illustrate Schafer's last criterion. A simple politically motivated action occurred in the late 1970s, when youth from the Jerusalem branch of the Black Panthers[3] stole bottles of milk from an upper-middle-class neighborhood and delivered them to lower-class, poverty-stricken areas. In 1979, representatives of this group broke into the house of the Israeli minister of welfare to put some rabbits inside as a symbol of the minister's lack of courage in dealing with Israel's socioeconomic problems. The Black Panthers clearly used a vocabulary of motives that linked their deviant behavior to such higher ideals as social justice and a more just allocation of resources.

As suggested in chapter two, my proposed solution for this problem is to examine the meaning of motivational accounting systems within the social, historical, and dynamic context in which they are produced, used, and change.

Summary.   The line between the political criminal and the political hero is a thin one, depending on which symbolic-moral universe defines it, why, and when. Furthermore, defining the motivation of a particular deviant act as political or not is in itself problematic. Consensus between symbolic-moral universes about the nature of morality, the specific characteristics and nature of the culture, and the distribution of power are all essential factors in the analysis of political deviance. Use of motivational accounting systems must be made, therefore, within the context of the action and the culture in which competing symbolic-moral universes negotiate.

In chapter seven, we shall see how two scientists (Jansky and Reber) were once viewed as deviants and many years later as heroes. Similarly, in chapter eight, we shall see a cycle of how an esteemed governmental minister (Abu-hatzira) was deviantized, and how this process was reversed and the minister was redefined as a hero.

Political Deviance from the Center to the Periphery

Political deviance that is aimed from the periphery to the center, challenging the center's legitimacy, was documented and includes such acts as political assassination, terrorism, tax and draft evasion, and spying. In recent years, however, more interest has been focused on political deviance that was aimed from the center to the periphery. This is the other category of political deviance, the one where so-called respectable members of society, ranking high in the hierarchies of morality and credibility, in or close to the centers of symbolic-moral universes, act in deviant ways for a variety of reasons. Deviant behavior that may be included in this category consists of such crimes as genocide, crimes against humanity, war crimes, slavery, racism, anti-Semitism, and disrespect for human rights, and finally, acts of deviance committed by a sovereign government itself. Furthermore, some members in the center may try to deviantize other members of the same center.

As early as 1898, Giddings wrote that one of the meanings of the term "political crime" " . . . is that of the crimes perpetrated by governments for alleged reasons of state and by politicians for alleged reasons of expediency or for political advantage . . . " (pp. xvii–xviii), and Proal's (1898) book is one of the early attempts to systematize this approach. This particular research effort has crystallized in recent years and has yielded some interesting results. Four types of such political deviance were identified: white-collar criminality,[4] government deviance,[5] professional deviance,[6] and corporate crime.[7]

Research into white-collar, professional, corporate, and government crime is exceedingly difficult to carry out. Officials typically employ vocabularies of motives that deny the "iceberg theory" in favor of a "bad apples" theory, clearly aiming to keep their legitimacy intact. After all, which government is likely to admit the widespread corruption of its officials and the subversion of the public interest? Some scholars even went as far as to suggest that white-collar offenders, by virtue of their respectability and high social status, are not "true" criminals at all. Vold's (reported in Conklin 1977, 9–10) motivational accounting system illustrates the point when he suggests that it is paradoxical to even think that the leaders of a community could be criminals. Ernest Burgess, reported in Conklin, stated that some scholars "say that although . . . [community leaders'] behavior may violate the law in a 'technical legal sense,' they are not real criminals because they do not see themselves as criminals and because they lack 'the spiritual attitude' . . . of the criminal" (Conklin (1977, 9–10).

Likewise, Tappan (1947) attacked the very concept of white-collar criminality and, among other things, implied that it is a term of propaganda (!). While this line of argument provides an excellent motivational accounting system for white-collar offenders, it fails to demand appropriate punishment for the deviants. Furthermore, in a cynical, somewhat crazy perspective, one could argue that, from the perspective of elite deviants, it is possible that they are not involved in deviance. They are the ones in the center of the symbolic-moral universe, they are those who create/negotiate/enforce morality—how, then, *can* they be deviant if they are the ones who help shape those societal moral boundaries (and behavioral codes) that provide the distinction between deviant and nondeviant?

Thinking about governments as deviants is not an easy exercise. However, if there *is* a case of deviance that is directed from the center to the periphery, then governmental deviance is one of its best illustrations. Because of its intrinsic and symbolic importance, I shall devote some space for this type of deviance.

An early statement in this area was made by Liazos (1972), who noted that contemporary writers:

> especially those of the labeling school, either state explicitly or imply that one of their main concerns is to *humanize* and *normalize* the deviant. . . . But by the very emphasis on the "deviant" and his identity problems and sub-culture, the opposite effect may have been achieved . . . by the overwhelming emphasis on the "dramatic" nature of the usual types of "deviance"— prostitution, homosexuality, juvenile delinquency . . . we have neglected to examine other, more serious and harmful forms of "deviance." I refer to *covert institutional violence* . . . which leads to such things as poverty and exploitation . . . unjust tax laws,

racism and sexism.... Despite explicit statements by these authors of the importance of *power* in the designation of what is "deviant" ... they show a profound unconcern with power and its implications. The really powerful, the upper classes and the power elite, those Gouldner ... calls the "top dogs," are left essentially unexamined by these sociologists of deviance.... (pp. 104–5).

Liazos pointed out that deviance was by no means restricted to the poor or the minorities but that a considerable number of deviant acts, especially violence, were committed by official institutions. He stated that institutions regularly violate basic human rights, harm the human body and human dignity, and destroy individuals' ability to govern themselves. Liazos illustrated his thesis with the example of the partial publication of the Pentagon papers in 1971, which "made public the conscious lying and manipulation by the government to quiet opposition to the Vietnam war" (p. 114)—scenes of deception in government and economy prior to the Watergate scandal.

Two recent examples seem to support the issue raised by Liazos. First, Klein (1981) examined how the Veterans Administration (VA) dealt with ill and injured veterans, especially of the Vietnam war. He concluded that the VA was not supportive, that young physicians tended to be unsympathetic or even abusive, that ethical norms regulating informed consent from those participating in human medical research were not always adhered to properly, that care for elderly veterans was poor, and that possible victims of Agent Orange were neglected. Second, Rosenberg's (1981) study of eighty-six governmental experiments with nuclear bombs between 1951 and 1963 showed that U.S. soldiers were exposed to the blasts in order to see how they would behave in nuclear combat. However, while the soldiers were informed that the quantity of radiation to which they would be exposed was harmless, this claim is suspect. Rosenberg strongly suggested that adequate safety measures were not taken, later resulting in health problems for those exposed to the blasts (for more, see Schur 1969; Smith 1982, and the more problematic Fuller 1984).[8]

All these examples converge to a point I made earlier: that governmental agencies, supposedly the bearers of legitimate power, may act in a deviant and violent[9] way.

Thio (1988, 443–61) pointed out that governmental crime, besides the physical harm it creates, also harms society more than other forms of crime. He quoted Supreme Court Justice Louis

Brandeis, who wrote in 1928 that: "If the government becomes a lawbreaker, it breeds contempt for the law; it invites every man to become a law unto himself; it invites anarchy" (p. 358). Thio hypothesized three reasons for governmental crime: the government's motivation to maintain its power; government officials' tendencies to become arrogant toward citizens; and the government's motivation to raise revenues beyond its actual need (assuming one can define what that "actual need" is). Governments and their officials are skilled in covering their crimes, and they rarely confess. Thio described five mechanisms, or types of motivational accounting systems (Pp. 443–61), through which governmental officials can neutralize the guilt and allegations associated with the accusations. These mechanisms are denial of the obvious, for example, denial that a specific act was committed or that it had a criminal nature; ignoring the crime, for example, government officials are suddenly unavailable for comment or give a "no comment" response; accusation of the accusers, for example, accusing journalists who exposed the crime of unethical behavior or even of treason (a specific example being the Nixon administration's attempts to "smear" Daniel Ellsberg, who leaked the Pentagon papers [see Roebuck and Weeber 1978]); promise of investigation, for example, under a strong pressure the government may promise to investigate the act, while in reality the investigative body may receive only a limited charter or may quietly ensure that the investigation is not seriously carried out (a specific example being the Agranat Committee assigned to investigate Israel's lack of preparedness at the outbreak of the 1973 war. The committee was chartered to investigate only the military level so that from the outset the government was freed of responsibility); and emphasis on the necessity of the act, for example, the government might implicitly admit a wrongdoing while arguing that it was necessary.

In a similar fashion, Simon and Eitzen (1982) argued that deviance committed by economic and political elites is intimately linked to the structure of wealth and power in the United States and to the processes that maintain such structures. They pointed out that elite deviance occurs because: (1) it helps maintain (or increase) the profit and/or power of economic and political organizations; (2) it is supported by the elite and/or by employees acting on the elite's behalf (pp. 28–29). Simon and Eitzen used the term "elite deviance" and thus referred to acts of deviance committed by an elite: political and economic.

These findings illustrate two points. First, Schur, Conklin, and others were probably right in their assessment that in the past white-collar criminals were rarely detected and that when they were captured they were punished lightly due to a specific morality and power configuration that worked in their favor. The mid-late 1970s, however, witnessed a change in moral boundaries (mostly due to the Watergate affair), coupled with an anti-white-collar crime social movement. This development intensified and gave legitimacy to the law enforcement efforts in this area. Second, the above-mentioned change of attitude toward detecting and punishing white-collar criminals supports my thesis that the meaning of deviance changes as a function of processes of social change and stability. Wheeler, Weisburd, and Bode (1982), who found that white-collar criminals *were* punished explicitly, stated that: "This suggests that our results might be extremely time-bound. If the study had been conducted in the 1960s, or in the early 1980s when a new political regime is announcing a renewed concern for violent crime, then [our] results might not be found" (p. 657). That is, as societal moral boundaries regarding what was right and appropriate and what was wrong and inappropriate changed, societal reaction (in the form of severity of punishment) toward white-collar criminals also changed. This conclusion is supported by Coleman's (1985, ch. 7) opinion that coping appropriately with *the criminal elite* requires some very serious societal changes and reforms.

Political Deviance vs. Political Justice

Political justice is associated intimately with political deviance. Widespread and entrenched feelings of injustice could motivate people into actions aimed to rectify what they feel is unjust (e.g., see chapter eight and Cohen 1986). Homans' (1961) notion of "distributive justice" is appropriate in this context. He defines distributive justice as the individuals' judgments regarding the appropriateness, or fairness, of a specific distribution of costs and awards. In other words, the principle of distributive justice explains expectations and their formation in various cultures.

Criteria for political justice, or injustice, are neither objective nor absolute, especially in situations where different competing and conflicting symbolic-moral universes meet, clash, and negotiate. The question of political justice itself is tied to questions of legal repression of political organizations, repression of hostile groups under majority rule, and political amnesty (see Kirchheimer 1961).

Many deviant acts in the form of various terrorist acts (e.g., see Wardlaw 1982; Stohl 1983; Schmid and Jongman 1987) may be justified by the perpetrators by using vocabularies of motives that explain these acts as originating from a sense of political misjustice.[10] Dror (in Crenshaw 1983, 65–90) rightly pointed out that terrorism constitutes a severe challenge and threat to the democratic capacity to govern. That is, acts of political deviance may threaten the social order itself. The lack of what is felt to be political justice may well lead into political corruption (e.g., see Heidenheimer 1970), bribery, and even assassinations (see Ben-Yehuda, forthcoming). The problem here is complicated by the existence of myriad of symbolic-moral universes.

One must examine whether feelings of political injustice, and consequently acts of political deviance, occur between symbolic-moral universes or within them. The location of such occurrences is crucial if we are to better understand the specific cases of political justice and deviance.

The question of political justice and deviance is also correlated with what Douglas (1970b) called deviance and respectability. The social construction of moral meanings can be conceptualized in terms of deviance (immorality) or respectability (morality). Both are linked to the problem of responsibility. Deviantization is always correlated with shame, disrespect, and irresponsibility. Politicization implies the opposite. That is why deviants sometimes try to politicize their actions and why those social actors in the center, whose authority and legitimacy are being challenged, try to reject this type of an interpretation and deviantize and criminalize the political challenge.

This problem of justice would become very salient in chapter eight.

Use of Criminal Procedure and Issues for Political Purposes

The use of the criminal code for political purposes is focused on the application of motivational accounting systems and vocabularies of motives from the criminal realm to the political realm and on using criminal issues for political purposes (e.g., see Fairchild and Webb 1985; more on this in chapters five and eight).

One immediate illustrative example for the topic of this chapter is police involvement in riot control; capture of terrorists; and enforcement of immigration rules, drug laws, and sexual taboos; as well as police corruption.[11] Liazos (1972) pointed out that: "police . . . enforce laws and prejudices of 'society' . . . " and relying on Cook (1968) he further stated that: "in a fundamentally unjust society, even the most impartial, professional, efficient enforcement of the laws by the police cannot result in justice" (p. 117). In this sense, the police, like other control organs, are an agent of stability, an agent whose job it is to prevent changes. DeFleur (1976) reported on a more subtle use of the police for political purposes. DeFleur examined drug arrest records in Chicago for the years 1942–1970 and showed that arrest rates reflected political attitudes toward drug abuse and changing policies rather than any real change in the nature of the phenomenon. DeFleur stated that: "police administrators indicated that they were making the kind of arrests that the public wanted"[12] (p. 90). Indeed, in chapter five we shall analyze how the Israeli police used inaccurately, and misleadingly, data about psychoactive adolescent drug use in order to help create a drug moral panic.

Lidz and Walker (1980, 252) stated that the drug crisis of the 1960s was a smoke screen for the repression of political and cultural groups. That is, the debate around drug abuse was seized by powerful moralistic groups as an opportunity to enforce *their* version of morality (more on this in the next two chapters). Nixon's motivational accounting system to the U.S. Congress on June 17, 1971, "raised the issue of drug use to the highest level of government concern and responsibility. . . . 'If we cannot destroy the drug menace in America,' Nixon informed Congress and the American public, 'then it will surely destroy us. I am not prepared to accept this alternative" (Goldberg 1980, 32). This statement is hardly based on a scientific vocabulary of motives, but it does draw sharp moral boundaries in a very powerful way. Nixon's efforts resulted in the federal budget for coping with drug abuse rising gradually from $101.9 million in fiscal year 1970 to $753.9 million in fiscal year 1974. Clearly, Nixon's powerful motivational accounting system to Congress and the creation of various agencies to combat drug abuse provide numerous official motivational accounting systems to justify the tremendous expansion of resources allocated to this problem. At least some of these resources were apparently given to doubtful activities.

Epstein (1977) noted that the Office of Drug Abuse Law Enforcement (ODALE), a special investigations agency, was created in 1972 by then U.S. President Richard Nixon without discussions or consent from the U.S. Congress. Epstein showed that Nixon managed to create an executive agency that was free of control by the U.S. Congress. Although some of Epstein's observations are questionable, ODALE's activities are fact. By accounting for illicit heroin use as a true menace and as the "Public Enemy No. 1" of the United States, ODALE justified its actions, some of which were illegal.

In sociological terms, and as I will show in depth in chapters five and six, the definition of drug abuse as a "social problem" involves difficult conflicts between various symbolic-moral universes. Thus, the "drug problem" may be thought of as deviantization and criminalization of specific life-styles and different symbolic-moral universes. In addition, in chapter eight, I shall illustrate how the weakening and failure of inner, informal control mechanisms among Israeli parties brought about increased reliance on external, more formal mechanisms, among them the criminalization of deviants. In one case, use of such a procedure backfired as a process of reversing deviantization was successfully activated by a particular deviant.

This particular issue will be found again in chapters six and eight.

Three more and relevant issues will be examined further in this chapter: *mental illness and political abuse, political trials,* and *political prisoners.*

Mental illness and political abuse.   Mental illness is another area where power and morality are expressed in deviantizing vocabularies of motives (e.g., see Pallone 1986). The nature of mental illness, especially the nonorganic, functional type, is very problematic. Determining who is mentally ill or abnormal is largely a question of social norms. A mentally ill person is one who seems to some to be violating normative and accepted definitions of social realities, as determined by dominant symbolic-moral universes (e.g., see Scheff 1966; Szasz 1961; Laor 1984; and Goffman 1961). Furthermore, Rosenhan (1973), Cumming and Cumming (1957), and Srole (1962) demonstrated the difficulties of interpreting the very concept of mental illness.

The low reliability of psychiatric diagnoses of mental illness coupled with a severe criticism of the medical conception of the term led to the view that mental illness denotes social misbehavior rather than a medical problem. The human rights movement of the 1960s directed attention to the role of the psychiatric profession in the political and social order. As such, clinicians were compared to priests or jailers as important control agents in a struggle to preserve society (Gallagher 1980; Menzies 1980). Furthermore, Davis (1938) claimed that psychiatrists were, in fact, "moralists," that the psychiatric ethic served the Protestant ethic, and that the "mental health" ideal was in reality a translation of middle-class morality.

Supporting Davis was Hollingshead and Redlich's study (1958), in which they found that diagnoses of a severe mental disturbance (mostly psychoses) tend to be given to lower-class people, while the upper middle class usually received lighter diagnoses (mostly neuroses). Likewise, Sarbin and Mancuse (1980) reject the concept of schizophrenia as a "true" disease and suggest instead that: "schizophrenia is a moral judgement, and like all moral judgements is conditional upon time, place, and person, and upon identifiable social features of the persons who declare the moral verdict" (p. 1). They showed that the label "schizophrenia" was applied to cases of unwanted or perplexing conduct (ch. 5). The authors provided a detailed analysis of such conduct, as well as the ideological premises that justify the disease model of schizophrenia (ch. 6).

Menzies' (1980) work presented a structural critique of the relationship between the political process and the sociological status of the mentally ill. He argued that mental illness was essentially a behavior that challenged normative views about the line between rationality and irrationality or sanity and insanity. Within this interpretation, so-called preventive medicine may be viewed as a step toward "psychiatric fascism" (Torrey 1972, 97–111).

The nature of the cultural category "madness" has, therefore, always been subjected to various conflicts involving different symbolic-moral universes and the use of power to enforce particular moral boundaries distinguishing between the "normal" and the "crazy."

What is considered "normal," or rational, or sane, is a direct consequence of the perspective of the individual, or group, endowed with the political power to define these norms for society in general. . . . In the final analysis, the determination of insanity is the end product of a sequence of value choices, in which the marginal, the deviant, and the unproductive . . . are grouped together under the trappings of prevailing definitions and taxonomies. . . . What is defined as sane, rational or wholesome is contingent upon what the rules are that societies—or those interest groups with the power to determine societal reality—formulate and represent as being relevant. (Menzies 1980, 12–13)

Hence, Halleck (1971) equated a therapeutic intervention to a political intervention, and Conrad and Schneider (1980) warned against the ascendance of a "therapeutic tyranny."

What follows is a relatively recent illustration for the above argument. In November 1985, the American Psychiatric Association (APA) suggested adding three new categories of mental illness: *paraphilic rapism*, which means "a persistent association . . . between intense sexual arousal" and fantasizing about or carrying out rape; *masochistic personality* disorder, which means "remain[ing] in relationships in which others exploit, abuse or take advantage of [the patient]" and "believ[ing] that he or she almost always sacrifices own interests for those of others"; and finally, *premenstrual dysphoric disorder*, which focuses on symptoms experienced by women the week before menstruation (see e.g., *The San Diego Union*, Nov. 17, 1985, p. A–17; *The New York Times*, Nov. 19, 1985, part 3, 1–3; and *Time*, Dec. 2, 1985, 19). The first and second categories aroused much turmoil, as they could be interpreted to mean that the APA provided medical vocabularies of motives that could give justifications and protection to both rapists and husbands who beat their wives. In the second category, the victim may even be thought of as the culprit.

The nature and history of mental illness may lead us, therefore, to the conclusion that people whose behavior violates accepted definitions of social reality were sometimes labeled as "sick." Political dissidents, by the same dynamic, were also labeled as sick, irresponsible, and in need of treatment. Thus, within this interpretation, we may conceptualize therapy as a form of social control and therapists as control agents (e.g., see Ben-Yehuda 1984; 1986b). Chapters five and six focus on illicit psychoactive drug use. There, *numerous* attempts were made to medicalize this nonconformist behavior and turn the user/addict into a "sick" and "disturbed" person.

Finally, one of the best available illustrations for applying deviantization and criminalization processes against political dissenters is the abuse of psychiatry by Soviet authorities who placed some Soviet political dissidents in mental institutions to be "treated" for something that was labeled as "counter-revolutionary paranoia" (e.g., Fireside 1979; Stover and Nightingale 1985).

Political trials. The exact nature and definition of political trials (Shklar 1986; Christenson 1986) are not entirely clear. Theodore Becker noted that: "If members of a ruling elite believe a particular individual or group to be imminently hostile to the prevailing pattern of value distribution, and if they activate the criminal process against him (or them) for that reason, what results is a political trial" (1971, xi–xii). This approach, however, is narrow. A criminal trial can be interpreted as a process whereby an answer is sought for a particular question. It is a process whereby an individual's (or group's) actions, representing one symbolic-moral universe, are being called into question and whereby one side (prosecution) attempts to get official recognition in the wrongdoing of another side—using a very specific and complicated set of rules—those of the law itself and of the criminal procedure. The question of whether or not a specific trial is a political trial, in my view, is not a binary question. The answer to this question must be, first of all, that it is a question of degree. Some trials can be viewed (at least retrospectively) as clearly political (e.g., those of Joan of Arc, Jesus, Socrates); in other cases, this conclusion may not be so obvious, (e.g., the trial of Patricia Hearst).

In a pluralistic, complex society, one symbolic-moral universe may use the power it has (with or without help and cooperation from other symbolic-moral universes) and through a political trial attempt to redefine and ascertain its definition of moral boundaries, hence its hegemony. European witch trials during the fourteenth to seventeenth centuries clearly fall into this category (Ben-Yehuda 1980, 1985). If one symbolic-moral universe has enough power and support, it would probably be able to negotiate successfully and enforce its own concept of morality and version of reality and gain more support for the symbolic-moral universe it represents. In other cases, success may not always be guaranteed. A political trial would, therefore, take place when the prosecution is reasonably confident that it can win, and hence make a moral and a political statement. Losing a political trial is not just a technical loss but also a blow to a specific symbolic-moral universe, especially because much attention is usually given to trials that are perceived as political. Thus, in many cases, it may be the prosecution's interest to present a case as apolitical and as criminal as possible, and in the defendant's interest to emphasize that it *is* a political trial. A strong and secure elite would probably not feel uncomfortable to deal with such a political challenge. A weaker and less secure elite would probably prefer to neutralize the political threat through criminalization. I would tend to state that trials where the threat potential to both the power and morality of groups that rule society are clear and visible are political trials par excellence. Where these elements are not clear, explicit, or visible, the degree to which a specific trial should be considered political decreases significantly. A political trial, after all, is one mechanism of social control that a coalition that has the power, and that wants its symbolic-moral universe to prevail, uses to cope with potential threats and challenges to its position.

Hence, political trials provide the parameters which structure the situation where those that are regarded as political criminals, such as war criminals, terrorists, assassins, political dissidents, and demonstrators, are prosecuted. In cases of political assassinations, the assassins (if at all caught) frequently adhere to their declared political motivation, while the prosecution emphasizes the "murder" interpretation. Consequently, the types of motivational accounting systems used in political trials obviously differ for the defendants and the prosecutors. These accounts reflect the macro symbolic-moral universe of each side to the conflict and the negotiations that take place during the trials to define and redefine these universes and, therefore, societal moral boundaries. For example, members of guerilla movements that try to "liberate" a land usually request prisoner-of-war status if captured, thereby denying authority and legitimacy of the court to judge them. The prosecution on the other hand, tries to depict such people as terrorists who plant bombs and endanger innocent citizens. The prosecution hence aims to deny the political nature, legitimacy, and motivation of the accused, focusing on what is regarded as the terrorist act itself. This conflict is salient in Spain with the Basques, Britain with the IRA, Italy with the Red Brigades, South Africa with ANC, Israel with the PLO, and others.

The distinction between a group of "freedom fighters" with national or ideological aspirations and a cell of bloodthirsty "terrorists" is meaningless. The character that one attributes to such a group is relative to one's viewpoint. Furthermore, these definitions can change. A respectable group of leaders can later be labeled criminals, such as the "gang of four" in China or former terrorists later seen as heroes. The nature of a terrorist or guerrilla movement, therefore, depends not so much on the acts the group commits,[13] but rather on its interpretation by both outsiders and members.

Bergesen (1977) compared witch-hunts with political trials and persecutions and suggested the term "political witch-hunts" to describe these phenomena. He illustrated his point with such political witch-hunts as those of the McCarthy era in the United States and the Stalinist purges in the Soviet Union, concluding that political witch-hunts constitute important rituals used "for the periodic rejuvenation of collective sentiments in national societies" (p. 220). Wallace (1966) presented a similar concept: "revitalization rituals," suggesting that the purpose of such rituals is to preserve stability and not to promote change.

Political prisoners.   Continuing the problem of political justice and political trials, one can see that the history of imprisonment is saturated with political elements, as shown by Foucault (1977) and Rothman (1971). The decision to imprison convicted (or "certified") deviants is in itself a moral-political decision; the nature of prisons and the role of incarceration versus rehabilitation are also significant.

For our purposes, two related issues demand attention: political prisoners and politicization of the prison. Political prisoners are those who have committed deviant acts that can be interpreted as challenging the power, legitimacy, and moral universe of those in the center ("authorities"); acts that have in turn led to their imprisonment, sometimes following a trial (e.g., see Goodell 1973; Simon and Eitzen 1982, 211–15). While such incarceration may follow a political trial, political prisoners may often find themselves in prison even without a trial, as a preventative measure. Britain's imprisonment of IRA activists and Argentina's reported kidnapping and imprisonment of citizens who were considered political dissidents are indeed well known. Such methods were also employed by Israel (e.g., see *Time*, June 13, 1988, 22–23), the Soviet Union and other Eastern bloc countries, South Africa, as well as by other nations (see annual Amnesty International Reports).

In many cases, political prisoners may have a different personal status from regular inmates in terms of age, education, and self-esteem. Such prisoners may later draw on their prison experience to enrich their careers and biographies.

The other element, the "politicization" of the prison (e.g., Atkins and Glick 1972; Wright 1973; Smith and Fried 1974), was brought to the public eye when former U.S. ambassador to the United Nations Andrew Young commented that U.S. prisons had a large proportion of political prisoners. On a basic level, when inmates begin to realize that they share a common interest and cultural heritage that goes beyond the immediate reasons for their incarceration, politicization begins.

Sykes (1978, 531–39) pointed out that in the 1960s and the early part of the 1970s ethnic militancy emerged as a cohesive force for a significant number of prisoners.[14] He reported that the early part of the 1960s saw several attempts (particularly by the Black Muslims) to organize inmates around Black consciousness, while the latter part of the 1960s witnessed in a number of prisons the development of a radical political movement that attempted to transcend ethnic lines. Quoting Pallas and Barber, Sykes wrote that:

> Nonwhite prisoners especially made quick connections between their struggles inside and the struggles of oppressed peoples

around the world. . . . These prisoners were joined by an influx of new prisoners, imprisoned for radical activities. Black, Puerto Rican, Chicano and other nonwhite men and women active in radical movements, and an increasing number of whites arrested for offenses stemming from their opposition to the Indochina war, brought their politics and organizing talents to prisons. (P. 537)

This development turned the prison struggle into part of an international struggle against such evils as oppresssion, racism, capitalism, imperialism, etc. Sykes remarked that the claims that a "revolutionary movement"grew in U.S. prisons is probably quite exaggerated, for it is difficult to evaluate the extent of ideological cohesion and integration among prisoners. However, while the nature of the political views of inmates is quite complex, prisons have undoubtedly contributed to the crystallization of political-moral views of the nature of the society in which these inmates lived.

The fact that some prison inmates developed "political consciousness" provides us with an excellent example of the development of motivational accounting systems by both inmates and authorities.[15] As Sykes pointed out, prison administrators usually react angrily when prison activists claim that inmates are really political prisoners. After all, few individuals willingly see themselves as agents of oppression of other peoples, especially if the "oppressed" are criminals like rapists, burglars, and thieves. To label felons as "political prisoners," a term usually associated with political dissenters, seems almost blasphemous. Most prison officials feel that the prisoners had been given a fair chance while a few feel that they were forced into crime, but in either case, the officials view prisoners as individuals who behave in an antisocial manner. This accounting system allows administrators to maintain the demarcation line between "decent" and "deviant."

A member of the "New Criminology," Krisberg (1975) devoted an elaborate discussion to the struggle inside prisons. He symbolically chose to open the chapter with a quote from Ho Chi Minh's "Prison Diary": "People who come out of prison can build up a country. . . . When the prison-doors are opened, the real dragon will fly out" (p. 80). Krisberg stated that: "From behind prison walls have come some of the most articulate and poignant statements about the nature of our social structure and the relationship of crime and privilege" (p. 80). One of the cases Krisberg cited is that of Black activist Angela Davis. In Davis' trial, "the state attempts to reduce the significance of political resistance by labeling it as a series of ordinary criminal events. . . . Prisons [to Ms. Davis] are places where the open expression of fascism can be seen" (pp. 83–84). Krisberg further stated (p. 80) that the "struggle inside the walls is the backbone of the New Criminology and the movement for social change."[16]

The development of a political consciousness that enables prisoners to "explain" their otherwise immoral, criminal, and anti-social behavior is an attempt to crystallize and legitimize a symbolic-moral universe and generate power. By claiming that a person is a criminal or a deviant because "society is rotten" and because, for example, the capitalist social order is itself the evil entity that forced the deviant into being what he/she is, an excellent motivational accounting system is created to explain deviance. For example, the motivational accounting system used by Eldridge Cleaver (1968) " . . . I did this [raping white women] consciously, deliberately, willfully, methodically . . . I felt I was getting revenge . . . " (p. 14), implying that every time a black man raped a white women he was making a political statement hence providing a political justification for black men to rape white women. In a sense, when deviants or criminals use a political motivational accounting system to justify their acts, they are using a mechanism like one of Sykes and Matza's (1957) neutralization techniques—the appeal to higher loyalties. Here, however, there is less a neutralization of guilt and more of a creation of a new morality, and the adherence to broad political conceptualizations justifying the deviance. Loyalty, thus, is to the interest of a general class of "oppressed" people with whom the delinquent supposedly identifies.

One should also remember that political consciousness as a motivational accounting system to explain deviance may often develop long after the actual deviant behavior occurred. Initially the deviant may have even admitted a nonpolitical motivation. However, long exposure to prison life, to various ideologies, and to persuasion can convert the prisoner and lead to the development of political justifications. I use the term "convert" here in a manner parallel to the religious conversion of an inmate. In the latter conversion, however, society is not held responsible for the inmate's past criminal behavior, which is perceived to have occurred because he lacked proper and correct beliefs and spiritual guidance. Religious conversion offers a religious motivational accounting system that not only helps the deviant to understand his past deviant behavior but also guarantees that it will not recur (if the conversion is successful).

Concluding Summary

In this chapter, I focused on a broad review of politics and deviance. This chapter constitutes an attempt to view the general area of politics and deviance through the theoretical prism presented in this book, with an emphasis on the relevant issues for the next chapters. I pointed out that the interpretation of particular behavioral acts as political deviances is itself the result of a process of negotiation. The real question, therefore, becomes not whether or not a particular deviant act is political but to what extent it is interpreted as such, by whom, and why (more on this in chapter eight). The determination of the extent to which a specific deviant act should indeed be regarded as political—and by whom—depends, first of all, on how explicitly and clearly this act challenges the power and symbolic-moral universes, especially of actors in the center of the universe, and vice versa.

Another set of variables that helps determine whether or not a specific deviant act will be defined as political is the process of negotiation between the sides to the controversy, as reflected in the motivational accounting systems they use, negotiate, change, and modify. In this sense, the label "political deviance" is in itself a particular result of a process of negotiation about how the nature of a specific behavior should be characterized.

We focused on two broad divisions: *political elements in regular deviance* and *political deviance.*

The first division consisted of a discussion that was aimed to explicate the political and moral elements in regular types of deviance. Having discussed the theoretical aspect of the issue, I illustrated the analytic point by focusing on therapy as a power contest.

The second division consisted of a discussion that was focused on political deviance. There, three challenges were identified. Two challenges were confined to the inside of particular symbolic-moral universes: (1) from the periphery to the center; (2) from the center to the periphery. The third challenge was focused *between* symbolic-moral universes. Finally, we touched the important and relevant issues of political justice versus political deviance, and the use of a criminal procedure for political purposes.

Part Three

The Politics
and Morality
of Deviance:
Cases

Chapter Five

A May 1982 Drug Scare
Toward a New Sociological
Synthesis of Moral Panics

INTRODUCTION[1]

This chapter, and the next, focus on the issue of illicit psychoactive drug use. In both chapters, we have macro societal reactions, directed from the center to the periphery, to an assumed form of deviance. In both chapters, we have illustrations of social actors from specific symbolic-moral universes who either generate or use power attempting to gain ascendancy for *their* version of morality and to stigmatize and deviantize other particular subpopulations that inhabit other symbolic-moral universes. The negotiations between these symbolic-moral universes are obviously the focus of cultural symbolic arguments, from where processes of social change may emerge and from where stability may be maintained.

This book is focused on the *symbolic* level of cultures. Processes that are aimed at achieving stability or inducing change on this level are typically initiated by particular *moral entrepreneurs*, representing the morality of the symbolic-moral universes to which they see themselves committed. Hence, this chapter, in a comparative perspective, analyzes the concept of *moral panics*. Based on a specific moral panic, a new sociological interpretation is suggested for understanding moral panics. The next chapter provides a comparative analysis of drug abuse social policy in two different cultures. This policy is typically the *result* of past moral panics, and the policy is examined with an eye to its impact and usefulness *as* a macro societal reaction to perceived deviance. In both chapters, attention is paid to the micro and macro levels.

Moral panics. The sociology of moral panics is one of the areas that is most relevant for the conceptual framework presented in this book. *Moral entrepreneurs* attempt to persuade others to adhere to a particular symbolic-moral universe (Becker 1963). An efficient way of doing this is to draw the public's attention to the moral boundaries that mark differences between symbolic-moral universes. Focusing on specified behaviors, attempting to stigmatize those behaviors and deviantize the actors, is the route to redraw moral boundaries. Thus, moral entrepreneurs typically start *moral crusades* aimed at transforming the public's attitudes toward specific issues, try to change legislation, and/or attempt to "deviantize" (Schur 1980) others.

Moral crusaders often create what Cohen's (1972) outstanding work called "moral panics": "A condition, episode, person or group of persons emerges to become defined as a threat to societal values and interests: Its nature is presented in a stylized and sterotypical fashion by the mass media; the moral barricades are manned by editors, bishops, politicians, and other right-thinking people; socially accredited experts pronounce their diagnoses and solutions; ways of coping are evolved, or (more often) resorted to; the condition then disappears, submerges or deteriorates and becomes more visible" (p. 9). Moral panics, and their creators, give much credence to the idea of control agents as creators and amplifiers of deviance, rather than preventing or suppressing it.

Moral panics typically involve telling what Bromley, Shupe and Ventimiglia (1979) called "Atrocity Tales," that is: " . . . An event which is viewed as a flagrant violation of a fundamental cultural value. Accordingly, an *atrocity tale* is a presentation of that event (real or imaginary) in such a way as to (a) evoke moral outrage by specifying and detailing the value violations, (b) authorize, implicitly or explicitly, punitive actions, and (c) mobilize control efforts against the alleged perpetrators . . . " (p. 43).

The success of moral entrepreneurs to create a moral panic depends on a few factors (e.g., Becker 1963; Eisenstadt 1984): first is their ability to mobilize power; second, the perceived threat potential in the moral issue for which they crusade; third, their ability to create public awareness to the specific issue; fourth, the type, quality, and amount of resistance they encounter; and last, their ability to suggest a clear, persuasive, and acceptable solution for the issue or the problem.

The concept of "moral panics" is intimately linked to politics and deviance as approached in this book because of several factors. First, moral panics provide a focal point between arguing and negotiating symbolic-moral universes. What is usually at stake in a moral panic are the definitions and redefinitions of moral boundaries of symbolic-moral universes. Thus, moral panics are deliberately created either to reaffirm older moral boundaries or to challenge those boundaries in order to define and legitimize a new symbolic-moral universe. Hence, moral panics are linked to major processes of societal change or stability. Second, Spector and Kitsuse (1977) implied that examining how particular patterns of behavior, or issues, emerge to be defined as "social problems" may provide us with a link between moral panics and the emergence of "social problems." This link may associate the sociology of social problems and that of moral panics to major societal processes of change and stability. Third, moral panics involve generating and using power as the different sides to the moral panic struggle to win sympathy, generate support, create legitimacy, and gain ascendancy, each attempting to deviantize the other. Fourth, it stands to reason that since moral panics involve competing symbolic-moral universes then the motivational accounting systems used by actors involved in the panics give direct, micro expressions to macro considerations (and vice versa) about the nature of the societal symbolic-moral universe and its boundaries.

Hence, the issue of moral panics is very intimately linked to contests of power and morality between different symbolic-moral universes. As such, moral panics involve a *moral crisis*. The societal reaction to moral panics has dynamics that could result in either reaffirming stability or helping create a process of social change. For example, the fourteenth to seventeenth century European witch-craze (see Ben-Yehuda 1980, 1985) as well as the McCarthy persecutions in the United States were moral panics aimed originally to preserve stability.

Moral panics are studied in a dynamic, historical, and political perspective and typically involve complex relationships between the center and the periphery as moral and political challenges are being raised and exchanged during the panic.

The above characteristics of moral panics mean that their interpretation does not lie with the sociology of deviance exclusively, but with sociology in general. All of the above make the study of moral panics almost a must for this book.

The origins of the concept "moral panics."   The sociological interest in moral panics crystallized within the sociology of deviance, particularly within the labeling approach.

The labeling approach (e.g., Goode 1978; Schur 1971, 1979; Becker 1963, Dotter and Roebuck 1988) stipulates that deviance is "a consequence of the application by others of rules and sanctions to an 'offender' . . . deviant behavior is behavior that people so label" (Becker 1963; 9). This approach focused attention on the societal reaction to a presumed act of deviance and emphasized the role of social control agents/agencies as amplifiers (or even manufacturrs) of deviance (e.g., Wilkins 1964; Ben-Yehuda 1980). According to Becker (1963), social groups create deviance by "making the rules whose infraction constitutes deviance" (pp. 8–9). These rules, however, are clearly the product of negotiations about the nature of morality among different social groups and individual actors representing different symbolic-moral universes.

The idea of social control agents who are engaged in an eternal battle aimed to initiate new moral legislation is a powerful, intellectual seedbed for the germination of sociological ideas focusing on moral panics. Indeed, Stanley Cohen's classical work, which appeared in England in 1972, *begins* with direct statements taken from the labeling approach. Cohen, however, makes it explicitly clear that moral panics are associated to the sociology of law, of social problems, *and* of collective behavior (more on this later in the chapter).

In his analysis (1972), Cohen S. relied on Gusfield's (1963) concept of a *symbolic crusade* and on Becker's (1963) characterization of a *moral enterprise*, which is: "the creation of a new fragment of the moral constitution of society" (p. 145). Hence, while the study of moral panics has remained within the sociology of deviance, the concept itself—as developed originally by Cohen—was certainly meant to be used in a broader, macro perception and analysis of cultures.

It is important to emphasize that the term "moral panic" in this context does *not* mean a very spontaneous collective reaction, but rather a much more deliberate, intentional, and planned action. To quote Goode (1989): "A 'moral panic' is a widespread feeling on the part of the public that something is terribly wrong in their society because of the moral failure of a specific group of individuals, a subpopulation is defined as the enemy. In short, a category of people has been *deviantized*" (Chapter One).

Two different and competing theoretical approaches developed in the sociology of moral panics. One approach emphasized the *moral* nature of the issue. The other emphasized that we should think about moral panics in terms of *interests*. While there were a few hints in the past that, perhaps, these two approaches should be combined, no real thorough effort was made in that direction.

Using a thoroughly documented national drug moral panic that occurred in Israel in May 1982, I will show that the two approaches in the sociology of moral panics are not mutually exclusive but complementary and thus create a new full synthesis in this area. The morality and interests approaches would be discussed by asking two separate questions about moral panics: that of *timing* and that of *content*.

Plan of the chapter. In the month of May 1982, the Israeli public learned that the rate of illicit psychoactive drug consumption among middle-class, adolescents, in what are considered good (even elite) high schools, was 50 percent. Following this news, a national drug moral panic developed and lasted until the end of the month. The fact that the actual rate has been between 3 and 5 percent in the last decade did not seem to have any noticeable effect on the panic.

First, the methods used to gather information for this chapter will be detailed. Second, the necessary data needed to acquaint the reader with the drug scene in Israel will be provided. No real understanding of the moral panic can be achieved without this background. Third, an historical account of the moral panic itself will be detailed. This account will follow the tradition of the "natural history of crime" approach and will detail, chronologically, how the moral panic developed and how it died.

Historically and sociologically, telling the "story" is, in itself, a necessary explanatory device—however, it is not sufficient. One has to *explain* the panic itself. The explanatory analysis in this chapter will focus on two axes.

First, the axis of *timing*: Why did this moral panic break when it did, and why did it end when it did? I argue that while the concept of moral universes in itself is an important variable in explaining moral panics , it does not sufficiently explain their origin and course of development. The specific political and economic interests of those involved in creating and sustaining the panic, as well as their ability to mobilize and use power also must be taken into consideration. This will make the explanation more structural and bring back active, living actors into the sociological analysis. In this type of analysis, one is not left only with the macrosociological variables (such as moral universes); the analysis is enriched with microsociological level variables (such as down-to-earth interests). Analyzing the specific interests of the actors involved in creating and sustaining the panic would enable us to explain its *timing*. This is the main reason I chose the natural history of crime approach. Detailing how the panic developed, how it was attenuated, and how it died is an essential tool for this type of analysis.

The second axis is the specific *content* of the panic—a drug moral panic. This question is important. Since the available studies suggest functional reasons for moral panics, one has to try to eliminate the ghost of the old functional equivalent problem, that is, we have to explain why a specific topic suddenly becomes the target for a moral panic—and why it is *this particular* topic and not something else. So far this question has not been addressed directly, and in this chapter, I shall treat this problem as a major topic. Using a theoretical scheme utilized before (Ben-Yehuda 1980) for a similar purpose, I will argue that the choice of "drugs" for the 1982 moral panic was not coinciden-tal. Here the question of morality would gain its justified importance. The symbolic-moral universe of drug abusers has usually been por-trayed as evil, inferior, dangerous, detested, and morally wrong. A clash between the negative moral universe attributed to *drug abusers* and the positive moral universe attributed to *abstainers* necessarily draws societal boundaries between the "morally right" and the "morally wrong" (e.g., see Young 1971). The use of illicit psychoactive drug consumption as a topic for a moral panic provides moral crusaders with a golden opportunity to delineate their version of a moral universe with virtually no real opposition. Also, the specific interests of at least one of the parties involved in creating and sustain-ing the panic (the Israeli police) dictated the choice of drugs.

Finally, I will show that while the sociology of moral panics stems from the sociology of deviance and the labeling approach par-ticularly, it is also connected to the sociology of mass delusions, social problems, and consequently change and stability

DATA AND METHOD

There are a few sources for the data used in this chapter. Between 1979 and 1982, I directed (on a part-time basis) the central Israeli drug abuse unit, the coordinating and administrative arm of the Israeli Interministerial and Interinstitutional Committee on Drug Abuse. The major task of the committee was to crystallize a national drug abuse intervention policy and to coordinate all drug abuse inter-vention activities in the country. The committee answered directly to the Israeli government, usually through the minister of social affairs. Almost any person in Israel who was connected with the area of drug abuse policy was on the Committee (which had thirty-six members). Because of my position, I was a direct participant observer to the events described in this chapter. I was invited to the fateful May 12, 1982, Parliament meeting (to be described later), and the following meetings, and I attended them all.

Thus, I was familiar not only with the nature of the Israeli drug abuse scene but also with the key figures and actors (with whom I had numerous formal and informal interviews before, during, and after the panic), as well as with the various agencies and departments that were involved in the panic. As the panic developed, I realized that an interesting and important sociological process was in progress, and I documented in "field notes," day-by-day, the various events as I witnessed them.

The media played a crucial role in this moral panic—as it did in other panics (e.g., Cohen 1972). The electronic and printed media provided the information that fueled the panic. Thus, I collected and filed systematically all the relevant printed media items that reported on the "information" leading to the creation and maintenance of the panic.[2]

ADOLESCENT DRUG ABUSE:
AN HISTORICAL ACCOUNT OF A MORAL PANIC;
THE PHENOMENON TO BE EXPLAINED

This section details the background and the historical development of the May 1982 moral panic in Israel. I shall first present the true magnitude of adolescent drug abuse in Israel. This part is necessary because the moral panic was based on distorted information. Then I shall detail the events preceding the panic, to be followed by a documented account of the panic. This account is crucial for answering two questions. One, that of *timing*—that is, why did the panic occur when it did? Second, that of *content*—why a drug moral panic?

Historical and epidemiological background   Public attention to the drug abuse problem in Israel started after the Six Day War, in 1967. Following the war, Israel was flooded with volunteers from Europe and North and South America. The perception continues that many of the Western volunteers brought to Israel a new form of illicit psychoactive drug use—leisure time drug use (mostly of hashish). It seems that such recreational drug use spread throughout the urban, middle-class youth, especially the kibbutzim (Ben-Yehuda 1979). While Israel has virtually no systematic data regarding the prevalence of illicit psychoactive drug use in the general population, efforts have been made to research the prevalennce of illicit psychoactive drug use among adolescents. Several studies were conducted on this topic between 1971 and 1983 that reveal a more or less consistent picture.

Peled (1971; see also Peled and Schimmerling, 1972) showed that about 5 percent of her subjects had used hashish. In 1974, Shoham et al. indicated that the percentage of users was approximately 3 percent. The Department of Statistics of the Tel Aviv Municipality conducted a 1975 study (Har-Paz and Hadad 1976), which showed that about 5 percent of the respondents had used drugs. Shoham et al, (1979; 1981) found a user percentage of 3.5 percent in 1977–78. Barnea (1978) found a user percentage of 3.1 percent. Kandel and Adler (1981) and Kandel, Adler and Sudit (1981) reported that about 3 percent of their respondents had used hashish. In 1979, Javitz and Shuval (1982) discovered a rate of 4.8 percent among their respondents. Burkof's (1981) study revealed that of the 2,800 junior high school students he studied, 2.7 percent admitted that they had tried hashish at least once, and 0.4 percent admitted having used LSD at least once. The final survey was conducted during 1982–1983 (in two stages) and revealed that reported use of hashish up to two times between 3.3 percent to 4.8 percent (Rahav, Teichman, and Barnea 1985). All the studies mentioned here examined lifetime prevalence and use mostly of hashish, or marijuana, in the fourteen- to eighteen-year-old population usually in high school. The use among high school dropouts was found to be usually higher.[3]

The above-mentioned studies indicate that the percentage of young, mostly high school adolescents who tried illicit psychoactive drugs (mostly hashish) from 1971 to 1983 remained stable: between 3 percent and 5 percent. The epidemiological picture is clear and has been consistent.

Background: preceding events   One important event that preceded the May 1982 panic took place in the same month. This event will be used later to explain part of the problem of timing. To understand this event, we have to go back to 1980. In July 1980, the Israeli police supposedly penetrated a large drug smuggling organization in the northern part of the country. The activities of the police led to a large-scale "mopping up" operation (code named "cleaning the valleys") in September. At that time, about seventy people were arrested and charged with smuggling and selling illicit psychoactive drugs. In May 1982, a key state witness in the trials that followed the operation— Amos Sabag— filed a statement to the Israeli Supreme Court. In that statement, Mr. Sabag not only denied his September 1980 testimonies; he also wrote that he had lied in court. This created much turmoil because Mr. Sabag's 1980 testimonies helped put about seventy people behind bars. Mr. Sabag appeared in the main edition of the Israeli television evening news on May 9, 1982, and repeated, very dramatically, his statement to the supreme court. The major daily newspapers gave large coverage to this event. *Yediot Aharonot* (May 9, 1982) quoted Mr. Sabag in a big headline:

" . . . 'I lied' claimed the state witness who caused the arrest of 70 drug dealers. He claims that operation "cleaning the valleys" in 1980 was staged and under police pressure; that he and a police agent "glued" accusations to various delinquents. . . . Amos Sabag, 26, from Tveria . . . claims that he and the police agent divided the hashish to small portions and put on each portion a name of a person, as if they bought the drug from him . . . . Sabag claims that most of the portions were meant to frame delinquents the police wanted to get rid of. In the night of Sept. 8, 1980, all the people against whom there were 'proofs" were arrested. . . . Sabag wrote in his statement [to the supreme court] that 'I decided to reveal the truth' . . . " (translated by the author).

The police used a common account and simply denied Sabag's claims. *Ma'ariv* of May 10, 1982 (p. 15), told its readers that the Israeli police were very angry at Sabag and that he was going to be investigated.

In early May 1982, theaters in Israel began the premier of the German-made movie *Christian F.* This movie is a shocking dramatized version of a book reputing to document the true story about a fifteen-year-old female herion addict in Berlin. The atmosphere in early May 1982 was therefore loaded with drug abuse issues and was very conducive to "drug abuse scandals."

The panic begins: discussions in the Knesset. The specific Israeli moral panic started, as perhaps one could expect, from the Israeli parliament—the Knesset—in May 1982.

On Wednesday, May 12, 1982, parliament member Mrs. Ora Namir convened the Knesset Committee on Education, which she chaired, for a discussion on drug abuse among youth. In May 1982, the Likud party was leading the governmental coalition. Mrs. Namir was a member of the Ma'arach, the major opposition party. It seems safe to assume that Mrs. Namir had a few "leaks" from some police officers prior to the fateful May 12, 1982, meeting of the committee. The meeting was well prepared, and quite a few public officials were invited to it. The meeting had a high attendance of reporters as well, who apparently "knew" that something dramatic was going to happen.

Mrs. Namir opened the meeting by stating that she had received some "alarming" information about drug abuse among young people. She then gave the floor to police officer Amnon Helfer, chief of detectives in the Tel Aviv police, youth branch. Mr. Helfer told the committee that, as a result of an intelligence youth drug abuse survey conducted in Tel Aviv (which is the major urban, metropolitan area in Israel), the police concluded that one out of every two high school elite adolescents had tried hashish at least once. The vocabulary of motives that Mr. Helfer used implied clearly that this situation probably characterized all of Israel. Mr. Zvi Ariel, head of the drug abuse unit in the national Israeli police headquarters, followed suit. He stated that about 22 percent of all schools in Tel Aviv, and about 19.5 percent of the youth clubs, had a drug problem.

The motivational accounting systems that were used by the police officers explicitly accused high school principals of avoiding cooperation with the police. This accusation found a dramatic expression in the media when, on May 13, it was repeated on the front page of *Yediot Aharonot*, a very widely circulated Israeli daily newspaper. There, the Hebrew headline read "Half of high school students experienced smoking hashish," and the item continued: "One of every two high school students in Israel experienced smoking hashish . . . this was told by . . . Amnon Helfer, head of detectives, youth branch, Tel Aviv to the education committee of the Knesset. . . . Policemen criticized high school principals for not cooperating with the police. . . . Parliament member Goldstein, from the Likud, who initiated the discussion, attacked the teachers and claimed that high school principals run away from the subject and introduce norms of permissiveness. . . . Shmuel Shimoni, principal of 'Tichon Hadash' in Tel Aviv, attacked the media for 'overblowing' the problem. . . . Yoseph Mechoulam, principal of a high school in Yahud, admitted that he had a drug problem and asked for advice from the committee. Chairperson of the committee, parliament member Ora Namir, accused the Ministry of Education of doing nothing about the problem. . . . She expressed her opinion that the increase of 10 percent in juvenile delinquency in 1981 was because adolescents burglarized houses and stores in order to finance the drugs . . . " (translated by the author). *Ha'aretz* followed suit, and on May 13 its major back-cover headline stated that "more than 50 percent of high school students experience hashish."

Members of the Interministerial Committee on Drug Abuse were present (including the author) but were permitted to question neither the data presented by the Israeli police nor the methodology used to obtain it. The above accusation, on May 12, gave other Parliament members of the committee a good opportunity and legitimacy to use accounts that attacked high school principals and the Ministry of Education for not doing enough about adolescents' drug abuse. One member argued that contemporary high schools were too liberal and that if pupils would wear uniform clothes (as was the case in the 1960s), all would be well. The session turned into quite a wild attack on high schools, on high school seniors, and especially on the Ministry of Education. Furthermore, a few members of the Knesset committee (e.g., Parliament member Meir Shitrit, Likud party) indicated that the tremendous efforts of the police in curbing the drug abuse problem were hampered by a "too liberal legislation." This attack clearly carried a moralistic, not technical tone. Most speakers expressed their concern about the apparently spreading "menace" of drug abuse among elite adolescents, supposedly the future leaders of the country. Illicit psychoactive drug use was attributed to loss of morality, too much liberalism, and morally confused parents.

The accusations that high school principals did not help or cooperate with the police received an unpleasant interpretation. It appeared as if the police *had* a clear and swift solution for the problem: law and order. High school principals' lack of action was interpreted to mean that they did not know what to do or wanted only to protect their school's reputation or indulge in too much liberalism. The reporters present throughout the discussion were obviously interested in this "drug scare" and intensively interviewed the committee members after the session.

The panic develops: media coverage. On the next day, Thursday, May 13, 1982, the Israeli public was "flooded" with drug abuse related media items. The major daily newspapers carried big, front-page headlines on the drug epidemic among high school seniors. A major morning radio talk show (*All the Rainbow Colors*) on Israel's second radio station had wide coverage on the topic—including interviews with high school students. The following two to three weeks witnessed a "drug festival" in the media.

On May 12, 1982, Mrs. Namir appeared on the main edition of the evening television news and told the Israeli public that there was a "government conspiracy to hide the true magnitude of drug abuse among Israeli youth," specifically blaming the Ministry of Education. When the interviewer questioned the data she used, her response was that the problem was not whether 3 percent or 60 percent of the young used drugs; rather the Ministry of Education was not doing anything about the problem (from the author's notes).

The "conspiracy theory" was an important issue because it contrasted two opposing symbolic-moral universes. One was portrayed as a governmental secret universe, seeking to mislead innocent citizens, hiding that which should not be hidden. The other universe was portrayed as nonplotting, nonsecretive, courageous, and seeking to share information openly and to cope with the problem directly.

The panic develops: police vs. Ministry of Education. The Israeli police kept mostly quiet as the panic developed. The media and the Ministry of Education, however, did not. A "moral panic" regarding illicit psychoactive drug use by middle-class, elite adolescents flourished on a full scale. One school in Tel Aviv called Tichon Hadash (meaning in Hebrew "New High School") was cynically renamed by the media "Tichon Hashash" (meaning "Hashish High School"), following accusations of a high rate of illicit drug use there. The fact that the principal of that school brought statistics showing that only one high school pupil was found using drugs did not help (from the author's notes).

On May 19, 1982, *Yediot Aharonot* (p.4) told its readers that "High school principals do not cooperate [with the police] in the war against drugs. A general attack on the Ministry of Education was carried out yesterday in the educational committee of the Knesset. . . . A principal of a prestigious high school in Tel Aviv said that there was no drug problem in his school. A secret police unit found out that at least 21 pupils in that school smoked drugs, almost regularly. . . . All present in the meeting said that high school principals did not cooperate with the authorities in order to eradicate the drug plague. . . . Mr. Turgiman, chief of Tel Aviv police, said that all high schools in Tel Aviv, which suffer from the drug plague, are precisely the prestigious schools in the north . . . " (translated by the author.) Furthermore, on May 20, 1982, *Ha'aretz* (p. 10)—a morning newspaper—claimed that principals of high schools hide and/or camouflage the true magnitude of the problem in order to keep the reputation of their high schools intact.

On May 17, 1982, a spokesman for the Ministry of Education accused the police of helping to create a "drug panic" and of using unreliable statistics, demanding that the police give the ministry the names of those pupils who had been suspected of drug misuse. His account was titled " . . . 'The drug festival' of the police. Every year . . . the police conducts its 'annual drug festival' on the educational system. The script almost repeats itself: police detectives discover a few adolescents who used some sort of drug, outside school, in a city. . . . Later on, police officers are invited to public forums to tell the nation about the achievements of the Israeli police in capturing adolescents who use drugs. . . . Suddenly we discover, God forbid, that we no longer deal with one city—but with all of Israel. . . . Following this, a friend told me that perhaps the Ministry of Education should sell some of the drugs it has to cover its budget deficits . . . after a few months, police notify (not always) the stigmatized schools that the investigation was finished and then . . . it is desclosed that [the problem] concerns only very few students. . . . The school's name, however, remains stigmatized. . . . This year, the police had gone too far. . . . The percentage of drug users in the educational system is low. . . . I call on the police to give us the namelists of the students who used drugs so that we would be able to treat them . . . " (*Ma'ariv*, May 17, 1982, 3, translated by the author).

At the same time, there appeared in the media police estimates that more than 100,000 high school students used hashish. The Ministry of Education demanded, again, to know even some names—to no avail.

Meanwhile, anxious parents began to pressure the Ministry of Education to "do something" about the "terrible drug problem" in high schools, threatening to keep their children away from school. High school students also expressed their anger and protested about the campaign, stating that all high school students—as a category— were smeared and stigmatized with no real justification. Some parents even began refusing to send their children to school because of the "drug menace" (see the daily newspapers of May 13 to May 18, 1982, and radio and television broadcasts; author's notes).

The panic continues: the second Knesset meeting. On May 18, 1982, the Parliament Education Committee had a second meeting on the youth drug abuse problem. I attended this meeting too. Before the meeting began, I was asked to Mrs. Namir's room. I gave her the accurate statistics and pointed out that the data used by her committee were probably biased or false and were methodologically flawed. I also protested that I was not given the right to speak in the previous session. Mrs. Namir rejected my arguments and pointed out that my turn to speak would be delayed. I was told that the scientist members of the Interministerial committee on drug abuse were biased and too "liberal" and thus not really very helpful or cooperative (author's notes). Furthermore, I was told again that the problem was not whether 3 percent or 60 percent of high school students were using illicit drugs but that no one was doing something about it, especially not the Ministry of Education. Mrs. Namir repeated her account that the Israeli public had not been given accurate information about the true nature and magnitude of the problem.

By this time, it was clear that the vocabularies of motives that presented accusations of "liberalism" and "lack of cooperation" became identified with a "soft" stand on the issue. A "soft" stand was usually interpreted to mean not showing enough combatant and militant spirit and the required conservatism "needed," supposedly, to squash drug abuse. One group of policy decisionmakers, parliament members, and police officers came forward with generalized motivational accounting systems that demanded quick, swift, and decisive action against the supposedly spreading menace of drug abuse among middle-class, elite adolescents. Members of this conservative symbolic-moral universe used vocabularies of motives that portrayed their imaginary antagonists as conspirators, lacking in fighting spirit, noncooperative, soft liberals, morally confused, and morally confusing. Inhabitants of this negative symbolic-moral universe, according to those in the opposing symbolic-moral universe, actually helped propagate and intensify the problem.[4]

The May 18 session started in a very tense atmosphere. Contrary to the previous session, only a handful of reporters were allowed in. The session began very dramatically when police superintendent Mr. Yehezkel Karti, national police chief of investigations, demanded to speak. Mr. Karti told the committee, in a very straightforward way, that they should not attribute much credibility to the figures given to them only a week earlier. He stated that the "study" was, in fact, an internal intelligence report based on a survey, not based on accepted scientific methods. The two police officers who presented the data only a week earlier were not present at the May 18, 1982, meeting. Mr. Karti's speech eased the tense atmosphere considerably.

Although a few reporters present started to leave the room, the police-Ministry of Education feud was not over yet. Tel Aviv police superintendent, Mr. Avraham Turgiman, claimed that the youth drug abuse problems in Tel Aviv characterized mostly prestigious high schools and middle-class and elite adolescents. He stated that neither high school teachers/principals nor students cooperated with the police. Other members of the committee and some invited guests attacked the Ministry of Education again. They pointed out that even if the problem was minor, the ministry was still doing absolutely nothing about it. They indicated that teachers, principals, and students had no address where to go and get help to deal with their drug abuse problems. While this meeting eased the tensions and put the magnitude of "the problem" in the correct proportions, the drug panic itself did not abate.

The panic continues: crystallization of main themes. The following two weeks witnessed major newspaper coverage on the issue of illicit psychoactive drug use employing such motivational accounting systems as "killing drugs" and the "white death" (heroin).[5] These vocabularies of motives attributed illicit psychoactive drug use to too much permissiveness, to liberalism, and to morally confused parents. Other newspapers used motivational accounting systems that explained youth drug abuse in Israel as characterized by a "silent conspiracy" that helped inflate the real magnitude of the problem. "Drug trafficking and drug consumption [in] the country are no longer a peripheral phenomenon, as it used to be. . . . Today . . . crime and corruption have become accepted norms. . . . Using the service of prostitutes . . . contributes in no small measure to moral deterioration, part of which is using drugs . . . " (from Aharon Shamir's "The Death Drug," *Yediot Aharonot*, May 21, 1982, supplement p. 11; translated by the author). *Hed Hakriot* (local newspaper, Haifa, May 21, 1982) associated drug abuse and teenagers promiscuous sexual practices (mostly abortions). *Yediot Aharonot* (May 23, 1982; 4) quoted Mrs. Namir as saying that " . . . kids under 13 years of age sell drugs and use guns because they know that due to their age they cannot be prosecuted," and pointed out again that the Ministry of education was doing nothing about educating students, parents, and teachers about how to cope with the problem.

In the period between May 12 and the end of the month, items on the "youth drug abuse plague" appeared in the national and local written and electronic media (author's files). The "moral panic" crystallized along five distinct lines.

First, the panic focused increasingly on illicit psychoactive drug consumption among middle-class, elite adolescents in middle-class, elite high schools. The portrayed danger here is obvious. If these particular groups adhere to the wrong moral universe, then the future of the country is in danger. The fact that much higher (and real) rates of illicit drug use existed among impoverished youth-in-distress did not seem to trouble anybody in particular (e.g., see note 3).

Second, motivational accounting systems that leveled strong criticisms about the lack of action by governmental agencies appeared in the media—especially the Ministry of Education. These motivational accounting systems typically expressed shock and amazement at the nature and scope of the problem among young people. They frequently associated adolescent drug abuse with general societal processes, such as permissiveness, motivation to experience almost everything, sensation seeking, lack of parental guidance and control, and general alienation. These popular analyses tended to acknowledge that, although the Ministry of Education should "get its act together" regarding drug misuse, the ministry was only one agency in "combating" drug misuse. It was pointed out that parents, family, and peers should take equal part in coping with the problem (see, e.g., *Yediot Aharonot*, June 6, 1982; 19, and June 7, 1982; 11; *Ha'aretz*, May 23, 1982, "Letters," 9). A few, however, warned that a whole generation of youngsters should not be stigmatized and that the police are to be equally blamed for the fact so many drugs are so easily available (see, e.g., *Ha'aretz*, May 23, 1982; 16, Adler's letter; Donevitz's column, 9).

Third, the electronic media gave advice, and the printed media provided articles on "how to find" and "what to do" if one's children used drugs. These articles gave accounts that included information about the dangers and hazards associated with the abuse of various chemical substances (see, e.g., *Yediot Aharonot*, June 7, 1982; 18, on "How to Behave with a Drug Abusing Adolescent"; and *Yediot Aharonot*, May 24, 1982, on "The Dangers of Hashish"). A survey of the daily newspapers for one year before May 1982 and one year after May 1982 (i.e. until May 1983) reveals that no such items on drug abuse appeared.

Fourth, toward the end of the panic, some items appeared in the media in which the public was informed that alcohol abuse among youth was the real problem and not hashish. These articles pointed out that alcohol abuse was far more dangerous than marijuana/hashish abuse (e.g., see *Yediot Aharonot*, June 6, 1982; 5).

The fifth, and last, line crystallized along an argument as to whether or not religious adolescents also used illicit psychoactive drugs, and whether or not a religious belief could be considered as a "good immunization" against the danger of illicit drug use. *Yediot Aharonot*, which is a secular daily newspaper, is a good source for the motivational accounting systems that were employed by one side. Its June 3, 1982, issue (p. 4) carried a big headline: "Drug abuse is prevalent among religious youth too." The news item that followed quoted Mr. D. Green, from the kibbutz movement, as making the statement in the headline: "Drug use is prevalent among religious and traditional youth too—this was disclosed yesterday by David Green, the head of the unit fighting drug abuse in the kibbutzim. He said that the drug use became a common social phenomenon and many adolescents are curious and want to try using drugs" (translated by the author). The news item quoted parliament member Rabbi H. Druckman as protesting the statement. Rabbi Druckman argued that research had proved that the prevalence of illicit psychoactive drug abuse among religious adolescents was about half the prevalence among nonreligious adolescents. On the very same date, *Hatzophe*, which is a daily Jewish-religious newspaper, published on its front page an account entitled "The Religious Education Prevents Drug Abuse," quoting Rabbi Druckman's statement: "Rabbi parliament member Druckman said that the claim that religion 'does not protect against the use of drugs' has no basis in reality. In a study that was published a year ago . . . in *Ma'ariv*, it was proven that drug use among religious youth is about 50 percent less than among non-religious youth. . . . This study proved that as the religious education runs deeper, and is more intensive, it provides a better protection against drug abuse. . . . " (translated by author). This last argument is particularly interesting because it confronted the accounts given by two different symbolic moral universes—secular and religious—regarding the abuse of illicit psychoactive drugs by adolescents, its reasons, and its methods of coping with it.[6]

The panic ends.   As time passed, it became clear that the sides of the argument were losing their initial zeal and vigor. The event that really stopped the drug panic, however, was the tension that was built up in Israel's northern border in late May and early June 1982. The Israeli invasion into south Lebanon on June 6, 1982, and the combat that followed between Israeli forces and the PLO and Syrian forces put the drug abuse moral panic to an end. One symbolic media item that illustrates this end appeared in *Yediot Aharonot*, June 18, 1982 (p. 6 of the "7 Days" supplement). There, a picture of a group of tired and proud young Israeli soldiers near their armored vehicle was given. The ironic explanation under the picture stated that: "a generation of which, until a year ago, it was pointed out in the streets as the one which [uses] drugs. . . . "

DISCUSSION

Moral panics and crusades, as explained in the introduction to the chapter, are inevitably and intimately linked to politics and deviance. They revolve around negotiations of power and morality, and they typically include campaigns that are aimed to shame vilify and deviantize (Schur 1980) other specific subpopulations. They are also linked to the processes through which societal control agents/agencies create or amplify deviance—a topic that was illuminated and emphasized by the labeling approach.

The historical description makes it evident that the May 1982 Israeli drug scare was, in fact, a moral panic, as characterized by Becker, (1963), Cohen, (1972), and others, and utilized an "Atrocity Tale" (Bomley, Shupe, and Ventimiglia 1979) about adolescent drug use in Israel. To follow Cohen's (1972) characterization, adolescent drug abuse emerged in May 1982 as a threat to societal values and interests. This threat was presented in a stylized and stereotypical fashion, using "Atrocity Tales," by the mass media by actors with high credibility and perceived morality. Actors announced diagnoses, solutions, and ways of coping. The panic then ended. The moral entrepreneurs were successful in creating the panic because they had power and were considered credible actors; the perceived threat potential in the drug issue was high; the moral entrepreneurs were successful in using the media and creating awareness of the drug problem; they encountered very little opposition; and they suggested a clear and acceptable solution for adolescent drug abuse. The nature of the panic and its historical development correspond to similar moral panics described by Cohen (1972), Dickson (1968), Ben-Yehuda (1985; 23–73), Zurcher et al. (1971), Zurcher and Kirkpatrick (1976), Johnson (1975), and Fishman (1978).

Two approaches have developed in the study of moral panics and crusades. One focused on the issue of morality and value systems and capitalized on how moral panics reflected a societal moral struggle (e.g., Becker 1963; Cohen 1972). The other approach focused on the issue of interests, showing that moral panics use moral themes in order to cloak a struggle between different actors or parties whose interests clash. In what might appear as cynical advocates of this approach imply that morality may be used for nonmoral issues (e.g., Dickson 1968; Chauncey 1980; Galliher and Cross 1983). Close to this approach is Brannigan's 1986 work, which suggested that researchers should not only pay attention to moral panics and moral crusades through the individual's perspective, but also pay attention to the politicial and institutional context. While there were a few hints in the past that these two approaches need not be thought of as mutually exclusive (e.g., Dickson 1968; 156), no theoretical or empirical attempts were made to integrate them. Dickson (1968; 142) even used the term "alternative explanation" to describe the "interest approach."

The May 1982 moral panic in Israel was based on distorted information, clearly aimed at sharply marking the boundaries between moral right and moral wrong. However, behind the public display about morality, there were other strong interests at work as well. The moral and interest perspectives can be used together to gain a better understanding of, insight into, and interpretation of the panic itself.

I shall first show that the question of *timing*—that is, why did the panic occur when it did—is best answered by using the analytical category of interests. Second, the question of *content*—that is, why a drug moral panic and not something else—ia best answered by using the analytical category of morality.

Moral panics and specific political/economic interests: the question of timing. The literature (especially Becker 1963; Gusfield 1963; and Cohen 1972) indicates that moral panics are the product of conflicts between bearers of different and competing moral principles, each trying to enforce their moral dominance over inhabitants of other symbolic-moral universes within the social system. In the broadest sense, the May 1982 drug moral panic in Israel supports this interpretation. A closer look, however, reveals that a better interpretation of these events must take into account various *interests* that find expression in a moral costume. The theoretical shift suggested here indicated that the exact nature and topic of a moral panic—while interesting in themselves—should not be the only major focus for analysis. Rather, one should analyze the specific political, economic, or other interests of the parties involved in the creation of the panic in order to find the true reasons for its occurrence.

The implication of this position is that the nature of the political/economic/social conflict that generates the panic should be a central focus for analysis. It is important to understand this shift because in Becker's (1963) analysis of "moral entrepreneurs" and "moral crusaders," as well as in those by Gusfield (1963), Schur (1979, 26, 252), and Cohen (1972), this point was hardly emphasized. They all focused on the *symbolic* value of the panics, the *moral* conflicts, and the threatened life-styles. Gusfield (1963) put it succinctly: "What is at stake is not so much the action of men, whether or not they drink, but their ideals, the moralities to which they owe their public allegiance" (p. 177). A theoretical shift to interests means that, instead of emphasizing only depersonalized social roles, one should analyze, among other things, the specific political interests of the specific political and social actors involved.[7] Thus, while the concept of moral universes is undoubtedly an important analytical concept, it is quite possible that "morality" and/or "values" are being used in moral panics to cloak actual, down-to-earth, and less ethereal interests. The shift in the theoretical focus I suggest here is tied in very nicely with the perspective of the political analysis of deviance. I do not challenge viewing moral panics as a *moral* contest between groups representing, prima facie, opposing symbolic-moral universes. However, what the May 1982 drug moral panic in Israel suggested is that it is quite possible for the relevant interested parties to *capitalize* on existing diversity and animosity between various symbolic-moral universes and to exploit this situation for their own benefit. This does not imply that the interested parties do not happen to believe in a specific moral universe. Rather, they take existing moral diversity and focus it in the public's mind, using the media for other than just moral reasons.

The perspective suggested here touches a somewhat older argument made by Lyman and Scott (1970). They argued that *interests* rather than *values* could, perhaps, better explain the social order. In a very specific sense, the development of ethnomethodology and sociological phenomenology supports this interpretation because the subjective and personalized worldview of the individual actor, emphasizing the individual's interests, is being taken as the central focus for analysis.

The Israeli May 1982 moral panic provides a golden opportunity for analyzing the panic using the interest perspective. The panic had at least two interested and powerful parties to it: the Israeli police and Mrs. Ora Namir, chairperson of the Committee on Education of the Knesset. Both are located in the higher echelons of the hierarchy of credibility and morality.

The police had two types of interests in creating the panic. The first is a long-standing vested interest to press the legislators into allocating more resources to the police fight against the "drug menace." The Israeli police are centralized and local city units are directed from national headquarters in Jerusalem. In reality, the police control fairly tightly what it "leaks" to the press or to other interested parties. The two young police officers who appeared before the parliament committee in its first meeting did so with the fullest approval of their superiors at national headquarters. Although their superiors knew fairly well that the scientific quality, validity, and accuracy of the "study" they brought was doubtful at best they nevertheless encouraged their appearance. The fact remains that they did not attend the second meeting, in which Mr. Karti—National Police Chief of Investigations—withdrew the "findings." The police interest in receiving more funds, however, is a long-standing one and did not have to be superficially timed to May 1982. Reporters receive information from the police, year round, about various and grandiose "drug raids" made every now and then. Indeed, Conklin (1986) noted that: "Rising crime rates have been used to justify higher police salaries and increases in police personnel, although police chiefs often acknowledge that police efficiency cannot be evaluated by crime data or arrest statistics" (p. 51).

The second, much more immediate, interest of the police was to deflect the public's attention away from the fact that a key state witness withdrew his statement and thus put in question the methods used by the police, as well as raising serious questions regarding the arrest of about seventy suspected "dope dealers." It was this second interest that, from the police point of view, was the most important. Regardless of the results of this dispute, the diversion of attention from the "state witness problem" to the "drug panic" was—one has to admit—very successful.

The second interested party, Mrs. Namir, then chairperson of the Committee on Education of the Knesset, was not only a member of the major opposition party, which at that time had some bitter arguments with Begin's coalition government, but she had always had very strong and explicit aspirations to become the minister of education herself. Mrs. Namir gave these aspirations a clear expression in interviews she willingly gave to reporters, to the media, and in informal interviews. Obviously, before election time these aspirations found expression frequently in the media. Being part of the major opposition party, Mrs. Namir could not become the minister of education. She was appointed instead, by her party, to the position of the chairperson of the Committee on Education. There can hardly be a question that Mrs. Namir had a strong vested interest to attack the Ministry of Education. This interest was first to attack the coalition party and thus to maintain a traditional opposition "watchdog" role. Second, through these attacks, Mrs. Namir was not only pointing out that there was something basically wrong with the way the Ministry of Education was functioning but that she had some better ideas as to what ought to—and could—be done regarding the problem of adolescent drug abuse. Furthermore, this moral panic gave Mrs. Namir (and others) a most convenient opportunity to present to the public the symbolic-moral universe she believed in and to contrast it with another moral universe that she (and others) portrayed as evil, as well as receiving exposure in the media—which seems to be an almost universal vested interest of Western politicians nowadays. This is an excellent example of how symbolic-moral universes clash and negotiate, how sympathy and power can be generated, and how one can legitimize one's own symbolic-moral universe by portraying a counter imaginary evil, antagonistic, and dangerous symbolic-moral universe. In this way, moral boundaries could be sharply drawn.

The motivational accounting systems that were used on the micro level by the parties are instructive. Both the police officers, but much more so Mrs. Namir, anchored their statements in a macro symbolic-moral universe. The danger portrayed by the interested moral entrepreneurs was not technical. For these parties, drug abuse constituted a significant symbolic threat of a moral degeneration, a threat to the country's youngest and brightest minds, a disintegration of its best high schools, and consequently an obvious danger to the future of the country. The motivational accounting systems that were used by these parties did not disclose anything about other interests. They actually could not because then no moral panic could be generated.

Thus, the interests of two parties that helped to create the May 1982 moral panic coincided almost perfectly. Drug abuse professionals who could, perhaps, cool the panic were divided among themselves and thus incapable of real coordinated action. Furthermore, those who were present in the discussion at the Knesset were prevented from stating their positions, and reporters were not eagerly interested in what they had to say. The analysis of the actions taken by the different parties points to their specific political/economic interests that led to creating and maintaining the moral panic. One, of course, is left puzzled about the dubious role played by the media—print and electronic—in helping this moral panic come about. There can hardly be a question that the media helped construct the social reality (Adoni and Mane 1984) where the panic flourished.

This analysis enables us to go one step beyond the older-traditional morality/role-type of approach to moral panics and to argue that moral panics may use (and abuse) moral themes for non-moralistic purposes.

The last decade witnessed the crystallization of a few studies that, together, tend to support the idea that, although moral panics may start because of moral reasons, one may also use an "alternative" (e.g., Dickson 1968) interpretation that emphasizes interests. Two analytically distinct types of interests can be isolated.

One type may be termed as *general political interests of system level* (e.g., Duster 1970). Let me use a few more detailed examples. Morgan

(1978) showed that the first antiopium crusade in U.S. history was directed against working-class Chinese brought over initially as cheap labor. By the 1870s, this crusade had become an ideological struggle, intimately linked to the desire to remove those workers from the labor force. Morgan drew the conclusion that the first opium laws in California were not a result of a moral crusade against the drug itself but resulted from a coercive action directed against Chinese laborers, who threatened the economic security of the white working class. Cook (1970) indicated that a similar fear of Chinese immigrants in Canada in the 1920s propelled the initiation of extremely harsh laws against the use and sale of opium, which was a behavior attributed to these immigrants. Likewise, Johnson (1975) illustrated how nineteenth-century antiopium moral crusaders created and diffused misinformation about drugs and equated "drugs" with "evil." Musto (1973, 221–33) and Bonnie and Whitebread (1974, 34–37) indicated that the passage of antimarijuna legislation in the 1930s in the western states in the United States was fuelled by prevailing hostility toward, and fear of, Mexican immigrants (Goode 1989, ch. one). Hall et al. (1978) analyzed a moral panic against a perceived threat of "mugging." They showed that this moral panic developed on the background of general societal fears from the spreading menace of "crime waves." Furthermore, this study implies that, as a result of societal moral concerns and fears, we may sometimes have anticipatory (preemptive) moral panics even before anything has happened. Bonacich's (1972) work also implied that ethnic antagonism "first germinates in a labor market split along ethnic lines" (p. 549). Bonacich explicitly wrote that: " . . . 'Antagonism' was chosen over terms like prejudice and discrimination because it carries fewer moralistic and theoretical assumptions" (p. 549). Thus, while deliberately avoiding any terminology even resembling a clash of symbolic-moral universes, Bonacich's work still implied that moral crusades against blacks originated in economic interests.

Hence, the above illustrations focus on the conclusion that anti-drug legislation was enacted, not so much because of objective fear from "the drug," but because of clashes between different groups of social actors, supposedly inhabiting very different symbolic-moral universes. Legislation symbolized the supremacy of a particular vocabulary of motives, and it was the final step in a long process of power negotiatioins regarding the nature of dominant and prevailing moralities and ideologies.

Another type of interest may be termed as *middle-level bureaucratic and/or occupational interest*. This chapter, as well as a few other studies, obviously illustrates how this type of interest motivated a moral panic. The first of the other studies is Galliher and Cross', (1983) study, which showed that the State of Nevada's conflicting ideas about morality have very little to do with moral value considerations but have mostly to do with economics. The State of Nevada makes a conscious effort to avoid any legislation that might harm the state's revenues from gambling, quick marriage and divorce, and legal prostitution in most counties. Nevada, however, also has what can be considered as very tough anti-marijuna laws, prohibition of state lottery, and the banning of prostitution in Las Vegas. Another study, by Fishman (1978), showed that media reports about a "crime wave" against the elderly in New York originated in a specific bureaucracy. This bureaucracy found itself lacking in activity and had an interest in creating a moral panic to justify its continued existence. In this case, too, official statistics indicated that there was a real decline in crimes against the elderly, contrary to the claims made by the moral crusaders. The third study, by Dickson (1968, which was reinforced solidly by Norland and Wright 1984), indicated that initiatives in antidrug legislation in the United States could be traced to the Narcotics Bureau (the Bureau was formed in 1930 and in 1960 was changed into the Federal Bureau of Narcotics and Dangerous Drugs [BNDD]). The Narcotic Bureau faced a nonsupportive environment and decreasing budget opportunities that threatened its survival. The moral crusade that the Narcotic Bureau created resulted in legislation and in a change in societal values. Finally, Chauncey (1980) argued that for organizational reasons the U.S. National Institute on Alcohol Abuse and Alcoholism portrayed teenage drinking as *significantly* worse and more serious that what it really was.

Morality, deviance, ideology, and moral panics: the question of content.   We noted earlier that both Lofland (1969, 14) and Horowitz and Liebovitz (1968, 282) focused on the "threat potential" in various deviant acts. We also noted Schur's (1980) term "deviantization process," referring to a process through which specific groups of social actors become deviantized. Schur stated that "stigma contests" are the major mechanism for such processes: "partisans in collective stigma contests are widely engaged in the use of propaganda: the manipulation of political symbols for the control of public opinion" (p. 135). Moral entrepreneurs, moral crusades, and panics therefore involve processes of "stigma contests" that focus on various and competing definitions of the boundaries between different symbolic-moral universes. As we shall see next, the area of illicit psychoactive drug use includes deviantization processes *and* a significant threat potential.

The "choice" of a topic for a moral panic is not just a random process. Moral panics are aimed to shame vilify and deviantize entire subpopulations and provide vivid illustrations for the clash of different symbolic-moral universes. Moral panics, therefore, are intimately linked to the basic nature of various cultures. Cohen (1972), who studied the creation of the Mods and Rockers in Britain as folk devils, pointed out that the specific content of a moral panic may vary, from a new topic to a revival of an old one. Gusfield (1963) studied how alcohol consumption became a topic for a moral crusade in the United States,[8] and Goode (1989, ch. one) analyzed the reasons for the development of a "moral panic" dynamics regarding the drug abuse issue in the United States in the middle of 1986. In different studies, Zurcher et al. (1971) and Zurcher and Kirkpatrick (1976) found that public support of a specific life-style and set of values was more important to the participants in antipornography moral crusades than the actual elimination of pornography. Another example is that of Anita Bryant in Miami. In the late 1970s, Bryant conducted an intensive moral crusade against homosexuals using such morally loaded motivational accounting systems as "save our children" (see Hills 1980, 106-7).

Drug abuse policies have been characterized in many parts of the world by moral panics, perhaps more so than any other form of deviance (for a recent example involving a drug panic around crack, see *Time* October 6, 1986, 30).

According to Lidz and Walker (1980), the drug crisis in the United States was "a phony creation of a variety of powerful people who felt threatened by the growth of expressive passivist beliefs in the youth culture and revolutionary politics among blacks. It seems that there was little reality to the belief that large sectors of the American population were about to become addicted to heroin" (pp. 251–52). Their conclusion was, therefore, that the drug crisis "was a smoke screen for the repression of political and cultural groups" (p. 252; see also Helmer 1975). Gusfield's (1963) famous work analyzed the Women's Christian Temperance Union, specifically its antialcohol activities. Gusfield stated that: "What prohibition symbolized was the superior power and prestige of the old middle class in American society. The threat of decline in that position had made explicit action of government necessary to defend it. Legislation did this in two ways. It demonstrated the power of the old middle class by showing that they could mobilize sufficient political strength to bring it about, and it gave dominance to the character and style of old middle class life in contrast to that of the urban lower and middle classes" (p. 122). As Gusfield pointed out, the symbolic message carried out by the end of Prohibition meant the end of the dominance of old middle-class virtues and the end of rural, Protestant dominance (1963, 126). Musto (1973), Kramer (1976), Goode (1972), Klerman (1970), Dumont (1973), Young (1971), Duster (1970), Conrad and Schneider (1980), Morgan (1978), Ashley (1972), Anderson (1981), and Trebach (1982) all illustrated how antidrug campaigns in the United States can be traced to ideological moral issues. Indeed, Goode (1989, ch. one) states that "much of the drug legislation passed in this century was motivated by political and moral reasons rather than by a genuine concern for the health and welfare of vulnerable members of the society." Thus, ample evidence exists that, in different time periods and in different cultures, drugs have traditionally been associated with moral-ideological issues. From this perspective, the "choice" of drugs for the creation of a moral panic was, obviously, not a unique Israeli invention.

The "choice" of drugs as a symbol for the creation of a moral panic, while perhaps not cognitively planned, was also no mere coincidence. Capitalization on the "drug menace" as a societal threat has at least two important aspects. First, drug scares are very attractive to both the media and the masses, especially drug scares concerning youth. It is relatively easy to use this issue in order to generate a moral crisis. The reason for this is that such drug scares can be considered as an effective ideology. Within our theoretical framework, let me suggest that ideologies provide, and help construct, the boundaries of symbolic-moral universes. In this specific respect, ideologies and morality share a common denominator. Ideologies provide their adherents with generalized motivational accounting systems, which are translated into vocabularies of motives at the micro level. These consequently help social actors to utilize the ideologically given rationale and justifications.

An analytical conceptualization of ideology that is consistent with the terminology I use here was suggested by Geertz (1964). According to Geertz,[9] the function of ideology is to provide authoritative concepts capable of rendering situations meaningful, and "suasive images" by which their meaning can be "sensibly grasped," and which can arouse emotions and direct mass action. That drugs can be used as a "suasive image" for corrupting youth and thus destroying the country's future seems clear. Thus, we find such expressions as "drugs destroy young minds," "drugs destroy the future of the country" (from the major daily media in Israel, May 1982) and the like. When these phrases are used within an authoritative framework, such as the Parliament, the press, and high ranking officials in the "hierarchy of credibility" and morality, an effective antidrug ideology is created, sustained, and used. Furthermore, as Szasz (1975) and others[10] have shown, the term drugs is an easy and safe enemy to create, magnify, portray in evil colors, and focus hatred on.

The second aspect is the fact that the moral statements used in the antidrug ideology help to draw and maintain moral boundaries, especially between those who use drugs and those who do not; those who are morally right and those who are morally wrong. A typical example for this point is the argument that was waged toward the end of the panic as to whether orthodox Jews were somehow more resistant (and perhaps even "immunized") to drug abuse vis-a-vis secular Jews. In this sense, two opposing symbolic-moral universes were sharply and visibly contrasted. Berger and Luckmann (1966) argued that when two such contradictory symbolic-moral universes meet a conflict is indeed unavoidable: "heretical groups posit not only a theoretical threat to the symbolic universe, but a practical one to the institutional order legitimated by the symbolic universe in question" (p. 124). In the moral panic described here one symbolic-moral universe fabricated a negative, morally wrong symbolic-moral universe of drug users and successfully campaigned against some of the "archenemies" who supposedly helped support this deviant, heretical symbolic-moral universe.

The symbolic-moral universe that said that it valued the work ethic, direct coping with everyday life problems, and maximum self-control claimed moral superiority. It portrayed an opposing negative symbolic-moral universe of drug users who supposedly symbolized moral degeneracy, loss of control, danger, lack of proper ideas, and irrationality.

The above situation is not unique. Elsewhere (Ben-Yehuda 1980), I illustrated that when the medieval Inquisition found itself without heretics to pursue it had an interest to find, or invent, a new type of heretic to justify the continued existence of its machinery. Thus, the Inquisition set about to introduce and develop a new form of heresy—that of witchcraft. A few Dominicans, and the Inquisition, fabricated a negative detested and fearsome moral universe—that of demonic witchcraft. That symbolic-moral universe was described as diametrically opposed to the positive symbolic-moral universe of the true believers. There can be little doubt that, based on this negative moral universe, the Inquisition was very successful in creating a devastating moral panic that lasted for a very long period of time. In a recent work,

Gusfield (1981) also showed that the development of the "myth of the Killer Drunk" (pp. 151–54), helps American society to maintain the illusion of moral consensus about such positive values as being sober, in control, rational, hard working, and the like. This point refers to the "boundary maintenance" function of deviance in moral panics, which was documented elsewhere (e.g., see Durkheim 1938; Erikson 1966; Lauderdale 1976; Ben-Yehuda 1985). All the previous illustrations indeed show that one possible and real result of moral panics may be a new legislation that can pave the way for a process of social change. Moral panics can, therefore, be *linked* in this way to major societal processes of change and stability, which is a basic theoretical focus of this book.

The way the various organizations, including the government, in Israel coped with what they perceived as the "drug menace" and the generalized accounts they chose to present their stance are instructive as to the underlying moral tones of the drug abuse issue in Israel. For example, AL SAM, the only Israeli voluntary citizen's association against the use of drugs, states officially on its letterhead that it has declared "war on drugs." In a country that has fought six wars in the last forty years (apart from antiterrorist battles and activities), this slogan carries a heavy moral tone.

Some of the motivational accounting systems that were used in governmental publications from the late 1960s and early 1970s were almost intended to create moral panics. For example, a poster published in 1971 by the Israeli government used a very interesting vocabulary of motives: "the number of hashish users in Egypt is approximately five million. In the Six Day War everyone could see the type and quality of the Egyptian soldiers. Don't delude yourself that there is no connection between these two facts." This particular motivational accounting system must have made sense in post-1967 Israel, when its youngsters felt perhaps like supermen. In the 1973 war, the Egyptian soldiers proved to be of a higher quality, so today when I show this poster to my students, they usually roar with laughter. Another poster from the early 1970s stated that: "If being a man means to have a strong and stable character, those who use drugs prove the opposite: apathy, lack of initiative and ambition, indifference." Obviously, these motivational accounting systems make clear and explicit moral statements by portraying the morally desired versus the morally undesired. In this context, it is not difficult to see why it is so easy to depict "drugs" as corrupting the innocent, perhaps morally confused, youth, while stigmatizing those who are morally perceived to be actually wicked, corrupt, and even evil.

In Israel, therefore, as in the United States, the drug issue has always been intimately associated with various moral and ideological issues. Thus, the rhetorical devices that were used in official publications on drug abuse, the motivational accounting systems given against using various psychoactive chemical substances, reflect the struggle between different symbolic-moral universes. These micro motivational accounting systems are not "technical" — portraying the "obvious" (or "technical") dangers of drug abuse; they focus instead on the type of person who, supposedly, *chooses* to use drugs and on the social and moral implications of such use.

Because a consensual definition of morality (and, therefore, of the actual meaning of deviance) in pluralistic societies becomes a complex issue, negotiations between different symbolic-moral universes become problematic in these societies. One way of solving this is to rely on the lowest, most "obvious" common denominator. Criminal law in complex societies, as a form of generalized motivational accounting system, becomes therefore increasingly relied upon as a formal mechanism of social control, providing an umbrella moral-symbolic universe, integrating all those who live within its political jurisdiction (Hills 1980; 35). The law symbolizes and reflects different moral ideas in society. As sociologists know all too well, the law may frequently reflect, perhaps more than anything else, the final product of a very long process of interaction and negotiation among different interest groups, representing different moral universes, and not always the reality of the legitimate needs of large sections of the population. Marijuana laws in the United States today reflect this problem: "marijuana has become the 'new Prohibition' in contemporary American society, with upwards of 40 million persons having used this illicit drug, perhaps one third of them using it on a more or less regular basis. Effective enforcement of this law has become impossible. The sale and use of marijuana remain illegal, however, primarily because most of the older adult public are *ideologically* opposed to total decriminalization. Use of the drug is symbolically associated in much of the public mind with many kinds of activities, life styles, and moral and political beliefs that these dominant groups find repugnant (for example, hedonism, sexual promiscuity, altered states of consciousness, radicalism, irreverence towards authority, and so on)" (Hills 1980; 38).

The drug abuse issue symbolizes something very important regarding the very nature of the Israeli complex collective conscience. In the Israeli context, this issue represents something that is very alien to the Israeli ethos of creating a *new* society, industriousness, asceticism, and machoism. Drug users, in this cultural context, *are* typically portrayed as *folk devils* (Cohen 1972).

In Israel, there might have also been an added factor helping the May 1982 moral panic to flourish. The educational system in Israel seems, somehow, to be prone to various "moral panics." For example, in 1979 and again in 1981 the Israeli public learned—through the media—about "terrible" problems of violence and vandalism in schools in Israel. Horowitz and Amir (1981), who researched this issue, indicated that the reports on violence and vandalism in schools were widely exaggerated. Eisenstadt (1984) pointed out that the panics about violence and vandalism in Israeli schools probably began, and were fueled by, the different groups whose interest it was to create such panics. For example, the teachers' union, which was negotiating the annual salary raises of teachers, wanted to show how hard their job was and parents who were against integrating schools (with students from different sex and ethnic groups) and who had an interest in showing that this integration had disastrous outcomes. Thus, another "moral panic" located within the educational system was, perhaps, associated in the public mind with what it felt were problems endemic to this system.

The May 1982 moral panic: morality and interests.   The argument so far explains why illicit psychoactive drug use is an almost natural topic for a moral panic. Drug abuse is an "easy enemy" (Christie 1984; Christie and Bruun 1985;Dumont 1973; Szasz 1975) and can be used in a moral panic as a boundary maintenance device in a clash between opposing symbolic-moral universes. The Israeli police, however, had a much more specific interest in using this topic for a moral panic. The state witness who retracted his testimonies in early May challenged the morality and integrity—indeed, the legitimacy—of the police anti-drug abuse action. Mr. Sabag's statement implied that the police used deliberately doubtful methods. The police denied Mr. Sabag's claims—and was stuck with the account. It had to justify what it did, neutralize Mr. Sabag's account, or divert attention from this challenge. It appears that the police decided to pursue the third alternative. The police "choice" of drugs for a moral panic was not coincidental. Since the challenge to the police was raised within the context of drug law enforcement, the proper reaction had to be within that area. There were three major messages that the police delivered during the drug moral panic it helped to create. First, the prevalence of drug abuse is very high, much more serious than what we "know." When the issue of "governmental conspiracy" was made, the police did nothing to negate this obviously wrong accusation. Second, middle-class adolescents in what are considered good (even elite) high schools are those that are massively involved in this dangerous illicit drug use. Thus, the cream of Israel's young minds are in danger. Third, while the police have the solution for this problem, lack of cooperation and liberalism undermine its efforts.

The police used a vocabulary of motives that projected an image of being engaged in a battle with an archenemy that corrupted and destroyed the morality of Israel's finest minds. Clearly, when such a battle is waged, a minor Lilliputian issue, as the claim made by Mr. Sabag, tends to disappear. At this point, even if the police had admitted to having made a mistake in the Sabag affair, the mistake would have become minute. After all, on the one hand, we have a symbolic-moral universe that pretends to project Israel's future and, on the other hand, only a questionable character. Diversion of attention here was very successful. After May 12, no one even seemed to remember the state witness problem.

Finally, two short remarks. First, this chapter raises the problem of whether the May 1982 moral panic and other panics were fabricated or based on monstrous exaggerations (or amplifications—see Wilkins 1964) of existing problems. The May 1982 panic was clearly based on a monstrous amplification of an existing problem. Similar amplifications occurred in the panics reported by Fishman (1978), Hall et al. (1978), Horowitz and Amir (1981). The studies by Erikson (1966), Bergesen (1978), and my previous work (1980) support the idea of fabrication.[11] Thus, fabrication or amplification depends on the specific case.

Second, the theoretical interpretation suggested here helps us understand why drugs were an almost natural choice for a moral panic. The social political background in Israel in May 1982, and the interested parties, explain why drugs were "chosen" as the topic. This interpretation also helps us to understand why the voices of scientists, and especially members of the Interministerial Committee, were hardly heard. While most of them knew what the actual facts were, neither the parliamentary committee nor the press were interested in these views since these facts did not help to "understand" the drug menace. Furthermore, these people were cast into the opposing symbolic-moral universe as "too liberal" and not caring enough; to some degree, although minute, their authority, legitimacy, and credibility were challenged. This challenge assumed one of two forms. The first was the fact that opponents to the moral panic were prevented from expressing their view both to the parliamentary committee and to the media.[12] The second was a claim that there was a governmental conspiracy to hide the "true" magnitude of the problem and that scientists were "too liberal." Thus, opponents to the panic always found themselves in an uncomfortable position of having to apologize and cope either with the problem of the conspiracy theory or with the accusation of being too liberal. Hence, aside from the two contrasting symbolic-moral universes, two hierarchies of credibility also were contrasted. On the one hand, we had the police and the politicians, on the other hand, the scientists. This analysis also helps us to understand why, in other similar situations (e.g., Ben-Yehuda 1980; Gusfield 1963; Cohen 1972; Bergesen 1977, 1978), the voices of those who had accurate information, although not supportive of the panic, were hardly, if ever, heard.

The moral panic did not focus only on drugs but on drug abuse among middle-class and elite adolescents, in middle-class and elite high schools. The threat potential and the amount of danger of illicit psychoactive drug use among this particular group are obvious and magnify the noise and impact of the moral panic. The fact that drug abuse among nonelite, peripheral, and problematic adolescents is probably much higher than among elite adolescents (see note 3) did not seem to bother the moral crusaders one bit.

Sociology of moral panics and sociology.   The moral perspective in moral panics emphasizes that these panics frequently help draw the boundaries between various symbolic-moral universes, in the neofunctional sense of the argument. The previous discussion as well as the various illustrations all point out that moral panics may be linked to social movements and may play a central key role in sociological processes that are so crucial from the theoretical standpoint of this book— societal process of change and stability (e.g., Bonacich 1972; Cohen 1972; Gusfield 1963; Morgan 1978; Ben-Yehuda 1985). These panics may either reinforce existing boundaries of symbolic-moral universes or introduce change into those boundaries. Power and morality obviously play a crucial role in these panics.

Moral panics may be connected to a few areas in sociology: social problems, law, labeling, and collective behavior. The sociological research in each of these areas *was* aware of the complex impact that power and morality had on deviance. Since this book explicitly attempts to reframe the sociology of deviance within the context of total social structures, history, and politics, it becomes necessary to examine to what other general areas in sociology is the sociology of moral panics related and how.

The connections between moral panics, labeling, and the law were already mentioned previously in this chapter.

The sociology of moral panics may also be related in two ways to the sociology of social problems (e.g., Spector and Kitsuse, 1977; Schneider 1985). First, repeated or prolonged moral panics about specific issues may give rise to the development of a dynamic characteristic of social problems, and hence either open the way for possible social changes or reinforce stability. The results of moral panics, and the negotiations between various symbolic-moral universes, depend on their ability to generate and/or use power and their abilities to negotiate morality. It is thus not possible to know the results of moral panics without getting into the details of particular cases. Second, in both areas researchers are faced with the need to cope with the problem of morality versus interests.

Another almost unavoidable issue relates to the relationship between public perception of a phenomenon and the "actual reality" of that phenomenon. This is a relevant issue since clearly it would be impossible to make statements about drug use among Israeli students that bear no relation to the real world and expect to be believed, unless the public were fairly uninformed about the phenomenon in question. As could be seen, in other and parallel cases of moral panics, similar gaps between public perceptions of a phenomenon and the "actual reality" existed too. In the specific moral panic described here and in other cases (see Fishman 1978; Davis 1952), it appears that the bridging mechanism was the media.

It is also worth our while to notice not only *what* the moral entrepreneurs did, but also *how* their messages were apprehended and reacted to by the public. Let me suggest, therefore, that these two issues—the gap between perception and reality and the public's reaction—connect the topic of moral panics to the general area of collective behavior.

Unfortunately, the sociological study of collective behavior itself is very problematic. In the minds of many sociologists, this area may even appear as a vast intellectual wasteland of redundant descriptions and sometime trivial theories.

Collective behavior is typically interpreted to mean a relatively spontaneous, unstructured, and extrainstitutional behavior of a fairly large group of social actors. This is a behavior that deviates from the usual, routine, everyday behavior (e.g., see Goode 1988, 505–29, for a short review). Collective behavior is assumed to include such topics as fads, fashions, crazes, panics, some riots, rumor, mass hysteria, mass delusions, crowds, and mass behavior—an impressive spectrum of behaviors indeed, all of which compose the material and non-material parts of culture. A related area is that of social movements. These movements, as usually characterized, "are organized efforts by large numbers of people to change or preserve some major aspect of society" (Goode 1988, 506).

While tending somewhat toward what may appear as esoteric, it is clearly the case that both collective behavior and social movements are fully capable of changing, or keeping stable, in the most profound way some very major aspects of culture and society.

In this regard, the concept of moral panics may be linked to those of collective behavior and social movements (e.g., see Gusfield 1963; Erikson 1966; Ben-Yehuda 1980). In both cases we have actors who try, collectively, to define the nature and boundaries of the social and moral reality in which they think they live. These attempts are aimed to socially construct particular symbolic-moral universes so that meaning could emerge, be grasped, and guide action. Future use of the concepts of collective behavior and social movements in general, and moral panics in particular, may provide us with an interesting and viable analytical tool to interpret processes of social change and stability.

One particularly interesting analytical parallel may exist between the topics of moral panics and of "mass delusions." In both cases, we have a public that does not have a clear idea of what is "really" taking place. In both cases, the media plays a crucial role in bridging the gap between reality and public perception. In fact, it is the media that may shape the public's perception by providing authoritative motivational accounting systems that help construct social realities and may direct mass action. In moral panics and mass delusions, there are systematic reasons (however, also specific to the case) why a particular public will believe a particular version of reality. There are a few examples for this: (1) Fishman's (1978) study of the fabrication of "crime waves" against the elderly: (2) my previous study (1980) of the production of the imaginary crime of witchcraft; (3) Cantril's (1940) and Koch's (1970) analyses of the now-famous "invasion from Mars" panic triggered by Orson Welles's 1938 radio show; (4) Medalia and Larsen's (1958) work on a Seattle panic regarding stories about damages to automobile windshields; (5) Johnson's (1945) work on the "phantom anesthetist" of Matoon. Goode (1988; 514–15) points out that the so-called cattle mutilation mystery (see also Summers and Kagan 1984) and the fabrication of the *Protocols of the Elders of Zion* also belong to the same category. Accepting the idea that on a very basic level there are at least two issues that imply that "moral panics" and "mass delusions" are connected may put both topics in another larger sociological frame of interpretation.

In a strange, indirect way, Stahl and Lebedun's (1974) study may support some findings in this chapter and may also provide a possible link between mass hysteria and moral panics. Stahl and Lebedun studied the sudden mass hysteria in a group of female workers. They found that those who were the most dissatisfied with their work situation tended to present the severest symptomatology (in the form of actual physical symptoms attributed to a "mystery gas"). These actors also reported having friends with similar, or even worse, symptoms. Here we have an association between dissatisfaction with work in a specific social network finding expression in a mass hysteria.

In this chapter, we saw that interests explained the onset of a moral panic. Thus, in both cases, mass hysteria and moral panics, collective behavior may be traced to individuals' problematic integration into an existing culture. The consequent strain finds expression in a mass hysteria or delusion. There may, however, be some profound differences between mass delusions and moral panics. One difference may be that mass delusions that do not involve—prima facie—moral issues may be different from moral panics. It is up to future research to examine whether symbolic-moral universes and/or interests may also be involved in such delusions.

CONCLUDING SUMMARY

The moral perspective gave the term "moral panics" solid support, while the interest perspective implied that the use of the word "moral" was, perhaps, inappropriate. While no change of term is suggested due to the new synthesis presented here, a new awareness to both perspectives is called for when analyzing moral panics.

The sociology of moral panics was analyzed as linked to other significant sociological traditions—those of the study of social problems, law, collective behavior, and the labeling approach. All the above approaches paid more or less explicit attention to power and to symbolic-moral universes. Consequently, the sociology of moral panics was reframed within the context of social change and social stability, particularly at the moral boundaries of different and competing symbolic-moral universes. In this way, another major goal of this book was achieved—linking the sociology of deviance with the mainstream of sociological analysis.

It is, perhaps, no coincidence that theoretical formulations in the sociology of moral panics have been divided along two "alternative" interpretations: the moral perspective and the interest perspective. Hence, the sociology of moral panics becomes part of social processes of change and stability. These processes indeed involve using the concepts of power and morality that are typically interpreted within an historical and dynamic perspective.

Using the May 1982 drug scare moral panic in Israel, I argued that, rather than viewing these two perspectives as competing, we should view them as complementary. This new theoretical synthesis was achieved by presenting two foci for theoretical inquiry: Why did the moral panic happen when it did, and why was a specific content—drugs—"chosen" for that panic. Answering these two questions fully necessitates the use of the morality and the interest perspectives in a combined, synthesized interpretation.

The specific interests of the parties involved in creating the panic primarily explain its *timing*. The political and social actors involved in the May 1982 drug moral panic in Israel deliberately ignored data contradicting their views and were successful in achieving their specific goals. The actual *content* of the panic was explained by resorting primarily to the concepts of boundary maintenance, morality, and ideology and secondarily to interests. Creating the moral panic provided an opportunity for actors adhering to one symbolic-moral universe to fabricate an antagonistic symbolic-moral universe, attack it, and thus redefine the moral boundaries between the morally desirable and the morally undesirable. The various motivational accounting systems that were used by the moral crusaders showing how macro-level elements were reflected and used in micro-level vocabularies of motives were examined as well. Thus, a genuine new theoretical synthesis was achieved by applying the two previously competing perspectives to the same moral panic.

The analysis presented in this chapter is tied in very intimately to the idea of negotiating symbolic-moral universes and the differential amounts of power these universes have and can use. As these two concepts are utilized throughout the analysis, the process of generating a moral crusade and panic, aimed to vilify stigmatize and deviantize particular behaviors and actors, connects the topic of moral panics to politics and deviance. This connection is done by employing an historical analysis, with an emphasis on both social structures and politics. As such, the analysis presented in this chapter is committed to, and coherent with, the conceptual framework of this book and presents a new synthesis for the sociology of moral panics as well. Furthermore, the chapter provided an analysis of a moral crisis and a challenge, as well as an attempted process of deviantization, which was directed from the center toward the periphery. The theoretical framework that was used was a non-Marxist conflict approach, coupled with neofunctionalism.

One may note, perhaps ironically, in conclusion, that the chapter deals with whether the rate of illicit psychoactive drug use by adolescents is 3 percent or 50 percent. This quantitative argument, after all, may have nothing to do with the real problem, which is qualitative, contrasting the symbolic-moral universe of illicit drug users versus that of nonusers. Here we have users—the only question is to what extent. Answering this problem relates directly to the problem of what the nature of deviance is. For the single user, the difference is clear and obvious. For a culture, there is a significant difference. When very few (later stigmatized and deviantized) individuals use illicit psychoactive drugs, it is relatively easy for powerful inhabitants of other symbolic-moral universes to try and define them as deviants. When, however, approximately half of the relevant population is involved in such a practice, the ability of inhabitants in other symbolic-moral universes to define them as deviants, and gain legitimacy and support for using such motivational accounting systems, decreases significantly.

Hence, the "danger" in widespread illicit psychoactive drug use is that of a *moral revolution* (e.g., Lidz and Walker 1980), where the symbolic-moral universe of users would gain legitimacy, power, and credibility and its boundaries would expand to include members that previously inhabited other, perhaps opposing, symbolic-moral universes.

Chapter Six

Drug Abuse Social Policy
in Comparative Perspective
When Symbolic-Moral Universes Meet

INTRODUCTION[1]

The connection to the analytical framework of the book. The way different cultures define particular patterns of behavior as deviant, or as social problems, is important for us. A society's "official" position toward a particular behavioral pattern, in the form of social policy, may be referred to—in our terminology—as a *generalized motivational accounting system.* Such a social policy originates either directly from a distinctive symbolic-moral universe or from a coalition of a few universes, and utilizes power to gain ascendancy for its version of morality and reality construction, as well as prevent other symbolic-moral universes from acting on the issue. After all, if some behavior is defined as problematic in some sense, then we ought to do something about it.

The crystallization of a societal generalized motivational accounting system in the form of a social policy is intimately linked to the topic of this book. In the case of an integrative drug abuse social policy (i.e., not *just* legislation), we have a societal reaction that was developed *after* the use of various psychoactive substances had been outlawed, stigmatized, deviantized, and defined as a "social problem." The crystallization of this particular social policy resulted from a confrontation between different and contesting symbolic-moral universes. This contrast signified the boundaries of these universes and reflected the different amounts of power and legitimacy held by these universes.

Thus, the issue of drug abuse social policy includes the issues of power and morality and the relations and negotiations between center and periphery. It also includes the issue of changing definitions regarding the very nature of deviance in a dynamic and historical perspective, and hence of the sociology of change and stability.

Following the general theoretical approach of this book, this chapter is based on an historical analysis, integrating into one analysis

135

the concepts of politics, power, and total social structures within the context of change and stability into one coherent sociological interpretation. The concepts of motivational accounting systems and vocabularies of motives will be used throughout the chapter to illustrate how, by using these concepts, the micro and macro levels of analysis are integrated.

In each of the other case-study chapters in this book, there is a "micro story" that is presented by using the natural history of crime approach and followed by a sociological interpretation. This chapter is somewhat different in the sense that the "story" it provides is on the macro level—the story of the crystallization of generalized motivational accounting systems taking issue with psychoactive drug use and of the symbolic-moral universes that either develop and use these motivational accounting systems or oppose them.

In the previous chapter, we saw how two parties with some very mundane interests were able to create a national moral panic regarding illicit psychoactive drug use by middle-class and elite adolescents in Israel. In that chapter, we also saw why it was that "drugs" became such a favored topic for moral crusades, and why they were specifically used in the May 1982 moral panic. Sometimes moral panics result in a successful social change—for example, a change in the social reaction to an assumed pattern of behavior. This chapter examines the "successful" results of a particular societal reaction in the form of a drug abuse social policy, in a comparative perspective. As such, the sociological interpretation presented in this chapter is a natural continuation of the analysis of "moral panics" presented in the previous chapter.

Goals and plan of the chapter. My goal in this chapter is to show that the generalized motivational accounting system in the form of social policy toward drug abuse in two different cultures—Israel and the United States—while stemming from similar moralistic assumptions, works very differently. This social policy clearly represents the victory of one symbolic-moral universe (that of "objectors" to psychoactive drug use) over the other (that of "nonobjectors").

However, the cultural differences between the two societies, particularly regarding the amount of power, consensus, and legitimacy that the symbolic-moral universe of "objectors" enjoys varies significantly. Hence, the use of very similar generalized motivational accounting systems produced dramatically different results in two cultures.

The reason for choosing Israel and the United States is that, although there are some obvious differences between these two cultures, there are some other similarities that warrant this comparison. Both are democracies, characterized by ethnic pluralism; in both societies, the same model of social policy toward drug abuse was implemented.

To make the comparison meaningful, I shall first describe the model itself; then I shall analyze the sociological nature of the drug abuse problem. Following this presentation, I shall provide a description of the relative success of social policy toward drug abuse in the United States and Israel, followed by a sociological interpretation of the existing differences.

Drug abuse. Drug abuse has been defined as "the use, usually by self-administration, of any drug in a manner that deviates from the approved medical or social patterns within a given culture" (Jaffee 1975, 284). Different psychoactive drugs have different histories (Austin 1978), but a justified generalization would be that prior to the twentieth century in most European and North American countries the use of various psychoactive drugs was perhaps considered immoral or bad, yet not illegal. This century, however, has been characterized by the passage of numerous laws, especially in the United States, against the use, possession, or manufacture of various psychoactive drugs. In other countries, (e.g., Norway), the intensive antidrug abuse legislation may even threaten basic civil liberties.[2] The first decades of this century witnessed a tremendous increase in public attempts to regulate drug use. Drug abuse was redefined by powerful moral entrepreneurs as an illicit act, especially with regard to such drugs as morphine and its various derivatives (e.g., heroin), cannabinoids (hashish, marijuana), cocaine, and other drugs. Gradually, these redefinitions brought about a change in legislation expressing the new moral boundaries.

The history of the societal reaction to drug abuse and the crystallization of generalized motivational accounting systems illustrate that this reaction developed in several stages: from lack of response and inactivity to increasing levels of social control, usually by the legal and criminal justice systems. This century has certainly served as a turning point in this development (King 1972; Brecher 1972; Duster 1970; Morgan 1974, 1981; Goode 1984a).

The works by Brecher (1972), King (1972), Bonnie and

Whitebread (1974), Galliher and Walker (1973), Musto (1973), Reasons (1974), Waldorf et al. (1974), Courtwright (1982), Himmelstein (1983), as well as others demonstrate how in the early decades of this century a few moral entrepreneurs conducted moral crusades that were aimed at outlawing various psychoactive substances, especially opiates and marijuana. These moral entrepreneurs generated moral crusades whose goal was to attack, vilify, delegitimize, and symbolically annihilate those symbolic-moral universes that permitted the more or less free and unrestricted use of a variety of psychoactive substances. They aimed to change the moral boundaries of these universes in such a fashion that use of psychoactive substances would be severely limited and controlled very tightly, if not banned altogether. This moral campaign generated myths, disseminated misinformation, and gradually changed the public attitude toward psychoactive drug use. These moral crusades were more or less successful in increasing antidrug legislation as an expression of changing moral boundaries in Europe. England, the United States, Canada, and other countries gradually made illicit psychoactive drug use a vile deviance, associated with a whole spectrum of other shameful and supposedly harmful behavioral patterns.

This social intervention caused the patterns of psychoactive drug use, as they existed in the late nineteenth and early twentieth centuries, to disappear as new patterns emerged. The widespread use of various psychoactive substances by female and middle-class users virtually disappeared and a new type of user emerged: lower class, mostly slum dwellers. This situation characterized predominantly the United States, and to a smaller extent Europe, until the 1960s. The 1960s witnessed another significant shift in the characteristics of the drug-abusing population.

The number of all substance abusers in both Europe and the United States (especially of marijuana and cocaine) has increased steadily since the 1960s. The most frequent users are young, urbanite, middle/upper-class males. Faced with this situation, governments, especially in the United States, where the problem was perceived as especially bad, felt they had to devise a credible social policy to cope with what these governments defined as a grave and serious problem.

History shows that the United States has assumed a most active role concerning social policies toward drug abuse. The social policy that crystallized in the United States was copied by other countries as well.

DRUG ABUSE SOCIAL POLICY

The model of social policy toward drug abuse as a particular form of a generalized motivational accounting system in the United States and Israel (as well as in other countries) was developed and crystallized in the United States.

The United States has issued a few policy documents regarding drug abuse. One of the earliest and most important, although most neglected, was the report submitted by the Prettyman Commission, which was appointed in 1963 by President Kennedy to review U.S. drug problems and to submit recommendations. The report's recommendations, however, were never fully implemented by the administration (King 1972, 240–46; Goldberg 1980, 24). A 1967 task force submitted a report to President L. Johnson on narcotics and law enforcement, leading to the establishment of the Bureau of Narcotics and Dangerous Drugs (BNDD) in 1968. The National Commission on Marijuana and Drug Abuse recommended in 1972 that antidrug laws (especially regarding marijuana use) be relaxed, but favored discouraging marijuana use (Morgan 1981, 161). The commission's recommendations led to decriminalization of marijuana use in some states. It was the Nixon administration, however, that gave the drug problem the highest priority it had achieved until then in the United States. As Goldberg (1980, 25–26) and Morgan (1981) noted, the need to reduce street crime, the growing public concern over heroin addiction, and the new approaches to controlling this problem all brought Nixon to declare "war" on drug abuse. Consequently, the federal budget for combating drug abuse rose dramatically during the Nixon years.

The continual a reported growth of drug abuse both in the United States and abroad demanded an integrative approach to the problem. The result was a new task force document, submitted in 1978, *The White Paper on Drug Abuse*,[3] which provided an elaborate suggestion for an integrative social policy. It has become one of the most important and influential documents in the history of drug abuse social policy.

The *White Paper* suggested a social policy that was based on two elements: supply reduction and demand reduction. Supply reduction includes activities aimed at reducing the quantity of illicit psychoactive substances available on the market. Such activities are largely handled by law enforcement agencies. Demand reduction includes activities aimed at reducing the demand for these illicit psychoactive substances. These efforts include prevention, treatment, and education.

If supply and demand reductions can simultaneously be achieved, then an overall decline or a check in the growth of illicit drug use can be expected. Israel, the United States, and several other countries implemented the social policy concept based on supply and demand reduction. Because this supply/demand reduction policy became so common, it has also become important to examine its results and effectiveness.

It is, however, virtually impossible to analyze the social policy and its results without establishing a prior base of understanding regarding the *sociological* nature of the problem. The next section (which is composed of seven subsections) does exactly this.

THE NATURE OF THE DRUG ABUSE PROBLEM:
A SOCIOLOGICAL PERSPECTIVE

In this section, I shall analyze the problem of illicit psychoactive drug use from a sociological point of view. I shall illustrate that attitudes toward such drug use have very little to do with "technical" problems—for example, the "objective" dangers popularly associated with illicit psychoactive drug use—but have *much* to do with moral views. The debates around illicit psychoactive drug abuse should, therefore, be thought of as confrontations between opposing symbolic-moral universes, each one attempting to generate sympathy, legitimacy, and power and to change the other's moral boundaries. The resultant generalized motivational accounting system, in the form of a social policy toward drug abuse, is hence the end result of complicated negotiations between these competing symbolic-moral universes. This social policy is, therefore, also based on generalized motivational accounting systems that were developed and used by social control agencies and that serve to justify their continued existence and actions. The vocabularies of motives used by the parties to the moral conflict around drug abuse illustrate and reflect, therefore, in the form of more micro motivational accounting systems, the macro struggle.

An historical discussion.   The history of the spread and use of various psychoactive substances is truly fascinating. Specific histories[4] vary according to the substance and its geographic location; yet they offer similar conclusions. In most countries prior to the twentieth century, the use of various psychoactive drugs was perhaps considered immoral or bad; yet it was not illegal. This century, however, witnessed a significant change in this perception. The first three decades of this century witnessed a tremendous increase in public attempts to regulate and stifle drug abuse. Numerous laws were passed against the use, possession, or manufacture of various psychoactive drugs, especially in the United States. Psychoactive drug use was redefined as an illicit act, thus marking new moral boundaries.[5]

For most psychoactive drugs, this social intervention succeeded in the sense that social patterns of drug abuse, as they had existed in the late nineteenth and early twentieth centuries, disappeared. However, the problem as a whole has not disappeared; it began to shift and change between different populations. Whether or not this transformation should be viewed as positive or negative depends of course on the evaluator's point of view.

There have been two exceptions to this historical process: tobacco and alcohol. Best (1979) showed that Europeans initially objected to the use of tobacco as early as the seventeenth century, but economic interests prevailed and smoking became widespread. Alcohol prohibition (see e.g., Gusfield 1963) not only failed to achieve its stated purpose, but it also contributed to the institutionalization of organized crime in the United States.

Over time, legislation against illicit psychoactive drug use became a means for dominant social groups to use their power to impose their moral standards on other groups, providing symbolic expression for existing social and moral hierarchies. To understand the societal reaction against the use of various psychoactive drugs, one must analyze two factors: the vocabularies of motives used to justify the reaction and the actual resulting social policy against illicit psychoactive drug use.

The initial opposition to psychoactive drug use imputed to it possible objective dangers (mostly addiction and a myriad of other health hazards), but particularly emphasized the moral dangers associated with drug use. The last decades of the nineteenth century and the first three decades of this century witnessed bitter moral arguments regarding the use of various psychoactive substances, of opiates in particular.

The nineteenth-century British Parliament was faced with many moral entrepreneurs who wanted to enact legislation against the use of opiates. The vocabularies of motives they used to justify their initiative implied that the use of these drugs crippled families, was debilitating, shortened life expectancies, and was demoralizing. For example, Dr. D. W. Osgood's motivational accounting system from 1878 stated that: "the continual use of opium . . . interferes with digestion, diminishing the secretions of the alimentary canal, producing constipation, loss of appetite . . . dyspepsia . . . difficulty in breathing . . . bronchitis and asthma. The smoker becomes anaemic and impotent. . . . The evil results from the continued use of opium . . . " (Scott 1969, 99–100). Reverend J. Hudson's motivational accounting system from 1874 added that: "I am but too familiar with the moral and physical evils wrought directly and indirectly by the use of opium . . . " (Scott 1969, 101).

These moral entrepreneurs were opposed by the opium dealers, who apparently had a vested interest in a free market for the drug (Conrad and Schneider 1980). This position received support from some physicians. For example, Sir George Birdwel gave in 1882 a motivational accounting system in which he stated that opium smoking was: "absolutely harmless. . . . Opium smoking, in itself, is as harmless as smoking willow bark . . . or vapour of boiling water . . . [it is] strictly harmless . . . " (Scott 1969, 99). Johnson (1975) pointed out that the British government itself had a vested interest in the opium trade: the state treasury received sizable revenues in the form of taxes.

The antiopium moral crusaders tried to generate sympathy and legitimacy for their version of how reality should be defined and to generate power and political support for their symbolic-moral universe. They organized a few groups, among them the Anti-Opium Society and the Society for the Suppression of the Opium Trade. In the second half of the nineteenth century, these groups published books, journals, and pamphlets that contained numerous vocabularies of motives that supported their cause. They were also involved in various political activities. Generally speaking, while the antiopium moral crusaders successfully raised public debate, they were not able to accomplish their purpose; in Great Britain, the economic value of the opium trade was considered more important than the dangers supposedly attributed to its use.[6]

While the British antiopium crusaders in the nineteenth century failed to achieve their primary goals, they nevertheless achieved some tangential and important ones. First, their moral crusades established a precedent that was to be emulated many times in later years and in different countries (see e.g., Gusfield 1963). Second, the struggle effectively helped to change public opinion. The moral crusades repeatedly used motivational accounting systems that claimed that the use of opium was inherently bad, evil, immoral, and dangerous. The social construction of opium use in this context began to be believable.

> The main legacy of the British anti-opium movement . . . was the institutionalization of anti-opium, but scientifically dubious, beliefs that opiates cause almost immediate and lifelong addiction, cause physical and moral harm to the user, cause crime, prostitution, gambling. . . . (Bruce Johnson, quoted by Conrad and Schneider 1980, 119)

However, opiate use was viewed by nineteenth-century American physicians in a more complex way: some viewed opiate use indifferently, some viewed it in a pragmatic and nonmoralistic way, some others were concerned about the addictive qualities of opiates, and still others viewed opiate use as sinful and immoral (e.g., see Terry and Pellens 1970).

Morgan (1974) stated that nineteenth-century America was characterized by strong beliefs in individual freedom, as well as by a national concern for productivity. Opiate users did not fit into this cultural context. They were viewed as "slaves" of a chemical, thereby losing their freedom and capacity for production. The following motivational accounting system, provided by Morgan, illustrates the point:

> . . . Narcotics allegedly made their user passive, devoid of free will. He was often compared to the helpless child, to the non-responsible insane person. . . . Opium was identified with Satan, who held men in bondage. . . . The addict of popular stereotypes thus lacked both the proper inhibitions and the stimuli of individual responsibility . . . drug abuse involved sexual license. . . . (Pp. 21–22)

Opiate users were thus seen as helpless sinners or sick people in need of treatment.

Two developments reinforced the perception of opiates as evil in the United States. First, the active ingredient in opium, morphine,[7] was discovered, and the hypodermic needle was developed while the American Civil War was being fought. The combined result was that soldiers who had been wounded became addicted to the opiates used during the course of treatment (e.g., see Courtwright 1982; Musto 1973). The second development was the construction of the transcontinental railroad (approximately 1864–1869). This gigantic enterprise employed thousands of workers from the Far East (especially in its western part), including China. Once the construction was finished (1869), many laborers became unemployed. Consequently, some segments in society viewed the Chinese as potential competitors in, and as a threat to, the job market. Consequently, a vicious campaign against these foreign workers began. When construction of the Southern Pacific Railroad began in the 1870s, newspapers were already using vocabularies of motives in which the Chinese "vice" of smoking opium pipes was emphasized. Some of the reports exaggerated the issue to mythic proportions. Thus, already in 1874 Dr. J. D. Newman, Chaplain to the United States Senate, constructed a motivational accounting system in which he stated that: "The Chinese . . . come to us *debilitated*, they have come enervated by the influence of opium" (Scott 1969, 100).

Morgan (1978) showed that the first antiopium crusade in U.S. history was directed by powerful social actors against working-class Chinese who had been brought to the United States initially as cheap labor. By the late 1870s, this crusade was transformed into an ideological struggle that was intimately linked to the desire to remove these workers from the labor force. Morgan concluded that the first opium laws in California were not really a result of a moral crusade against the drug itself, but resulted from a coercive action against the Chinese laborers, who threatened the economic security of the white working class. This is an important interpretative observation because it lends additional support to the basic argument that I made in chapter five. In both cases, we have examples of moral crusades and panics that were created and sustained for other than moral reasons.

The motivational accounting systems that were constructed by the newspaper crusade against Chinese opium-use soon led to a connection between opium and immoral sex, popularizing anew the previously made connection between prostitution and opium. Ashley (1972) noted that: "in 1913 *The Insidious Dr. Fu-Manchu*, the first of Sax Rohmer's twenty novels featuring the evil doctor appeared. . . . The insidious Doctor had a plan. . . . Fu-Manchu intended to enslave the white world with his evil drugs. . . . The Fu-Manchi novels . . . were very popular" (p. 115). Conrad and Schneider (1980, 20) confirmed that after 1860 U.S. consumption of opium, mostly by the Chinese, rose markedly. It was estimated that about 35 percent of the Chinese immigrant population smoked opium with some degree of regularity. Morgan (1974) stated that in the fifty years prior to 1909, legal importation of opium rose sevenfold. The vocabularies of motives used by *The*

Insidious Dr. Fu-Manchu, and the motivational accounting systems it used, reflected a changing cultural matrix that was ripe to accept, perhaps even embrace, such stereotypes. These motivational accounting systems provided a clear explanation and justification for existing fears from the "yellow danger" and could direct future action against this danger.

These developments began to show their effects in the late 1860s, when "some anxiety began to be voiced that women and the young may be particularly vulnerable to addiction . . . and many middle class, respectable citizens were addicted" (Conrad and Schneider 1980, 119–20). Duster (1970, 8) stated that U.S. newspapers, like the British press, were reluctant to publish antiopiate articles because the opium trade provided a major source of revenue for them in the form of advertisements. However, publishing motivational accounting systems that warned against the spreading Chinese menace were not considered like publishing direct antiopiate accounts. It is one thing to publish accounts warning against a human danger (e.g., Dr. Fu-Manchu) and another to publish alarming motivational accounting systems warning against drugs. After all, a substance may be thought of as, perhaps, not so dangerous. It is the way people use it that makes it more or less dangerous.

Such developments in the United States, and even more so in England, created ready-made, easily accessible reservoirs of motivational accounting systems and vocabularies of motives, all aimed against psychoactive drug use. This development prepared the ground for initiatives to change opium laws in the early decades of the twentieth century. The accounts propagated by the early antidrug moral crusaders served as a basis, and justification, for future action.

North American and European cultures underwent a series of rapid and profound changes in the last one hundred years, particularly in their moral boundaries. In their struggle to preserve older symbolic-moral universes and moral boundaries intact, moral crusaders were successful in associating psychoactive drug use with some basic fears and anxieties that these changes induced, with most ills of modern society and with lack of proper, even debased morality. The new legislation eventually drove heroin, marijuana, and other substances underground, "predominantly to the lower classes" (Duster 1970, 10). Thus, through the efforts of moral entrepreneurs, legislation against opiate use was passed in the first few decades of this century, and international cooperation against drug trafficking emerged (Duster 1970; Musto 1973; Conrad and Schneider 1980). By the 1930s, "narcotics had joined prostitution and alcoholism as major moral problems in the minds of Americans" (Duster 1971, 23).

Hagan (1985, 68–77) reviewed about fifteen studies done on the origin of antidrug and alcohol laws and came to the conclusion that: "These studies collectively made the point that some of the most important North American alcohol and drug statutes developed alongside one another during the progressive era as part of a cross-national effort to protect middle-class values against the alleged threat posed by users of habit forming chemicals" (p. 68).

Implications of the moral struggle: demography   The historical developments described in the previous section paved the way for the emergence of a perception that placed opiate used into a symbolic-moral universe that was identified with immorality, slavery, promiscuity, laziness, irresponsibility, irrationality, and the like.

As Duster (1970), Musto (1973) and Morgan (1974) reported, the use of opiates was very popular in nineteenth-century America, perhaps more so than in any other previous period in history. Ray (1978, 308) even suggested that at least 1 percent of the U.S. population was then using opiates. Much of the population using opiates in nineteenth-century America probably consisted of middle-class females. Local authorities had conducted epidemiological surveys in the last decades of the nineteenth-century in order to estimate the number of drug abusers, especially those using heroin (or morphine). Conrad and Schneider (1980) summarized the main findings of those surveys: "A Chicago study in 1880 reported that . . . it was among the middle class that we find the great majority who are today opium eaters. . . . The Iowa . . . survey noted [that] the age at which the habit is most common is fifty and sixty. . . . It has been estimated that 60% to 75% of the addicts were women" (p. 116). The growing success, however, of the antidrug moral crusades and the increasing number of antidrug laws and control bureaucracies were accompanied by some paradoxical social developments. A major result were two dramatic shifts in the social-demographic characteristics of drug users.

The first shift began at the turn of the century and lasted almost until the 1960s. During this period, the percentage of opiate users from the lower class, especially males, in many cases blacks and other impoverished minorities living in ghettos, increased dramatically (e.g., Finestone 1964; Brecher 1972; Courtwright 1982; King 1972; 1984a). Using heroin by this particular subpopulation has been the result of attempts to escape from, or protest against, unbearable and degrading life conditions, as well as challenging conventional morality. Treatment of this population was relatively straightforward. First,

drug abuse within this population was portrayed as intimately linked
to profit-oriented crimes aimed at securing the funds necessary to
purchase the drugs at inflated prices. Therefore, social intervention in
the form of law enforcement became a major focus in coping with this
type of drug abuse.[8] Second, some physicians in the first decade of
this century tried to provide morphine to those who wanted it, in
so-called morphine maintenance clinics (e.g., Waldorf, Orlick and
Reinarman 1974). These clinics, for a variety of reasons, fell into
disrepute and were forced to close their gates. Later, the medical profession attempted to detoxify addicts. Two of the most famous places
for this were in Fort Worth and Lexington. This method consisted of
primarily detoxification only (and no rehabilitation), and lasted well
into the 1970s. Only with the realization that this method was not efficient (Brecher 1972; Delong 1972; Duvall et al. 1963; Hunt and Odoroff
1962; O'Donnell 1964; Vaillant 1966), and with the advent of
methadone maintenance in the mid 1970s, this method was aban-
doned by the medical profession as a major treatment route. Illicit
psychoactive drug use and users were thus dealt with either through
medical or legal channels. The societal generalized motivational
accounting systems explained illicit psychoactive drug use either as
immoral and dangerous or as a sickness.

Even in the medical model, where the user was viewed as sick
and lacking in responsibility, he/she was also viewed as morally weak,
wrong, and disrespectful. The social characteristics of the population
prone to use illicit psychoactive drugs from approximately the 1920s
until the 1960s in the United States only reinforced existing
stereotypes, and a vicious circle of a self-fufilling prophecy was set
in motion.

Several factors contributed to this puzzling shift in the type of
population using illicit psychoactive drugs. One major factor was the
activation of social control (Goode 1972, 1984b). Outlawing opiates
caused their prices to soar and their quality to fall; their illegality also
provided various subpopulations with a means to challenge the
authorities, not to mention providing an escape for a powerless and
deviantized minority population from unbearable living conditions as
well as a sad message of hopelessness. The middle class, mostly
females, gradually dropped out of the circle of users, to be replaced
by desperate, young, powerless lower-class males. The black, lower-
class, "cool cat" heroin user perhaps best exemplifies this type
(Finestone 1964).

Illicit psychoactive drug users between the 1920s and the 1960s
could be described as lower class, deprived minorities, lacking in

power and needing a crystallized and credible symbolic-moral universe. These actors resorted to psychoactive drug use as a desperate escape from a disgraceful and hopeless life-style. These users' moral universe posed no threat to dominant elites, certainly not to their symbolic-moral universe. The moral universe of these drug users was portrayed, for a long time, in such negative and degrading vocabularies of motives that, coupled with their lack of power, called for no real action and that could be used to clearly demarcate the profound differences between those living in the morally correct symbolic-moral universe and those living in the morally incorrect universe.

Goode (1972) pointed out that: "legislation and enforcement practices on drugs appear to have *created a problem* out of whole cloth" (p. 193) and that: "It is obvious . . . that the first half of the 1920s witnessed the dramatic emergence of a criminal class of addicts—a *criminal class that had not existed previously* . . . [p. 194] . . . the most important contribution that law enforcement had made to the problem of addiction is *the creation of an addict sub-culture. . . . It was the criminalization of addiction that created addicts as a special and distinctive group"* (p. 195).

The second demographic shift in the type of drug users occurred in the 1960s. Drug abusers of the late 1960s did not confine themselves only to opiates, for they had a variety of drugs from which to choose: cigarettes, alcohol, opiates, marijuana, barbituates, sedative-hypnotics, tranquilizers, cocaine, amphetamines, and hallucinogenics. This selection of psychoactive substances was further enriched by other practices that had psychic effects, like glue-sniffing, gas inhalation (e.g., halothane, nitrous oxide, metallic sprays), inhalation of poisonous gases (e.g., fingernail polish, gasoline fumes), even shoe-polish sniffing and banana peel smoking, or a combination of a few substances.

From the 1960s onward, however, a new type of illicit psychoactive drug user appeared on the scene. This new drug user "discovered" the existing wide selection of available psychoactive substances and did not limit his/her consumption to only heroin or marijuana. The new users started using "speedballs" (a combination of amphetamines and opiates) and "speed" (amphetaminess; e.g., see Grinspoon and Hedbloom 1975). Alcohol use was combined with barbituates and sedatives; opiate use was supplemented with Valium and placidyls; hallucinogenics (e.g., LSD, STP, DMT* to name only a

---

*Lysergic acid diethylamide; Serenity, Tranquility, and Peace; Dimethoxy amphetamine.

few) became very popular. Eventually, polydrug abuse became the pattern. The new drug users began, therefore, experimenting with various substances to get what they thought was a safe, chemically produced "high." Sometimes physiologically dangerous drugs (or mixtures of drugs) were ingested, often with tragic results. This experimentation developed against the social background of the developing new countercultural movements, some of which promoted openly the use of various psychoactive drugs to achieve personal growth and fulfillment (see e.g., Haar 1976).

Another factor in the growth of these new forms of drug abused was the establishment of methadone programs (beginning in 1967) for treatment of opiate abusers. Methadone, an addictive artificial substance whose effects may last for up to twenty-four hours, was suggested as an alternative drug for addicts who could not detoxify from heroin (see Brecher 1972; Wilmarth and Goldstein 1974; Ben-Yehuda 1981; Newman 1977). Methadone programs became very popular and thousands of addicts turned for help to what Nelkin (1973) called "the technological fix." However, not all the addicts who turned to methadone programs did so out of a sincere desire for therapy and change. For many addicts, ambulatory methadone programs provided a safe and sheltered environment, away from the streets, the police, and the need for money. These addicts wanted to get high as quickly and as often as possible. While methadone programs have the technological means to detect such abusers (e.g., urine analysis), addicts can in fact fool a program for an extended period of time (Ben-Yehuda, 1982). They can take the licit opiate (methadone) and supplement it with alcohol, Valium, amphetamines, and the like to achieve a "high."

Illicit psychoactive drug use, moral universes, and ideology   The existence of a wide selection of potent psychoactive substances and the ease with which many of them could be obtained do not fully explain how the demographic transformation of drug abusers took place or why illicit psychoactive drug use became so widespread, especially in the 1960s.

The major reason for these developments occurring since the late 1960s was that the symbolic-moral universe that was characterized by the older, conservative ideology that had deterred illicit psychoactive drug use came increasingly under attack, its legitimacy questioned, and its power base eroded. An alternative symbolic-moral universe, characterized by a radically different ideology, developed and was embraced mostly by young people. This new symbolic-moral universe emphasized that drug use was a legitimate *means* to achieve desirable altered states of consciousness, to fulfill one's individuality, freedom and creativity. This particular ideology rose to prominence, especially regarding marijuana use, and numerous motivational accounting systems were developed and used to justify this new morality. Hence, Haar (1976, 161) emphasized that: "private use of marijuana within the home must be unimpaired as long as others are not brought into contact with it against their will"; this motivational accounting system was obviously aimed at changing previous moral boundaries.

This new ideology, which used a sophisticated vocabulary of motives, did not flourish among lower-class minorities; it rose on university campuses, among intellectuals, and among the middle class. One figure who certainly symbolized this ideology and the new moral boundaries was Timothy Leary, the Harvard LSD prophet.

Kramer (1976) indicated that the new ideology was actually sanctified by such historic figures as Baudelaire and William James, who reported having celestial visions through psychoactive drug use. This new symbolic-moral universe, expressed in the ideology of individuality, emphasized that some drugs, especially psychedelics, possess sacred powers that impart wisdom and enlighten or even transform the character of the user. Thus, "people accept socialization into drug culture because they find the culture attractive in terms of solving problems which they face; they do not 'catch' drug addiction, they *embrace* it" (Young 1971, 42). Feldman, Agar and Beschner (1981) also indicated that young PCP abusers typically placed a positive value on the taking of illicit drugs. While these abusers apparently understood the dangers associated with PCP consumption, they were nevertheless willing to take the risk.

This ideology not only characterized a particular symbolic-moral universe, but emerged together with the social movements and social unrest of the late 1960s, including the civil rights movement, the students' revolts, and other social reform movements. Every individual's inalienable right to achieve self-fulfillment and individuality through any means that do not harm others was increasingly emphasized by many of the adherents to this new symbolic-moral universe, as well as by those many who joined the various social movements of the 1960s. This ideology challenged openly the motivational accounting systems given previously by different moral entrepreneurs and that had attributed a variety of medical and physiological "dangers" to opiate and marijuana use. This challenge was very serious: It attacked the validity of an ideology that was adopted by powerful social control agencies as a generalized motivational accounting system that provided these agencies with *the* justification for their actions. Indeed, it is not difficult to see that the challenge was also aimed at the morality, power base, legitimacy, and integrity of these social control agencies themselves.

The late 1960s and 1970s witnessed, therefore, an emerging and crystallizing struggle between two different and opposing symbolic-moral universes, on the background of popular and widespread feelings that a genuine social revolution was also taking place. On the one hand, we had those who felt that they had the right to pursue their happiness in any way—as long as they did not hurt anyone. If this pursuit meant taking drugs, they were willing to fight for it and delegitimize those who denounced such patterns of behavior as immoral and dangerous. On the other hand, moral entrepreneurs who adhered to the older conservative symbolic-moral universe felt that illicit psychoactive drug use should remain illicit because it was immoral and dangerous, and they fought for this idea. We must realize that the struggle between adherents to these different symbolic-moral universes was not only about whether new moral boundaries would be drawn but also about the differential amounts of power and legitimacy each universe had and was capable of using.

Another ideological confrontation emerged from institutional sources. Both Becker (1963) and Dickson (1968, 1975) pointed out that over the years there had developed a large institutional framework that dealt with drug abuse. Because these institutions had a self-interest in survival (see also Goode 1972), they became prime sources for the antidrug moral campaigns. Dickson (1968), for example, stated that when the Federal Bureau of Narcotics (FBN) realized that its power and budget were slowly being reduced it placed survival over impartial considerations and began a major campaign against what it defined as "the drug menace," hoping to increase its own scope of operations.[9]

As pointed out in chapter five, drug scares should not be understood in simple technical terms. Drug abuse is generally perceived as a grave threat to the very essence of the moral organization of society. The danger implicit in drug use, therefore, is the possibility of a moral revolution. Klerman (1970) pointed out that the public's concern over drug abuse involves more than a concern for health and law enforcement; rather, it is based on a fear of social change promoted by the youth culture. A restrictive legislation reflects the dominant adult symbolic-moral universe, as well as its dominance in terms of power. From such a stand, it should not surprise us that the "junkie" is portrayed as a dangerous political enemy (Dumont 1973). Furthermore, Goode (1972) indicated that "the passage of laws [on drug abuse] is basically a nonrational process that represents an ideological, moral and political victory of some segments of society over others" (p. 186) and that therefore the "solution" for the drug abuse problem: "would be to undertake a massive program to totally restructure the society to insure that all Americans live a life that they consider meaningful" (p. 212). Goode concluded that: "the only realistic approach to the drug problem is to develop methods not to eliminate drug use or even to drastically reduce it, but to live with it and to make sure that drug users do not seriously harm themselves and others" (p. 212). In the 1984 edition of his book, Goode clearly stated that the terms and expressions used by various moral agents (pro or con) in the drug abuse debate "assume the abstract correctness of the social system in which we live" (pp. 11–12) and that the politics of reality, that is, the way in which certain assertions come to be regarded as true (p. 13) is a crucially important process to watch if we are to understand the drug abuse controversy. It appears that much of the drug abuse controversy is centered around processes where different moral agents attempt to persuade other members of society of the correctness and appropriateness of *their* view.

Like Lidz and Walker (1980), Helmer (1975) stated that the drug abuse issue had become mythologized and served as a "front" for deeper moral and power conflicts in U.S. society. Taking a Marxist approach, similar to Foucault's (1977) analysis of prison workers in Paris in previous centuries, Helmer's account pointed out that periods of unemployment were characterized by industrial unrest and working-class militancy as well as by heightened political conflict. The usual response on the political level was increased law enforcement and repressive policies. According to Helmer, public concern over the drug menace and the resulting law enforcement efforts are all functions of unemployment. The campaign against drug abuse, therefore, is not a technical problem of treatment or stigmatization, but is a moralistic political struggle.

Thus, I have given the reasons why the area of drug abuse has attracted so many moral entrepreneurs, moral crusaders, myths (Saper 1974), and misinformation. The issue of illicit psychoactive drug use involves basic ideas about the structure of society, so that the moralistic struggle between supporters and opponents of drug use involves opposing views of actors from very different symbolic-moral universes regarding the moral nature and boundaries of society.

Until the 1960s, most of the illicit drug-taking population was politically unorganized, powerless, and mute, but then a new illicit drug-taking population arose. The new users felt that they belonged to new symbolic-moral universes that they felt presented alternatives to conventional morality. These new and young moral entrepreneurs were actively involved in generating power, sympathy, and legitimacy in an attempt to change moral boundaries. Among their ranks were social actors who ranked high on various hierarchies of credibility, such as university professors, students, musicians, authors, poets, actors, among others who were involved in organizing political activity (Rock 1977). Drug use for this population became a means for expressing their newly discovered collective identity and for a political moral revolution, as part of the 1960s' experiential revolution: "It is a revolution that assumes that all change begins with the 'mind' or 'self' rather than with the external social world" (Horowitz 1977, 105).

In contrast to the ideology denouncing drug abuse as evil and immoral, a moral counterattack developed. This new ideology emphasized the good and beneficial aspects of psychoactive drug use, especially marijuana. Robert DuPont (who was the director of NIDA for five years) gave the following account about this development: "During the sixties and seventies there was a tumultuous change in values in the United States. . . . The emphasis was on the present tense and not on the future, and also on the individual's personal pleasure and not on responsibilities to others in his or her life, or in society. This was something new and entirely out of character in terms of the previous history of our country. *The leading edge of this cultural change was marijuana use*" (Mann, 1985, 31). The crystallization of this ideology as part of an explicit symbolic-moral universe, and the continued attempt of the most active leaders of this counterculture to generate legitimacy and power, resulted eventually in increased rates of illicit psychoactive drug use, as measured by independent surveys.

The 1960s thus bred a new type of morality. The rise of this new ideological movement challenged severely what it saw as the "hypocrisy" of the previous moral entrepreneurs and the symbolic-moral universe that they supported. The validity and reliability of the vocabularies of motives used by the old moral entrepreneurs were challenged, as well as the idea that using drugs is inherently bad, immoral, or dangerous. The challenge not only was a moral one but also was scientific and legal. Many of the movement's supporters were educated young people who could read scientific literature, conduct experiments, and use scientific vocabularies of motives to create sophisticated motivational accounting systems to justify their cause. Thus, they were able to challenge some of the findings previously reported in the literature, and by using accurate information, they could devise motivational accounting systems that accused various social control agencies and moral entrepreneurs of withholding information from the public. Scientists increasingly concluded that many of the social, medical, pharmacological, and physiological damages attributed previously to drugs were actually the result of their being outlawed.

Eventually, there arose a whole middle-class subculture that published journals (e.g., *High Times*) and that was politically active in struggling to generate power and legitimize their symbolic-moral universe, supporting psychoactive drug use. Adherents to this symbolic-moral universe maintained that it was each individual's inalienable right to pursue happiness via the use of psychoactive drugs (especially the private use of marijuana), as long as other individuals were not forced into contact with drugs.

One can acquaint oneself with this type of motivational accounting system by browsing through any issue of *High Times*. This journal provided prices of drugs, positive personal stories of drug users, and where to buy drug paraphernalia. The journal was lavishly illustrated and emphasized "the good life" and sex. Specialized motivational accounting systems were developed, and some cultlike symbols were created. Another example is the 417-page *High Times Encyclopedia of Recreational Drugs*, published in 1978 by the Stonehill Publishing Company (N.Y.). This encyclopedia openly endorsed the recreational use of drugs, informing its readers that such prestigious social actors as Pope Leo XIII, Thomas Edison, Emile Zola, Jules Verne, and Sigmund Freud were all regular users of cocaine. The book detailed how, where, when, and on what substance one can get "high"; how to grow marijuana plants; and the like. It is well worth our time to examine the type of motivational accounting systems that this encyclopedia employs to describe what happens when one injects intravenously amphetamines (rather than take it in a pill form): "The high from injected amphetamine differs in quantity and quality from the pep-pill high. The shot-for-the-stars rush, the instant gratification, the feeling of 'where has this ecstatic, powerful me been all my life?' makes the needle . . . seductive" (pp. 239–240). One of the most interesting and controversial components of this subculture was NORML—National Organization for the Reform of Marijuana Laws—formed in 1971 in the United States. NORML's formal stated goal is to bring about a change in the U.S. drug laws so that people could openly and legally use marijuana (Anderson 1981).

To illustrate the struggle between the different symbolic-moral universes, let me use two items that appeared in 1981 in *High Times*. The degree of accuracy of these reports at best is secondary. What is important is the very fact that they appeared at all in *High Times*. The first example is King's (1981) report on the National Anti-Drug Coalition (NADC). This organization, according to the report, send young representatives armed with antidrug literature on a house-to-house campaign in U.S. cities and suburbs. They "declared war on drugs" and solicited contributions. They claimed that marijuana destroyed the young brains of America and caused youngsters to move on to hard drugs. The report stated that the NADC was active in at least twelve U.S. states, supporting a monthly newsletter with a circulation of about 30,000. In his article, King exposed the connection between the NADC and the National Caucus of Labor Committees (NCLC), an extreme rightist group. King claimed that he had considerable evidence pointing to intimate links between NADC and organized crime. Lyndon LaRouche, a major figure in NCLC's moral crusade against the use of drugs, was also known, according to King, to be very much involved with both the NCLC and with organized crime. King also pointed out that the NCLC and the NADC integrated anti-Catholic, anti-Semitic and antiminorities propaganda with their anti-drug campaign.[10] For example, King noted that one particularly contemptible NCLC book stated that Zionism constituted a way to legitimize drug money and that America was being destroyed by a subhuman species of Jewish bankers from London.

The second example of the moral-ideological struggle being waged around drug use consisted of a coalition of parents and community leaders who supposedly met in New York's LaSalle Junior High School auditorium in March 1981 to rally against drug use among young people. *High Times* (King 1981), which attributed this gathering to the organizational efforts of the NCLC, stated that it was led by the "Anti Drug Coalition prima donna Carol White . . . [and] was something of a charade, a Trojan horse, a front for recruiting converts to the arcane social philosophy of Lyndon LaRouche, failed presidential candidate and guru to the cult like U.S. Labor Party" (pp. 19, 29).

The amount of accuracy included in the accusations that were published in the accounts given by the pro-drug use *High Times* is not significant here. The important point is the fact that ideologies regarding drug use are integrated into larger moral struggles about the nature of reality and the moral-ideological shape of our society. That is, a struggle between different symbolic-moral universes is superimposed on the drug abuse issue and vice versa, the drug abuse issue becomes a way to express larger moral problems.

So strong was the counter moral attack during the 1960s and 1970s that it might have caused some problems with scientific research on drug abuse. In 1976, I heard a guest lecture by Howard Becker at the University of Chicago. Becker, by all accounts, cannot be considered a moral crusader against the use of marijuana. He made the point, however, that it was difficult to publish an article that used scientific data that could be interpreted to discourage the use of the drug. The qualitative reactions to such an article were so intense that editors were reluctant to publish it. Becker was concerned about the biased atmosphere in which drug studies were conducted and published and expressed his worry that scientific objectivity may fall victim to the moral struggle in this area.

The type of analysis brought above led Bakalar and Grinspoon (1984) to the conclusion that: "We will all have to learn to live with more compromise and ambiguity on drug issues. There is something absurd and irrelevant about the martial imagery often evoked: drugs versus society, a war on drugs. A drug-free society remains a mirage. We must learn to live with drugs in a way that, as Mill would say, promotes individuality, self-development, variety of human situations, the highest and most harmonious development of human powers. The complexity of modern society and the powers of modern technology make this harder to do. So does the growth of leisure time and disposable resources. And attempts to control drugs are subject to the conflicting influences of a decline in enforceable moral authority and a heightened consciousness of the need for public protection against common risks" (pp. 143–44), and that "Ultimately, the problems surrounding drug use can be neither solved nor dissolved" (p. 152; see also *Time*, May 30, 1988).

The real problem is probably one of price and risk. Either to continue drug enforcement as it exists, paying such prices as: thousands of sick and persecuted addicts, high crime rates, and high level expenditures for an almost hopeless battle. Or to legalize/decriminalize drugs (for more on this see Kaplan 1983; Trebach 1982; Goode 1989). The debate between these two approaches regarding the evaluation of the acceptable risks and prices is waging almost endlessly (e.g., see *Time* [International Edition] May 30, 1988 [#131. No. 22], pp. 20–26).

Implications of the moral struggle: motivational accounting systems. The micro motivational accounting systems provided by drug users reflect the changing societal definitions and explanations regarding illicit psychoactive drug use. Addicts of the 1950s and 1960s used motivational accounting systems that largely agreed with the official view. For example, Wakefield's (1963) anthology uses a vocabulary of motives that asked questions like "Why doesn't the potential addict quit before he's hooked?"; "Why do 9 out of 10 addicts return to the habit once they've kicked it?"; "What torture must an addict endure to break the hold of the heroin?" and the like. Hughes (1961) and Larner and Tefferteller (1964) *emphasized* the *stereotypical* image of addicts. More recent books and anthologies, however, especially on hallucinogenics, emphasized the positive experiences of using drugs. They also tended to use more positive vocabularies of motives when describing the drug subculture and typically argued that the negative effects attributed to drug abuse were actually by-products of the law enforcement efforts (e.g., Gould et al. 1974). Pope (1971), for example, edited a volume that described "voices from the drug culture," relating the bad aspects of drug use, but also indicating its positive experiential aspects. The author admitted: "I was as much a participant as an observer . . . in the drug scene" (p. 9). In what can be considered a strong antiestablishment statement, Fiddle (1967) was ahead of his time by suggesting that drug users alter their lives significantly and that therefore psychoactive drugs should be called "existential drugs" (p.4). Fiddle's vocabulary of motives enabled him to write the following motivational accounting system: "Existential drugs can be seen as personal expeditions to explore what man is really like and how far he can go and still remain human" (p. 4). The positive emphasis in individual and institutional motivational accounting systems reflects the shift in morality regarding drug use. The changing nature of the motivational accounting systems given for and against the use of drugs actually reflects deeper changes in the symbolic-moral universes that constitute the mosaic of culture.

The symbolic-moral universe that projected an image in which the work ethic was valued, as well as an emphasis on direct coping with everyday life problems and maximum self-control, claimed moral superiority. Social actors from this particular universe protested that drug use symbolized moral degeneracy, loss of control, lack of proper ideas, and irrationality. They accused the drug subculture of futilely attempting to solve problems by using chemicals. On the other hand, prodrug moral entrepreneurs claimed that society persecuted addicts just as fifteenth and seventeenth-century Europe persecuted witches. Szasz (1975) even called the persecution of addicts "drugcraft." Downes (1977) illustrated how drug addicts were portrayed as "folk devils," and Kramer (1976) indicated that social policies on drug abuse resulted from overreaction to minor or nonexistent dangers, leading to the "demonization" of drug use and the persecution of drug users. Christie (1984) and Christie and Bruun (1985) pointed out that illicit psychoactive drug users became "easy enemies."

This sociological analysis suggests that the nature of the drug abuse problem is most reasonably understood *not* as being a general "technical" or "medical" problem (such as the problematic nature of the amount of "dangerousness" hiding in specific psychoactive substances). Rather, the issue of drug abuse was created and used by various moral entrepreneurs to assert, or force, a particular type of symbolic-moral universe and hence specific moral boundaries.

One should not mistakenly think that "moral entrepreneurship" is a simple issue, for in fact it is a very complex one, demanding an intimate knowledge of the culture in question. Such entrepreneurship must take into consideration the full spectrum of people and organizations working for, or against, a specific cause, their interests' and the power configurations (e.g., see Himmelstein 1983). Over time, legislation against a specific pattern of psychoactive drug use may become a means for dominant and powerful social groups to impose the moral boundaries of their own symbolic-moral universe on other groups, providing symbolic expression for existing social and moral hierarchies of dominance. Hence, Hoffman and Silver (1987) pointed out that calls for a "war on drugs" typically have very little to do with drug abuse, but *a lot* to do with controlling citizens.

Consequently, drug abuse legislation is primarily focused on moral boundaries. Hence, Eldridge's (1971) observation that the debate over the use of narcotics is focused on uneasy moral questions. Packer (1968) noted that: "In a society that neither has, nor wants, a unitary set or moral norms, the enforcement of morals carries a heavy cost in repression" (p. 265). Blumberg (1975) observed that the area of drug abuse is not only associated with moral and value problems, but it also turns drug enforcement into a cynical and corrupt enterprise. Any police force that presents itself as providing a much needed service is faced with serious problems when the laws it is supposed to enforce are not regarded as good or valid by a large segment of the population.

Implications of the moral struggle: treatment and myths. The fact that the debate regarding drug abuse has a very basic moralistic, or ideologic, nature filters down to specific questions regarding such issues as prevention, treatment, education, law enforcement, and social policy.

Before moving to social policy, let me give a few illustrations for this filtering process.

One area affected by this moral debate is that of treatment. When Dole and Nyswander (1967, 1968) began the first methadone (a synthetic narcotic) program in New York City in 1967, the major motivational accounting system that they used to justify the treatment were medical. They claimed that addicts suffered from a metabolic imbalance and thus needed a regular intake of narcotics to counteract the imbalance. They developed an ideology that used a respected medical vocabulary of motives to enable authorities to allow the use of methadone maintenance as a legitimate treatment for heroin addicts. U.S. authorities, who felt that the heroin epidemic was ruining the moral fiber of society, supported this alternative. The first reports on using methadone for therapeutic purposes were so positive and promising that the programs quickly became a very popular method of treatment. Since the mid 1960s, thousands of addicts have enrolled in methadone programs in the United States and abroad.

Two competing ideologies, however, arose against the methadone treatment, Because methadone programs competed with the suppliers ("pushers") in the streets, the "pushers" started spreading misinformation and rumors that "methadone gets into your bones," that "one cannot detoxify from methadone," that "heroin is safer," that the federal government had records on all participants in methadone programs, and the like. The addict was faced with the dilemma of whether to believe the friendly pusher in the streets or the official motivational accounting systems that were used by the program.

The second attack came from Therapeutic Communities. They endorsed very aggressively a totally drug-free life-style (e.g., see Yablonsky 1965; Brook and Whitehead 1980; Ofshe 1976), and opposed almost fiercely methadone treatment. Therapeutic Communities used vocabularies of motives that claimed that methadone treatment did not really solve the problem of addiction, for it substituted one addiction with another, nor did it really change the addicts' pathological life-style. They further claimed that methadone treatment was a fraud because not only did it not free addicts from their dependency, but methadone was actually more addicting (and therefore harder to detoxify from) than heroin. Therapeutic Communities offered a particular type of symbolic-moral universe based either on a specific ideology or on a charismatic leadership. In most cases, Therapeutic Communities' morality emphasized, even exaggerated, both conventional values and life-style. Therapeutic Communities' graduates were portrayed as joining the ranks of the average citizens, exhibiting very few patterns of deviant behavior even when compared to other people. Methadone patients, on the other hand, even after adopting a conventional life-style, were portrayed as continuing to deviate by taking methadone, a dependency-producing drug, something that many social actors found hard to understand.[11]

The struggle between Therapeutic Communities and methadone programs was not only over the treatment *technology* but also over the definition of the very *nature* of the life-style of the addict. Most methadone programs were medically oriented and worked for the long-range goal of detoxifying their patients. In the meantime, most programs were satisfied if the addicts abstained from crime and found regular employment—in short, if they started to function as productive citizens, despite their daily need for methadone. Therapeutic Communities, on the other hand, operated according to a social change model (Siegler and Osmond 1974). They helped addicts to stop using drugs as soon as possible without substituting one drug for another. They demanded from addicts to change their life-style completely. Methadone programs and Therapeutic Communities, in short, propose *very* different interpretations about the nature of reality and promote very different symbolic-moral universes. One is medically oriented, and the other socially oriented.

The second area that is directly connected to the moral nature of illicit psychoactive drug consumption is the generation of a large amount of myths. The area of drug abuse has virtually been flooded with various myths and misinformation that provide us with rich vocabularies of motives. These, in turn, generate a variety of motivational accounting systems that have been used by different symbolic-moral universes to persuade others of the validity of believing in a specific symbolic-moral universe. A few examples should suffice to illustrate this.

To begin with, we must remind ourselves about the ironic and paradoxical situation where the use of cigarettes and alcohol has been relatively uncontrolled, even though the pharmacological, physiological, and social harm caused by these substances has been well documented. On the other hand, opiates, whose physiological dangers are more limited (mostly to addiction and overdose), have become controlled. The dangers of recreational marijuana use are even less than those attributed to opiates or alcohol; yet marijuana use has also been controlled throughout this century.

Moral agents are fond of the vocabulary of motives provided by the "stepping stone" theory. According to this theory the abuse of "soft" drugs (like marijuana) "inevitably" (one may add or omit this word according to one's views) leads to abuse of "hard" drugs (like heroin). This theory had not been scientifically proven, and there are no indications for its validity. Thousands of marijuana users seem to control their use fairly well. Furthermore, Feldman et al. (1981) even showed how social groups can, and do, control individual use of PCP.

The drug-crime myth, in its classical form, states that illicit drug users become criminals in order to finance the superinflated price of the drug. Yet there are thousands of marijuana users who have not become criminals. Furthermore, studies indicate that in many cases drug abusers who do commit crimes do not have exclusively drug-related motivations. They had usually been involved in a criminal career long before they began to use illicit psychoactive drugs, which later became part and parcel of their social interactions and life-style. Once drug abuse was established, however, it could change an individual's crime patterns to easier, less sophisticated, quick profit oriented street crimes (Austin and Lettieri 1976; McGlothlin et al. 1978; Nurco et al. 1984).

The rhetorical devices that are used in drug education provide a good clue to the nature of the moral struggle involved in the drug abuse problem. Such popular motivational accounting systems as "war on drugs" or "the drug plague" (or pestilence) illustrate this. On June 17, 1971, President Nixon gave the U.S. Congress a motivational accounting system that stipulated that either illicit drug use would be eliminated in the United States or the country would be destroyed. This motivational accounting system did not reflect so much a scientific fact as much as a specific moral conviction stemming from a particular symbolic-moral universe. As such, the statement simply gave expression to a particular value system. When given such a clear-cut choice, one becomes willing to declare total war on drugs. This type of motivational accounting system, coming from someone whose position on the hierarchy of credibility is so high, could be used to justify almost any action against the "menace" of drug abuse. It should really not surprise us, therefore, to discover a contemporary antidrug federal agency that was "born" illegally (i.e., the U.S. Congress did not even know about its formation) and that performed illegal acts during the course of its "war" on drugs (e.g., see Epstein 1977).

The expression "once a junkie, always a junkie," so popular among various moral entrepreneurs who aim to eradicate illicit psychoactive drug use, does not really hold because, in fact, most addicts mature out of opiate use in their midthirties (Scher 1966; Winick 1962). Furthermore, this statement contradicts well-established clinical facts showing that "junkies" can be treated and not remain "junkies."

Another commonly held belief is that "one cannot control the drug habit." In fact, Powell (1973), Graven (1977), and Zinberg (1979) showed that there are occasional heroin users who control their drug use fairly well. Robins' (1973) classical study showed that the overwhelming majority of U.S. soldiers in Vietnam who used heroin there controlled their habit fairly well when they returned to the United States and simply stopped taking the drug. Biernacki's (1986) recent work added strength to this approach.

When lower-class, uneducated social actors used illicit psychoactive substances, the generalized motivational accounting system, which came out as the societal reaction, was focused around pathologization and law enforcement activities. However, when young, educated, middle-class people began to use drugs and to develop ideologies favoring such use, the societal reaction changed to such generalized motivational accounting systems that emphasized the therapeutic, educational, preventive, and even, finally, decriminalization.

Another myth concerns the so-called addictive personality. While many social agencies use this term, accounting for and explaining why addicts use drugs, such a personality apparently does not really exist (Platt and Labate 1976, ch. 8; Austin and Lettieri 1976). This particular motivational accounting system had wide appeal in the 1950s, when the pathologization of deviance was prominent. When, however, in the late 1960s and 1970s upper-middle-class, "normal" actors began to use drugs, this motivational accounting system lost much of its appeal.

Implications of the moral struggle: drug education.   The above-mentioned mythical and misleading vocabularies of motives have very little to do with actual facts. Nevertheless, these myths have been used in various drug education programs aimed at preventing drug use. Today, we know that scare tactics and horror films "not only don't work, but can be counter-productive" (*A Perspective . . .* 1973, 7).

In Israel, many efforts have been made in the area of drug education, and as in other countries, scientists and other members of the higher echelons of the hierarchy of credibility were recruited to generate and use motivational accounting systems against the use of illicit psychoactive drugs. I shall next bring several examples for the types of motivational accounting systems against drug use that were developed and employed in Israel.

The first example is an official motivational accounting system that was issued on June 2, 1970, by an obscure body called the Advisory Psychiatric Committee to the Government Health Council. The document stated that the committee: "is united in its opinion that hashish use constitutes a serious danger for public and individual health. The hashish user's social adaptability and ability to function maximally and efficiently in society is damaged . . . to the degree of [developing] mental illness" (Rubinstein 1975, 27). While this motivational accounting system may occasionally be true, it would be more appropriate to use it to describe alcohol abuse (or chronic hashish use).

A second example concerns the choice of particular rhetorical devices in drug education. Some of the governmental publications from the late 1960s and early 1970s were *intended*, explicitly, to create a moral panic. One such example was a 1971 poster published by the Israeli government and which associated illicit drug use with weakness and the Egyptian loss in the 1967 war (see previous chapter, p. 124).

Finally, one of Israel's most aggressive moral entrepreneurs, B.L. (not real initials), traveled around the country's high schools in the 1960s, actually scaring teenagers over the moral and physiological dangers of drug use. B.L. exploited both his academic title in pharmaceutics and his relatively high position in one of Israel's ministries. Here is a quote of a motivational accounting system from one of the documents[12] B.L. distributed:

Hashish can cause psychotic reaction, a feeling of faked euphoria, serious damage to the memory, indifference and apathy. It sets the stage and creates the motivation and the actual push to use drugs such as L.S.D., and 91% of youth detoxified from drugs return to use within one year.

It is difficult to resist the temptation to deny categorically the validity of these motivational accounting systems. Certainly the last claim was true for opiate users only (mostly heroin) and not hashish users, and then only for treatment methods and data from the 1960s; furthermore, how is one to interpret "faked euphoria"?

Perhaps one of the best available examples for the intentional and deliberate use of a motivational accounting system that included obvious misinformation was generated in the United States:

On March 6, 1971 Dr. Wesley Hall, the newly elected president

of the American Medical Association, was quoted by UPI as saying that a study completed by the AMA left "very little doubt"
that marijuana caused a considerable reduction in sex drive. Dr.
Hall noted that a thirty-five year old man might find his sex drive
diminished to that of a seventy year old man if he used marijuana and he hinted that certain evidence demonstrated that
marijuana caused birth defects. . . . About three weeks after the
statement was made, Dr. Hall said that he had been misquoted
but added in an interview: "I don't mind . . . if we don't wake up
in this country to the fact that every college campus and high
school has a problem with drug addiction, we're going down the
drain not only with respect to morality, but . . . the type of
system we're going to have" . . . When [Dr. Hall] was asked
whether misleading statements such as his own might damage
the credibility of the AMA, Dr. Hall said: "I'm tired of these
problems about the credibility gap. *We're talking about the morality
of the country . . . and respect for authority and decency."* Apparently,
Dr. Hall "not only disapproves of marijuana but also exploits
such drug use as a vehicle for expression of his own ideological
views towards other kinds of activities and attitudes that he
deplores. (Goode 1972, 15–16)

On a different level, one could posit that Dr. Hall was using his influential high position on the hierarchies of credibility and morality,
backed by the prestige of the AMA, to relay inaccurate information
and biased motivational accounting systems about marijuana. In this
way, he could influence popular, (micro level) opinion against marijuana use, as well as the activities and attitudes of law enforcement
agencies (macro level). Specifically, Dr. Hall's symbolic-moral universe
compelled him to use a particular vocabuary of motives and generate
a motivational accounting system that was aimed at reducing the
motivation of other social actors to use marijuana.

A more contemporary illustration for an alarmist approach, giving expression to the older "conservative" symbolic-moral universe, is
provided by Mann's (1985) book. The "Forward" to the book was
signed by no less than Nancy Reagan, who, among other things, gave
the motivational accounting system that: "*Marijuana Alert* is a true
story about a drug that is taking America captive. . . . Drugs are a
plague that is ruining the minds and bodies of our children . . . "
(pp. ix–x). Mann quotes a motivational accounting system that was
constructed by Carlton Turner (who, in 1983, was appointed special
assistant to the president for drug abuse policy): "We must realize that

there will be no free ride for marijuana users. Unless we come to grips with this problem, they may take our nation with them on this downhill course, one which we never traveled before" (p. 34). Mann's style and level of sophistication in presenting her vocabularies of motives obviously surpass those made by Dr. Hall; yet the motivational accounting systems used by both reflect and express the same basic moral position.

Likewise, in 1988, Harvard psychiatrist Robert Cole voiced his objection to legalize the use of illicit psychoactive drug use because it would be a: "moral surrender of far-reaching implications about the way we treat each other" because it would send a message of unrestricted hedonism which Dr. Cole was "not prepared as a parent, as a citizen or as a doctor" to accept. Mitchel Rosenthal, president of Phoenix House (a drug rehabilitation program), added that "to legalize drugs would give us a vast army of people who would be out of control" (*Time*, May 30, 1988, 24).

Final notes: morality, power, former addicts, and professionals.   There are two other issues that are intimately linked to the problem of drug abuse and symbolic-moral universes: *one* is the former drug user as a professional, the *other* is the drug abuse professional. I shall start with the second.

The drug abuse professional (psychiatrist, pharmacologist, social worker, or sociologist, among others) often acts as a consultant on the municipal, national, or even international level. Professionals are frequently consulted about such issues as the nature of drugs, the populations at risk, and the consequences of addiction, and they are frequently asked to suggest recommendations for a possible social policy. My analysis indicates, however, that the high position of the expert on the hierarchy of credibility may become very problematic. The knowledge that the expert brings may frequently have very little to do with basic problems regarding such central issues as drug abuse social policy. Because the *nature* of these issues is moralistic-ideological, the professional may find him/herself in an impossible situation because his/her symbolic-moral universe may not necessarily be any better than that of those who seek his/her advice, and may even contradict it. Hence, drug abuse "experts" may find themselves in situations where they are supposedly asked for "professional" opinions—but in reality, those opinions may have to do more with one's symbolic-moral universe than with one's professional knowledge (e.g., the problems regarding decriminalization or legalization of drug use; the choice of specific treatment modalities). Hence, and in a strange fashion, the knowledge of the expert that forms the very basis of his/her and credibility may become irrelevant to the expert's moral views, and even useless when applied to some very crucial questions (e.g., legalization of drugs; see *Time*, May 30, 1988, 20–26).

The other issue has to do with former addicts who are employed as counselors. Drug abuse is probably one of the few areas where a deviant experience may be utilized later to advance a career. Former addicts often find careers as counselors, educators, and administrators in drug abuse treatment and educational programs. In this way, they utilize their past deviant career as an asset in their new position. They are at times regarded as respected experts because they are *ex*-drug addicts. By contrast, few if any individuals are able to advance their career as ex-prostitutes, ex-murderers, or ex-thieves. One obvious reason for this is that the existence of the social category of the former drug addict, in itself, gives evidence to a clear moral statement: "I was wrong. Now I am right. I could do it—so can you." It is a case of a person who moved from what is perceived as a negative symbolic-moral universe to a positive one, hence "purifying" and "cleansing" oneself from the "deviant symbolic dirt" (Scott 1972). In a moral struggle, such cases are among the best tools (or weapons) to use in order to persuade those who are already in the struggle (or in prevention efforts), to move from what is regarded as the morally wrong universe to that which is regarded as the morally right one. Support for this idea may by found in Pallone's (1986) and Covington's (1984) works. Covington illustrated how heroin addicts used motivational accounting systems that politicized their drug problem. These motivational accounting systems provided the addicts with an effective defense in minimizing their self-rejection (in fact, in the summer of 1988, and toward the elections to the Israeli parliament, a group of addicts tried to create their own party and compete in the elections).

METHOD OF COMPARISON

Comparing the results and effectiveness of a similar social policy, on a global scale, in two different countries and cultures necessitates a selection of variables for comparison. In theory, a successful social policy aimed at reducing the prevalence of a specific phenomenon should either reduce, or at least freeze, the prevalence of that phenomenon. Certainly, a consistent and gradual increase in illicit psychoactive drug usage cannot be considered a success for the d e m a n d / supply reduction model.

I shall therefore examine the prevalence of illicit drug usage in Israel and the United States in order to see whether the societal reaction to drug abuse, in the form of the supply/demand reduction social policy, can be considered successful in these countries. Fortunately, both countries have independent and reliable surveys on the prevalence of illicit drug use. Hence, we do not have to rely solely on official statistics, which are problematic since they may indirectly indicate, more than anything else, the amount of resources spent by specific agencies to control a particular pattern of behavior. Unfortunately, the U.S. data are much better and more systematic than the Israeli data. Both sets, however, are sufficient to make a meaningful comparison possible.

SUPPLY AND DEMAND REDUCTION
AS IMPLEMENTED IN THE UNITED STATES

We must first raise the question of whether there was a decrease, or at least a freeze, in illicit psychoactive drug consumption in the United States.

Examining the available data reveals that the answer is negative. The National Institute on Drug Abuse (NIDA) has conducted annual national surveys in the United States for the major part of the last decade. The studies conducted by Rittenhouse (1977), Richard and Blevens (1977), Johnston et al. (1981), Fishburne, Abelson and Cisin (1979), Miller et al. (1983), Johnston et al. (1984) all point to a similar conclusion: the prevalence of illicit drug use had increased steadily from the early 1970s for most types of drugs across all age groups (see also *Time* May 30, 1988).

The selected data[13] brought here support this conclusion. In the twelve-to-seventeen age group, the percentage of teens who has used[14] marijuana rose steadily from 14.0 percent in 1972 to 30.9 percent in 1979; hallucinogenic use rose from 4.8 percent in 1972 to 7.1 percent in 1979; cocaine rose from 1.5 percent in 1972 to 5.4 percent in 1979; alcohol consumption rose from 54.0 percent in 1974 to 70.3 percent in 1979. In the eighteen-to-twenty-five age group, use of marijuana rose from 47.9 percent in 1972 to 68.2 percent in 1979; cocaine from 9.1 percent in 1972 to 27.5 percent in 1979; use of stimulants rose from 12.0 percent in 1972 to 18.2 percent in 1979. In the twenty-six and over age group, marijuana use rose from 7.4 percent in 1972 to 19.6 percent in 1979; cocaine rose from 1.6 percent in 1972 to 4.3 percent in 1979; hallucinogenics rose from 1.3 percent in 1974 to 4.5 percent in 1979.[15]

These figures indicate a consistent increase in illicit drug consumption. Additional surveys by Johnston et al. (1981, 1984, 1986) also indicate a steady increase in illicit drug consumption in almost all drugs from 1975 to 1979.

Johnston's et al. (1981, 1984) and Miller's et al. (1983) data suggest that there may have been a gradual and very moderate decline in the use of some drugs, especially of marijuana, since 1979. However, Johnston's et al. 1986 work indicates that the rather steady decline of the past four years in overall illicit drug use among high school seniors appeared to have halted and that there was a significant increase in cocaine use. One has to remember, first, that despite the possible small decline in marijuana use the rates of its use (and of some other drugs) was (and is) still relatively very high and, second, that the possible gradual decline in use since approximately 1979 has been from previous relatively high prevalence levels of use. Furthermore, one must contrast this possible decline with the tremendous increase in cocaine use (e.g., Gonzales 1984; Johnston et al. 1986), and the use of new drugs (e.g., so-called designers' drugs; crack; see *Time* (International Edition), August 18, 1986, 20–21; *Time* (International Edition) Sept. 15, 1986, 26–36, Special Report on drugs; *Time*, (International Edition), May 30, 1988, 20–26; see also Jensen, Jurg, and Babcock 1987).

The situation was perceived to be so problematic in the second half of 1986 that President Reagan and his wife, Nancy, gave the drug abuse issue a *very* high priority. In fact, on September 14, 1986, President Reagan and his wife delivered a televised speech to the nation about the country's drug problem. Certain claims in that joint speech are instructive indeed: "Drugs are menacing our society. They're threatening our values and undercutting our institutions. They're killing our children. . . . It is an uncontrolled fire. And drug abuse is not a so-called 'victimless crime' . . . There is no moral middle ground. . . . I implore each of you to be unyielding and inflexible in your opposition to drugs. . . . We seek to create a massive change in national attitudes which ultimately will separate the drugs from the customer . . . to take the user away from the supply. . . . Drug abuse is a repudiation of everything America is" (quoted from the official text, distributed by U.S. Information Service; see also *Time*, September 22, 1986, [#128], pp. 29–30). While listening to and reading the speech, one must remember, ironically perhaps, that the supply/demand reduction model was *the* social policy in the United States at least since the early 1970s, and it was meant to prevent exactly the situation referred to in the president's speech.

In other words, the supply/demand reduction model of social policy, as implemented in the United States, was *not* very successful, to say the least. Hence, a major U.S. police chief was quoted as saying: "The fight against drugs for the past 70 years has become one glorious failure" (*Time*, May 30, 1988, 22; see also Gonzales 1982; *The New York Times*, Nov. 17, 1986; Jensen, Jurg, and Babcock 1987).

SUPPLY AND DEMAND REDUCTION AS IMPLEMENTED IN ISRAEL

With the exception of one survey that used a national representative sample and focused on patterns of illicit psychoactive drug use in the general Israeli population (Levi 1982), no systematic or dynamic collection of data exists in Israel regarding the prevalence of illicit psychoactive drug use. Is is thus virtually impossible to say anything definite, meaningful, or valid about the true nature of the problem in that country. The figures from that 1982 survey indicated that 6.5 percent of the respondents admitted that they had used illicit psychoactive drugs, and about half of them used it only once. These numbers, however, do not mean very much because we lack the relevant comparative epidemiological picture before or after 1982.

The public and government concern over drug abuse, however, focuses mainly on drug abuse among young people. Much effort has been invested in this question, and the several studies conducted between 1971 and 1983 reveal a more or less consistent picture.

The data regarding the prevalence of adolescent illicit psychoactive drug use were fully given in chapter five. However, because the data are very important for this chapter as well, let me briefly restate the main conclusions. The several studies conducted between 1971 and 1983 reveal a more or less consistent picture: the percentage of young people who tried illicit psychoactive drugs (mostly hashish) from 1971 to 1983 remained more or less stable: between 3 and 5 percent.[16]

While the percentage of drug use among high school students remained more or less stable, two changes did occur. The first change has been the increased involvement of the Israeli police in drug arrests between 1966 and 1988. The data in Table 1 illustrate this.

The second change was the increased frequency of "drug moral panics" in the Israeli media from 1967 onwards (see chapter five and Ben-Yehuda 1988). These panics emphasized the dangers of drugs, the

TABLE 1[a]

Drug Charges Brought by the Israeli Police
Between 1963 and 1988: Number of
Investigation Files Opened and
Number of Individuals Accused

	Files opened:		Individuals accused:	
	Number	% Change from Previous Year	Number	% Change from Previous Year
1963	227	–	357	–
1964	282	+24.20	411	+15.10
1965	282	0.00	401	– 2.40
1966	417	+47.80	554	+38.20
1967	555	+33.10	826	+49.10
1968	744	+34.10	1,071	+29.66
1969	1,053	+41.50	1,480	+38.20
1970	1,678	+59.40	1,725	+16.55
1971[b]	1,308	– 22.10	1,863	+ 8.00
1972	886	– 32.30	1,274	– 13.60
1973	920	+ 3.80	1,386	+ 8.80
1974	1,306	+41.95	1,928	+29.10
1975	1,691	+29.50	2,542	+31.80
1976[c]	1,053	– 37.70	1,042	– 27.50
1977	1,916	+81.95	2,370	+28.70
1978	2,168	+13.15	2,711	+14.40
1979	3,057	+41.00	3,070	+13.20
1980	3,900	+27.60	3,633	+18.30
1981	3,938	+ 0.90	3,487	– 4.01
1982[d]	3,707	– 5.90	3,108	– 10.90
1983	4,326	+16.70	4,602	+48.00
1984	4,415	+ 2.06	3,225	– 29.92
1985	4,366	– 1.11	3,515	+ 8.99
1986	5,139	+17.71	6,598	+87.71
1987	6,047	+17.67	7,549	+14.41
1988	6,345	+ 4.91	7,187	– 4.80

[a] Sources: Annual police reports: The "master plan" of the interministerial committee on drug abuse (released 1982).
[b] In 1971, the registration was transferred to a computer system, and some redefinition and reclassification of offences took place. Until 1971, the "No. of files" is more reliable than "No. of accused." From 1972 on, both measures are reliable.
[c] In 1976, the drug market "dried up" due to the civil war in Lebanon.
[d] The Israeli invasion into Lebanon and the national effort that followed probably caused the slight decline.

number of drug-related arrests, and the growing menace and threat of drug abuse. News about "intelligence reports" regarding young users in prestigious high schools, usually followed by arrests, can be found in the Israeli press every now and then.

One should not ignore the fact that, while the Israeli police force has intensified its efforts and created many drug panics, the prevalence of illicit psychoactive drug usage among high school youth has remained more or less stable (at least until 1983, which was the time of the last survey). Thus, although in other Western societies the young population is usually characterized by the highest rates of drug abuse, in Israel the percentage of drug abusers from this particular age group has been so far relatively low.

DRUG ABUSE POLICY: THE UNITED STATES AND ISRAEL

The figures that indicate the breadth of illicit psychoactive drug use in the United States over the last decade also suggest that the supply/demand reduction social policy there, as a form of a generalized motivational accounting system, has not been very successful. The possible trend for lowering some drug use in the last three to four years should be contrasted, *first* of all, with the very high rates of use of those drugs prior to the small decline. After all, how much higher could such figures climb? *Second*, the small decline paralleled a decline in the economy and the rise of a particular symbolic-moral universe that emphasized health and longevity (the use of cigarettes and alcohol is in strong conflict with these newly embraced ideals of physical well-being), as well as a significant rejuvenation of the older, conservative, and materialistic symbolic-moral universe. *Third*, parallel to the small decline has been a significant and tremendous increase in cocaine use, as well as in new patterns of illicit psychoactive drug use (e.g., designers' drugs, crack). The supply/demand reduction policy seems to have had very little to do with these macro societal changes. [17] I shall next offer an interpretation, based on several factors, of the relative failure of the generalized accounting system represented by the supply/demand reduction social policy model in the United States.

Technical considerations. The first cluster of factors concerns the "technical" feasibility of implementing the supply/demand reduction social policy. I shall show that even the "technical" aspect is very problematic. First, while social control agencies know, theoretically, how to reduce supply (although they often seem to lack all the resources supposedly needed to do so), they do not know how to reduce the demand.[18] As a result, most efforts are directed toward reducing supply, and relatively little is done to reduce demand.

Second, if some biochemical theories that attribute the origin of drug use and drug addiction to inherent metabolic deficiencies prove to be valid (especially regarding opiates), then all the efforts to reduce demand are useless; it would be similar to outlawing insulin for diabetics.

Third, efforts aimed at supply reduction usually create an unreliable supply, resulting in an increase in the drug's price and the creation of "dirty" drugs (due to more "cuts" — mostly in opiates). In turn, health risks for users may increase (indirectly costing more in medical and rehabilitation bills), and addicts may also resort more frequently to crime to secure funds to buy the drugs.[19]

Fourth, arresting drug dealers may create an artificial process of "natural selection," whereby the unsophisticated, crude drug dealers are imprisoned and the more sophisticated dealers may dominate the market. In the long run, law enforcement agents may not be able to control these stronger, more protected, and more sophisticated dealers.

Fifth, not all law enforcement agencies operate from the same ideological base, or capacity, to process drug users and dealers, thereby creating problems for a unified law enforcement action. For example, the police's ability to capture drug dealers is greater than the court's ability to process these dealers or the prison's ability to accommodate them. Furthermore, police ideology does not always coincide with those held by the court, the probation officers, or the social workers.[20]

Sixth, social control agencies cannot always destroy or control the production of illicit psychoactive drugs at their source. Some nations in which illicit psychoactive drugs are grown, or processed, have a vested interest in producing these drugs because they constitute an important revenue for their gross national products.[21] Two examples should suffice. Bags of heroin sold in New York streets during the 1970s contained, on the average, 2 to 5 percent heroin, the remainder being pure junk. Following the revolution in Iran and bumper crops of opium poppies in the "Golden Triangle" in Southeast Asia in 1979–1982, the percentage of pure heroin in the same bags rose to 8 to 13 percent.[22] Second, the Israeli invasion into Lebanon in the summer of 1982 opened the border between the two countries, and illicit psychoactive substances (mostly heroin and hashish) began to pour into Israel. Lebanon, it should be noted, is a major source of both heroin and hashish in the Middle East.

Moralistic considerations. Up to this point, I have listed the technical reasons why using the supply/demand reduction model is problematic. While I had mostly the United States in mind, these technical reasons are not confined to the United States only. There is, however, a particular cluster of reasons that makes the use of this model distinctly very problematic, and these reasons have more more to do with the basic moralistic assumptions of the model.

The most important point is that the supply/reduction model, as based on a broader generalized motivational accounting system, assumes that a reduction in the use of various psychoactive substances is a desired, consensual societal goal. This assumption, however, is obviously not valid in the United States. As we have seen, the sociological analysis of the drug abuse problem indicates that it is not a technical-medical problem but is rather a reflection of deeper conflicts between different symbolic-moral universes, involving struggles and negotiations about redefinitions of societal moral boundaries within changing cultures. Starting in the 1960s in the United States, it has become increasingly clear that a respectable (and growing) section of the population accepts, endorses, and embraces the use (licit or illicit) of a variety of psychoactive substances as a necessary and legitimate way to achieve personal growth and happiness—especially marijuana. Efforts at demand reduction, with this background, are necessarily doomed to fail. In turn, lack of societal consensus about the basic assumptions of the model makes supply reduction difficult because a large section of the population would simply not cooperate with the police. Enforcement of drug laws in such an atmosphere becomes a very unpleasant task.

Decriminalization is an interesting illustration to what happens when even anti-illicit psychoactive drug use moral crusaders admit failure. The fact that some states in the United States have decriminalized the use of marijuana should not mislead the reader. Since 48 percent to 60 percent of specific upper-middle-class age groups used psychoactive drugs, supply/demand reduction became meaningless. Decriminalization became a necessary course of action when a high and significant percentage of the population literally mock drug use legislation, the written law becomes "dead letters," and enforcement of these laws becomes a tasteless and sad job.

Like the United States, Israel's official social policy against drug abuse utilizes a supply/demand reduction model. The basic assumptions of the Israeli model are much like those in the United States, that is, to reduce the prevalence and use of illicit psychoactive drugs. The moral nature of these assumptions is reflected in the final report of the Israeli Interministerial Committee on Drug Abuse.[23]

The committee's report, in its final form, states that (p. 92) no social or political system can totally eradicate illicit drug use, especially not a pluralistic and a democratic system. Such an eradication, the committee noted, would clash with basic civil rights and liberties. Yet the committee stated that illicit drug use presents a grave danger both to the individual and to society, and it recommended that all necessary actions be taken toward a moral education opposing, and thus preventing, the use of illicit psychoactive drugs. The committee stated that preventive drug education should emphasize that drug use is only one symptom of a defective life-style and that it deters the formation of a positive personality, which can be integrated into Israeli society, with its positive symbolic-moral universe. This statement is obviously value-laden, totally rejecting the idea that illicit psychoactive drug use could have positive results, or that it could have a legitimate place in Israeli society.

In contradistinction to the United States, the figures discussed earlier indicate that the breadth of illicit drug use in Israel (at least among middle- and upper-class adolescents) over the last decade remained more or less stable and that the supply/demand reduction model is quite successful. A few factors are important in explaining this phenomenon.

As in the United States, a few "technical" factors contribute to the relative success of the model. First, Israel has been in a state of war with its neighbors since its founding in 1948.[24] As a result, the Israeli borders have been sealed and closely guarded; therefore, it is much more difficult to smuggle drugs into Israel than into European or North American countries.

Second, most Israeli youth between the ages of 18 and 21 are recruited into the army, which is considered to be a source of prestige. Youth know that a previous police drug record would either disqualify them from select units or from service altogether. The patriotic drive thus deters them from using illicit drugs. Furthermore, actual abuse while in the army is made difficult by tight supervision and control. This situation prevents a large part of the population of potential drug abusers in Israel from becoming involved with drugs.

The major reason for the relative success of the supply/demand reduction model in Israel, however, probably lies elsewhere: in the realm of symbolic-moral universes. In contrast to American society, which emphasizes the *individual's* search for happiness, Israel is not yet characterized by such a high degree of individualism. A national consensus does in fact exist, defined historically and nationally. A high level of social pluralism is perceived as a threat to the Zionist spirit, which still emphasizes and reflects a symbolic-moral universe set on melting pot ideologies, as illustrated by Israel's failure to legitimize the use of ethnicity as a framework for politics, life-style, and education. Israel instead is characterized by attempts to crystallize a central symbolic-moral universe and a value system and to negate the idea of pluralism on a cultural-political basis. The national consensus is reflected not only on the theoretical level (i.e., in national historical issues on a very broad, moralistic level), but on the practical level as well. For example, a national consensus exists on many issues ranging from military service, love of nature, landscapes, and geographical tours[25] to a wide repertoire of folksongs and dances.[26] Thus, Israel presents strong elements of both mechanical solidarity and civil religion.[27] This consensus is further reinforced by the existence of pressures and tensions — political, economic, psychological, and military — which together create a feeling of an ongoing and continuing crisis and of "togetherness."

The penetration of powerful and popular Western pro-drug use symbolic-moral universes and ideologies has been largely neutralized and balanced by the national-historical Israeli myth and ethos and by Israeli society's self-image for the future. Despite the noticeable decrease in the 1980s of values emphasizing collective action and the increase of values emphasizing individuality, the sense of belonging to the collective, through which meaningful activity is performed, is still very strong in Israel. This national, integrative and unifying ethos cannot coexist with symbolic-moral universes that reflect pervasive ideologies of individualism and egoism and the use of psychoactive drugs as a legitimate route to happiness or fulfillment. Furthermore, the center in Israel is not broken, or fragmented, into peripheral centers, to the same extent as in Europe or the United States.[28] Compared to the complex and pluralistic type of societies in Western Europe and North America, Israel is much simpler and less pluralistic.

The national consensus in Israel makes the acceptance of the supply/demand reduction model easier. In sentencing a convicted drug abuser, an Israeli judge used a motivational accounting system that stated that "most of the public in Israel shy away and denounce drug use" (Rubenstein 1975, 29). Rubenstein's analysis indicated that the Israeli public is unified in its resistance to illicit psychoactive drug use. This judge, and Rubinstein, use vocabularies of motives that help construct clear moral statements with no real irrefutable direct empirical support.[29] By constructing and supporting these motivational accounting systems, however, the judge and Rubinstein illustrate how they have become moral entrepreneurs themselves.

Thus, the supply/demand reduction model has been more successful in Israel than in the United States because the issue has not created or was used in a conflict between two or more viable symbolic-moral universes. A pro-illicit psychoactive drug use symbolic-moral universe (or ideology) never fully crystallized or was actively and collectively adopted in Israel. A national consensual symbolic-moral universe condemning illicit psychoactive drug use does in fact exist in Israel—and it is not really counteracted or challenged seriously.

The introduction of open borders (and consequently an influx of external, acceptable, and respectable alternative life-styles) and an increase in the legitimacy of cultural pluralism and individuality (as happened after 1967) would mean a change in the moral boundaries of Israeli society; the rise of alternative centers with their enveloping symbolic-moral universes would almost certainly induce an increase in psychoactive drug use, as well as an increase in the popularity of various religious and civil groups or cults.

Finally, one must notice that despite this consensus Israel has always had a lower class, distressed, slum-dwelling population that has traditionally used drugs as an escape from unbearable conditions, much like in the United States and Europe. Such speculative developments as described at the end of the previous passage would hardly affect drug abuse patterns among this population (see Ben-Yehuda 1989).

CONCLUDING DISCUSSION

In the previous chapter, we examined the sociological issue of moral panics. In this chapter, we noted that moral panics may bring about a change in legislation or in collective attitudes and behavior. Hence, moral panics may help to initiate a process of social change. Moral panics may also be aimed at stabilizing moral boundaries. In this chapter, we examined, in a comparative perspective, a result of past successful moral panics—a societal reaction in the form of an integrative social policy aimed at controlling and containing an assumed form of deviance: illicit psychoactive drug use.

Social policy reflects the statement of those organizations in society whose job it is to isolate social problems, define them as such, and act so as to alleviate, neutralize, or solve the problem or the threat in it. As such, statements of social policy can be thought of as generalized motivational accounting systems—explaining observable patterns of behavior and justifying future action and allocation of resources. Social policies reflect assumptions about the nature of reality and desired short- and long-term goals and express specific symbolic-moral universes.

In this chapter, I made a comparative examination of an integrative social policy that was constructed to cope with illicit psychoactive drug use in two cultures: Israel and the United States. It is important to note that this specific societal reaction (social policy) toward patterns of deviant behavior (illicit psychoactive drug consumption) must be understood and interpreted within the analytic context of conflicting and negotiating symbolic-moral universes located within cultures that are constantly changing. Clearly, understanding deviance in this case would be unsuccessful without understanding the more general societal context. Throughout the chapter, I examined the motivational accounting systems used by the different parties to the conflict, as they represent various symbolic-moral universes focused around the drug abuse issue.

The available data[30] indicate that, although both the United States and Israel use the supply/demand reduction model for drug abuse social policy, the model has been much more successful in achieving its explicit goals in Israel than in the United States. To understand the differential success of this social policy model, an analysis of the sociological nature of the drug abuse problem was offered. The thrust of this analysis was that, sociologically, the drug abuse problem focuses around moral-ideological problems, not technical ones (e.g., medical). Once the nature of the drug abuse problem was illuminated in this way, it became easier to explain the differential impact of the suppy/demand reduction model.

It was pointed out that the relative failure of the social policy in the United States could be attributed primarily to the type of pluralistic, individualistic cultural beliefs prevalent there. In the United States, there was a clear and active clash between opposing symbolic-moral universes: one with much power and legitimacy, the other in the process of crystallizing legitimacy and generating power. The result of this clash was that social definitions of reality about, and motivational accounting systems given for, psychoactive drug use in the late 1970s were very different from those in the late 1950s or early 1960s. The movement was from a negative view about the use of various psychoactive substances to a positive view.

The relative success of the same social policy in Israel was attributed primarily to its much less pluralistic, more collective-oriented culture. There, a *real* and active clash between opposing symbolic-moral universes never took place. Furthermore, it was pointed out that a few technical considerations should also be taken into account when comparing the two cultures. First, the problem of the borders of the two countries: open in the United States, closed in Israel. Second, the compulsory army draft in Israel of almost all youth at an age at which these adolescents are most vulnerable to illicit psychoactive drug experimentation and the lack of such a draft in the United States. Third, the activities of the Israeli police.[31] The relative success of the Israeli police is also due, in part, to the supporting culture in which it operates. Most of the Israeli public does not view the police activities in drug enforcement as problematic. Also, the much smaller size of Israel and its closed borders make police efforts much more efficient.

It is thus easy to see how the analytical and empirical comparison that was made in this chapter focused on a particular form of deviant behavior in a dynamic and historical perspective. The analysis took into consideration total social structures and processes of what is considered as nondeviant as well.

The collective societal reaction of Israel and the United States to the perceived danger of illicit psychoactive drug use, and the results of this reaction, can not really be interpreted without using the concepts of power and morality—both to explain the initiation of the reaction and to evaluate its consequences.

Comparing the two cultures illustrates how the meaning and interpretation of deviance can be negotiated and relativized in different social contexts. This situation is most certainly the logical outcome of the fact that arguments rgarding the definition of the *nature* of drug abuse constitute the focus of debates between different symbolic-moral universes. The nature, force, magnitude, and meaning of these debates are very different in Israel and the United States. The power and amount of legitimacy that characterize the symbolic-moral universe that does not object to illicit psychoactive drug use or even endorses a particular aspect of it (i.e., legalizing the use of marijuana) are *very* different in the United States and Israel. Consequently, the ability of the symbolic-moral universe that wants illicit psychoactive drug use to remain illicit to enforce this morality is signficantly higher in Israel then in the United States.

Thus, through the prism of a comparative analysis of a particular social policy aimed to control and contain a specific form of deviance, we gained a better and deeper insight not only into the nature of the policy but also into the nature of deviance and the social reactions to it.

Finally, a few words of caution. Obviously, a cross-cultural comparison on a global scale, as was done here, is difficult to perform — conceptually, ideologically, and empirically. Let me try to cope with at least one possible problematic point. One could argue that the cultural differences between the United States and Israel are such that the results of the analysis presented here could be predicted even without it and that perhaps the cultural differences explain the differences in the patterns of drug abuse without invoking the supply / demand reduction model as a variable reflecting generalized motivational accounting systems. There are two problems with this argument. Its logic negates almost any cross-cultural comparison because no two cultures are alike. Second, if, in fact, one assumes that the supply/demand reduction model of social intervention in drug abuse is an epiphenomenon once the cultural differences are considered, then the very basis of using this model in different cultural matrixes is omitted. The fact is that this model is used worldwide and has even been adopted by the United Nations (with slight and insignificant modifications); thus, it becomes our obligation to examine its effectiveness, and the meaning of its use, in the different cultural matrixes that use it. The analysis presented in this chapter indicates that there are specific sociocultural conditions that should be thought of before and during the use of this model as a legitimate way of coping with drug abuse.

If one wishes to continue this type of analysis, then some possible future directions for such research could be to introduce other cultural matrixes, where the supply/demand reduction model is being used, into the analysis. While this chapter is not necessarily aimed at social policy decisionmakers, it might be fruitful, for this particular audience, to try to isolate, in specific cultural matrixes, which side of the model works best and which worst—the reduction of supply or of demand.

Chapter Seven

Deviant Sciences
Early Radio Astronomy: A Case Study in the History and Sociology of Introducing an Innovation into Science

INTRODUCTION[1]

Science and deviance. Science may be thought of as a more or less definable and cohesive symbolic-moral universe, distinguishable by its own moral boundaries (as differentiated by each separate discipline). Socialization into this particular universe of knowledge is complex, long, and difficult. Science uses socially acceptable and approved methods to make certified statements about the environment—in the broadest sense of the term—in which we all live.

Science may be also viewed as an organization of social actors within particular subdisciplines, each resembling a separate universe of knowledge. While each of such universes is a micro system of power, science in general is a structured system that generates, utilizes, and processes power (for a discussion of power in science, see Bourdieu 1975; Law 1986). Science also interacts with the culture in which it functions, and this interaction is characterized by an obvious element of power (for a recent interesting example, see Shanks's 1986 review of archaeology and politics in Israel). The symbolic-moral universe of knowledge called "science" (and the subuniverses called "disciplines") is arranged by hierarchies where power, prestige, and morality play a crucial role. Those actors in science who guard its moral boundaries and who are occupied with negotiating, processing, and generating power are necessarily involved in politics.

Being dedicated to making certified statements about the environment in which we function, science, paradoxically, is simultaneously committed to two contradictory ideas. On the one hand, science presents a conservative trend and does not wish to revise its body of knowledge without what it feels is a sufficient and

181

justified cause, that is, science tries to maintain the *stability* of its boundaries. On the other hand, science is committed to revise its body of knowledge along new findings or ideas, that is, science tries also to *change* its boundaries. From this perspective, examining deviance within science is a natural, and almost ideal, topic for this book. Because the boundaries of science are inevitably speculative, the aims and values of science may stimulate deviant belief systems. These, in turn, may shift the boundary lines of orthodox science. The problem, therefore, becomes how is innovation greeted in science.

Elsewhere I argued (1985, ch. 4, 5) that the concept of deviance may be utilized to examine how innovations, or changes, are introduced into science and how they are reacted to by the relevant scientific communities. I argued that there are two relevant types of deviance that should be thought of in this context.

The *first* type is what we may call deviance in science. Here we have cases of fraud, fabrications, falsifications, etc. (e.g., see Ben-Yehuda 1985, ch. 5; 1986a; Bechtel and Pearson 1985; Greene et al. 1985; Chubin 1985; Kohn 1986; Salinger 1986). There, the reaction of the relevant scientific community to cases of deviance, particularly in the forms of motivational accounting systems and of actions, helps redraw the boundaries of the relevant discipline, as well as to relate to the more macro, generalized motivational accounting systems that maintain the boundaries.

The second type may be termed "deviant science." This is a symbolic-moral universe of knowledge that by virtue of its hypotheses and/or methodology, is reacted to by the relevant scientific establishment as deviant. Deviant sciences usually have a statement to make about the "true" nature of the world. As such, they challenge orthodox science regarding the very nature of the scientific endeavor. In principle, such claims can shatter conventional theory or methodology or both, thus changing completely a specific scientific symbolic-moral universe.

Naturally, we can expect the relevant scientific community to take such attempts seriously and to resist them. This resistance can assume many forms, from shaming vilification and deviantization of the claimants themselves, to public denouncement of the whole approach, to ignoring the innovator/innovation (e.g., see Ben-Yehuda 1985, ch. 4; McClenon 1984; Grove 1985). Clearly, the negotiations and controversy that a deviant scientific claim creates are focused on change and stability in the realm of the boundaries of particular scientific disciplines. The micro and generalized motivational accounting systems that are utilized in such a controversy reflect the power struggle between supporters and opponents of the deviant scientific claim, as well as the arguments about the boundaries.

The generalized motivational accounting systems used by the symbolic-moral universe of science to define its boundaries are reflected in the micro motivational accounting systems used by specific scientists. These micro motivational accounting systems may also change the macro generalized motivational accounting systems.

Connection of deviant science to the book and plan of the chapter. Looking at deviant sciences is intimately linked both to my previous work (1985) and to this one. When a new knowledge claim is brought into science, it may be defined or reacted to as deviant (or, as an innovation). This definition/reaction has to do with the nature of the new knowledge claim (i.e., its substance or the methodology that was used to generate the claim, see Ben-Yehuda 1985, ch. 4), that is, with what may be acceptable and what not. New knowledge claims may change completely the moral boundaries of specific scientific disciplines. For example, the old and bitter argument between quantum physics on the one hand and the more "objective" physics (which Einstein tried to develop) on the other hand, exemplified by Einstein's famous response to the uncertainty projected by quantum physics when he stated that "God does not play dice" (e.g., see Davies 1982: 35). Or the differences between the more positivistic structural-functional sociological discourse, and ethnomethodology or phenomenology.

The negotiations about the nature, implications, and meaning of new knowledge claims do not revolve exclusively around redefinitions of the moral boundaries of the different disciplines. These negotiations also involve a very strong element of bargaining about and generation of power and legitimacy. A very important element in defining which knowledge claim (and claimant) would be deviantized and which not is the social and professional standing of the social actor(s) who actually make(s) the claim. The *higher* the position of the claimant on the hierarchies of morality, credibility, and power, the *lower* the probability that the claim and the claimant will become deviantized, and vice versa (e.g., see Ben-Yehuda 1985).

Hence, examining deviant sciences forces us to interpret a particular form of deviance within the broader context of a total social structure (science), in the dynamic context of change and stability. To interpret the phenomenon of deviant sciences in a meaningful way requires using the concepts of power and morality. This is so because a new knowledge claim may threaten to change—in the most significant way—the boundaries of specified symbolic-moral universes that represent the different scientific disciplines. Furthermore, the relations between the scientific center and the periphery become crucial for the understanding of the dynamics involved in negotiating the nature and meaning of possible deviantization attempts aimed against various knowledge claims and claimants.

My purpose in this chapter is to continue, in a much more focused manner, my previous analysis (1985, ch. 4) and to examine the ways in which a very specific deviant scientific claim—that of early radio astronomy—was generated, presented to scientists from relevant symbolic-moral universes of knowledge, and reacted to.

As elsewhere in this book, there is also a "story" to be unfolded—that of early radio astronomy—interpreted sociologically and following a "natural history" approach. Following this fascinating "story," I shall discuss the nature of science, and change and stability in it. The early days of radio astronomy will be interpreted by an analysis clustered along three axes: (1) the degree to which the work done by Jansky and Reber—the pioneering figures in the field—was accepted/rejected by contemporary scientists; (2) the amount of "deviancy" presented by their work; and (3) the differential importance of Jansky's and Reber's work.

By examining early radio astronomy as a deviant knowledge claim, I shall examine change and stability in the boundaries of the symbolic-moral universe of one specific scientific discipline—that of astronomy. This will constitute a research effort into the nature of deviance within a total social structure, power, and politics. Full attention will be paid to the way in which the various motivational accounting systems were constructed, negotiated, and utilized in an ongoing process of attempting to determine the boundaries of the symbolic-moral universe of knowledge called astronomy.

THE STORY:
THE EARLY DEVELOPMENT OF RADIO ASTRONOMY:
AN HISTORICAL DISCUSSION

Introduction.   Until the late 1940s, astronomy was mostly based on optical means. Only in the late 1940s did radio astronomy begin to emerge as an independent and important scientific discipline within astronomy. Today, without radio-astronomy, one can hardly imagine such major astronomical breakthroughs and discoveries as pulsars, quasars, and radio galaxies, as well as the development of the "big bang" theory (see Silk 1980; Weinberg 1977; Trefil 1983; Barrow 1983;

Silk 1980; R. W. Smith 1982; Gribbin 1986), and the empirical finding of the background low microwave radiation, to mention only a few cases.

However, while since Maxwell's and Hertz's work in the late nineteenth century one could have perhaps expected radio astronomy to develop, in reality this did not take place until almost the middle of the twentieth century. It is interesting to note that, although radio technology developed for commercial purposes very rapidly, the same instruments were not utilized to advance scientific astronomical knowledge. Hence, it becomes important, historically, sociologically, and philosophically, to examine how early radio astronomy developed as a science.

Nineteenth-century developments. In 1887, Heinrich Hertz demonstrated experimentally the existence of radio waves predicted earlier (in the 1870s) by James Maxwell's theory of electromagnetic radiation. These discoveries did not encourage physicists or astronomers to seriously search for extraterrestrial radio waves. There were, however, a few attempts in the late nineteenth century in France, Germany, and England to search for and detect radio waves from the sun (Sullivan 1982).

In 1890, Thomas Edison tried to detect solar radio emissions (Edge and Mulkay 1976, 9; Sullivan 1982; Shane 1958). Later, between 1897 and 1900, Sir Oliver J. Lodge, in England, also tried to detect these radio emissions (Sullivan 1982, 141), and in 1896, Johannes Wilsing and Julius Scheiner made a similar attempt in Potsdam (Edge and Mulkay 1976; Sullivan 1982). In 1899, Nikola Tesla reported the actual reception of extraterrestrial radio and electric transmission from unknown sources that he felt "were due to intelligent control" (Sullivan 1964, 179; Kraus 1981, 10). A long period of time elapsed before Charles Nordman, from a research station high in the French Alps in 1902, tried to repeat earlier attempts to detect radio emissions from the sun. In the same year, Henri Deslandres and Louis Décome suggested another similar experiment (Sullivan 1982, 143, 150–63). These attempts (excluding Tesla's report) failed to detect any radio emissions. There can be hardly any doubt that these failures were primarily due to the low sensitivity of the equipment that was used.

However, one has to remember that, although some isolated searches for extraterrestrial radio emissions indeed took place, there were no strong and encouraging contemporary incentives to engage in such searches. Hey (1973) even points out that at the time it was thought that an ionized reflecting layer in the Earth's upper atmosphere prevented extraterrestrial radiation longer than twenty meters from entering earthly based antennas.[2] Furthermore, Westerhout (1972) indicated that the development and acceptance of Max Planck's radiation theory could be interpreted to mean that extraterrestrial radiation could not be detected. These theoretical developments, coupled with the late nineteenth-century failures to detect extraterrestrial radio emissions, probably explain why no interest in radio astronomy developed until the 1930s.

Karl Guthe Jansky. If anything, Karl Guthe Jansky's accidental discovery of radio waves of extraterrestrial origin constitutes a true case of serendipity.

Jansky graduated from the University of Wisconsin in 1927 and joined the staff of Bell Telephone Laboratories in 1928. He was stationed at Bell's field research laboratory in Holmdel, New Jersey, and was assigned to uncover the causes of static noises interfering with long-distance telephone calls (mostly radio-telephone conversations over transatlantic short-wave links of the Bell system) (Jansky 1958).

About March 1929, Jansky began to plan, and later to build, a 14.6 meter rotatable, directional antenna system and the corresponding receiving apparatus. In an open field, Jansky built the first directional radio telescope. It resembled a 30-meter wing frame of an early Wright Brothers' biplane, and it rotated on a circular track on four rubber tires from a Model-T Ford (Jansky 1958; Sullivan 1982; Hey 1973; Edge and Mulkay 1976; Struve 1962; Kraus 1966, 1981).

It took Jansky only a few months of data recording to establish the fact that the noise in question could be sorted into the following three categories: noise from lightning in nearby thunderstorms; noise from distant thunderstorms; and an unexplained, thin, persistent hiss[3] that did not vary with changes in the weather and that appeared to be synchronized with the stars (not with the sun as Jansky first thought).

By the end of December 1932, Jansky had data taken throughout an entire calendar year on the hiss static. By 1933, after checking maps of the stars, Jansky demonstrated that the source of the hiss was a band coincident with the Milky Way. Being somewhat hesitant about his own conclusions, Jansky suggested the construction of a new antenna, specifically designed to find out what was going on in the center of the Milky Way.[4] In April 1933, he concluded in a written report[5] presented before the International Scientific Radio Union in Washington that the origin of the hiss noise could definitely be attributed to extraterrestrial sources (Jansky 1958, 14).

Jansky published his findings in 1932 in the *Proceedings of the Institute of Radio Engineers*, presented them in 1933 to the International Scientific Radio Union, and received wide publicity through Bell Telephone's various press releases and radio programs. While Bell Telephone was partly interested in some of the sensational[6] aspects of Jansky's innovative work, the problem originally assigned to him was solved, and Jansky was not provided with additional funds to continue his research.

It is worthwhile, in concluding with his work, to note that Jansky himself was not satisfied with his discovery of extraterrestrial radio noise and wanted to explain it as well. Jansky noticed that the hiss sound was similar to "a sound produced by the thermal agitation of an electric charge in a resistor" (Haddock 1958, 4; Jansky 1935) and therefore gave the account that the radiation could be attributed to "some sort of thermal agitation of charged particles such as found not only in the stars, but also in the . . . interstellar matter" (Haddock 1958, 4; Jansky 1935).

Thus, by 1935, Jansky made the tremendously important discovery of identifying extraterrestrial radio emissions within the very structure of our galaxy, the Milky Way. Taken very liberally, his account explaining the source of the extraterrestrial radio noise might be considered close to later, much more accurate and valid explanations.[7] There can hardly be a question that, by right, Jansky should be credited with the actual work in pioneering radio astronomy and in helping to put this field on a good, reliable, and measurable track. It is no surprise that Jansky is considered by many to be the actual "father" of radio astronomy.[8] Jansky died in 1950, at the age of forty-four, being able to realize to what developments his work led.

It is imperative to emphasize that at that time (the 1930s) the very idea of radio waves coming from celestial bodies or from the interstellar void was almost totally impervious to most optical astronomers' symbolic-moral universe; they simply ignored the revolutionary aspects of Jansky's work. Kraus (1966, 8) reported that at a convention held on July 3, 1935, scarcely two dozen people came to listen to Jansky.

An important observation is that, although Jansky was probably aware of the significance of his discoveries (and theoretical developments) for contemporary astronomers and had the technical tools and level of sophistication needed to create the appropriate motivational accounting systems that could convince the skeptics (Kraus 1966), he apparently made very little serious effort to interact with contemporary optical astronomers. Most of his work was either published in or presented before professional radio engineers (Sullivan 1982, 5–41).[9] Out of the six papers that Jansky published between 1932 and 1937, four were published in the *Proceedings of the Institute of Radio Engineers*, which was a professional journal for radio engineers proper. All of Jansky's important works, reproduced in Sullivan (1982), are from that journal. Of the remaining two papers, one was published in 1933 in *Nature* and was actually a very modest one-column note. The other paper was published in 1933 in *Popular Astronomy*, carefully entitled "Electrical Phenomena that Apparently Are of Interstellar Origin." One cannot fail to notice the rhetorical devices "electrical phenomena" and "apparently." Furthermore, *Popular Astronomy* was not a professional journal but was aimed at a more general audience.

Grote Reber.   Jansky's fundamental and important discoveries made very little impression. Radio engineers, for obvious reasons, were not too interested in extraterrestrial radio emissions, and optical astronomers were either uninterested, ignorant, or simply misunderstanding of the meaning of Jansky's work. This state of affairs, no doubt, was also due to Jansky's lack of strong initiative to interest optical astronomers in his work. The next step in radio astronomy was taken by Grote Reber. Herein, I feel, lies one of the most fascinating stories of modern astronomy.

Grote Reber, a young radio engineer from Wheaton, Illinois, graduated from the Illinois Institute of Technology in 1933. He was not only a radio engineer, but also an avid ham radio operator. Having read and appreciated Jansky's papers, Reber decided to pursue Jansky's findings at his own expense and in his spare time.

While Reber understood the significance of Jansky's work, he also realized that without improved equipment no real progress would be possible. First he had to build a radio telescope. Thus, in 1937, Reber personally constructed the world's first genuine radio telescope.[10] He assembled it piece by piece and completed the entire project in four months, from June to September 1937, at a cost of $1,300 in 1937 dollars (which represented about two-thirds of Reber's annual salary). Reber built the radio telescope on the sideyard of his home in Wheaton, and then he began his observations. He would observe the sky from midnight until six o'clock in the morning and then commute thirty miles to Chicago to his work designing radio receivers. He would return home, sleep after supper until midnight, and start his observations again.

The structure of Reber's radio telescope is reminiscent of modern-day radio telescopes. Sullivan (1982) noted that: "The magnitude of his engineering skill and ingenuity can only be appreciated by realizing that this part time, backyard project produced what was undoubtedly the largest antenna of its kind in the world" (p. 42). It was a nine-meter diameter, steel dish capable of rotating around its horizontal axis, but fixed in azimuth (to coincide with the meridian of Reber's home). While continually improving his equipment, Reber, to the amazement and wonder of his puzzled neighbors and various curious tourists,[11] made the first systematic radio survey of the sky, producing its first radio maps. Kraus (1966, 10) evaluated these maps as "remarkably good, even compared to present-day maps."

The theoretical orientation of Reber's attempts to listen for extraterrestrial radio waves rested on Jansky's earlier formulations (Sullivan 1982; Reber 1958). Reber initially accepted Jansky's idea that the extraterrestrial radio emissions were due to random movements in a hot material and therefore assumed that one could predict where to search for this radiation by consulting Planck's law of black-body radiation. With the equipment he used, he expected to obtain not only a higher angular resolution than Jansky; he also expected to detect a stronger signal if, as Jansky suggested, the radiation was similar to that of a black body. These expectations were never met, indicating to Reber that perhaps the extraterrestrial radiation was not thermal in origin and that the application of Planck's law of black-body radiation to extraterrestrial radio emissions was not valid.

This failure did not discourage Reber. In 1939, he detected and confirmed Jansky's previous findings, that is, that in fact there were radio emissions from the Milky Way. Reber's (1958) account was that by early April of 1939 "It was . . . apparent that cosmic static from the Milky Way had really been found and that it was of substantial strength" (p. 20). During the summer of 1939, Reber examined a variety of celestial objects, attempting to detect radio emissions from them. With the exception of the Milky Way, nothing significant was found. Reber's success in 1939 "further whetted my appetite on the basis of 'if a little is good, more is better'" (1958, 20). Encouraged by his success, Reber purchased more equipment and improved the quality of his receiver. He also bought an automatic recorder that released him from spending his nights observing and recording data. In 1941, Reber felt he was ready to begin a radio survey of the sky. He published the preliminary results of the survey in 1942 in a professional journal of radio engineers (Reber 1942).

Reber was prevented from doing the systematic survey he planned because his work was interrupted when he went to work for the Navy. He resumed the survey in 1943. From 1943 to the middle of 1944, Reber continued his observations and published the results of his work.[12]

As can be seen from the above description, Reber—much like Jansky—was not satisfied with observations only and tried to understand and to account for the nature of the phenomenon he was observing. His early work, especially his attempts to examine if the extraterrestrial radiation originiated in thermal energy, was guided by theoretical considerations. In Reber's first paper, in 1940, he suggested an explanatory account for the extraterrestrial radio waves: "space is filled with positive particles and high speed electrons (of a few volts energy). These particles may be encountered in a variety of ways. The one of interest here is a free-free transition; that is, an electron approaches a positive charge from one direction and is acted upon to leave in another direction. In 1923 Kramer deduced . . . [and later Eddington and Gaunt developed this idea] that when an electron encounters an ion in such a free-free transition, energy will be radiated at the expense of the electron" (in Sullivan 1982, 50–51).

It is very clear that Reber made a genuine attempt to explain his observations by using not only Kramer's 1923 work, but those of Eddington (in 1926), Gaunt, (in 1930) and Einstein as well (Sullivan 1982, 50–51). As Sullivan (1982) pointed out, while Reber's 1940 original theoretical development had many errors, it "is nevertheless illuminating" and "we should not . . . let these errors detract from the genius in Reber's work" (p. 43).

Reber invested his personal resources not only in building a radio telescope and in spending time collecting data; he also made many attempts to interest optical astronomers in his work. To better understand his observations, Reber even took a course in astronomy at the University of Chicago. Having completed his work, Reber took his maps and charts to Yerkes Observatory, trying to persuade the optical astronomers there that he had something of value, but to no avail. Most optical astronomers either could not or would not realize the significance of Reber's findings.[13]

Reber's publications become an important issue because they established the way and means through which he communicated his discoveries to others. Reber's first paper was published in 1940. This work was published in a professional journal for radio engineers. Reber's second paper was submitted to the prestigious *Astrophysical Journal* in 1940. The attempt on Reber's part to publish his early results in such a journal, totally outside of his "official" area of studies and specialization, should indicate a serious attempt on his part to communicate his work and ideas to the group that should have been interested the most in his work—astronomers. The fact that he did it so early indicates that Reber was right in his intuition that the phenomenon of extraterrestrial radio waves should interest astronomers more than radio engineers. There are two versions of what happened when Reber submitted his work, and fairness compels me to detail both.

Ferris (1977, 88) noted that in 1940, when Reber submitted his paper to the *Astrophysical Journal*, the referees rejected it by giving the motivational accounting system that it was unbelievable. Dr. Otto Struve, who was the editor of the journal at the time, found himself torn between his deep conviction in the novelty, validity, and importance of Reber's work and his professional obligations, for the referees' rejections made him cautious, and he did not want to publish an article that might later prove to be incorrect or inaccurate. In a 1945 letter, he provided the following motivational accounting system: "This is one of those cases where an editor does not want to take responsibility for rejecting what might conceivably be of utmost importance, but where he does not have of his own knowledge sufficient evidence to feel convinced that the work is good" (Sullivan 1984b, 13). Dr. Struve got motivational accounting systems from astronomers who complained that they could not understand the radio terminology, totally ignoring the significance of the discovery. When Dr. Struve sent the paper to radio engineering referees, they understood the terminology but could not comment on the astronomical implications. Hence, Dr. Struve found himself in the position of not having even one reviewer who was willing to give an account recommending or defending the paper. The last avenue that Dr. Struve pursued was to establish Reber's credentials. First, he noted that Reber was a member of the Institute of Radio Engineers, and in desperation, he wrote to the institute's headquarters to find out if it could supply any information on Reber's qualifications and reputation. Dr. Struve received a prompt reply stating that Reber was a member in good standing of the institute, who paid his dues regularly. Second, it seems that Dr. Struve decided to travel himself to Wheaton, where he inspected the radio telescope and talked at length with Reber.[14]

Sullivan's (1982, 43–44 and 1984a:b) version is somewhat different. Sullivan stated that Dr. Struve and the other astronomers at the Yerkes Observatory had never seen such data as those presented by

Reber and were apparently confused and unsure about the data's reliability. According to Sullivan, Dr. Struve "sent a delegation from the University of Chicago, including Gerald Kuiper and Philip Keenan, to Wheaton. It was this visit that convinced the optical astronomers that Reber knew what he was doing *experimentally*. Apparently, they felt that the *theoretical* interpretations, however, should best be left to 'real' astronomers."

At this point, Dr. Struve had all the reasons he needed to reject Reber's contribution; however, he decided to take the risk and publish the paper. Years later he explained that he felt a good paper rejected would have been a greater evil than a poor paper accepted.[15]

Thus, Reber's paper appeared in the *Astrophysical Journal* in 1940. Basically, this paper is almost identical to his previous paper, which appeared in the *Proceedings of the Institute of Radio Engineers*. There is, however, an important difference between the two. While Reber's original paper included a theoretical section giving his own explanation in the form of a synthesis and interpretation of the free-free radiation idea and the galactic structure, the article in the *Astrophysical Journal* did not have that explanation. As Sullivan pointed out, immediately following Reber's paper: "Struve inserted ... [a paper] by Hengey and Keenan, which contained a more rigorous and correct development of the free-free radiation theory."[16]

After publishing these two papers in 1940, Reber published two more papers, in the *Proceedings of the Institute of Radio Engineers* in 1942 and again in the *Astrophysical Journal* in 1944, refining his earlier formulations and presenting better data.

It is important to note that while Jansky had made no attempt to actively seek out optical astronomers and to share his discovery with them, Reber, in contrast, tried to establish such contacts. He took a course in astrophysics at the University of Chicago and brought his initial results to Yerkes Observatory. Edge and Mulkay (1976, 84, 263) stated the obvious when they wrote:

> ... it is perhaps not surprising that the scientific community would not immediately notice the work of a largely self-taught amateur working under such conditions. ... Reber's results seemed *theoretically* implausible. ... The optical astronomers ... were, of course ... rather doubtful about the reliability of the information presented by this unknown amateur. ...

Reber's papers appeared during World War II and caught the attention of a few Dutch[17] astronomers who grasped their meaning and importance (Kraus 1966; Edge and Mulkay 1976). The Dutch scientists were not the only ones to realize the importance of Reber's work; groups of scientists in Britain, Australia, and Canada simultaneously started to work on radio astronomy. Thus, significant postwar developments in radio astronomy took place in those places, with the United States lagging behind. Discoveries during the war years, especially in radar technology (mostly in Britain), gave a great boost to radio astronomy.

Hence, since the last decades of the ninetenth century and the development of electromagnetic theory, one could expect astronomers to search for extraterrestrial radio emissions; this in fact did not take place until the 1930s, and even then it was not done by astronomers, but by radio engineers.

DISCUSSION

Science Change and Stability

Science: a matter of definition. Some clarification regarding the nature of science is necessary before we continue. Unfortunately, defining science is not a simple undertaking and would be truly presumptuous here. A few notes about it, however, are necessary. According to Merton (1968): "the institutional goal of science is the extension of certified knowledge" (p. 606). Truzzi (1979) distinguished between the social institution called "science" and the basic method of science. By accepting this distinction, scientific knowledge becomes defined not so much by its *content* as by its *form*. Dolby (1979) suggested that: "the most reliable immediate indication of what is scientific is provided by the mature judgment of the relevant expert scientists. . . . Orthodox science is that which commands the approval of all the leading scientific experts of the time" (pp. 10–11). In other words, what is (and what is not) science is determined by the scientific elite. In this perspective, the crucial variable is the *reaction* to new ideas by key and powerful scientists (those high on the hierarchies of credibility and morality and closer to the center). Thus, reactions of referees in professional journals, as well as in conferences (and to grant applications), become very important. Thus, a definition of something as "scientific" always involves a social evaluation. Zuckerman (1977) chose to focus her definitions on the normative structure in science. She distinguished between two classes of analytically separable norms: the cognitive (technical) norms and methodologies, which specify what should be studied, and the moral norms, which specify what the attitudes and behavior of scientists should be in relation to one another.

Thus, it is possible to generalize and claim that science aims to discover something true and valid about the world. The degree of "truth" and "validity" of any particular knowledge claim are determined by the scientific elite, using its power legitimacy and position on the hierarchies of credibility and morality. This approach means that two important processes take place in science: first, there is a *social* process that "certifies" knowledge; second, there is a *cognitive* process that discovers or creates new knowledge. There can be a contradiction between these two processes. Generating new knowledge claims may contradict the social process of certification, and it can especially challenge old certified knowledge. Thus, innovations in science can have a definite deviant nature. Furthermore, the process of certification may well hint that what is and what is not defined as "science" depends, to a very large extent, on how significant others, especially those in or close to the center of the scientific symbolic-moral universe, will react to it. It is virtually impossible to ignore at this particular point an obvious comparison to the labeling approach in deviance, which stated that what is and what is not considered as deviant "lies in the eyes of the beholder" (Becker 1963). In both cases, the relevant (moral and powerful) experts and (social) control agents and agencies, decide which particular behavioral patterns, or knowledge claims, will be deviantized.

Viewed in this fashion, one may conceptualize the various scientific disciplines as different scientific centers, enveloped by different symbolic-moral universes. Each of these disciplines, a focus of a micro system of power, is characterized by its own specialized jargon and discourse. These are micro and generalized, particular and distinguishing vocabularies of motives, which in turn give rise to specific motivational accounting systems and focus of research (both in terms of contents and methodologies). Each of these disciplines strives to maintain its stability *and* to change its boundaries along new, accumulated and certified knowledge. Thus, the various symbolic-moral universes of the different disciplines exhibit a basic and chronic tension that is generated by the polarity of the two opposing forces — change and stability.

Objectivity versus relativity.   Another relevant problem that arises at this point is the one relating to the issue of subjectivity or relativity versus objectivity. A possible implication of what was said so far may be that there may be nothing "real" or "objectively true" about scientific knowledge and that what constitutes "valid," certified scientific knowledge is, simply put, what other scientists have to say about it.

The problem of viewing scientific knowledge as "relative" versus viewing it as "objective" is linked to Plato's famous allegory. Liberally paraphrased, Plato's allegory portrays a cave in which people labor for extended periods. They are born in the cave and they die there. They do not really know what goes on in the outside world, but they can see that the intensity of the light changes; they perceive shadows, feel variations in temperature, and hear sounds. From this data, they try to construct a model of the "real" world outside the cave. For Plato, the concrete world that we research is nothing but a reflection of another real, unchanging, and eternal reality. Indeed, this metaphor was greatly reinforced by scientific research and innovations from the mid-nineteenth century on, and it was further upheld when Maxwell crystallized his equations in the 1860s in the theory of electromagnetic fields.

The view that there is something eternally true "out there" that can only be experienced indirectly is an essential ingredient of ortho-dox positivism. This positivism was reflected not only in the natural sciences but also in the social sciences. Freud's theories and Durk-heim's measurements of suicide rates are merely two examples of this view, which is reminiscent of religious or transcendental worldviews, which also assume that there is an eternal truth. The Mertonian concept of science seeking "certified knowledge" is easily under-standable in this context because it may be taken to imply that there is "something" true out there that *can* be certified.

As strange as it may sound, the Mertonian formulation may implicitly also support the opposing view as well. "Certification," in the positivistic sense, implicitly assumes that if elite key scientists approve a particular "knowledge claim" as valid, then it may mean that this specific knowledge claim is perhaps closest to the "objective truth." But one may ask, how or why should these key scientists "know" what is closer to the "objective truth"? The opposite view assumes either that there is nothing "objectively true" out there or that if something like that exists we really do not possess the knowl-edge, or technology, to measure or understand it. Obviously, scien-tific disciplines that focus on interpretations (e.g., sociology, history, anthropology, psychology, quantum physics) would be better hosts for the relative, subjective position. It is possible, in some of the symbolic-moral universes in the natural sciences (e.g., chemistry, medicine), that the subjective, relative position would be harder to defend. Solv-ing this problem (if at all possible) is clearly beyond the scope of this volume. However, I would focus in analyzing the case of introducing radio astronomy into science, on the reactions of the relevant scientific communities to a prima facie objective reality—that of the existence of *measurable* extraterrestrial radio waves.

Change in science. The early development of radio astronomy, especially Jansky's and Reber's work, provides us with an interesting case of attempts to introduce change into science and the ways in which contemporary science reacted to these attempts. In Mauskopf's (1979) terms, the acceptance of early radio astronomy by the relevant contemporary scientific community should be thought of as a case of "reception of unconventional science." The problem of the reception of "deviant" ideas or observations is linked intimately to the problem of change in science in general.

Scientific knowledge does not remain unchanged, and the question of how change is introduced into the boundaries of science, and conversely how stability is maintained, has received much theoretical, as well as empirical, attention. A number of scholars, notably Kuhn (1962; see also Barnes 1982; Cohen, B. 1984), analyzed various mechanisms through which changes were introduced into science or stability was kept. The history of science indicates that, on the one hand, many scientific ideas once accepted as valid and reliable were later rejected (e.g., phlogiston theory in chemistry, the ptolemaic worldview in astronomy). On the other hand, many scientific ideas once rejected were later accepted as valid and reliable (e.g., continental drift and plate tectonics theory, see Frenkel 1979; Greene 1984: Messeri 1988). Some ideas may be considered for long periods of time as problematic (e.g., UFOlogy, astrology, etc.; see McClenon 1984; Ben-Yehuda 1985, 1987).

However, since scientific explanations and interpretations before, during, and after certification are embedded within a more general worldview, it becomes evident that science itself may become a belief system. Thus, an acceptance or rejection of specific hypotheses and data and the existence of scientific controversies (e.g., Bachelard 1985; Rudwick 1985) are areas that are difficult to research because the meaning of any type of explanation is doomed to be problematic (Barnes 1977).

The way that the development of science has been portrayed leaves a strong impression that science progresses toward some objective truth "out there" and that science's major effort is to find, describe, and analyze that truth.

Truzzi (1979), however, indicated that the development of science demonstrates a much more discontinuous process than what is usually perceived. Kearney's (1971) study of the scientific revolution in the sixteenth and seventeenth centuries showed that it was not a slow and gradual process of change, but it exhibited instead a very complex interaction among three different traditions, paradigms. These are: the organic, the magical and the mechanist traditions (chapter 1). The scientific process is so removed from the normative portrayal of it (i.e., gradual and accumulative) that Brush entitled his 1974 paper in *Science* "Should the History of Science Be Rated X?"

Polanyi's (1967) interpretation suggested that there are cases when experimental data should be dismissed, when the data violates current scientific conventions. He also suggested that, if the data relate to something that is real, the results would probably be produced again. If this occurs consistently over time, then, and only then, should change be considered. Polanyi stated that "deviant" experimental data usually occur as a result of errors; the effort required to detect the errors, or fraud, can be of such magnitude that it is preferable to simply ignore the results rather than waste time in finding the error. Ben-David (1977) reviewed discoveries that had at first been dismissed in the nineteenth century but were later rediscovered and found to be significant. His account was that the surprising factor was not to be found in the prevalence of various attempts to suppress ideas, but rather "the fact that they so rarely succeeded and that at no point was there any doubt among those with different prejudices that the contest of views could be resold by accepted scientific procedures" (p. 286). Reber's continuation of Jansky's ideas lends some support to Ben-David's and part of Polanyi's ideas. It appears that Reber's experience with the *Astrophysical Journal* illustrates the resistance he encountered in his attempts to communicate his ideas. The fact that optical astronomers totally ignored Jansky's previous paper (even that which appeared in *Popular Astronomy*) only supports this conclusion.[18]

The Kuhnian conception of change. The description of science as a belief system, or as a specified symbolic-moral universe that envelopes a particular center, necessarily brings us to the conception of science developed by T. S. Kuhn (1962).

The orthodox view portrays the sciences as developing in a linear and progressive manner, built up by accumulation of data in a continuous effort to discover the truth. Kuhn's account suggested that, while science develops *from* something, it does not evolve *toward* anything specific. According to Kuhn (1962), what he calls "normal science" enjoys widespread acceptance by the particular scientific community that shares a specific theoretical and empirical paradigm. This paradigm provides guidelines for research methodologies and for prioritizing research goals, and it establishes criteria for accepting or rejecting data and hypotheses. According to Kuhn, the history of science can be characterized by the dominance of specific paradigms. A scientific paradigm constitutes, for a longer or shorter period of time, the worldview, or the definitions of reality, of specific scientific disciplines. A scientific paradigm may be viewed as synonymous with our symbolic-moral universe. This paradigm delineates the moral boundaries of the relevant discipline, and within it, specific accounts may be used and others may be discarded. While a specific paradigm reigns, it will provide criteria for what is "sensible" and what is "nonsense." Phlogiston theory in chemistry, relativity in physics, Parsonian or ethnomethodological theory in sociology, psychoanalysis in psychology, and the idea that the earth is the center of the universe can all be used as examples of specific paradigms, or competing symbolic-moral universes of knowledge. Ultimately, the existence and persistence of many anomalies will force an entire field into a state of crisis. This crisis situation generates questions relating to the very basic assumptions, validity, and reliability of a specific paradigm. Kuhn stated that a crisis situation is solved by what he called a scientific revolution that creates a new paradigm that will dominate the field until the next revolution occurs (for some recent illustrations see Cohen, B. 1984).

The Kuhnian conception of change and stability in science projects a very different view from the one fostered by orthodox science. As empirical historical analyses indicate, however, the Kuhnian view is not always valid. Furthermore, Kuhn's account takes very little note (if any) of the social processes involved in a scientific revolution (Mulkay 1972a, 1972b).[19] The important points for our discussion are not only Kuhn's view of change in science, but the implication of his work that science is conservative and resistant to change.

I shall illustrate this point through two concrete examples of mechanisms in science that maintain stability. The first example is the classical statistical hypothesis testing that gives most probability in favor of existing knowledge. When alpha is set for .05 or .01, it means that 95 percent or 99 percent, respectively, are being given to Ho (i.e., to existing knowledge); this is a statistical admission that science is 95 percent or 99 percent conservative. The second example is the review process through which papers and books (or grant applications) are accepted for publication by what are considered to be prestigious and reliable journals and publishers. This procedure can be thought of not only as a good safeguard against the publication of nonsense, but also as an excellent mechanism for maintaining stability. In such a process, obviously, it becomes very important who the reviewers are, and thus, editors have much power in helping (or preventing) a specific report to be published,[20] simply by selecting the reviewer/referee.

In addition, the concept of professional technical competence (i.e., the recognition that a particular individual's work is reinforced by years of accumulated experience in the field) creates sets of vested interests and controversies over the nature of a phenomenon under study. For example, Barbara McClintock, recipient of the Nobel prize in medicine in 1983 for her work in genetics, was very clear in interviews she gave to the electronic and print media[21] that in the 1950s her colleagues called her crazy, that she could not find a job, and that she was ridiculed. Her work on the so-called jumping genes ("transposition," see Keller 1983, ch. 8) was certainly considered deviant (Lewin 1983; Judson 1979, 460–61). It took the scientific community about thirty years to acknowledge that McClintock was not, after all, crazy.

Brush (1974, 1107) succinctly summarizes this point, quoting the famous scientist Max Planck's bitter remark about the fact that new theories "rarely get accepted by rational persuasion" and that "one simply has to wait until the opponents die out" (see also Planck 1950, 33). As the new Darwinian orthodoxy swept through Europe its most brilliant opponent, Karl Ernst von Baer (an embryologist), remarked "with bitter irony" that "every triumphant passes through the following three stages: first it is dismissed as untrue; then it is rejected as contrary to religion; finally it is accepted as dogma and each scientist claims that he had long appreciated its truth" (Gould 1977, 160).

Resistance to innovation.   Resistance to change and innovation in science has a few sources. Disciplinary paradigms, as part of a myriad of symbolic-moral universes of knowledge, are a major source of resistance because they provide the backbone of the specific discipline's symbolic-moral universe. Peer review is also a source for resistance to change because in many cases referees see themselves as the gatekeepers of the relevant scientific discipline (e.g., see Crane 1967; Schlussel 1983). The rhetorical devices and motivational accounting systems used by peers reflect the boundaries of the disciplines. These peers have the actual power to decide what is "relevant" and "scientific" and what not.

Barber (1961) distinguished between two forms of resistance to change in science. The first is "passive resistance," which implies that new ideas are simply ignored. The second is "active resistance," where scientists actively try to debunk new innovations. Cole (1970) used the term "delayed recognition" to include both forms of Barber's resistance to change. The reaction to deviant sciences can assume all three forms of resistance: passive, active, and certainly delayed recognition. This state of affairs explains why it is so difficult and risky to introduce new facts or new interpretations. While a well-established, prestigious scientist can afford to take risks, others who do not enjoy that status can be expected to exhibit more restrained and risk-avoiding behavior. Young scientists in particular are faced with a difficult dilemma: for those seeking academic careers, taking risks can be quite dangerous if they do not have a prestigious scientist to back them up. On the other hand, a successful risk can boost their careers tremendously.

It is important to understand the basic mechanisms of change within science and to note that the rhetorical devices (and hence the motivational accounting systems) employed to describe the phenomenon is of great significance. For example, terms such as scientific conservatism, resistance to change, and stagnation versus innovation, revolution, change, and modification are all emotional laden and implicitly reflect the user's attitude toward the subject matter. For our purposes, and in accordance with this book's theme, I have chosen the terms "stability" and "change."

Finally, when approaching the problem of change in science, one needs to decide whether to regard this change as "revolution" or "evolution." These two concepts imply totally different approaches. Let me suggest that it is impossible to solve this controversy. The choice of terms reflects, more than anything else, the symbolic-moral universe of the one who makes the choice (see also note 29).

Deviant sciences.   Contrary to Polanyi's suggestion that deviant results should be discarded, Agassi (1975) suggested that there may be times when we should ignore evidence in favor of an hypothesis. Feyerabend's (1975) controversial formulations argue that science does not progress according to a rational method but, rather, by breaking away from rules. Since Feyerabend is convinced that scientific work and decisions are based on, and saturated with, power and prestige, he argued that creativity in science seems to have always had a deviant nature. Furthermore, Laudan's (1983) account clearly implied that we ought to drop our older notions regarding the demarcation lines between what is considered "scientific" and what is not. In a restricted sense, Feyerabend's, Agassi's, and Laudan's works seem to support the Kuhnian perspective.

Every scientific discipline, therefore, that constitutes a belief system or a symbolic-moral universe makes claims about the general nature of reality and specific disciplinary claims. Within these universes puzzles are raised, anomalies are recognized or denied, and the plausibility of various types of explanations is weighed.

The acceptance of new ideas and the rejection of others, as well as the problem of "resistance to innovation," are all directly linked both to science as a symbolic-moral universe and to the fact that every scientist operates on the basis of, and within, an extensive and complex matrix of existing beliefs and vocabularies of motives that are prevalent in this universe. This matrix includes the prevailing disciplinary paradigm and the scientists' criteria for evaluating knowledge claims. "Plausibility" and "explanation" are therefore defined within this matrix of existing beliefs (Barnes 1977).

In a previous section, it was pointed out that defining science is a difficult task. Likewise, defining "deviant science," and demarcating "science" from "nonscience" are not simple or easy undertakings (Nowotny and Rose 1979; Gieryn 1983). Generally, we can claim that deviant sciences challenge regular scientific disciplines and, in particular, the paradigms (in the Kuhnian terminology) of normal science. The term "deviant science" hence refers to "strange observations, to anomalies that are not recognized as such by normal science, and to bizarre interpretations about the nature of reality. A deviant science's claims always seem to threaten paradigms of normal science, which partially explains why deviant sciences are so fiercely rejected and stigmatized by the science establishment and its powerful gatekeepers (e.g., see Crane 1967; Zuckerman and Merton 1971; Higgins 1983). The reaction to deviant sciences and especially to those adhering to them is similar to reactions to regular deviance: rejection, isolation, stigmatization, ridicule, expulsion from jobs, and the like.

Dolby (1979) suggested that deviant science: "is that which is rejected by the orthodox scientific experts, and which they label 'pseudo' science" (p. 11). Thus, what constitutes scientific and nonscientific can become, to a very large extent, a matter of social evaluation and recognition by powerful experts. Wynne's (1967, 1979) analysis of the J-phenomenon, Frankel's (1976) analysis of how the wave theory of light was adapted over the corpuscular system of the early nineteenth century, as well as other works by Wallis (1979),

Mauskopf (1979), Hanen, Osler, and Weyant (1980), and McClenon (1984) on parapsychology all seem to support Dolby's view.

Deviant sciences challenge the motivational accounting systems and boundaries of particular scientific symbolic-moral universes. They often try to break the scientific monopoly in terms of power and legitimacy, regarding what are acceptable as definitions and explanations of some important aspects of the world's nature. Therefore, an essential element in almost all scientific debates and controversies is an explicit, or implicit, argument about the nature of reality. Obviously, the amount of challenge of each contemporary deviant science varies and depends on a variety of conditions.

Just as in regular deviance, not *all* patterns of deviant behavior pose the same threat and are not always reacted to in a similar or uniform fashion. Radio-astronomy elicited a different response, much more quiet, than such knowledge claims as parapsychology, Däniken's "ancient astronaut hypothesis," Velikovsky's theory of catastrophe, the field of unidentified flying objects, and others (e.g., see Hines 1988). Negotiations and arguments about the nature of reality have obviously not been confined to the natural sciences.

Theoretical approaches in sociology, such as ethnomethodology (Garfinkel 1967) and the sociology of the absurd (Lyman and Scott 1970), exemplify this. Furthermore, the dramaturgic approach to the analysis and interpretation of social interactions, as fostered by Goffman and by symbolic interaction as well, demonstrates not only that reality can be negotiated but also that the claim that there really is "something out there" is problematic at best. Phenomenological research in deviance, exemplified by Douglas' (1967) work on suicide and Blum's (1970) work on mental illness, illustrates this claim. Even the more eclectic interpretations in sociology and psychology, such as those made by Marx and Freud, respectively, also focused on particular reality constructions, hinting perhaps at "ultimate truths" (not to mention works in so-called speculative history, such as those by Toynbee).

The social position, in terms of credibility, legitimacy, and power, of those adhering to various deviant sciences, especially within the symbolic-moral universe of a particular scientific community, is of crucial importance if we wish to understand why a "deviant" suggestion becomes legitimated, and vice versa. To a large extent, power plays a crucial role here. Following Lofland's (1969, 14) definition of deviance, it is possible to maintain that in many deviant sciences we have an individual, or a very small group of scholars, who are feared by a sizable group of colleagues. Indeed, the reality and specific scientific claims made by the minorities can potentially challenge the agreed-upon paradigms, or symbolic-moral universe, of the dominant normal or orthodox science. The Velikovsky affair illustrates the clash between two opposing symbolic-moral universes.

In brief, Velikovsky's formulations suggested that various religious myths had solid basis in reality. He claimed that there were physical upheavals of planetary and global proportions in historical times and that these upheavals were caused by extraterrestrial events (mostly changes in the structure of the solar system). McAulay (1978) pointed out that when Velikovsky presented his ideas to Harlow Shapley (an eminent and powerful contemporary astronomer) in 1946, Harlow Shapley responded by writing an angry account to his colleagues stating that: "if Dr. Velikovsky is right, the rest of us are crazy" (p. 317). Later, a campaign against Velikovsky was organized. In this campaign, Macmillan publishing company was threatened by Harlow Shapley and asked not to publish any of Velikovsky's books. The American Philosophical Society gave, in April 1952, an opportunity for its members, and associates to attack Velikovsky but did not allow him to publish a rebuttal. These two examples only demonstrate the type of organized fierce resistance Velikovsky encountered (for more on this see McAulay 1978). McAulay suggested that organized "opposition to Velikovsky among segments of the scientific community was partially mobilized along informal lines by mail, direct contact and, apparently, the personal authority of Harlow Shapley" (1978, 331).

When a deviant scientific idea is brought forth a controversy is usually generated. During this controversy or debate, the status of the scholars or scientists who suggest or support the deviant ideas certainly helps to determine whether they will be accepted or rejected. The frequent flare-up of such an argument arouses debates about the integrity, competency, past achievements, and scientific solidity of both the supporters and the rejecters. The more secure, high, powerful, and prestigious a scholar's position in the scientific hierarchy of credibility and morality, the more attention and consideration would be given to his/her opinion.

Processes of change in science do not resemble a democratic procedure. Deviant sciences must inevitably face scientific and political struggles for recognition and legitimization by the symbolic-moral universe of a relevant scientific community. These struggles are usually fierce because deviant sciences frequently propose not only a competing symbolic-moral universe to the paradigms of orthodox science (e.g., spiritualism, Velikovskism, UFOlogy, and the like), but they sometimes also posit a different form of rationality. Furthermore, such a proposed change may well mean a restructuring of social positions and a redistribution of power within a particular symbolic-moral universe of knowledge. Hence, it is quite possible that many good and valid ideas have simply been forgotten because they were developed "before their time" (i.e., before the symbolic-moral universes of the relevant orthodox scientific disciplines or were ripe enough to deal with them). Such innovative ideas may be ignored or ridiculed, often at a very high personal cost to the original developers of the idea /innovation who felt that they had made a genuine discovery. This phenomenon is coherent with Truzzi's observation that: "like any form of deviance within a social group, unconventional ideas in science are seldom positively greeted by those benefiting from conformity" (1979, 131).

The challenges of deviant sciences encounter contradictory claims and debunking efforts from orthodox science. This debate, no doubt, helps each side to redefine, sharpen, and crystallize its own symbolic-moral boundaries (Grim 1982). Gieryn (1983) pointed out that, while demarcation is routinely accomplished in practical, everyday settings, the "actual" boundaries and demarcation of science from nonscience are very ambiguous. Gieryn also noted that "boundary work" will occur: (1) when the goal is expansion of authority or expertise into domains claimed by other professions or occupations (in this case, boundary work contrasts rivals); (2) when the goal is monopolization of professional authority and resources (in this case, boundary work would exclude rivals from within, labeling them as "outsiders," "pseudo," "deviant," or "amateurs"); (3) when the goal is protection of autonomy over professional activity (in this case, boundary work exempts members from responsibility for consequences of their work by putting the blame on outside scapegoats).

Thus, the question of scientific innovation and change and the labeling of specific ideas as deviant or pseudoscientific have much to do with the culture (paradigm), or specific scientific belief system (its moral symbolic universe) that prevails in a particular scientific discipline, at a specific time (see Brannigan 1981; Latour and Woolgar 1979). Introducing innovations into science therefore always involves power struggles and sometimes involves bitter arguments about the nature of reality and about what constitutes evidence (or fact). Science does not operate in a vacuum and is influenced by prevailing sociopolitical ideas (i.e., via funding); in turn, science can support sociopolitical ideas (e.g., in rehabilitation of deviants). Thus, to a limited degree and in different disciplines, facts and truth can be shaped socially. Certified knowledge can be geared to specific goals either within or outside science.

Deviantization of various knowledge claims and of adherents to a deviant symbolic-moral universe of knowledge is a process that develops gradually and in degrees. On the one hand, some knowledge claims may elicit such reactions that the suggested innovation and the innovators be fully stigmatized and rejected (e.g., Velikovsky, Däniken, UFOlogy, etc.). On the other hand, other knowledge claims may be ignored or rejected without full stigmatization. Not all deviants are treated in the same manner. In the process of deviantization bearers of deviant knowledge claims are frequently isolated, ridiculed, stigmatized, their competency challenged, and frequently prevented from continuing their work. Analyzing the conditions under which a "deviant science" label will be evoked, maintained, or eliminated is a complex task. If an unorthodox scientific motivational accounting system is made and generates a controversy, then one possible way to solve the controversy is through experiments. When empirical experimenting is inconclusive, or impossible, a complicated negotiating process starts. The end result of that process can be the declaration of an unorthodox idea as deviant or as a new scientific specialty. The negotiating process is intimately linked to the prevailing relevant scientific symbolic-moral universe and to the amount of threat presented by the new challenge.

The reaction of adherents to "deviant sciences" in itself is important in determining the magnitude of the reaction of the relevant scientific community. For example, if a scholar presents an innovative, new, speculative idea and gets very negative reactions, that scholar could either drop the idea or keep pursuing it. The amount of success or failure of the new innovation depends not only on its validity, or on its being certified as "genuine," but also on complex political processes of persuading other colleagues, that is, generating power, support, and legitimacy. Thus, whether or not a specific innovation becomes defined as a "deviant" science is the result of a lengthy process of negotiation and is not based on just one event.

This process is similar to identity negotiation processes in other types of deviance—mental illness, homosexuality, drug use, and the like (e.g., see Goode 1984a; Thio 1988). In these cases, the negotiation process focuses on attempts to generate accounts that would be capable of characterizing the nature of the reality in question and to evaluate it in terms of "deviant" or "nondeviant," and hence draw moral boundaries. As is often the case in such deviances as mental illness, drug use, and the like, the nature of the behavior in question (or the innovation) is not the only factor to be evaluated, but the deviant himself and his past behavior are all interpreted and reinterpreted.

For example, the quality of anthropologist Margaret Mead's work was questioned recently. The fall 1983 issue of the *Skeptical Inquirer* had an article by Martin Gardner documenting some bizarre beliefs supposedly held by Mead (mostly on UFOs, dowsing, psychic phenomena). The article suggested that it was not only Mead's work that was questionable but that her integrity as a person was questionable. Likewise, when Struve had to cope with Reber's "bizarre" paper, he checked Reber's credentials in the association of radio engineers. Thus, both the validity of an innovation and the credibility of those who try to advance it are questioned. Also, one must make a distinction between the case where actors external to the relevant scientific discipline define an idea or observation as deviant and when actors inside the relevant scientific discipline invoke this label.

The concept of "deviant science," I feel, is a very important one. It shows how significant actors in a particular and relevant symbolic-moral universe react to challenges on moral boundaries. The demarcating process in science can be thus thought of as a process of redefining the boundaries of orthodox science's symbolic-moral universe. Deviant sciences may introduce important changes into the boundaries of particular scientific moral-symbolic universes or may reemphasize the older boundaries when they are ignored, rejected, stigmatized, or deviantized. The motivational accounting systems that are used by adherents to either orthodox sciences or to deviant sciences reveal the nature of this moral struggle about the future of specific moral-symbolic universes.

Following the Mertonian approach, earlier in this chapter we made a distinction between the "cognitive" and the "social" aspects of science (p. 249). However, and following this section, if we conceptualize the production of scientific knowledge as a *socially constructed* activity, then the "cognitive" aspect may be *included* in the "social." Such a conceptualization may lead us to conclude that the social construction of scientific knowledge (e.g., see Mendelsohn, Weingart, and Whitley 1977) also involves constructing the criteria which are required to evaluate different knowledge claims.

Hence, the rhetorical device/s that we use to refer to different knowledge claims carry a value judgment. There are obvious differences between the social and evaluative meaning attached to the following labels of various knowledge claims: deviant science; marginal science; unconventional science; on the fringes of science;

esoteric science; pseudo science or even non-science. Mauskopf, for example, seemed to have moved from a definition of "unconventional science" to "marginal science" (see 1979 and 1989). This book makes it obvious why I prefer "deviant science," which I defined as: " . . . a science that by virtue of its hypothesis or methodology, is regarded by the relevant scientific establishment as deviant. Deviant sciences usually have a statement to make about the 'true' nature of the world. Thus, they challenge orthodox science regarding the very nature of the scientific endeavor . . . " (1985: 106).

EARLY RADIO-ASTRONOMY AS A
DEVIANT KNOWLEDGE CLAIM

Jansky and Reber versus optical astronomers. The introduction of radio astronomy by Jansky and Reber illustrates how a major contribution to science, which was not a result of a slow and gradual process within science, was reacted to. This early work *broke* with optical astonomy in both theory and methods, indicating that pursuing knowledge in astronomy could be done in a way that was radically different than that of optical astronomers. Furthermore, Jansky and Reber demonstrated that using radio astronomy could provide researchers with new knowledge about the universe that could not be gathered in any other way.

Ben-David indicated that in two nineteenth-century scientific innovations outsiders played an important role: in the emergence of bacteriology and psychoanalysis. Ben-David (1960) stated that: " . . . 'revolutionary' inventions are usually made by outsiders, that is, by men who are not engaged in the occupation which is affected by them, and are, therefore, not bound by professional custom and tradition" (p. 557). While both Jansky and Reber were "insiders" in radio engineering, there is no doubt that they were both "outsiders" to physics and optical astronomy. In this sense, their case supports Ben-David's study.

The early work in radio astronomy does not support Ben-David's notion of the creation of an economic incentive to change one's role. However, Ben-David's (1960) concept of "role hybridization" describes accurately Jansky's and Reber's work: "the process whereby a person in role A is set to achieve the aim of role B can be described as 'role hybridization'. The innovation is the result of an attempt to apply the usual means in role A to achieve the goals of role B" (p. 566). According to this theory, significant innovations and changes were introduced into one symbolic-moral universe by actors located on its periphery or by actors from other universes. Furthermore, Ben-David also indicated that what were later interpreted as important preliminary discoveries in bacteriology and psychoanalysis were done so during the course of attempting to solve practical rather than academic problems. Jansky's work for Bell Telephone, where he tried to solve a practical problem and found extraterrestrial radio waves, illustrates this point.

How hard was it for the two pioneering figures, Jansky and Reber, to get their ideas and findings accepted by the relevant scientific community?

The problem of how the relevant scientific community accepted Jansky's and Reber's work is complicated by the question of *who* that "relevant" community was.

There were three types of professionals who could be interested in this work. The first and most obvious group was that of radio engineers. Radio engineers were likely not only to discover extraterrestrial radio waves but also to comprehend the nature of the discovery without objection. They felt comfortable with the new instruments and understood the terminology that Jansky and Reber used. It fitted well into the type of work they were doing and with the instruments they developed and worked with. It was this group that gave solid support to both men by letting them discuss their works in their meetings and publish their work in their professional journals. However, the theoretical and practical meaning of Reber's and Jansky's discovery for this group was minimal. Jansky's and Reber's work did not affect significantly the way radio engineers worked.

The second potential group of relevant scientists constituted those who inhabited the symbolic-moral universe of physics. The discovery of extraterrestrial radio waves should not have surprised this group, but it could change, in a most significant way, some of their formulations. However, this group showed very little, if any, interest in Jansky's or Reber's work. Reber wrote to me (January 8, 1984) his account of how powerful scientists in the center of this particular symbolic-moral universe reacted to what they saw as Reber's deviant ideas: "During 1936 I tried to discuss the subject with Walter Bartky, Dean of the Department of Physical Sciences. He was absolutely sure Jansky had made a mistake for a reason very plausible to him. The celestial radio waves could not get down to the surface of the earth through the ionosphere. H. G. Gale was head of the Physics Department. He had no ideas and did not want to hear about the subject. As late as 1949 I. I. Rabi had never heard of solar radio waves." The reactions to Reber indicate how one of the most significant discoveries of this century was originally ignored, and passively and actively resisted, by major physicists who were then at the center and located in high positions in the hierarchies of morality, power, and hence credibility. Bartky objected because the paradigm he believed in did not allow for the discovery. Gale did not even want to hear what he must have felt was quite a serious threat for the boundaries of the discipline.

In 1935, R. M. Langer, a physicist, did mention the problem of the extraterrestrial radio "noise" in a short abstract in the *Physical Review* (49, 209). Also, it appears that Fred L. Whipple and Jesse L. Greenstein, an instructor and graduate student at Harvard College Observatory, who were also avid ham radio operators, showed some interest in Jansky's work in 1936. They tried to explain Jansky's findings but failed (see Sullivan 1982: 2). However, Whipple and Greenstein were astrophysicists and should not be considered as physicists proper. In any event, despite these insignificant cases, the discipline of physics in the 1930s was not at all interested in the discovery.

The third group of professionals, clustered in the symbolic-moral universe of optical astronomers, should have been most interested in Jansky's and Reber's work. The discovery of extraterrestrial radio waves meant for this group a new, radically different, and very fruitful way of "seeing" and understanding the universe. However, those for whom this discovery meant the *most* were the *least* interested.[22]

Jansky's and Reber's work presented a new, unconventional scientific specialty. Their specialty had no identity, no structure, and no support or recognition by optical astronomers. This new specialty meant that new rhetorical devices had to be developed and used, that new instruments had to be built, that new work routines and skills had to be developed. What Jansky did not understand (perhaps because of his situation at Bell Laboratory and his shyness) and that Reber did, was that one cannot simply wait passively until one's discovery is recognized. Reber, more than Jansky, identified correctly, and very early in his work, that the relevant scientific community for his work was the one inhabiting the symbolic-moral universe of optical astronomers. Thus, Reber made an effort to become an inhabitant of this universe. He studied astronomy and went to great lengths to make sure that his work would be recognized, its full meaning grasped, by optical astronomers. It seems that Reber also realized that if no astronomers were to commit themselves to do work in radio-astronomy, the new discipline would never develop.

Reber's relative success can be attributed to a combination of several factors. First, he had very persuasive, real, reliable, and replicable "hard" data. These data were collected through the use of equipment that was apparently examined by either Struve or a delegation of optical astronomers.[23] Second, he studied some formal astronomy at the University of Chicago and could demonstrate that he was not just another ignorant amateur with some crazy ideas. Third, while Jansky published and appeared mostly before his peers—that is, radio engineers—Reber tried to publish in a prestigious astronomical journal and was involved in some very active efforts to communicate with contemporary optical astronomers his ideas and findings. Fourth, Jansky's work, but more so Reber's, was done on the background of sporadic attempts to detect extraterrestrial radio waves from the sun, which began already in the late nineteenth century. While Jansky and Reber were probably ignorant of these attempts, others were not. Thus, it could be said (in a very restricted sense) that the ground was almost (but not quite) prepared for such discoveries as those made by Jansky and Reber.[24] Furthermore, Jansky's and Reber's reputations, solid stands, and credentials as impeccable radio engineers, coupled with the fact that the symbolic-moral universe of radio engineers provided them with solid support, gave their claims, especially Reber's much needed legitimacy and credibility. However, it was Reber who took a formal course in astronomy and who took his results to Yerkes Observatory. Thus, it was Reber's "work . . . more than Jansky's, which made a strong impression on astronomers. It was frequently discussed in meetings" (Struve and Zebergs 1962, 96–97).

Hence, Reber actually created the new role of "radio astronomer"; he built the instrument, structured a work routine, and produced a new map of the galaxy. In other words, Reber provided the blueprint, including the content, boundaries, and vocabularies of motives, for a new symbolic-moral universe, that of radio astronomy.

Jansky's and Reber's work, therefore, clashed with the work of optical astronomers because it meant that new boundaries for astronomy could be crystallized. However, to accept and incorporate the discovery meant that optical astronomers had to break away from their old habits, had to learn a new language (electronics), and had to acquire a new vocabulary of motives and adopt new motivational accounting systems. They had to acquire new skills, to devise new instruments and working routines, and, in short, to *think* in different terms (electronics versus optics). While their resistance—personal as well as collective—was, perhaps, understandable, it was not justifiable.

Optical astronomers were deeply immersed and entrenched in their own symbolic-moral universe, which had acquired a very strong legitimacy, and they had all the power they needed. Thus, the dice in the confrontation between optical astronomers and Jansky and Reber were clearly lined against the latter. Jansky and Reber stood a very slim chance that optical astronomers would be genuinely interested in changing the boundaries of their symbolic-moral universe.

While Jansky and Reber worked in a very orthodox way in radio engineering, their "orthodoxy" was also very alien to optical astronomers, who simply could not understand it. While there can be no doubt that Jansky's and Reber's work broke the older methodological boundaries of optical astronomy, they were both acutely aware of these boundaries and tried to "play the game by the old rules."

The problem for optical astronomers was how to incorporate a radically new way of "seeing" the universe and how to cope with an unknown new methodology and terminology. In other words, how could optical astronomers recognize and incorporate a radical change into the boundaries of their "optical" symbolic-moral universe.

In this matter, one cannot downplay Struve's most important role. It is very clear that Struve wanted to overcome his limitations and to give a chance to what could be a very important discovery, although he could not be sure of that. Struve's behavior, and decisions, can only serve as examples for a truly curious scientific mind, willing to take risks on controversial but important matters. Struve's decision must be appreciated against the background that most optical astronomers presented various degrees of resistance to the innovations presented by Jansky and Reber, as many of them felt that there was no place for radio waves, or radio telescopes, within contemporary optical astronomy.

Early radio astronomy as a deviant science. The early work in radio astronomy leaves very little room to doubt the fact that it definitely constituted a "deviant science" for both physicists and optical astronomers. Jansky and Reber had to convince optical astronomers of the validity of a whole new way of observing and interpreting the universe. One should remember that Jansky's pioneering work was virtually ignored by optical astronomers. It took a powerless, outsider amateur to grasp the true meaning of Jansky's work and with an admirable personal effort, totally outside any contemporary recognized research institute, to actually make the quantum leap that almost threw radio astronomy into the skeptical optical astronomers' halls. One can hardly avoid reading Reber's (1983) cynical note that: "astrophysicists could not dream up any rational way by which the radio waves could be generated, and since they didn't know of a way, the whole affair was at best a mistake and at worst a hoax" (p. 5).

One should also remember that, although he made a significantly more intense effort than Jansky to interest optical astronomers in his work, Reber was not *very* successful. Radio astronomy developed mostly after World War II and not in the United States (Edge and Mulkay 1976). Certainly, contemporary, prestigious, and central figures in physics and optical astronomy paid virtually no attention to either Jansky or Reber.[25]

The applicability of the Kuhnian idea of a "scientific revolution" to the early days of radio astronomy is problematic because it supports the Kuhnian thesis only partially. The major support lies with the fact that introducing radio astronomy as a scientific change was resisted by optical astronomers, and introducing this change was not gradual. Optical astronomy constituted a symbolic-moral universe that, in Kuhn's terms, was a normal science, dominated by a specific paradigm. However, it would not be correct to suggest that puzzles or anomalies within this paradigm brougnt about the development of radio astronomy. Reber and Jansky were totally outside optical astronomy, and their work did not solve any puzzle or anomaly within it. On the contrary, optical astronomy in the 1930s was at its peak. In this sense, the case of Jansky's and Reber's innovative work does not support the Kuhnian perception of the conditions under which a scientific "revolution" takes place. Furthermore, Jansky's and Reber's work did *not* occur on the background of a major, Kuhnian type of crisis in optical astronomy. Optical astronomers really *had* no compelling good inner disciplinary reasons to listen to Jansky or Reber.[26]

In a very broad sense, one could claim that, although radio astronomy certainly changed and revolutionized the discipline of astronomy, it did not change its central paradigm. The dominant paradigm of optical astronomy was based on understanding the universe through observing stars and galaxies, which transmit large amounts of light. Optical astronomy's "mistake" was in not realizing that the energy generated in the universe—in the void between the stars and in galaxies—also finds expression in radio waves. The discovery of extraterrestrial radio waves did not change the dominant paradigm of optical astronomy. Adherents to this position are quick to suggest motivational accounting systems that suggest that *optical* astronomy is a technology, and so is *radio* astronomy. Unfortunately, adhering to these motivational accounting systems may obstruct us from realizing that, in fact, the discovery of radio astronomy not only expanded the older optical astronomy paradigm greatly and significantly; it also revolutionized astronomy—in more ways than one. First, the symbolic-moral universe of radio astronomy illustrated the tremendous importance of intergalactic gas. Second, radio astronomy provided a new tool, which meant that optical astronomers had to learn and acquire new skills. Third, it forced astronomers into *electronic* thinking instead of *optical* thinking exclusively. One should not underestimate the significance of this particular shift in boundaries. For example, this shift meant learning a new terminology, language, and vocabularies of motives for older optical astronomers. It meant that the universe could be "seen" and interpreted in a very different way than before. Fourth, radio astronomy gave a great boost to, and enabled the development of, new theories as new discoveries were made. For example, the discovery of pulsars[27] and the discovery of the microwave background radiation in 1965 by Arno Penzias and Robert Wilson, which gave a major support for the "big bang"[28] cosmology, to mention only two examples. Fifth, radio astronomy provided new maps of the universe. Sixth, radio astronomy meant new work routines. In summary, the introduction of radio astronomy revolutionized the symbolic-moral universe of optical astronomy in a very profound way and clearly changed its boundaries.[29]

Jansky's and Reber's discoveries and vocabularies of motives were both ignored by optical astronomers and physicists. Cole's (1970) concept of "delayed recognition" also describes very well the early days of radio astronomy. However, when Cole used the criteria of five years, his analysis could not take into account such a cataclysmic event as World War II, which twisted channels of communication and caused an even longer delay in properly recognizing new innovations.

Optical astronomers could easily use motivational accounting systems that gave legitimacy to discard and ignore the early innovations in radio astronomy as "deviant" due to several factors. To begin with, both Reber and Jansky were true "outsiders" to optical astronomy in two important ways. First, neither had a full, formal education or training in astronomy, and their professional identity as radio engineers put them outside the closed circle and communication network characteristic of the moral-symbolic universe of optical astronomers. Ben-David (1960) indicated that, in the cases of bacteriology and psychoanalysis, those with marginal positions in the relevant research networks were the ones responsible for introducing significant innovations. Jansky and Reber, one must remember, were not only not in the margin of the research network and universe of optical astronomers, but were in fact totally outside it.[30] Second,

Jansky's and Reber's methods were certainly considered deviant, misunderstood, and unintelligible to optical astronomers. Reber (1983) noted that contemporary astronomers viewed "electronic apparatus . . . as black magic" (p. 5).

To appreciate Jansky's and Reber's deviancy, one must also remember that the role of amateurs in astronomy has been considerable. Lankford (1981) documented the major (albeit usually neglected) advances that amateurs had contributed to the development of astronomy and astrophysics. Lankford pointed out that it was the amateurs who were willing to take the risks[31] in new specialties in the early days of the discipline. Since 1900, however, professional astrophysics developed so rapidly, and the price of equipment rose so sharply, that it was no longer possible for amateurs to compete and contribute. Thus, on the one hand, Jansky, and even more so Reber, continued a respected line of amateurs who contributed significantly to astronomy. On the other hand, however, neither *was*, in fact, an amateur astronomer. Both were competent, highly qualified radio engineers, which only reinforced their deviant role.

Multiple discoveries and the central message.   One very important issue in science is the one associated with creditation of new discoveries. The prestige, recognition, and awards go to the *first* scientist who made the discovery, not to the second, third, or fourth. Consequently, the competition to arrive *first* to the discovery and reap the rewards may sometimes be quite fierce and may lead to twisting the historical facts and to deviant acts concerning the question of who *really* made a specific discovery.[32]

Contrary to the popular and accepted view, Merton (1973) noted that: "the pattern of independent multiple discoveries in science is, in principle, the dominant pattern . . . all scientific discoveries are in principle multiple" (p. 386). Schmookler (1966) challenged the Mertonian formulation and stated that the claim that a few scholars arrived at the same conclusion and/or ideas simultaneously is misleading because there had been in fact important and significant differences in the work of the different scholars. For example, Elkana's (1970) analysis illustrated that the law of conservation of energy, usually cited as a case of multiple discovery, was not, in reality, such a case.

Patinkin (1983) examined the subject of independent multiple discoveries in science, using as a case example the alleged multiple discovery of the theory presented by Keynes in economics. Patinkin concluded from his study that inadequate attention was paid in the sociology of science to two essential points in multiple discoveries: (1) precise definition of the discovery; and (2) the extent to which the discovery was part of the scientist's central message.

In Patinkin's (1983) view, the scholar who carries the "central message" is the one who is himself convinced of the validity of his work because he "really means it" (p. 1) and is therefore able to persuade fellow scientists in the truth of the discovery. Patinkin's concept of the "central message" can thus become an important analytical tool if one wishes to assess correctly the differential importance of various multiple discoveries.

Jansky's and Reber's work does not present a clear case of "independent multiple discoveries." Reber knew about Jansky's work and was stimulated by it to begin his own work. However, the time difference between the two is not very significant, and Patinkin's concept of the "central message" can, and should, be used[33] to assess the differential contribution of Jansky's and Reber's work.

Which of the two beginners, Jansky or Reber, should be credited with the most important contribution in the early days of radio astronomy? Most texts credit Jansky as the "father" of modern radio astronomy (e.g., Edge and Mulkay 1976), and Reber seems to share this view.[34] I have to disagree with this position: the historical and sociological analysis indicates that Reber's role was by far more important. Interestingly, this question and the answer are aimed to give a different account than the accepted one, and thus to change one of the accepted symbols of a specific symbolic-moral universe: that of the history of radio astronomy. In terms of power and morality, this particular issue seems to fit very well the topic of this book.

Reber was much more successful than Jansky in communicating his discoveries to the relevant scientific group—optical astronomers. Jansky's discovery was true serendipity, a coincidence. While it is true that he was prevented by Bell Telephone from continuing his revolutionary work, he also did not try too hard. Jansky's work was financed by Bell, and he enjoyed the benefit and security of a steady job. He presented most of his work before sympathetic audiences of radio engineers and even seemed to enjoy the exposure of his work in the mass media. He really did not try very hard to deal directly with the more suspicious and hostile optical astronomers (Sullivan 1984a). As Edge and Mulkay (1976) put it: "Jansky made . . . no attempt actively to seek out astronomers. He acquired the astronomical knowledge necessary for his research from his colleagues at Bell Laboratories, and by consulting basic astronomy textbooks" (p. 263). While his publication of one paper in *Popular Astronomy* in 1933 could perhaps be considered as an attempt to communicate his findings to optical astronomers, this attempt cannot be taken too seriously. Jansky, in short, did not take too many risks and did not invest too much of his time or resources to make the nature and magnitude of his discoveries known to the relevant scientific community. Compared to Reber, it seems that Jansky did not really "mean it," in Patinkin's terms.

The amazing fact about all this is that, for a short time in the early 1930s, Jansky held in his hand the key to an instrument that could provide many new scientific insights into the very nature of the universe (as indeed it did years later), but somehow he let the key go.

Reber (1983,) on the other hand, realized that "it was obvious that K. G. Jansky had made a fundamental and very important discovery" (p. 16), and "Here was a scientific opportunity—a first class discovery had been made and nobody was going to do anything about it. No matter what I did in this new area, it seemed that I just couldn't go wrong" (Sullivan 1984b, 1). Reber, however, was a radio engineer with very little, if any, knowledge of astronomy. Nevertheless, he decided to pursue this matter. His work was certainly not coincidental. He planned it both empirically and theoretically—taking a course in astronomy at the University of Chicago; investing a great deal of his personal time and money building a radio telescope; spending a tremendous amount of time observing and recording extraterrestrial radio emissions on no one's expense account. In short, he took all the risks. Furthermore, he had to withstand bitter disappointments in 1938, when his predictions did not yield any valid empirical results, and he therefore had to change some of his methods. He decided to begin, and to continue, his observations despite several objective difficulties and, in fact, no benefits. One important aspect of Reber's work is that he tried, time and again, to communicate his ideas and results to physicists and optical astronomers, who displayed various degrees of misunderstanding, ignorance, and even hostility. Unlike Jansky, who continued his work with Bell Telephone, totally leaving radio astronomy, Reber actually left the universe of radio engineering and shifted gradually into the symbolic-moral universe of radio astronomy.

Thus, it is easy to see that, while Jansky's choice was not to confront optical astronomers, Reber's was totally different.

An interesting question is why did Jansky and Reber pursue different routes in communicating their work? Basically, I feel that it had to do with the fact that it was Reber who grasped the true meaning and tremendous importance of the new discovery. He presented a much more rigorous attitude and self-confidence in his work than Jansky did; Jansky seemed more hesitant and unsure.

While these differences could be attributed to different personalities, some of Jansky's hesitation could perhaps be attributed to his
superior in Bell Laboratories—Harald T. Friis. Sullivan (1984a)
pointed out that Harald T. Friis was a difficult, aggressive, and very
practical administrator, who did not encourage Jansky to pursue his
work on extraterrestrial radio waves. Friis himself wrote years later
that Jansky was free to pursue his work on the cosmic noise if he had
only wanted to, but with the absence of encouragement and support
from the scientific community, Jansky did not want to (Sullivan 1984a,
pp. 25–26). Sullivan's (1984a) conclusion was thus: "It . . . seems
that . . . Friis did not allow Jansky to continue his work in any major
way, but also that Jansky did not press the point on those occasions
when he had been turned down" (pp. 27). As Sullivan noted, one
must remember that Jansky's reluctance to confront his superior could
also be attributed to Jansky's poor health, the Depression, and
possibly his fear that he might find himself with a young family to
support without a good and secure job.

Patinkin's "central message" is a key analytical concept if we are
to appreciate correctly Jansky's and Reber's work. Radio astronomy
was a "central message" for Reber, not for Jansky. While both "saw"
extraterrestrial radio waves, it was Reber who saw, understood, and
grasped the true importance and magnitude of the discovery. In
Patinkin's terms, Reber provided a precise definition of the discovery
in question, both empirically and theoretically, providing a role
model, an instrument, a work schedule, a routine, and a new radio
map of the Milky Way; so it was Reber who "really meant it." Reber
announced his discoveries very early and repeatedly. In Whitehead's
(1917) words, quoted by Patinkin (1983), Jansky came very near a true
theory, but it was Reber who grasped its practical application.

Finally, therefore, and without downplaying Jansky's important
role, it seems to me that when we take all the facts and discussion into
consideration, the unavoidable conclusion must be that, contrary to
the way the story is usually told, it was Reber and not Jansky who was
the more important figure in introducing the symbolic-moral universe
of radio astronomy into modern-day astronomy since it was Reber
who carried the "central message."

CONCLUDING DISCUSSION

Science can be characteized as composed of a myriad of different
symbolic-moral universes in the form of various disciplines. Each of
these universes envelopes a center and is distinguishable by its moral
boundaries. Each of these universes strives to achieve two almost con-

tradictory goals—to maintain the stability of its boundaries *and* to introduce necessary change and revise the definition of its boundaries along new knowledge.

Deviant sciences were presented in this chapter as knowledge claims that by virtue of their content, or methodology, are deviantized by scientists who inhabit the symbolic-moral universe representing the relevant scientific discipline. These scientists are typically located in the higher echelons of the hierarchies of power, morality, and credibility in the center. The reactions to what is defined as a deviant knowledge claim may range from ignoring to full stigmatization, not only of the claim, but of the claimant as well.

Obviously, a knowledge claim that had once been defined as deviant, may be later accepted, certified, and become either part of orthodox science or create new symbolic-moral universes in the form of new orthodox sciences. Other deviant sciences are doomed to remain deviant. Deviant knowledge claims may thus serve either to introduce change into the boundaries of stable moral-symbolic universes—the relevant scientific disciplines—or, conversely, to enhance stability. This is done by provoking reactions that use vocabularies of motives and producing motivational accounting systems that either emphasize existing knowledge and reject the new knowledge claime or that help change the universe of knowledge. Some of the possible motivational accounting systems used in such controversies were surveyed in chapter two.

In this chapter, I detailed the early days of radio astronomy, which was described as a deviant knowledge claim. I detailed how it emerged as a deviant symbolic-moral universe, how it was reacted to, and how it was finally accepted and revolutionized astronomy by changing its boundaries and its vocabulary of motives.

The original knowledge claims made by Jansky and Reber were certainly deviantized. However, while Jansky and Reber themselves were considered as deviants by contemporary optical astronomers, they both did not experience very strong deviantization processes. This, perhaps, is somewhat unusual because in many other similar cases the claims *and* the claimants stood a reasonable chance of being deviantized (e.g., see Ben-Yehuda 1985, 106–67). This occurrence may have something to do with the fact that, while both Jansky and Reber were considered as aliens to physicists and astronomers, they were very much integrated into the symbolic-moral universe of radio engineers. Furthermore, Jansky basically withdrew from the confrontation. While Reber had the "fighting spirit" and was willing to wage a battle, he really did not stand much of a chance without firm and massive support of optical astronomers (or physicists), which he simply could not mobilize. The fact remains that both Jansky and Reber were later turned from deviants into heroes.

Examining Jansky's and Reber's pioneering work in radio astronomy during the 1930s required a description and analysis of the ways in which the early innovations in radio astronomy came into being and how the relevant scientific symbolic-moral universes and communities—radio engineers, physicists and optical astronomers— reacted to this innovative work. Ben-David's (1960) concept of role hybridization was used to explain Jansky's and Reber's work. Dolby's (1979) concept of "deviant science" was used to explain how and why optical astronomers ignored the early innovations in radio astronomy. Finally, Patinkin's (1983) concept of the "central message" was used to assess the differential contribution of Jansky's and Reber's work, concluding that it was Reber who was the important figure in the early days of radio astronomy.

This chapter has thus focused an analytical interpretation on a particular form of deviance in an historical and dynamic context. The interpretative analysis took into consideration total social structures, as well as negotiations about power, morality, and legitimacy between the center and the periphery, and the motivational accounting systems which were used. The interpretation emphasized both elements of power and morality, showing how a discovery that was once regarded as deviant became an orthodoxy.

Chapter Eight

The Politicization of Deviance
Resisting and Reversing Degradation, Stigmatization, and Deviantization

INTRODUCTION: CONNECTION TO, AND PLAN OF, THE BOOK[1]

One major analytical argument made in this book was the association between negotiation processes regarding social definitions about the *nature* of deviance and broader social processes of change and stability. The preceding three chapters were focused on this topic, as well as this chapter.

The analysis of politics and deviance, as presented here, implies that deviantization may be a possible mode of interaction when different symbolic-moral universes meet, conflict, and negotiate. Deviantization, as one form of a societal reaction, is directly linked to the labeling approach in deviance research (Becker 1963; Schur 1971, 1979; Goode 1978; Pfuhl 1986; Dotter and Roebuck 1988). There, deviance is perceived to be more a property *conferred upon* specific types of behavior rather than a property *inherent* in the behaviors in question (Erikson 1962). Thus, becoming deviant (Matza 1969) is not a product of a one-time act of control agents or agencies but rather is a product of a process. This lengthy and complicated process is composed of a few important ingredients, two of which are stigmatization (Goffman 1963) and degradation (Garfinkel 1956).

The labeling approach emphasizes that the process of becoming deviant, or of being deviantized (Schur 1980), can be conceptualized as a process of negotiations between the deviants and the social environment. These negotiations focus on the scope, intensity, length, meaning, and consequences of the deviantization process. On the one hand, potential deviants can resist such a process, alter its meaning, and change its consequences; on the other hand, potential deviants can be very helpful in this process by cooperating with the control agents or agencies.

221

The way deviantizers and deviantazees meet, clash, and negotiate is of crucial importance for us because this process serves as an analytical and empirical focus for change and stability. It is at this point that we can observe how motivational accounting systems are manufactured, utilized, and help to negotiate the meaning and interpretation (and hence relativization) of deviance, in a dynamic and historical process. Questions relating to power and morality are obviously and intimately integrated into the negotiations about power and morality. In this analytical context, an interesting and important theoretical and empirical question becomes whether a process of stigmatization and deviantization can be neutralized or even reversed, under what conditions, and at what stage.

The idea of politics and deviance implies that deviants may either play a crucial part in processes of stabilizing and/or changing moral boundaries or that deviance may play a crucial role in politics. Socrates is an example for the first case, while Robin Hood is an example for the second.

Deviants may, under specific conditions, try to use their deviancy as an asset in a political career or as a political statement. In this chapter, I shall provide an historical analysis of the Abu-hatzira affair, which took place in Israel. The essence of the case is that Abu-hatzira, while occupying the important governmental position as minister of religion, was officially deviantized and criminalized. However, he was able to exploit his deviances to advance his political career quite significantly. This case provides us with a fascinating historical illustration of how a social actor who was in the focal point of processes of stigmatization and deviantization was able not only to *neutralize* these processes but to actually *reverse* them. The main focus of this chapter is to examine sociologically how such a reversal was possible and what the impact and meaning of this case were for Israel as a total social structure.

The main conclusion of this chapter is that processes of deviantization, stigmatization, and degradation can in fact be effectively resisted, neutralized, and even reversed.

If a specific social actor who is being labeled as a deviant can politicize what would otherwise be viewed as a "regular" type of deviance, subsequently making a political statement within the context of an effective ideology geared to mobilize a receptive audience, then the probability of an effective reversal of the deviantization process increases significantly.

To illustrate the above argument, a full analysis of the Abu-hatzira affair will be provided. As in the previous chapters, there is a "story" to be told here—that of the case itself—within a particular historical and political context, considering the total social structure of Israeli society. As we shall see, the case affected in a most significant way Israeli culture and society and touched some very basic issues in and exposed some delicate nerves of the Israeli social structure and culture. The different motivational accounting systems that were used by the different social actors will be emphasized, and we shall be able to see how the micro-macro levels interacted.

Using the natural history of crime approach, the case itself will be presented first, to be followed by an analytical discussion, clustered along two axes. The first axis details how and why Abu-hatzira was successful in reversing processes of stigmatization, degradation, and deviantization aimed against him. This success can be partly, but secondarily, attributed to his background. Of greater, and primary, importance was his ability to manipulate and use an ethnic dispute in Israel in his favor. The second axis focuses on the politicization of deviance, the theoretical implications of the case, and possible generalizations from it.

TRANSFORMING DEVIANCE:
THE CASE OF ABU-HATZIRA.
THE PHENOMENON TO BE EXPLAINED

General background. The State of Israel was established in 1948. It is still a young country, fighting not only for its existence and survival but also struggling to establish and legitimize social and political patterns, norms, and institutions (e.g., see Horowitz and Lissak 1989). It is no surprise therefore to discover heated debates in Israel about what does or does not constitute an acceptable, valid, and honest political norm,[2] as well as how the governmental system should work. Furthermore, in its early years, the State of Israel had quite a few scandals that received wide coverage in the media and made people aware of some inherent problems in the functioning of the political system (e.g., Eisenstadt 1968). After a relatively quiet period in terms of scandals involving political figures lasting from the mid 1960s to the mid 1970s, the late 1970s witnessed a chain of scandals involving major political figures that virtually shook the country. Brief reports about six such cases follow.

The first case involved former Israeli Prime Minister Itzhak Rabin. In March 1977, an Israeli reporter in Washington discovered that the Rabins has a U.S. bank account with about $20,000 in it. While Rabin's wife, Leah, was in charge of the account, it was still a serious violation of an Israeli foreign currency regulation. Rabin took the blame upon himself and resigned his office, an act that was followed by much admiration in Israel. The second case involved former Israeli Minister of Foreign Affairs Abba Eban. He too was charged in April 1977 with having a U.S. bank account, also in violation of foreign currency regulations. This case created much turmoil. Hardly anyone seemed to have paid attention to the fact that in June 1977, Eban was cleared from all suspicions. The third case happened in April 1977, when accusations were raised against late Professor Yigal Yadin, a famous archaeologist from Hebrew University, who later became the deputy prime minister. The accusations were that Yadin, in violation of Israeli law, smuggled abroad archaeological artifacts. Again much turmoil was created, but Yadin was acquitted. The fourth case also began in April 1977. Samuel Rechtman, from the Likud party, was accused of corruption, kickbacks, and bribery. Rechtman was an important figure—the mayor of Rehovot (a small town near Tel Aviv) and a candidate for the Israeli parliament. While the investigation against him was still being conducted, he was able to persuade his party to give him a seat in the parliament. On July 18, 1980, Rechtman was officially accused with seventeen items, concentrating on usurpation and abuse of power, bribery, and the like. While Rechtman denied all the accusations, on February 2, 1981, the court found him guilty and sent him to serve a long prison term. An appeal to the Israeli Supreme Court did not help as Rechtman went to prison and gave his seat in parliament back to his party (not without a struggle). The fifth case took place in October 1979, when then secretary of energy Modai was suspected of fraud and tax evasion in his previous position as general director of the Revlon cosmetic corporation (Israel). While Modai was proven innocent, the case did raise a great turmoil.[3] The last case focuses on a very ugly, still mysterious incident that constituted a calumny in January 1981. The then Israeli Chief of Police Herzl Shafir was dismissed quite suddenly by Minister of Police Dr. Joseph Burg. While Minister Burg claimed that he had dismissed Shafir because they could not work together and because Shafir did not follow his directions, Shafir hinted that he was dismissed in order to prevent, and stop, the Israeli police from investigating charges raised against some political figures (possibly from Burg's own political party).

This climate, which began to crystallize in 1977 and exposed public figures in Israel to public investigations, created distrust in political figures and evidently shook the public's attitudes toward its elected representatives. Before 1977, there were a few isolated and sporadic cases where major Israeli public figures were involved in scandals. The volume, intensity, and rapidity of such accusations before 1977 did not parallel what happened after 1977.

The mid 1970s clearly witnessed a major change in the way Israeli political parties dealt with their deviants. Three elements of this period are very salient. First, the vulnerability of high political figures to suspicion and investigation, with full exposure in the media, became evident.[4] Second, many of the accused did not accept responsibility and used motivational accounting systems that blamed "the system." Many of them claimed that they were "only" doing what others had done before them and that "the system" had to carry the blame. Let me provide two examples. The first example is that of Mr. Yadlin, who was one of the most important political figures in the Ma'arach (Labor) party. He was accused in the late 1970s of mismanaging public funds and of corruption (mostly kickbacks and bribery). Mr. Yadlin was put on trial, found guilty as charged, and sentenced to serve time in prison. The motivational accounting systems that Mr. Yadlin used in public implied that what he did was a very common practice in "the system." The second example took place in 1980 and involved the then chief of the military police, Baruch Arbel, who was accused of abuse of his authority and of corruption. A military court found Arbel guilty. The vocabulary of motives that he used in his trial conveyed the very clear impression that he had "just" done what others had regularly done before him and that if he was to be found guilty then "the system" was guilty as well.

The legal advisor to the government proved to be a key figure in all these cases. It was up to him to decide on the opening of an investigation, on who was to be investigated, and on where and when to make formal accusations, and he had the authority to bring a case before a court or to close it. Hence, the power and independence of the advisor are great.

On this background, the Abu-hatzira case broke with fanfare, glamour, and full coverage in the media, between 1980 and 1983.

The case of Abu-hatzira: personal background. It is essential to understand Abu-hatzira's family and social background before describing and analyzing the case itself.

Aharon Abu-hatzira is the son of a famous Jewish family from Morocco. While the background of this family is an important issue, it is very difficult to trace and validate that history and to separate myth from reality. For example, many Moroccan Jewish families claim to have originated in seventeenth-century Palestine. However, these stories are quite standardized in folklore of Moroccan Jews, and it is impossible to validate or refute them. The following description, therefore, is based on the way the Abu-hatzira family chose to project its image in public. The reader should be cautious about the accuracy of this public image. The projection of this particular public image, however, is important.[5]

The Abu-hatzira family gives the account that it is originally traceable to seventeenth-century city of Jerusalem, when family members moved to Syria and Morocco. The branch of the Abu-hatzira family that settled in Morocco became highly respectable. Many members of the family were even considered by the local Jewish community as saints. The family had many famous rabbis.[6] Aharon Abu-hatzira's family is related to a very famous Moroccan "Admor"[7] — the Baba Sally (his uncle), who was regarded by many contemporaries as a true saint. The Baba Sally evidently certainly enjoyed the admiration of many Moroccan Jews who felt he was endowed and blessed with a rare divine grace — similar to the *baraka* (e.g., see Westermarck 1926, ch. 2, 3) known with regard to Moroccan Moslem saints. This divine grace is considered to be a positive supernatural power given to only a few. Itzhak Abu-hatzira, Aharon's father, was a well-known figure in Morocco. He supposedly helped to conquer the southern part of Morocco, for which it is claimed that he won a royal decoration. In 1925, the father visited Palestine for one year and made many contacts. He later returned to Morocco to receive a royal welcome from the Moroccan king. Aharon Abu-hatzira was born in 1939 in Morocco. When he was ten years old, all the Abu-hatzira family immigrated to the newly established Jewish state, Israel.[8] The family left virtually all of its considerable wealth in Morocco when it came to Israel. The family came to the town of Ramla,[9] where the father, Itzhak, was officially appointed chief rabbi of the town. Unofficially, it appeared that very many North African Jews in Israel considered Itzhak Abu-hatzira as their rabbi. Other members of the family have also received respectable and prestigious public positions. Thus, the father's brother became an "Admor" in "Netivot";[10] his son became the deputy mayor of Ashkelon; two other members of the family became rabbis of other Israeli towns. It is thus evident that Aharon Abu-hatzira descends from a prestigious, religious, well-to-do family.

Aharon Abu-hatzira, the oldest son, studied in schools in Ramla and Jerusalem and later studied literature and history at the religious Bar-Ilan University (in Israel) for four years. In 1968, he married Jarmen, who also descended from an established and respectable

Jewish-Moroccan family (Aharon and Jarmen now have six children). In 1969, Aharon Abu-hatzira began an intensive political activity and career within the Mafdal[11] party. Within a short period of time, he established himself as an important figure in that party. He held various political positions, among them the mayorship of Ramla (in 1970), where much of his political power was based. In 1973, Abu-hatzira won a seat in the Israeli parliament, the Knesset. After some political maneuvers, Abu-hatzira was successful in obtaining the position of the minister of religion in Begin's coalition government in 1977. This, certainly, was the peak of Abu-hatzira's political career. The position of minister of religion is a powerful one because the budget of this ministry is not a small one, and much of its funds are distributed at the minister's own discretion and/or recommendation.

The case of Abu-hatzira, an historical account. In the summer of 1980 the Israeli public learned from the media that Abu-hatzira was suspected of bribery and of abusing state funds. In October 1980, a few personal advisors to Minister Abu-hatzira were arrested, and Abu-hatzira himself was interrogated by the police. On December 2, 1980, Abu-hatzira was formally accused of taking bribes and abusing his position and public funds for personal and party goals. On January 12, 1981, the Israeli parliament decided to revoke Abu-hatzira's parliamentary immunity, and on January 16, 1981, for the first time in the history of the State of Israel, a government minister was officially indicted. The actual trial began on February 2, 1981, in Jerusalem.

The trial took place before three judges and lasted continuously until May 24, 1981. The court's discussions made headlines almost every day in the Israeli media, and heated arguments about the nature of the motivational accounting systems given during the trial proceedings were carried out publicly and privately throughout this period. Eventually, Minister Abu-hatzira was acquitted of the charges and found nonguilty, mostly because the prosecution could not prove the accusations "beyond the shadow of a doubt." The acquittal, however, was not a simple one. All three judges (Asher Landa, Eliezer Goldberg, and Yehuda Cohen) leveled devastating criticisms on the work methods and integrity of both Abu-hatzira and the Ministry of Religion. Abu-hatzira's working methods were defined by the court as "shocking" and as representing "a degraded and low level of public morality." One of the judges even held that Abu-hatzira apparently believed that politics and morality did not go hand in hand and that it was possible to use the state's funds, strictly allocated to the Ministry of Religion, for party needs.

During this trial, two other important events took place. The first was that another investigation and set of charges against Abu-hatzira began in January 1981. The general prosecution decided in February 1981 to formally indict Abu-hatzira again with new accusations of bribery and abuse of state funds. The second event was that new elections took place in Israel on June 30, 1981. The last day to submit the names of parties and candidiates for the Israeli parliament was at midnight on May 26, 1981. On this very date, in the evening, Abu-hatzira dramatically announced that he was leaving the Mafdal party in order to establish a new party, Tami.[12] The new party was officially registered just a few minutes before the midnight deadline. Appearing on Israeli television, Abu-hatzira's verbal and televised motivational accounting systems did not hide that the Tami party was intended mostly for Sephardic (or more specifically, Moroccan) Jews and that his disillusion with the Mafdal party propelled him to establish the Tami party.

Thus, the Tami party entered the election race for the tenth Israeli Knesset with little planning and budget and with hardly any preparations. The Tami party was not only in a rough, difficult, and sometimes violent election race, but it was also trying to crystallize itself as a party with its own identity and definable symbolic-moral universe and boundaries. The election took place on June 30, 1981, and Tami won three seats out of 120 in the Israeli Knesset, an impressive achievement by all accounts. The party eventually entered Begin's coalition government, and Abu-hatzira became the minister of labor and social affairs. This took place while the second investigation against him was still in process.

The second investigation against Abu-hatzira ended in May 1981, and he was formally accused a second time, on May 25, before a court in Tel Aviv, with charges of theft, fraud, and abuse of authority. The second trial was also a lengthy one, with full daily coverage in the media. On April 19, 1982, Abu-hatzira was found guilty as charged. He was fined and received a conditional prison sentence on April 24, 1982. During his second trial, Abu-hatzira resigned from his position as minister of labor and social affairs and devoted all his time to the trial. He did not, however, resign from his Knesset position.

Abu-hatzira appealed to the Israeli Supreme Court (criminal appeal no. 281/82), but he did not succeed. On August 7, 1983, and in a long and carefully reasoned verdict, the Israeli Supreme Court stated that Abu-hatzira had received an overly lenient sentence and decided that he must go to prison for three months. In reality, however, the Israeli police transformed Abu-hatzira's three-month prison sentence to so-called external work, meaning that he spent eight hours every day working in prison and returned to his home at night. Abu-hatzira began to serve his transformed prison sentence on October 2, 1983. At that time, he still retained his parliamentary position and was very active in politics, especially as the Tami party's undisputed leader.

Far from causing his criminalization and his disappearance from public life, it would appear that the criminal case against Minister Abu-hatzira was used by him to bolster his political career, establish a new party, gain three seats (out of 120 available) in the Israeli parliament, and enter the government. How was this possible? How and why was Minister Abu-hatzira able to transform what were *obvious* processes of degradation and stigmatization into events that worked in his favor?

The Abu-hatzira case can be approached from many different angles. Sociologically, I feel that the most important and fruitful approaches to it would be through religion and ethnicity, on the one hand, and politics and deviance, on the other hand. The dimensions of religion and ethnicity, very strong in this case, basically explain how and why Abu-hatzira was so successful in turning something that was supposedly a liability into an asset. The dimension of politics and deviance will be used to develop a general interpretative approach to this case, and to others.

RESISTING DEGRADATION, STIGMATIZATION, AND DEVIANTIZATION: THE RELIGIOUS AND ETHNIC DIMENSIONS

It appears that Minister Abu-hatzira's success in resisting and reversing processes of degradation, stigmatization, and deviantization was based on the convergence of a few conditions. To begin with, one must give credit to Abu-hatzira's stamina, which enabled him to withstand vilification, stigmatization and degradation. Had he been a weaker person he would probably not have survived. But this is only one of the conditions.

Abu-hatzira's major victory was his successful attempt to gain legitimacy and to mobilize support from at least the 44,466 people[13] who voted for him in the 1981 election. The support of and legitimacy given by these people (and presumably others who did not vote for him) throughout his trials, eventual conviction, and subsequent success in establishing a new party gave him his strength and enabled his success. Who were the people who voted for Abu-hatzira? Analyzing the votes of those people indicates that they were predominantly Jews who either came directly from Morocco to Israel or were the direct descendants of such, and who see themselves as "traditional" (i.e., observant Jews) in religious terms. Hence, Abu-hatzira's support was based on two major sources: religion and ethnicity.

When the first trial began, Abu-hatzira's initial reaction was to deny the accusations. Like Nixon and others before him, in August 1980 Abu-hatzira claimed that "the accusations against me are a provocation — it is all lies."[14] At that time, Abu-hatzira used a motivational accounting system that implied that a political attempt was made to smear all of the Mafdal party. He hinted then that some political figures in the Mafdal party were "after him" and would stop at nothing and even ruin the whole party. Retrospectively, it appears that in September–October 1980 Abu-hatzira realized that he had to do something about the serious allegations against him or else. It seems that he chose one more implicit line of defense and two other explicit lines of action. The implicit, but nonetheless very powerful, line of defense was to rely on his family's aura of Baraka and sacred halo of religiosity. The first explicit line was to try to mobilize the support of as many of the Moroccan Jewish community as possible, and Sephardic Jews generally. This implies an attempt to generate political power and influence and to get involved in a process of legitimization. Thus, this line also implied an attempt to redefine the moral boundaries of the Moroccan Jewish community in Israel and to try to negotiate for a possible inclusion of other Sephardic Jews within these boundaries. The second explicit line was an attempt to shatter the belief in the objectivity and fairness of the Israeli police, that is, to delegitimize the investigation. These two lines of action characterized Abu-hatzira's actions until 1984.

The religious dimension. This analysis indicates that Abu-hatzira was able to use in his favor his own (and his family's) religiosity, capitalizing on his uncle's (the Baba Sally) and father's reputations as respected and revered religious leaders. He was clearly able to manipulate the divine grace, similar to the *Baraka*, which was supposed to have been bestowed upon his relative, the Admor Baba Sally, into his own needs. A la Weber, when the symbolic confrontation was between the legal/rational symbolic-moral universe of the secular, civil laws of the modern State of Israel versus the traditional symbolic-moral universe of the traditional, religious law of the Moroccan Jewish community, and when Aharon Abu-hatzira was perceived to be part of a holy family, blessed with something supernaturally powerful as the *baraka*, then evidently Abu-hatzira could not be perceived by actors who saw themselves as inhabitants of his own symbolic-moral universe as doing something wrong. It must therefore be the secular symbolic-moral universe that was wrong.

The ethnic dimension. The religious dimension, however, was only one of the resources Abu-hatzira used. My analysis clearly indicates that Abu-hatzira was successful in creating a new party of his "own" people—that is, a significant portion of Jews of Moroccan roots who rallied after him. Strictly speaking, Abu-hatzira's appeal was limited mostly to members of his own community, sharing the same symbolic-moral universe, and his party did not attract many other voters. This is also the place to note that, while a significant part of Moroccan Jews supported Abu-hatzira and gave him legitimacy, clearly not all of them supported him.

One must notice, however, that this was also the first time in the history of Israel (since 1951) that anyone was able to create successfully a viable party along strict ethnic lines.[15] In the past, Israel's major political parties have tried to present a so-called ethnically balanced list of members. Their attempts, however, were not always successful and created many controversies. Tami's achievement should not be underplayed because the Zionist ideology strongly emphasizes the melting pot idea and is vehemently opposed to political organization along ethnic lines. One has to note, however, that this official ideology was not translated successfully into the structural level. Herzog's (1986) impressive work indeed documented the continuous failure of attempts to crystallize political parties along an ethnic platform. Indeed, Israeli society never legitimized such a crystallization. In this respect, Tami's success may be thought of as a possible breakthrough in the Israeli political scene, and hence as a possible opening for future social changes. The establishment of Tami could well mean the beginning of a process that would legitimize political organization along ethnic lines. It should be noted that in its official presentations Tami tried to avoid an ethnic identification, attempting, perhaps, to create an appeal to a larger audience. In reality, however, there could be no mistake as to who was the leader of this party and to exactly which audience it was addressed. Thus, Abu-hatzira's deviancy was used within the process of a major process of societal change in Israel—that of crystallization of ethnic consciousness geared toward enhancing the moral boundaries of particular ethnic symbolic-moral universes and of generation of political power and legitimacy for those universes.

Tami's achievement must not be taken for granted. We have to understand the successful appeal of Abu-hatzira to many members of his own symbolic-moral universe in terms of an ethnic group. To do so, we must also understand some aspects of the process of absorbing immigrants into Israeli society.

The Jewish population in Israel is composed of a variety of ethnic groups that originated in different parts of the world. One of the major, albeit very crude, divisions along ethnic lines in Israel is the one between Ashkenasic Jews and Sephardic Jews. The former are Jews from western and northern Europe, America, Canada, and Australia, who seem to have their own symbolic-moral universes clustered under the general umbrella of Ashkenasi. The latter are Jews from the Arab peninsula and from northern Africa. They also have their own symbolic-moral universes, clustered under a parallel umbrella. One *must* remember that this is a very crude division and that each ethnic group consists of a large and complex mosaic of other groups.

Moroccan Jews form a large ethnic group among the North African group of Sephardim. Most Moroccan Jews found Israel a difficult place. Many of them are lower working class whose settlement in Israel has been anything but easy. Consequently, the overwhelming majority of delinquents and deviants come from this specific ethnic group, which has acquired some negative stereotypes since the 1960s. In recent years, many conscious attempts have been made by Israeli officials, political parties, and some Moroccan Jews themselves to change the status and image of members of this group. Among the complaints brought by speakers for this group are accusations that Ashkenasic Jews have taken advantage of Moroccan Jews; that Moroccan Jews are underrepresented in management positions, government, army, universities, and parliament, but they are overrepresented in jails, juvenile delinquency, crime figures, and lower-class manual jobs.

In short, many Moroccan Jews feel that they are abused by "the establishment," predominantly dominated and controlled by Ashkenasic Jews. The confrontation between the symbolic-moral universe of Sephardic Jews in general and Moroccan Jews in particular and the symbolic-moral universe of Ashkenasi Jews is therefore clear. This confrontation, however, has existed in a very problematic culture. The symbolic-moral universe portrayed and dictated by the Zionist ideology emphasizes that Jews are *one* people. This ideology does not encourage a pluralistic culture where many clear and different symbolic-moral universes would coexist. Israel's official egalitarian ideology only reinforces this (e.g., see Cohen E. 1983).

Furthermore, for a very long time, many spokesmen for the Ashkenasi group denied the interpretation that Moroccan and Sephardic Jews were deliberately and systematically discriminated against. Because for a long period of time Sephardic Jews in general and Moroccan Jews in particular failed to generate a reliable, credible, and militant leadership (including academicians), their ability to develop generalized motivational accounting systems for their own symbolic-moral universe to explain past and to justify future behavior was virtually nil. In other words, Moroccan Jews were unable to develop a credible and persuasive vocabulary of motives and sets of political motivational accounting systems. When their symbolic-moral universe clashed with that of the Ashkenasi elite, they were stigmatized and deviantized by a variety of motivational accounting systems that pointed out their supposed inferiority and inadequacy in coping with the modern world.

In the last several years, a few leaders for this group arose (including a few intellectuals) who were more successful in developing and delivering generalized motivational accounting systems explaining the misery of this group in political (not psychological) terms. The crystallization of this ethnic group along or around these new leaders was very weak, however, and not significant.

Abu-hatzira, no doubt, *used* this friction between the symbolic-moral universe of Ashkenasi Jews and that of many Moroccan Jews in his favor. He was able to manipulate one side of this confrontation to support him. By doing this, he redefined the moral boundaries of many Moroccan Jews' symbolic-moral universe, giving inhabitants of this universe a better and stronger sense of togetherness, hence of an identity and cause. This redefinition of moral boundaries also gave actors a particular vocabulary of motives and plenty of motivational accounting systems. Abu-hatzira thus used the general existing bitterness and resentment of many Moroccan Jews to counteract the deviantization process. How was this done?

Abu-hatzira's utilization of the ethnic dispute and attempts to discredit the Israeli police. Throughout his trial, Abu-hatzira appeared very little in the media and hardly, if ever, granted an interview. For many, this qualified him for the "silent hero" role. However, his close associates appeared frequently in the media with absolutely no restraints. The motivational accounting systems given by these people implied that

Abu-hatzira was a victim of the elite Ashkenasi group in the Mafdal party. The motivational accounting systems they used made clear distinctions between Sephardic and Ashkenasic Jews, thus helping to draw the moral boundaries between these two symbolic-moral universes.

At the beginning, Abu-hatzira himself used his parliamentary immunity and refused to be investigated. After pressure from Prime Minister Menachem Begin and the legal advisor to the government (himself an Ashkenasic Jew) Abu-hatzira agreed to be investigated in October 1980. At that time, the minister for police affairs was Dr. Joseph Burg, himself an Ashkenasic Jew and from the Mafdal party. On August 29, 1980, Abu-hatzira announced that he would not intervene or stop the police investigation. Editorials that began to appear in late August 1980 in the Israeli daily newspapers urged Abu-hatzira to quit his position until his trial ended.

Already in September 1980, a few prominent Sephardic Jews began to organize and mobilize support for Abu-hatzira. While this early mobilization emphasized that it was *for* Abu-hatzira and not *against* anybody in particular, some of the statements made implied that the Abu-hatzira case was just one more attack by Ashkenasic Jews against Sephardic Jews. The fact that the two symbolic-moral universes were confronted so early only hinted at what was going to unfold later.

In early September 1980, it became known that a central witness in the Abu-hatzira case was Israel Gottlieb, an Ashkenasic Jew, then the mayor of Bnei-Brak.[16]

In October 1980, Minister Abu-hatzira was first interrogated by the police. Afterward the police stated that the minister did not answer, or avoided answering, the questions put to him. Abu-hatzira said that he was innocent, that he had to face loaded and biased questions, and that he did not intend to answer any more unfair questions. Later that month, Abu-hatzira and his close friends demanded that the Israeli police reveal the nature of the evidence against him and implied that the police officer in charge of the investigation, Mr. Ziegel, was an Ashkenasic Jew who wanted to degrade Abu-hatzira because the latter was a member of the Moroccan Jewish community.

The months of October–November 1980 witnessed an actual public fight between Abu-hatzira and the police. Editorials in the daily press expressed concern that Abu-hatzira was actually discrediting the Israeli police.[17] This "war" escalated when on December 2, 1982, it was decided to formally accuse Abu-hatzira, and the Knesset started to debate revoking Abu-hatzira's parliamentary immunity. Under this immunity, a Knesset member cannot be brought to trial unless he/she willingly gives up the immunity or unless the Knesset takes immunity away from that member.

On December 12, 1980, the legal advisor to the government formally asked the Knesset to revoke Abu-hatzira's parliamentary immunity so that prosecution would be possible. Abu-hatzira objected fiercely. He hired two prominent and expensive lawyers to help him. From December 12, 1980, until January 12, 1981, the three of them fought against revoking Abu-hatzira's immunity. The way this fight was handled is most instructive.

The discussion regarding revoking Abu-hatzira's parliamentary immunity took place in a parliamentary committee. In general, the reason for such a discussion is not to determine whether or not a specific parliamentary member is guilty, but to make sure that no political motivation lies behind the accusations. Abu-hatzira's lawyers turned this discussion into a public political debate. They tried to show that, in fact, there was a political conspiracy against Abu-hatzira. Already on December 12, 1980, Abu-hatzira's lawyers issued a public statement indicating that the media and the police were conducting an intentional and deliberate campaign to smear Abu-hatzira and gave the account that he "was found guilty" even before a trial had actually begun. During the discussions in the Knesset's committee, the representatives of the Israeli police found themselves constantly under heated questioning by Abu-hatzira's lawyers. Very gradually this debate moved toward focusing on ethnic issues. As early as December 3, 1980, Dan Margalit, an influential journalist, wrote in the daily newspaper *Ha'aretz* that the only action that could probably help Abu-hatzira would be to use his ethnicity. Later, parliament member Saadia Marziano (himself of Moroccan descent) told the public that he would organize street demonstrations for Abu-hatzira because he saw the accusations against Abu-hatzira as directed against all Moroccan-descended Jews. Furthermore, on December 18, 1980, the Israeli public learned[18] that rich Sephardic Jews in New York had contributed $100,000 for Abu-hatzira's defense.

Formally, however, the ethnic issue was not brought up by Abu-hatzira in December 1980. The main motivational accounting system that he used at that time was that he was persecuted because some members in his party, the Mafdal, wanted to get rid of him. He also accused the Israeli police of conducting an unfair and biased investigation.

There can be little doubt that Abu-hatzira, consciously and

intentionally, used the discussions in the parliament committee to generate positive public support and to discredit the police at the same time. So successful was this effort that on December 16, 1980, Mati Golan wrote in Ha'aretz that: "judging by what is happening these days in the Knesset's committee . . . one might get the impression that the real accused is not Abu-hatzira . . . but . . . the police and the legal advisor to the government. . . . " Abu-hatzira himself gave an account in which he admitted,[19] on December 12, 1980, that he used the publicity of the discussion to create a "positive exposure" for himself. This technique implies that Abu-hatzira was involved in a process where morality was negotiated. He used every opportunity he had not only to accuse his accusers but also to show that despite all the allegations he believed in his innocence and was not so bad as the accounts of his accusers implied.

Abu-hatzira's first trial.   On January 12, 1981, Abu-hatzira's parliamentary immunity was finally revoked, and his trial began on January 16, of that year. Abu-hatzira denied all the allegations. The trial was accompanied by clear and blunt ethnic statements, and it was this trial that enabled Abu-hatzira to emerge as *the* "tormented and persecuted" Sephardic Jew.

Already on February 18, a key state witness in the trial (an Ashkenasic Jew) was attacked and beaten by unknown people. The defense in the trial literally "grilled" each and every witness for the prosecution. One of the most important state witnesses, Israel Gottlieb, changed his testimony while on the stand. During his testimony, it was disclosed that the police had used an undercover agent to persuade Gottlieb, an Ashkenasic Jew (then mayor of Bnei-Brak), to testify against Abu-hatzira. This undercover agent recorded his conversations with Gottlieb, and transcripts of these conversations were made public.[20] There can be hardly any question that during those conversations the undercover agent defamed Abu-hatzira, using dirty stereotypical language specifically aimed at Moroccan Jews.[21] That in itself obviously aroused much turmoil. On February 20, 1981, two more witnesses for the prosecution changed their testimony.

On March 9, 1981, Abu-hatzira himself took the witness stand. The motivational accounting systems that he used denied all the accusations against him and implied that Ashkenasic members in the Mafdal party (he actually gave names) tried to reorganize some party members along ideological lines. According to Abu-hatzira, these members' ideology was that Abu-hatzira was a dangerous person because he supposedly wanted to make sure that the Mafdal party would be dominated by Sephardic Jews thereby putting an end to the traditional Ashkenasic dominance. Abu-hatzira insisted that *this* was the reason for his being persecuted.

This defense was very interesting. On the one hand, Abu-hatzira's motivational accounting system attributed the accusations to a party conspiracy against him. On the other hand, the same motivational accounting system implied that it was not "just" an inner party dispute but also a dispute along *ethnic* lines. In other words, Abu-hatzira maintained his innocence and presented himself as one more "persecuted" Sephardic Jew.

Although the judges leveled a devastating criticism against Abu-hatzira, he nevertheless was found not guilty.

Following the announcement of this verdict, on May 25, 1981, many of his supporters (who came to the trial daily), carried him on their shoulders to the sacred Wailing Wall in Jerusalem yelling and shouting "he is holy," "he is a saint," which seems almost natural for people who apparently believed that Abu-hatzira was blessed with the sacred *baraka*.

Abu-hatzira's second trial. As can be remembered, another trial against Abu-hatzira was carried out throughout 1981–1982. Let me remind the reader that between these trials Abu-hatzira established his new party, Tami, and won three seats in parliament during the 1981 general elections.

The second trial, in many respects, was similar to the first one. Some state witnesses changed their testimony at the last minute; the trial generated many discussions on ethnicity and certainly served as one more catalyst in solidifying many Moroccan Jews against those that they perceived as their oppressors. The ethnic language in this trial was more blunt and explicit than in the first trial. At one point (December 12, 1981) Abu-hatzira's lawyers wanted to resign because they claimed that the judge presiding over the case had expressed a stereotypical anti-Moroccan Jews statement. This specific controversy arrived at the Israeli Supreme Court, which on January 6, 1982, discarded the whole episode as overblown beyond any reasonable proportion by Abu-hatzira's lawyers. In the minds of many Sephardic Moroccan Jews, however, this particular turn of events was taken as yet another indication that the whole trial was biased. In a few instances, the judge had to put witnesses in their proper place. For example, when Abu-hatzira's wife testified (January 1, 1982), the judge, Victoria Ostrovsky Cohen, had to tell her that the court was not a theater. She also had to tell Moshe Gabai on January 22, 1982: "don't try to make us look like fools." On January 21, 1982, the police had to place twenty-four-hour guards around the judge because of anonymous threats against her and an attempt to blow up the gas tanks in the house where she lived.

As in the first trial, Abu-hatzira's supporters crowded the court house whenever he was there. When, on April 19, 1982, he was found guilty as charged, a wild scene in the court house developed into a small riot. The police had to use force, and some Moroccan Jews threatened that they would "turn Israel upside down." So bad was this incident that the president of Israel and the president of the Israeli Supreme Court expressed their amazement and shock at what had happened. On April 23, 1982,[22] both warned publicly that the occurrences in Tel Aviv on April 19, 1982, could in fact threaten the basis of law in Israel.

Crystallizing a symbolic-moral universe.   Obviously, Abu-hatzira was able to tap a deep and bitter reservoir of feelings. When some Sephardic Jews felt they could give a more or less free expression to their hostilities, the Israeli public was literally stunned to hear some of their ideas. For example, a young Moroccan Jew appeared on a talk show on Israeli television stating that he felt he was at war with Ashkenasic Jews.[23] Another, much worse incident took place in the form of writings on public walls. As is well known, Ashkenasic Jews suffered the most during World War II, when the Nazis exterminated about 6 million European Jews. Many survivors of Hitler's death camps found their new home in Israel. One can imagine the anger, anguish, and amazement of Ashkenasic Jews to discover a "new" word appearing on public walls: ASHKENAZI, which is a combination of ASHKENASI and NAZI, aimed against Ashkenasic Jews.

Abu-hatzira, at that time, used motivational accounting systems in which he claimed that he was trying "to contain the dangerous ethnic fire" and again accused the "system" of persecuting him. He stated that he was about to shatter some elements of the system to which he had fallen victim. The establishment of Tami by Abu-hatzira, and his success in the 1981 elections, should be interpreted in this context.

What Abu-hatzira did during his two trials was to crystallize in his support the feelings of a significant part of the Moroccan Jews in Israel. Among the other processes that Abu-hatzira activated and used, he also transformed his two otherwise regular criminal trials into *political trials.*

He was also successful in attracting the support of a small number of non-Moroccan Sephardic Jews. He brought to focus feelings of being discriminated against and of not getting a fair share of the "national pie." The nature of Abu-hatzira's family helped this process, for some of his relatives were held to be saints, and he was considered by many as another saint. How could a saint be wrong? How could anyone from such a family be found guilty? Thus, Abu-hatzira could, and did, play the role of a quasi martyr, *the* prototype symbol of the Sephardic victim in the Ashkenasic system, giving clear expression to hidden feelings. Abu-hatzira helped Moroccan Jews rebuild a symbolic-moral universe and redefine its moral boundaries. This universe building provided many Moroccan Jews with plenty of motivational accounting systems to explain why they were where they were (e.g., a result of systematic Ashkenasic discrimination), and it gave them the opportunity to generate political power.

This is also the place to reemphasize that, although Abu-hatzira attracted a significant number of Moroccan Jews, not all of them supported him. A few even objected to Tami, and many other Moroccan Jews felt that they had succeeded as a result of their own efforts and were not, consequently, bitter or frustrated. It is interesting to note that Tami attracted a few Sephardic intellectuals who felt that they were discriminated against and thought that they could contribute to Tami's ideological aspect, not to mention to bolster their own careers.

A possible alternative explanation, Zeitgeist.   Finally, one must consider another problem. Is it possible that the ethnic tensions in Israel reached such a point during the early 1980s that the cultural and political climate was ripe for an ethnic explosion? In this sense, the Abu-hatzira incident could be thought of as a timely catalyst, but it is also possible that somebody else could have done the same. This, of course, is the ghost of the Zeitgeist type of explanation.

While it is virtually impossible to totally rule out this possibility, there are few good reasons not to adhere to it too tightly. First, the fact is that Abu-hatzira, and not someone else, served as a catalyst is something that should not be ignored. Other Sephardic Jews tried to do the same before him without the same results. When the Abu-hatzira case exploded, other Sephardic Jews were trying to integrate the Sephardic Jewish community in Israel (perhaps on a less radical or militant platform), and they were not successful. Second, in the 1981 elections, there were other parties, competing for seats in the Knesset, that were clearly based on ethnic lines; their success was virtually zero. Third, one must notice that the voters for Tami were predominantly traditional Moroccan Jews. My guess is that had Abu-hatzira tried to establish Tami before his trials he would not have succeeded as well as he did after the trials. His trials gave him a golden opportunity (which he was clever enough to understand) to focus and crystallize a significant part of the minority subculture of Sephardic Jews into one political party. This crystallization could not have taken place prior to his trials, at least not on such a large scope. The public exposure of the case gave Abu-hatzira almost free access to the mass media. He used this exposure to create a positive image of himself in the eyes of many Moroccan Jews. Finally, therefore, the interpretation presented here, both in ethnic terms and in the resulting politicization of deviance concept, to a very large extent weakens the possibility of a strong Zeitgeist explanation.

Summary.   Abu-hatzira was very successful in resisting and reversing strong stigmatization, degradation, and deviantization processes aimed against him. He not only resisted these processes but, in fact, used them to bolster his political career. By using his ethnicity, family religious background, and reputation, Abu-hatzira manipulated feelings of general resentment by many Moroccan Jews in particular and Sephardic Jews in general. He emerged successfully as *the* person upon whom, supposedly, Ashkenasic "hatred" was aimed, and for many of his own ethnic group, his trial symbolized their plight and fight for recognition. Against this background, Abu-hatzira's trials were turned into political statements and became an actual asset for him. It is doubtful whether he could have won three seats in the parliament without the trials.

By neutralizing the accusations against him and reversing deviantization, Abu-hatzira was successful in at least putting his previous party, the Mafdal, the Israeli police, the legal advisor to the government, and the Israeli legal system under a heavy shadow. In this sense, Abu-hatzira's trials are certainly more than just a passing episode in the political or ethnic history of Israel. These trials touched some very *basic* tensions in contemporary Israeli society, bringing into the open implicit conflicts and direct threats in the very delicate Israeli social fabric. Thus, an affair in deviance turned into a significant process of social change in Israel. One must remember, however, that despite all this Abu-hatzira's success was accomplished *within* the existing Israeli "rules of the game" — political as well as legal, although sometimes bordering on the very edges of these rules.

Furthermore, after Abu-hatzira finished serving his prison term in 1983, he was apparently accepted by all major Israeli political leaders as their equal, with no stigma attached. He even played a major political role in March 1984, when the Israeli Knesset decided on rescheduling the general elections in the country.[24]

RESISTING AND REVERSING DEVIANTIZATION: POLITICIZATION OF DEVIANCE

The case of Abu-hatzira evidently involves open and explicit questions focusing on issues of power and morality. Furthermore, I have stated before that there is a clear relationship between the moral status of a particular type of deviants and the social position of that group (e.g., Rock's 1973b ideas about the societal system of moral stratification and Becker's 1967 concept of hierarchies of credibility). Lower social and moral position of deviants increases the probability that they will in fact be regarded as deviants (i.e., deviantized) and eventually acquire a deviant identity. A change in the social position of the deviant will also change the moral meaning of the deviancy.

Abu-hatzira used his high position in a few hierarchies—religious, government, and ethnic—to gain credibility and to generate support for his version of events and to avoid acquiring a deviant identity. In accordance with Rock's (1973b) thesis, Abu-hatzira was certainly actively involved in a deliberate attempt to organize and persuade other people to redefine "important sectors of the world," hence redefine boundaries of symbolic-moral universes.

Contrary to Douglas' (1970b) thesis that "deviance" and "respect ability" are diametrically opposed, Abu-hatzira proved that "deviance" could, under a specific set of conditions, be politicized and used to gain respectability. Abu-hatzira did this by using micro motivational accounting systems that helped to transform, change, and crystallize generalized motivational accounting systems of many members of the Moroccan Jewish community. Doing that necessarily meant changing moral boundaries. Furthermore, Abu-hatzira was not only involved in generating legitimacy for his own version of reality but was also actively involved in generating political power so as to give his symbolic-moral universe added strength. Abu-hatzira was able to put himself within the center of the symbolic-moral universe of many Moroccan Jews. It is true that even before his trials he was a very prominent leader among this ethnic group, but the criminal trials that he turned into political trials gave him the opportunity to become much more prominent and salient. In the eyes of many Moroccan Jews, Abu-hatzira and his trials symbolized their own plight. Thus, Abu-hatzira did not only occupy a respectable seat in a center and its enveloping symbolic-moral universe; he also changed, molded, and redefined the moral boundaries of that universe.

Labeling theory generally posits a one-way directional process of stigmatization and degradation. Is it possible to neutralize or even reverse the direction of this process? Better yet, is it possible to *use* these processes for the deviant's own advantage? Using the Israeli case of Abu-hatzira, this chapter illustrates that a positive answer to these questions is possible. Abu-hatzira, who was accused of being involved in such down-to-earth violations of the law as theft, mismanagement of state funds, abuse of position, falsification of documents, and the like, was able not only to neutralize these accusations but also to harness the trials against him to reverse the deviantization process for his own political advantage.

In counteracting processes of stigmatization, degradation, and deviantization, Abu-hatzira first denied the allegations against him; then he attacked and accused his own accusers, very much in accordance with one of Sykes and Matza's (1957) techniques of neutralization. However, one has to realize that the Abu-hatzira case goes far beyond neutralizing the process of deviantization.

Neutralization of accusations means that, although the accusations are neutralized, they do not disappear. Such cases as those of former President Nixon and Watergate and of Ted Kennedy and the Chappequidic incident illustrate how deviances were neutralized. However, neither Nixon nor Kennedy were able to *resist* the deviantization process, much less *reverse* them. By contrast, Abu-hatzira was able not only to neutralize the accusations against him but in fact to resist and reverse them. In the eyes of many Moroccan Jews, Abu-hatzira was never stigmatized or deviantized, on the contrary. Many Moroccan Jews in Israel gave Abu-hatzira their full and enthusiastic support because they could see in him, as one journalist put it,[25] their tormented "Moroccan Prince," carrying the entire burden of their own long plight. Using this source, Abu-hatzira was able to politicize a regular type of deviance.

The interpretative motivational accounting systems Abu-hatzira offered for why he was accused negated all guilt and transferred guilt and evil from him to his accusers. Furthermore, these micro motivational accounting systems fitted very well into macro motivational accounting systems and gave acceptable and credible social interpretations for the plight of Moroccan Jews in Israel. Having done that, and using his high position in a few selected hierarchies of credibility, he was able not only to resist but actually to reverse the process of stigmatization, degradation, and deviantization. Put otherwise, Abu-hatzira turned these processes upside-down.

Abu-hatzira and his supporters were involved in negotiating, creating, and marking new social and moral boundaries. The vocabularies of motives that fueled the societal reaction of part of the non-Ashkenasic Jews to Abu-hatzira's deviance were transformed and removed from the personal level into the collective level. Abu-hatzira, and his adherents, relied on the symbolic-moral universe of the traditional Moroccan Jews. They focused and crystallized the resentment of many of these Jews against what they portrayed as their arch-enemy, the Ashkenasic Jews.

The Ashkenasic symbolic-moral universe was portrayed as the cause for all the problems of Moroccan Jews in general and the plight of Abu-hatzira in particular. In this fashion, Abu-hatzira and his followers were involved in publicly creating and reinforcing new social-moral boundaries between two ethnic groups. Their portrayal clearly helped many of the Moroccan Jews to understand not only their past plight but also the agonizing process one of their most prestigious figures had to endure. Abu-hatzira's camp portrayed a struggle that supposedly was taking place between the Ashkenasic and the Sephardic symbolic-moral universes. Their portrayal of this struggle, and the vocabularies of motives that they used, lend much support to Berger and Luckmann's (1966) concept of "universe maintenance" and to their observation that when two contradictory symbolic-moral universes meet a conflict is unavoidable. "Heretical groups posit not only a theoretical threat to the symbolic universe, but a practical one to the institutional order legitimated by the symbolic universe in question" (p. 124). Furthermore, Berger and Luckmann suggested the concept of "nihilation," meaning an attempt by inhabitants of one symbolic universe "to liquidate conceptually everything *outside* the same universe" (p. 132). Nihilation denies the legitimacy of reality interpretations, or motivational accounting systems that originate in other symbolic-moral universes. That the inhabitants living in the symbolic-moral universe that Abu-hatzira defined were involved in attempts to nihilate what they saw as the opposing Ashkenasic symbolic-moral universe is irrefutable.[26] Members of Abu-hatzira's symbolic-moral universe tried to deviantize those who they felt were deviantizing Abu-hatzira, that is, deviantizing the deviantizers.

The conditions required for Abu-hatzira's success. There were a few conditions that enabled Abu-hatzira's success. First, the existence of two potentially antagonistic symbolic-moral universes in Israel, divided by a deep ethnic conflict. Abu-hatzira was identified as an inhabitant of one of these symbolic-moral universes, one of the underdogs. Second, Abu-hatzira's success was reinforced because he was able to harness and coordinate a religious consciousness along the ethnic dispute and therefore appear in the focus of these two symbolic-moral universes combined. Third, many Israeli Moroccan Jews' perceived Abu-hatzira as a "fighter" for their cause. The micro motivational accounting systems he and his supporters used were translated by inhabitants of this symbolic-moral universe into generalized motivational accounting systems. This translation became possible because it illustrated for this particular group how a Sephardic Jew may suffer from the dominant Ashkenasic Jews.

What was the nature of the vocabulary of motives and the types of motivational accounting systems that were used by Abu-hatzira? He denied the allegations against him; later he attributed these allegations to a party conspiracy against Sephardic Jews;[27] he was very active in attempts to delegitimize the police and the legal advisor to the government as projecting Ashkenasic moral and social dominance. Members of the minority group who shared a symbolic-moral universe with Abu-hatzira could accept his motivational accounting systems as credible interpretations of reality because they "made sense" to them and appeared sincere (in the Goffmanian sense of the term, that is, the actor truly believes in what he/she says). These motivational accounting systems "made sense" to members of this particular subculture because they felt part of an excluded and disadvantaged group. Abu-hatzira, as a potential spokesman for them, used motivational accounting systems that were understood and widely shared by members of his minority community *because* they provided ready-made and credible interpretations for what they saw as their social and moral essence.

The uniqueness of the case. One may finally ask: What is so unique about the Abu-hatzira case? After all, scores of politicians in Israel and in other countries have been accused of a variety of crimes. The answer to this question lies in three points.

First, very few, if any, politicians (in and outside Israel) were able in the past to manipulate formal, public contemporary criminal accusations against them into real electoral assets.

One could, perhaps, argue that such examples as Hitler's imprisonment after the Beer Hall putsch, the trials of Ku Klux Klan and other militant segregationists in the U.S. South, and Robert Kennedy's prosecution of Jimmy Hoffa make the Abu-hatzira case *not* unique. Such comparisons, however, are obviously wrong and irrelevant. Hitler did *not* use his criminalization as the main impetus for bolstering his political career. Abu-hatzira did. Abu-hatzira's criminalization *was* the central process that he managed to reverse. Furthermore, Abu-hatzira was an *important government minister,* located very high in the societal hierarchies of respectability, morality, and credibility when the processes of criminalization and deviantization occurred. I am not aware that *any* of the above examples (or other similar ones) fit this. These characteristics most certainly make this case unique in its historical dynamics and implications.

As I pointed out earlier, there seems to be at least one category of deviance where being deviantized and stigmatized can be potentially used for the deviant's own benefit and that is so-called political deviance. Many successful politicians have utilized their past "political" deviances as an asset.

For example, past participation in a "liberating-revolutionary" movement is often employed by politicians to help gain legitimacy and support. That members in such movements probably commit dozens of acts of deviance (e.g., bank robberies, kidnapings, bombings, etc.) seems to have virtually no negative impact. In some instances, a past "regular" criminal record was used as an asset in political careers. This was clearly the case with politicization of prisons[28] or with such motivational accounting systems as the one attributed to Eldridge Cleaver (1968, 14) and that implied that whenever a black man rapes a white woman a political statement is being made. Menachem Begin, former Israeli prime minister, was the commander-in-chief of the Irgun (ETZEL), a group that was defined as "terrorist" and persecuted by the British mandate forces in Palestine in the 1940s. There can hardly be a question that Begin utilized his position in the ETZEL as a political asset because it was regarded by many Israelis as a true resistance movement. Likewise, many people regard the Italian Red Brigades, Irish IRA, and the Palestinian PLO as "terrorist groups," while others regard them as true liberating movements.

However, while different political figures were able to politicize various past deviances and use their past "deviant" record to bolster a later political career, being part of a contemporary and legitimate political system and *then* being accused of such crimes as theft, abuse of authority, mismanagement of public funds, and the like is a very different issue. After all, how could a social actor who was located in the upper echelons of the hierarchy of credibility and who was, presumably, a symbol of conventional morality and guardian of a symbolic-moral universe, justify such an act to other members of the same symbolic-moral universe? The obvious answer is that this actor cannot do it satisfactorily. A possible way out of this dilemma is to invoke the influence of another, preferably contradictory, symbolic-moral universe.

Attributing assumed deviance to accusations made by inhabitants of another and opposing symbolic-moral universe was the technique Abu-hatzira used. Abu-hatzira presented the accusations against him as persecutions on the part of Ashkenasic Jews propelled by a political motivation against Sephardic Jews in general and Moroccan Jews in particular.

While in the past criminal procedures were used for political purposes to smear and stigmatize those who were suspected of being political opponents, Abu-hatzira's case illustrates that such processes can be reversed and have a "boomerang effect." In this case, a process of criminalization and deviantization was used to advance a political career. Instead of a criminalization of political dissent, a politicization of deviance took place.

This is also the place to note that while other politicians in similar situations could neutralize deviantization they could not reverse the process. These politicians were perceived as the upkeepers of morality, and once a deviantization process began, the most they could do was to neutralize it. They could not rely on a symbolic-moral universe in the form of a minority group that embraced and supported their motivational accounting systems; hence, they were not able to mobilize and generate enough power and support in their favor.

Second, Abu-hatzira's trials were, without doubt, very important events in the contemporary history of Israel. These trials, more than anything else, served as a focal point to crystallize and sharpen the demarcation lines and political conflicts between Sephardic and Ashkenasic Jews in Israel. It was the first time in the history of the country that this implicit conflict generated an institutional organization, culminating in the successful establishment of a small party based on ethnicity. This party was generally perceived as representing the grievances of Moroccan Jews in particular and Sephardic Jews in general. Tami's existence gave legitimation and direct expression to hidden feelings that had never before had such a direct and respectable voice.

Furthermore, Abu-hatzira's trial was another trial in a list of many others that started in the 1970s. Following the 1973 Yom Kippur War, the authority and legitimacy of political figures in Israel were eroded, and trust in these leaders decreased. It seems that parties in Israel shifted the focus of social control mechanisms from inside, informal ones to formal and external ones like deviantization and criminalization. The growing list of public figures accused of a variety of deviant behaviors testifies to this.

The Abu-hatzira trials thus constituted two peaks in a long process that consisted of a combination of three factors: (1) deep changes in Israel's party mechanisms of social control; (2) decreasing trust of Israel's public in its leaders; and (3) an increasingly aggressive role assumed by the media.

Third, one should note the fascinating way in which Abu-hatzira was able to politicize a criminal accusation and make an important political statement with it. This process does not happen very frequently.

Possible generalizations. The question about possible generalizations from this case is an important one. The most obvious generalization relates to an important issue in the theory of deviance. The Abu-hatzira case evidently demonstrates that, under a specific set of conditions, processes of degradation, stigmatization, and deviantization not only may be neutralized but also may be resisted and even reversed. This is an important observation. We have cases where various types of regular deviance were attributed to political figures and where those figures were able to neutralize the accusation (e.g., Kennedy and the Chappequidic case, Richard Nixon and Watergate, Willie Brandt and the spy caught in his staff, etc.). We even have cases where different social actors accused of various types of regular deviance were able to politicize these accusations (e.g., Angela Davis' case, the politicization of prisons, or some claims made by black militant leaders in the United States). Being able to politicize deviance and successfully reverse its effects, however, is less common and, for obvious reasons, much more interesting.

This brings us to another possible generalization that is about the way resisting and reversing a process of deviantization may operate.

The case presented in this chapter points out that the first step in this process is to politicize a "regular" type of deviance (or crime). For such a politicization to be successful, the micro motivational accounting systems for deviance must be transformed into a generalized and politically meaningful motivational accounting system in a way that would mobilize social forces (e.g., using an ethnic dispute). Furthermore, this generalized political motivational accounting system must be directed to a population that not only is willing to listen but also could be persuaded to adopt and use these generalized motivational accounting systems and to act (e.g., the existence of a disadvantaged, excluded minority group). In short, a symbolic-moral universe, or an ideology, has to be found or invented.

The concept or ideology that is referred to is again (see chapter five and note 9 in that chapter) that of Geertz (1964, 47–76). The function of ideology here is to provide authoritative concepts capable of rendering the situation meaningful and "suasive images" by which their meaning can be "sensibly grasped," and that can arouse emotions and direct mass action so as to relieve existing strain. In this framework, it is easy to see how Abu-hatzira became a "suasive image" in, and a moral crusader for, the specific symbolic-moral universe of Moroccan Jews. He provided a vocabulary of motives that was capable of "explaining" their feelings of being systematically discriminated against by resorting to an interpretation that posited him as the contemporary "Moroccan Jewish Prince" who fell victim to the old Sephardic-Ashkenasic conflict. With this explanation, he was able to transform the process of deviantization and stigmatization against him into a credible and powerful political motivational accounting system. Thus, an association with a symbolic-moral universe, or with an ideology, seems to be also crucial for resisting and reversing processes of degradation, stigmatization, and deviantization.

What the Abu-hatzira case implies is that a social actor, located at a high position in the social hierarchies of morality, respectability, and morality, was able to turn the tables on the state by crystallizing and generating an independent power base that questioned the legitimacy of the state, from an ideological point of view. It was the Abu-hatzira case that actually gave a previously politically mute group an opportunity to express itself loud and clear.

While the case of Abu-hatzira is very specific in terms of culture and time, the analysis provided in this chapter indicates that whenever similar conditions (obviously, in different cultures) are created one may expect similar results. One must remember that ethnicity was the major factor that enabled Abu-hatzira to do what he did, after all, and ethnic disputes are certainly not a unique characteristic of Israeli society.

CONCLUDING SUMMARY

This chapter examined a reversal of a process of deviantization by a major political figure in Israel. This process was described and interpreted within broader processes of social change in Israel. The reversal of deviantization by Abu-hatzira cannot be understood without understanding some of the major ethnic tensions in Israeli society, as well as some of the political transformations in the Israeli political system during the 1970s. Although Abu-hatzira was obviously interested in his own career, his actions crystallized and gave expression to a large minority group. As such, the reversal of Abu-hatzira's deviantization also gave legitimation and respectability for political organization along ethnic lines—something that was not perceived as legitimate prior to the establishment of Tami.

In this chapter, we could see not only how deviance and reactions to it were relativized but also how they became central elements in a major process of social change.

In the Abu-hatzira case, an important social actor from the societal center, positioned very high on the hierarchy of morality and credibility, recruited the periphery to help him reverse a process of deviantization and criminalization that was directed against him from the center itself. This process was analyzed in a dynamic and historical perspective, taking into consideration total social structures. We saw how in the process of deviantization, and of its reversal, different symbolic-moral universes clashed and negotiated power and morality.

The micro accounts used by Abu-hatzira and his supporters were integrated with the generalized macro motivational accounting systems in an attempt to achieve the desired synthesis between the micro and the macro levels of analysis.

The central question that this chapter addresses is whether, and under what conditions, processes of degradation, stigmatization, and deviantization can be resisted and reversed. Having analyzed and documented the case of Abu-hatzira, one must admit that, in fact, these processes *can* be reversed.

The analysis and interpretation of the Abu-hatzira case was clustered along three axes.

First, the case itself was documented.

Second, the success of Abu-hatzira in resisting and reversing processes of degradation, stigmatization, and deviantization was explained. A few factors, and tensions, explain the success of Abu-hatzira. First, there was Abu-hatzira's strong character. Second, Abu-hatzira was able to rely on a popular perception of many Moroccan Jews that he was a member of a family blessed with the sacred *baraka*. Hence, he was perceived as having a religious charisma. Third, Abu-hatzira used a bitter and deep ethnic dispute that exists in Israeli society between Ashkenasic and Sephardic Jews by using motivational accounting systems that gave Moroccan Jews a plausible structure of interpretation for what they felt was a long and systematic discrimination against them. To use Levi-Strauss's (1963, ch. nine and ten) example, Abu-hatzira manufactured motivational accounting systems that "made sense" to these traditional Moroccan Jews because they turned an unclear and threatening situation into something that was meaningful and comprehensible, together with a "suasive image." Fourth, it can be argued that the case of Abu-hatzira represents a conflict between the Weberian traditional and legal/rational bases of authority. The Weberian conceptualization is helpful in this particular regard because it enables us to understand that, while Abu-hatzira may have behaved in a "normal" manner for someone operating from a traditional base of legitimacy, this behavior became to be defined as "corruption" under the legal/rational basis of legitimacy. Hence, the Abu-hatzira case also illustrates another major cleavage in the newly crystallizing Israeli society—the one between traditional and legal/rational bases of legitimacy and authority. Thus, the interpretation of the Abu-hatzira case becomes even more pronounced within *major* societal processes of change and stability in Israeli society.

Third, it was pointed out that the way to resist and reverse processes of degradation, stigmatization, and deviantization was found to consist of politicization of a "regular" type of deviance by translating micro and personal motivational accounting systems into credible and meaningful generalized political motivational accounting systems that would redefine the boundaries of particular symbolic-moral universes. This in itself was not enough. This process had to occur within the context of an effective ideology geared to mobilize a receptive audience that would be willing to embrace and to act on the generalized vocabulary of motives. In other words, to crystallize a symbolic-moral universe and to redraw its moral boundaries.

While this chapter focused on a particular case within a specific culture, the analysis goes beyond this specificity indicating that whenever similar conditions are created one may expect similar results.

Part Four

Concluding
Discussion

Chapter Nine

Concluding Discussion

This last chapter of the book has two goals: first, to summarize its main arguments and, second, to explore some of the theoretical implications of the approach taken in it.

SUMMARY OF MAIN ARGUMENTS

The concept of deviance was used in this book in a different way than its usual application. The work in this book continues the argument I made in my previous book (1985): to place the concept of deviance within mainstream sociological analysis. The emphasis here is not only on *morality* but on *power* as well. The book has four theoretical foci.

First, I integrate the concept of deviance within the more general sociological analysis of change and stability. Furthermore, emphasizing change and stability necessarily means that our analysis must be historical and dynamic. This type of analytical orientation stems from both classical and modern, criticisms that the sociology of deviance has in fact become trivialized by extreme phenomenalism (Rock 1973a) and by a lack of theoretical integration (e.g., see Piven 1981; Scull 1984; Terry and Steffensmeier 1988).

I argue that deviance should be analyzed as a relative phenomenon in different and changing cultures, vis-à-vis change and stability in the boundaries of different symbolic-moral universes. Deviance is interpreted as the product of negotiations about the nature of morality *and* the use and legitimization of power.

In this way, deviance is being put into a wider sociological context of change and stability, which, while contradictory, still expresses essential and central processes that characterize all social systems. Furthermore, this approach takes deviance out of its marginal status and puts it within a central context of the sociological tradition.

Second, I argue that the way to examine deviance within the context of change and stability is by looking at the myriad of different symbolic-moral universes that constitute the wider societal cultural mosaic. Reactions to deviance, in this context, would help either to redefine the moral boundaries of these symbolic-moral universes in a rigid way or to break them and introduce elements of flexibility and hence change. In this way, deviance becomes not only relativized but must also be interpreted as a specific *process* of either *deviantization* or *politicization*. Any distinctions between the creation of categories and sanctioning of individuals must be made within this more general sociological context.

Third, I suggest that vocabularies of motives and particularly the concept of motivational accounting systems be used, not only to help us understand deviance itself and the symbolic-moral universes involved in it, but also as a bridging mechanism between processes in the macro and micro levels of analysis. These motivational accounting systems are used by deviants, and social control agents and agencies, to justify past behavior and to justify (and motivate) future behavior. The appropriateness and acceptability of motivational accounting systems vary between different cultures and within one culture over time. Thus, changes in motivational accounting systems reflect much deeper and more pervasive processes of change in moral boundaries. As such, these personal micro motivational accounting systems reflect higher macro processes. Also, as moral entrepreneurs and moral crusaders promote changes in motivational accounting systems on the micro personal level, these motivational accounting systems may diffuse to the macro level and help promote changes in symbolic-moral universes and in moral boundaries. Obviously, strong repression of new motivational accounting systems that are aimed at promoting change might generate instead more rigidity and lack of change. In the past, change in moral boundaries was usually conceptualized on the macro level and the mechanisms that produced change on the micro level. The analytical discussion in this book attempts to integrate the two levels into one coherent interpretation.

Fourth, the theoretical introduction establishes that deviance, as an empirical phenomenon and an analytical concept, is an important sociological construct. It makes deviance "an omnipresent phenomenon" and "part and parcel of all social realms" (Terry and Steffensmeier 1988, 58). The importance of deviance lies with the fact that deviance and the reactions to it may be utilized as key analytical concepts if we wish to better understand change and stability; the ways symbolic-moral universes meet, negotiate, and clash; and how the societal moral boundaries of these universes change or, conversely, remain rigid. Terry and Steffensmeier (1988, 70) stated that " . . . deviance is under attack . . . and appears to have lost some of [its] initiative," hence their pessimistic conclusion that sociologists of deviance "have been left to fight the rear-guard holding actions, actions that may delay, but not avoid the inevitable outcomes. We suggest that they should at least go down fighting" (p. 70). As my previous book (1985), and this one (as well as Ben-Yehuda, forthcoming) clearly imply, while I tend to agree with the diagnosis, I totally disagree with the conclusion and prognosis.

The concept of deviance that emerges from this book, and from my previous one (1985), is anchored in specific theoretical frameworks, focused on an *interpretative analysis*, aimed at *understanding* the phenomenon of deviance (e.g., see Orcutt 1983, 59–62). What this theoretical complex implies is that the process of negotiating motivational accounting systems is continuous and ongoing all the time between deviants and the social environment in which they live and function. Consequently, deviance is almost eternally socially negotiated and socially constructed (e.g., see Dotter and Roebuck 1988, 23–24, 28–29). Since the motivational accounting systems that are used in this process are anchored in broader ideological structures, in the form of symbolic-moral universes, the label "deviant" is much more than just a label. The invocation of this label is part of a long and complex process of negotiation about social identities. Once this label is given, and accepted, it reflects the end result of a particular process of identity negotiations—for a given time in a given social system. This label can be neutralized and even reversed. The process of deviantization, therefore, is never final. The main parameters for this whole process of identity negotiations are power and morality. Understanding this particular point illustrates vividly how intimately the phenomenon of deviance is interwoven with other phenomena in the mainstream of society. Examining the interface of politics and deviance seems almost ideal for this type of analysis. It is thus clear from the analysis presented here that the reality of deviance that emerges from my work is problematic, negotiable, and fluid.

This book implies that deviance is a relative phenomenon. The specific content of what is, and what is not, defined as deviance depends on the culture in which a particular form of behavior takes place. Thus, the links among deviance, change, and stability are strong and intimate. This approach negates the opposite absolutist, or normative, and narrower approach (e.g., see Hills 1980, 8–11; Douglas and Waksler 1982, 8–25; Orcutt 1983, 3–29; and a similar argument by Woolgar and Pawluch 1985.[1] Furthermore, deviance in this context is perceived as a voluntary act, and its subjective aspect is emphasized.

Having detailed my general theoretical commitment, I move on to deviance, power, and morality. I argue that the concept of power is essential because it basically helps us understand who can deviantize who. The concept of power alone, however, is insufficient. Symbolic-moral universes provide the necessarily legitimacy of power. Different centers enveloped by symbolic-moral universes confront, conflict, and negotiate with one another. Through these negotiations power may be generated and moral boundaries defined. This means that the powerful do not necessary deviantize the powerless, as others have suggested. The powerless may persuade inhabitants of other symbolic-moral universes in their cause, or may engage themselves in power generation and negotiate a compromise. Discussing politics and deviance necessitates therefore using the concepts of power, symbolic-moral universes and boundaries, moral entrepreneurs, moral crusaders, hierarchies of credibility, and motivational accounting systems.

Politics and deviance were characterized in chapter three as: problematic behavioral acts that take place where boundaries of different symbolic-moral universes meet and touch, that are directed from the periphery of a symbolic-moral universe toward its center and vice versa, and that involve challenges (use or abuse) of power and morality. The cases that were analyzed in this book are fully compatible with the above definition.

Having clarified my theoretical orientation toward the idea of politics and deviance, I argue that this area should be divided into two distinct domains. One domain is political deviance proper; the other consists of analyzing political elements in so-called regular deviance.

Political deviance proper consists of three classes of deviant acts. One class consists of acts done by one person or by a group in the periphery and that challenge the authority and legitimacy of those in the center. These acts usually aim at transforming symbolic-moral universes and changing moral boundaries. The second class consists of deviant acts by those in the center who were invested with power and legitimacy and are, supposedly, the guardians of the symbolic-moral universe and its boundaries. Sometimes these guardians abuse their power and twist and mock their moral obligations, committing despised and harmful acts of deviance. The third class involves a clash between social actors from two or more different and opposing symbolic-moral universes (or cultures). Chapter four provides a review of the classes in the domain of political deviance, using the theoretical conceptualization provided in the first three chapters.

The designation of particular behavioral patterns as deviant contains some important, although often implicit, political elements — that is, elements of power and morality. Exposing these elements is not always an easy task. The very attempt to define a particular behavioral pattern as deviant is inherently a political act. Such attempts are based on using power to impress the view of a specific symbolic-moral universe upon other universes. Applying a process of deviantization does not necessarily mean that the application would be successful and would culminate in the actual identification of one person (or group) as deviant. This process can be neutralized or, as I illustrated in chapter eight, even reversed. Counter ideologies and symbolic-moral universes may rise and generate enough power to counteract processes of deviantization. In chapter seven, I illustrated how societal reactions toward drug abuse may be interpreted by using this framework.

Finally, I chose four specific cases of deviance to illustrate my theoretical approach. Each of these cases is described by using the natural history of crime approach. *All* the cases were interpreted within the context of change and stability, in a dynamic, historical, and political perspective. In each of these cases, the negotiations between different symbolic-moral universes were emphasized. The motivational accounting systems that were employed by the different participants to the relevant drama of deviance were presented.

Chapter five provides a novel integrative approach to the study of moral panics, taking into consideration both the moral and the interest perspectives. In May 1982, the Israeli public learned that about 50 percent of its middle-class adolescents use illicit drugs. The actual figure was between 3 percent and 5 percent. Following this "news," a national drug moral panic developed and lasted for the month of May. I first provide an in-depth documentation of the panic, based on participant observations and a systematic analysis of the relevant reports in the electronic and print media, following the natural history of crime approach. Then I analyze the panic along two axes. One axis argues that a better interpretation of moral panics should take into consideration not only morality but also the specific political/economic interests of those involved in creating and sustaining the panic. This axis helps us to explain the *timing* of the panic; the other axis explains its *content*. I argue that illicit psychoactive drug use is utilized as a boundary maintenance device when two opposing symbolic-moral universes clash. The concepts of power, morality, and ideology are used to develop this interpretation.

Chapter six provides a comparative analysis of societal reactions, in the form of generalized motivational accounting systems called "social policy," to the perceived threat of illicit psychoactive drug use. The United States and Israel have implemented the same social policy toward illicit psychoactive drug use: a supply/demand reduction model aimed at minimizing illicit drug usage. The chapter examines the crystallization and results of this social policy in both countries, concluding that this social policy achieved a relative success in Israel while relatively failing to achieve its explicit goals in the United States. The sociological nature of the drug abuse problem is analyzed, indicating that this problem is not a technical-medical problem, but one that is focused around issues of power, morality, and dominance. Once the sociological nature of drug abuse is cleared, an explanation for the differential success of the supply/demand reduction model is offered. The degree of complexity and pluralism of the U.S. society is infinitely larger than that of Israeli society. The interpretation argues that the different symbolic-moral universes and boundaries that exist in the two cultures basically and primarily explain the differential success of the same social reaction. U.S. society gave rise to symbolic-moral universes that *legitimized* the use of illicit psychoactive drugs. Such a development did not occur in Israel.

Chapter seven analyzes deviant sciences in general and early radio-astronomy in particular. Science was presented as a more or less coherent symbolic-moral universe of knowledge identifiable by distinct moral boundaries. Since the frontiers of science are inevitably speculative, the aims and values of science may stimulate deviant ideas. Some of these deviant ideas aim to change the scientific symbolic-moral universe and its boundaries (e.g., parapsychology, astrology, UFOlogy, to mention only a few). The success of many deviant sciences, in terms of introducing changes, is at best problematic. However, some knowledge claims were reacted to originally as deviant, only to be accepted later as legitimate. Such knowledge claims, and claimants, may have been ignored, vilified, deviantized, rejected, or ridiculed—much like those committing other forms of deviant behavior. Such claims, like radio-astronomy, were later successful in introducing profound changes into scientific symbolic-moral universes and boundaries. The reactions of the relevant scientific disciplines to deviant knowledge claims illustrate how science grapples with one of its endemic problems—to preserve its boundaries intact or to introduce change.

Chapter eight examines the possibility of reversing processes of degradation, stigmatization, and deviantization. While in the past sociologists of deviance thought that such processes could be neutralized, the possibility of *reversing* such processes has not yet been documented or thoroughly researched—theoretically and empirically. I argue that deviantization processes can, in fact, be reversed, and using the empirical case of Abu-hatzira, I illustrate how, in reality, such a reversal was accomplished successfully. I suggest that to accomplish a reversal of deviantization successfully one has to politicize "regular" deviance (i.e., change the nature of the vocabulary of motives), subsequently creating a credible politicized system of motivational accounting systems within the context of an effective ideology, geared to mobilize a receptive audience. In other words, one has to become a moral entrepreneur, generate power by either creating, capitalizing on, or revitalizing a viable symbolic-moral universe.

SOME THEORETICAL CONSIDERATIONS: MOTIVATIONAL ACCOUNTING SYSTEMS, CONFLICT AND NEOFUNCTIONALISM

This book raises the age-old Hobbesian question "how is the social order possible?" by focusing on the Hegelian concept of antithesis. This general plot is occasioned by directing attention to how, why, where, and when challenges to the status quo emerge and function as catalysts for processes of social change or stability.

To answer the above question and to sustain the theoretical framework of this book, as well as the specific analysis in each of the cases, I used—in an integrated way—three different theoretical perspectives. The first emphasized subjectivism, symbolic interactionism, and motivational accounting systems. The second was conflict (focused on the "interest group" point of view and not on any particular version of a Marxist point of view; e.g., see Orcutt 1983, ch. 10). The third was, neo-functionalism.

Using these three perspectives, in itself, should indicate clearly that the three are not necessarily mutually exclusive and can, in fact, be brought together to create a meaningful and coherent synthesis that is aimed at explaining a specific sociological problem. As Turner (1986, vii) pointed out, the barriers between the different theoretical perspectives in sociology have been in a slow process of crumbling.

Non-Marxist conflict theory presents a rather straightforward orientation. According to Goode (1984a), lacking what some view as the Marxist ideological bias, this approach agrees with the Marxist approach that: (1) the interests of the powerful are translated into, and are protected by, the law; (2) reaching societal consensus regarding what type of behavior should be criminalized is difficult if not impossible; and (3) deviantization and criminalization rarely, if ever, protect the interests of society as a whole. In this process, some societal segments profit and others will be hurt. Non-Marxist conflict theory emphasizes that: (1) not all conflicts are between economic classes; conflicts may occur between different ethnic/age/sex groups; (2) some conflicts are over symbolic issues (e.g., prohibition, drug abuse, prostitution, homosexuality); and (3) deviance and crime exist and will continue to exist in all societies. No utopian perspective is suggested here because theorists feel that conflict is endemic to all societies (pp. 40–41; see also McCaghy 1985; and Orcutt 1983, ch. 10). Dotter and Roebuck (1988) present a close theoretical perspective (which they call "interactional conflict") that: "recognizes a level of tenuous agreement held together by the actions of participants. . . . It assumes the existence of multiple, competing interest groups . . . [and] it allows for a degree of freedom among individual actors to pursue collective political goals" (p. 22). Viewing complex and pluralistic social systems as characterized by a multiplicity of symbolic-moral universes, constantly competing with one another for limited resources, necessarily introduces the conflict perspective. However, conflict is introduced in this way not from the point of view of any particular conflict theory, but from the much more specific context of the subjective interests of the contesting individuals and groups.

From the three perspectives, the use of symbolic interactionism, motivational accounting systems, and the (non-Marxist) conflict approach seem to be straightforward and nonproblematic. The use of neo-functionalism may appear to be more problematic, especially because its use became somewhat controversial in the last decade and attacking it became somewhat fashionable. I would, therefore, like to expand some more on this particular issue of neo-functionalism.

While the functional approach in sociology (e.g., see Turner and Maryanski, 1979; Johnson 1981; Turner 1986, 37–128; Ritzer 1983, 221–39 for short reviews), and in the sociological study of deviance (e.g., see Wright and Hilbert, 1980) were severely attacked (e.g., see Pfohl 1985, ch. 6; Jensen 1988), they have regained some new attention and legitimacy (e.g., Alexander 1985, 1986; Page 1985; Huaco 1986; Faia 1986; Knoepler 1986; Forster 1986; Ritzer 1986; Warner 1986). Since my work implies some support in the revival of functionalism, it is imperative to try to cope with some of the major criticisms leveled at the functional approach.

Three main criticisms have usually been aimed at functionalism (e.g., see Pfohl 1985, 195–97; Jensen 1988). The first is that functionalism tends to view society as a total "system" that acts as such. This view may imply an overly mechanistic image of society. There are at least two answers to this. First, the word system (or social order) can be used as an analytical abstraction to represent an empirical reality. While an unjustified and indiscriminate use of the term may indeed lead to an overly mechanistic view of society, careful and reasonable use of the term should avoid it. Second, the new type of functionalism does not deal with the total "system" (e.g., see Jensen 1988, 3) but with specific components.

Erikson's (1966) analysis indicated which specific sectors of the social system were involved in manufacturing deviance and why; so did Weisman's (1984) and Gusfield's works (1963, 1981). All these studies focused on questions of who deviantized whom, when, and why. Neofunctionalism certainly uses the natural history of crime approach, in an historical-dynamic perspective (as suggested by Scull 1984 and Piven 1981), isolating, in the various cases of deviance, whose interest it was to deviantize whom, why, and when. This approach analyzes not only how various forms of deviance emerge but also how they mature and when and how they die. By using such terms as "symbolic-moral universes" and by analyzing the negotiations among these universes, the neofunctional analysis of deviance is not diffuse but is rather specific. It frequently associates deviance-production with actors or with defined groups of actors, examining the complex relationships among various groups (sometimes in harmony and sometimes in conflict) that function together in a social system.

The second criticism may claim that the functional analysis seems circular, verging on the tautological. This criticism may be coupled with the ghost of the "functional equivalent" problem (e.g., asking whether the same function can be attained by some other pattern of behavior). To begin with, it is clear from neofunctionalism that together with showing that some patterns of behavior are functional (i.e., positive in some sense to particular actors in the social system), the analysis also indicates and illustrates to whom and why it was dysfunctional (e.g., Lidz and Walker 1980; Ben-Yehuda 1980, 1985; see also ch. five, six, and eight of this book). Furthermore, much theoretical effort was invested in questions relating to the *specificity* of particular forms of deviance (e.g. see Ben-Yehuda 1985, 23–73; Cullen 1983.)

Neofunctionalism seems to be successful in avoiding a circular logic and in eliminating the ghost of the "functional equivalent" problem. Thus, in my previous analysis of the European witch craze of the fourteenth to seventeenth centuries (1980, 1985), as well as in the analysis presented in chapter five of this book, I address this problem directly. I asked why specific actors or organizations were involved in either helping to fabricate imaginary forms of deviance or moral panics. The answers focus on why and how these actors or organizations, and not others, were involved in the aforementioned activities.

Second, a few criticisms of functionalism (e.g., Gans 1972; Pfohl 1985; 196) use imaginary examples stating that: "with enough imagination we can find" or "when stretched to its imaginative limits," to the extreme of Gans's (1972) fascinating and cynical example on the functions of poverty. The point is not what *may* be done using functionalism or what *may* happen if we stretch it to its limits, but what *was* actually done. I find it difficult to accept criticism on what, perhaps, could have been done, but was not really done. Obviously, any sociological interpretation (including neofunctionalism) must be judged in the final analysis by the degree to which it makes sense and its plausibility. The fact that some wild imaginary stretchings may bring a quasifunctional analysis to sheer absurdities and nonsense should not deter us from admitting that sensible and plausible neofunctional analysis has some very strong benefits.

The third criticism accuses functionalism of maintaining and harboring a conservative view. Pfohl (1985, 195–97) reflected this position when he mentioned that functional analysis has a conservative bias. To begin with, Merton's (1968, 114–36) analysis of "Manifest and Latent Functions" most certainly disposed of the conservative biased argument. Second, one must realize that such a criticism reflects a position that does not like so-called conservatism—in itself clearly biased as well. Third, neofunctionalism does not necessarily reflect a conservative view. Lidz and Walker (1980), Galliher and Cross (1983), and my own work (1980, 1985, and this book), to use just a few examples, do not reflect in any way what can be termed a "conservative" stand. Certainly, neofunctionalism does attempt to understand who exactly benefits from manufacturing or controlling deviance, and who does not, in a social ecology of cultures that are constantly changing and where symbolic-moral universes almost eternally negotiate power and morality. The analysis of political deviance in the context of neofunctionalism should be a good illustration for this point.

Much of the criticism leveled at functionalism, therefore, is biased, inaccurate, and to a large extent outdated. Neofunctionalism seems to have learned from past problems and offers a type of analysis that is free of many of the defects attributed previously to functionalism.

Alexander's (1985) analysis implied that neofunctionalism: " . . . indicates a tradition. . . . [It] provide[s] a general picture of the interrelation of social parts, a model in a more descriptive sense. Functionalism models society as an intelligible system. It views society as composed of elements whose interaction forms a pattern that can be clearly differentiated from some surrounding environment. . . . Functionalism suggests . . . open-ended and pluralistic rather than monocausal determinism. Functionalism concentrates on action as much as on structure. . . . [It] is concerned with integration as a possibility and with deviance and processes of social control as facts" (pp. 9–11; see also Turner and Maryanski 1988).

Furthermore, while the analysis presented here was influenced by neofunctionalism, it also integrated a non-Marxist conflict approach and symbolic interaction (with motivational accounting systems) as well. In this way, the explanatory power of the interpretations gains from two sources: from the logic of *consequences* implied by neofunctionalism and from the logic of *causes* implied by the conflict perspective (e.g., see Cohen 1978; Jensen 1988). My basic view is that the social order should be thought of and represented by a model of negotiation. It is clearly the case that any social system has many conflicting actors, roles, and symbolic-moral universes. However, it is also clearly the case that many actors, roles, and symbolic-moral universes in this very same social system live together in peace, cooperation, and harmony. Therefore, what we have is a situation of ongoing negotiations where conflict and consensus intermingle and coexist. The addition of the conflict and the symbolic interaction perspectives also helps to neutralize any "conservative" bias that might be left in functionalism.

Part Five

Notes and Bibliography

Notes

Chapter One.

1. This part continues chapter 1 of my 1985 book.

2. Sagarin's (1985) programmatic paper advocated, uncompromisingly and sharply, what I view as an obsolete absolutist position. Typical of this approach, Sagarin's paper failed to take into serious consideration the problem of power and the vitally important role of the relevant societal reactions. The really interesting problem is not whether or not a particular behavioral act is defined as deviant but rather who wants to define it as deviant, where, when, why, and under what conditions such social actors may be successful in enforcing their views upon the rest of society.

3. For a fuller review, see Ben-Yehuda 1985, 3–10. For some recent formulations on the Durkheimian views, see Inverarity, Lauderdale, and Feld (1983) and Inverarity (1987).

Chapter Two.

1. I reflect here the traditional view that the Durkheimian approach does not quite mix with the perspective of symbolic interactionism. See Stone and Farberman (1967) and Byrne (1976) on the possibility that the two perspectives are, perhaps, closer than what has been implied in the traditional view.

2. In the third, new version of the *Diagnostic and Statistical Manual* (DSM III), homosexuality is not defined as mental illness. Treatment of homosexuality is indicated only when the patient himself desires it.

3. For a more recent empirical and theoretical examination of this concept, see Minor (1981).

4. Darley and Zanna (1982) indicated that moral judgments are specific culturally transmitted excuses that are generally believed to absolve people of blame for harming others.

5. See also Sharrock and Watson's (1984) response to one of these papers.

267

6. Some contemporary scholarly efforts in the sociology of science attempt to use the concepts of "accounts" and "discourse analysis." See, for example, Gilbert and Mulkay (1984); Fuhrman and Oehler (1986); Woolgar (1986).

7. We should not overlook, however, the interpretation that in some cases the medicalization of deviant behavior (e.g., homosexuality and drug abuse) was an important step in decriminalizing these behaviors.

8. I did not include in the survey the studies conducted, in sociology and other disciplines, under the somewhat overgeneralized title of "discourse analysis." See, for example, Gilbert and Mulkay (1984); Burton and Carlen (1979); Potter and Wetherell (1987). I feel that the term "motivational accounting systems" is more accurate and better suited to my purposes.

Chapter Three.

1. See Clinard (1957); Rubington and Weinberg (1971); Sykes (1978); Hagan (1977); Taylor, Walton, and Young (1973, 2-3); Davis (1975); Gibbons and Jones (1975); Conrad and Schneider (1980).

2. Perhaps the best-known and most frightening forms of both internal and external controls can be found in Orwell's imaginary work *1984*. Six significant theoreticians are typically mentioned in the area of control theory: Durkheim's (1951) study on suicide; Matza (1964, 1969. See also Beyleveld and Wiles 1975); Reiss (1951); Reckless (1967); Nye (1958); Hirschi (1969).

3. It is even possible that the term "social control" should not be used to describe both approaches.

4. Control theory is not problem free. Micro control theories were usually formed using data on juvenile delinquency. The universal validity of such data for other age groups is problematic. Furthermore, the assumption that actors are prone to deviate when no controls are present is philosophically complex and only begs the question.

5. For an interesting comparison of Marixst-oriented theories about the origin and the cause of crime with the positivist, non-Marxist approach, see Miller (1973). See also Goode (1984a, 38–41) for a short, critical review of Marxist and non-Marxist conflict theories.

6. It is well worth noting that in 1973 Denisoff and McCaghy edited a volume on deviance, conflict, and criminality. This volume consists of works by various authors exploring the complex relationships between the conflict perspective and deviance.

7. Hagan's (1977, 41) analysis reinforced this view because it pointed out that deviant behavior is probably much more prevalent than most of us imagine and that attention to and choice of specific types of deviance as a foci

for societal reactions are not incidental. He also stated (pp. 144–54) that analysis of both power and morality is crucial if we are to understand deviance. This, naturally, is close to Douglas' (1970b) analysis of deviance and respectability (and responsibility), which are perceived as the polar opposites of deviance.

8. For more on value incommensurability, see Cohen and Ben-Arie (1985).

9. While a few exceptions do exist, it appears that many professional groups have been able to manipulate the relevant political powers to allow them to police themselves.

10. The sociological concept of a "subculture" is close to the concept of a "symbolic-moral universe." Because the emphasis in this type of work is on a *symbolic interpretation*, I feel that the concept of a symbolic-moral universe is much more appropriate and accurate than that of a subculture.

11. Durkheim (1933) himself recognized this possibility when he stated (in the preface) that various occupational groups in such societies could have their own collective conscience (i.e., different professional ethical systems) specifying meaningful values and conduct for members of that group.

Chapter Four.

1. Turk (1975) stated that political criminals are those who, because of their morality or ideology, constitute a potential (or current) political threat to a specific regime or social system. Packer's (1962) analysis argued that political offenses are either forms of behavior that threaten the very existence of the state (e.g., espionage or treason) or forms of behavior that interfere with what is felt to be the orderly and just administration of the public social order (e.g., bribery and corruption). Thus, in the narrowest sense of the term, political deviance may be defined as "an offense against the state" (Lauderdale 1980, 3) or as violations of laws created to protect the state (Quinney 1964). As such, political crime includes such deviant acts as treason, espionage, terrorism, political assassination (Packer 1962), sedition, revolution, subversion, membership in illegal organizations, draft evaders, civil disobedience, and passive resistance.

2. A quasi-messianic, religiously orthodox movement, dedicated mainly to settling a Jewish population in Judea and Samaria, with the eventual goal of annexation. It is virtually impossible to give a detailed account of *Gush Emunim* here. For a recent and general description of the development of *Gush Emunim*, see Aran (1987) and Shprinzak (1986).

3. A group consisting mainly of Sephardic Jews living in poor neighborhoods (see Cohen E. 1972; Bernstein 1979).

4. See Ross (1907); Sutherland (1940); Clinard (1952); Cressey (1953); Conklin (1977); Edelhertz (1970); Gies and Stotland (1980); Wheeler, Weisburd, and Bode (1982); Wickman and Dailey (1982); Simon and Eitzen (1982); Braithwaite (1985); Coleman (1985); Hirschi and Gottferedson (1987); Thio (1988, 419–42).

5. See Schur (1969); Douglas and Johnson (1977); Sherman (1978); Ermann and Lundman (1978); Douglas and Waksler (1982, 348–59); Coleman (1985); Thio (1988, 443–61).

6. See Coleman (1985); Ben-Yehuda (1986); Braithwaite (1985).

7. See Clinard and Yeager (1980); Schur (1980, 168–83); Ermann and Lundman (1982); Wickman and Dailey (1982); Clinard (1983); Hochstedler (1984); Coleman (1985); Frank (1985); Hills (1987).

8. Similarly, in the months June–July 1986, the Israeli public learned that some of the key officers (including the commander-in-chief) of its general security services (Shabac) lied deliberately to at least two official investigative committees. This "cover up" was intended to hide the fact that the service was involved in the killing of two Arab terrorists (who had kidnaped a civilian bus) after they were captured by Israeli commandos who stormed the bus (e.g., see *Time, 128,* (#2):21, July 21, 1986).

9. For a case example of institutional violence against drug addicts, see my and Einstein's work (1984). There, we show how since 1981 hundreds of drug addicts were "treated" with methadone in the midst of the largest garbage dump in Israel.

10. See, for example, Stohl (1983); Clutterbuck (1973); Watson (1976); Hacker (1976); Kupperman and Darrell (1979); Alexander and Kilmarx (1979); Lodge (1981); Freedman and Alexander (1983); Mickolus (1980); Hyams (1974); Crenshaw (1983) to mention only a few sources on terrorism. On political assassinations see Rapoport (1971); Crotty (1971); Havens, Leiden, and Schmitt (1970); Clarke (1982); Wilkinson (1976); Kirkham, Levy, and Crotty (1970); Ford (1985); Ben-Yehuda (forthcoming).

11. Ironically, McCaghy (1985, 216) opened his chapter on police corruption with a quote from actor Woody Allen: "I like policemen. It gives me a very secure feeling, knowing that it's that blue uniform that is all that stands between me and him robbing and killing me. . . . " For more on police corruption, see Douglas and Waksler (1982, 353–59); Sherman (1978); Punch (1985).

12. DeFleur (1976) also used this study to warn researchers against biases that exist in so-called official statistics.

13. Such acts, of course, are not totally irrelevant. The degree of violence, aggression, and damage that such groups inflict contributes to its image as a terrorist or guerrilla group.

14. We should note, however, that the idea of the prison system as a source for social revolution is certainly not new. See, for example, Enquist and Coles (1970).

15. For an interesting field study on this problem, see Fairchild (1977). Based on prisoner interviews, Fairchild suggested that the average prisoner has had political socialization experiences that resulted in alienation, but not in ideological estrangement from the political order. Second, the politicization processes, when coupled with failure in rehabilitation efforts, made the political model very attractive for prisoners. Administrators, of course, cannot accept either the theory or the process.

16. Contrary to this view, one cannot help but recall the Soviet Archipelago as described by Solzhenytsin and others, where numerous political prisoners were incarcerated for years and where many perished. No social revolution began inside the Archipelago or in similar "camps" in other countries. Krisberg's (1975) idea may be, therefore, applied in particular types of prisons in very specific cultures. The higher (and more controlled and lethal) the level of repression, the lower the probability for Krisberg's idea to materialize.

Chapter Five.

1. This chapter is based on a significantly different version that was published in *The Sociological Quarterly*, 1986, *27* (#4):495–513.

2. One may ask, at this point, about the nature of the connection between the presentation of information in the media and the reaction of the public to that information. That is the difference between the media's role as *presenting* or as *creating* a social reality. Obviously, the media are a symbolic cultural product. If something happens and is not reported, from the public's point of view it is as if it did not happen. The impact, however, of reports in the media is more complex because they help to construct particular social realities. This happens because of the choice of particular vocabularies of motives, of topics, as well as the space/time given to specific items. As Cohen (1972, 16) pointed out: "a crucial dimension for understanding the reaction to deviance both by the public as a whole and by agents of social control, is the nature of the information that is received about the behaviour in question."

Checking the media reports leaves no room for hesitation regarding the fact that the media created a social construction of a panic. Did the public react to the panic as such? As in other cases, the dynamics of a panic are such that polling before, during, and after the panic was not feasible. However, and as the indications (i.e., reactions of parents, students, teachers) that were used in the chapter show, there is no reason to doubt that the public reacted *as if* the reports were accurate, and a moral panic was in progress.

Furthermore, unlike Well's radio transmission on the "invasion from Mars," nothing in the May panic required an immediate and dramatic action.

Most researchers of moral panics have no choice but to rely heavily on reports in the media. These reports typically project the moral positions of the different and contesting symbolic-moral universes, as well as reflecting the end results of the panic in such macro and formalized terms as legislation. Hence, using the media as a source for studying moral panics is simply a must and *was* used in this fashion by previous researchers who helped to establish the field. "The student of moral enterprise cannot but pay particular attention to the role of the mass media in defining and shaping social problems. The media have long operated as agents of moral indignation in their own right: even if they are not self-consciously engaged in crusading or muck raking, their very reporting of certain 'facts' can be sufficient to generate concern, anxiety, indignation or panic" (Cohen 1972, 16).

3. Drug use among "youth in distress" (i.e., those adolescents who are not part of any formal educational system) and juvenile delinquents is probably much higher. Wolanski (1981) and Wolanski and Kfir (1982) asked street guides who work with youth in distress to fill out questionnaires regarding their estimate of drug abuse among their clients. In 1981, the estimated rate of use was reported as 14.2 percent and in 1982 as 23 percent (the daily estimated use in the last survey was 5.5 percent). From a personal communication with Dr. M. Horowitz, chief of corrections (youth and adults) in Israel until January 1986, I learned that his indirect estimate (based on reports from his probation officers) was that about 50 percent of his clients used drugs (mostly hashish). However, one has to take these estimates with great caution due to the indirect, crude measurements used (see also Ben-Yehuda 1989).

4. At one time during the panic, I was asked to give a talk to a group of parents. Having explained the situation and given the statistics, I was asked why the interministerial committee was not doing enough about the problem. I guess that I realized at that point that the question came from someone who had paid more attention to the media than to the talk, so I responded cynically and sarcastically and stated that, after all, we really did not want to solve the problem because had we solved it we would all be out of jobs, and that it was our vested interest to keep the problem going and increasing. The absurdity and irony of that answer made its impact, and the rest of the evening was much more relaxed and rational.

5. For just one example, see *Yediot Aharonot*, May 21, 1982, weekend special edition.

6. For a somewhat similar debate between these two symbolic-moral universes on the issue of treason, see Cromer's (1986) fascinating work on an Israeli spy (Udi Adiv).

7. Closer perhaps to the type of analysis presented by Banfield (1961).

8. For similar attempts to create an alcohol-free utopia in England, see Dingle (1980).

9. Geertz (1964) limits his discussion to situations in which the need for cognitive and moral reorientation are the result of the emergence of "autonomous polity," namely, the differentiation of the political from the religious. However, widespread need for such reorientation is caused by every process of significant institutional differentiation and change, a situation that is a hallmark of modern societies characterized by continuous change, alienation, anomie, centerlessness, and atomized individuals (Lasch 1979).

10. Christie illustrated the validity of this argument in the Norwegian culture too (personal communication, February 1985. See also his 1984 paper and Christie and Bruun 1985.)

11. It is possible to claim that even in these cases there was a high degree of amplification. I tend to disagree. Even if there was amplification, it was on such a magnitude that fabrication describes the process more appropriately and accurately.

12. At one point, I spent two hours with a reporter from Israeli television and another hour with a reporter from *Yediot Aharonot*, attempting to prepare reports on the true magnitude of the problem. Nothing came out of this effort because the editors felt that what I had to say was not "newsworthy" — perhaps not sensational enough.

Chapter Six.

1. This part is based on a significantly different paper that was published originally in Hebrew in *Delinquency and Social Deviance*, 1982, *10* (#1–2):7–43. A different version appeared in *The International Journal of the Addictions*, 1987, *22* (#1):17–45.

2. Personal communication with Christie, January 31, 1985.

3. Subtitled: *A Report to the President from the Domestic Council Drug Abuse Task Force.*

4. For a concise summary of these histories, see Austin (1978).

5. See, for example, King (1972); Duster (1970); Morgan (1974, 1981); Brecher (1972).

6. In 1895, a Royal Commission (Indian Hemp Commission), appointed by British Prime Minister William Gladstone, submitted a seven-volume, 2500-page report. The report's accounts stated that the dangers attributed to opium were exaggerated and that outlawing opium would cause significant and unnecessary economic problems and setbacks (Scott 1969). For example, the report stated that India's economy could not afford to lose the revenues from opium production.

7. Heroin was developed in 1898 as a derivative of morphine.

8. DeFleur (1976) illustrated that increasing or decreasing number of drug arrests in Chicago had more to do with political pressures than with real changes in the scope and magnitude of the phenomenon.

9. The FBN (1930–1968) played an important role in creating and sustaining the drug panic, even though Musto (1973) and Galliher and Walker (1973) stated that its role was less significant than generally claimed.

10. For more on this, see Berlet (1981).

11. The fourth annual report (1981) of the U.S. National Institute on Drug Abuse to the U.S. Congress stated (p. 27) that 69.1 percent of all addicts in treatment in the United States were in drug free programs, while only 11.6 percent were in methadone programs. These figures certainly reflected a victory for the antimethadone movement.

12. The document is not dated, but was probably published in the early 1970s.

13. Data are based on national representative surveys.

14. The statistics refer to the category of those who had tried the respective drug at least once.

15. Data quoted from Fishburne, Abelson, and Cisin (1979).

16. See note 3, chapter 5, and the corresponding pages in the chapter.

17. One can, of course, argue that the situation could have grown much worse without this policy. Such an account cannot be answered by scientific tools. However, in the case of the decriminalization of marijuana, there were no significant changes in illicit drug usage after decriminalization (*A First Report* . . . (1977); *An Evaluation* . . . (1978); Cusky et al. (1978); *Marijuana* . . . (1977); *The Decriminalization of Marijuana* . . . (1979); Single (1981); Johnston (1980).

18. While there may be some actions that are presumably very efficient, they contradict the values of a free, democratic society.

19. Both *A Perspective* . . . (1973) and *The Nation's Toughest Drug Law* . . . (1977) emphasized that "get tough" laws usually had undesirable side effects. *The Nation's Toughest Drug Law* . . . (1977) pointed out that the tough New York State drug laws did not affect the prevalence and patterns of drug use and that crime was hardly affected.

20. This ideological incommensurability is illustrated in Israel as well. While sentences provided in the Israeli law for illicit psychoactive drug use are quite severe, El-Roy's (1981) work illustrated that the Israeli courts do not

exhaust the severity of punishment provided by the law and that most criminals sentenced for illicit psychoactive drug use (first offense) receive lenient sentences.

21. See, for example, *Newsweek* and *Time* cover stories (International Editions) in the last week of February 1985 about cocaine.

22. This increase has several implications. First, physical addiction occurs faster. Second, there was a 264 percent rise in drug-related deaths in New York during those years. The tremendous increase in the quantity and quality of illicit opiates available in the United States and Europe caused a great deal of concern. See, for example, *Newsweek*, May 1981 (International Edition) and the April through September 1981 issues of *Narcotic Control Digest*.

23. The final report was presented to the Israeli government in the summer of 1983. As a member of the committee and director of its executive headquarters unit (1979–1982), I had access to all of its documents.

24. The peace treaty with Egypt in the late 1970s is the sole exception.

25. This love has become almost a national obsession, and the Society for the Protection of Nature in Israel enjoys a tremendous popular support.

26. Both community sing-a-longs and folk-dancing groups enjoy tremendous popular support and active participation. These activities clearly enhance mechanic solidarity.

27. For more on civil religions, see Bellah (1968); Coleman (1970); Roberts (1984, 384–92). On civil religion in Israel, see Liebman and Don-Yehiya (1983).

28. This interpretation also explains why there is a minimal number of esoteric, individualistic social movements in Israel and why those that exist do not win widespread popularity.

29. In a previous work, Ben-Yehuda and Einstein (1984) illustrated that the Israeli public in general as well as actors positioned in high places in the hierarchies of credibility and morality show much indifference to drug abuse issues. One possible interpretation for this is the same as the one offered by Cumming and Cumming (1957), that is, that the community does not wish to blur the symbolic boundaries between the morally right and the morally wrong.

30. One could, perhaps, argue that this comparison could have been performed by using a quantitative multivariate analysis. Unfortunately, such an analysis is not feasible because it requires comparative quantitative data that are simply not available. However, as we could see, a meaningful com-

parative interpretation was made even without such an analysis. Furthermore, such an analysis, even if possible, would not have added very much to the conclusions and would have complicated the analysis and interpretation unnecessarily. It would have also required making some statistical assumptions that are problematic. This particular problem has brought this type of analysis increasingly under attack by different statisticians (e.g. Hannan Selvin, Louis Guttman). The analytical and presentational tools that were used in the analysis are straightforward and help to make the conclusions clear and understandable.

31. Data about the activities of the U.S. police are much harder to get and to interpret. The United States has federal police agencies fighting drug abuse (e.g., the Drug Enforcement Agency), and local, state, county, and city drug abuse law enforcement units. I avoided bringing partial data from U.S. law enforcement agencies so as not to confuse the issue. As can be seen, Israeli police data are all national, unified, and easier to interpret. Furthermore, police data do not play a very central role in the analysis and are only used to supplement other data.

Chapter Seven.

1. This part focuses a new integration of parts of chapter four of my 1985 book (*Deviance and Moral Boundaries*) and a paper on radio astronomy that was presented in the section on the sociology of science at the 1984 annual meeting of the American Sociological Association, San Antonio, Texas.

2. Hey's observation was, and is still, valid. That is the reason that one has to observe short wave lengths, less than twenty meters. As technology developed, this became more and more feasible.

3. It is interesting to note that in 1928 Gordon Stagner, a young radio operator in the Manila RCA station in the Philippines, also noticed this peculiar hiss. Although he wanted to investigate further, he was instructed not to pursue the matter. Only after reading Jansky's papers did Stagner understand that the strong hiss occurred on those antennae directed toward the Milky Way (see Kraus 1981, 18). Reber (personal communication, August 16, 1982) noted that Stagner "did not have enterprise or perseverance to follow matters up."

4. There is no documentary evidence that Jansky tried to formally submit a proposal to do this. While this account keeps appearing, it seems that the source is that Reber says that this is what Jansky and Kraus (1966, 9) told him. There seems to be no other direct evidence for this (personal communication with W. T. Sullivan, May 10, 1984).

5. Jansky described his findings in a series of papers, published in journals of radio engineers or presented before meetings of radio engineers.

For a concentrated presentation of his most important papers, see Sullivan (1982, 5–41).

6. As an example of intense public interest, the May 5, 1933, *New York Times* carried a front-page report, "New Radio Waves Traced to Center of Milky Way" (see Hey 1973, 7; Sullivan 1984a, 11). At 8:30 p.m. Eastern Standard Time, on Monday, May 15, 1933, the National Broadcasting Company Blue Network announcer began: "Tonight we will let you hear radio impulses picked up from somewhere among the stars" (see Kraus 1981, 11).

7. Kraus (1981, 12) pointed out that if we take the term "thermal agitation" to mean "electrons moving at a high velocity in a magnetic field," then the similarity to later explanations is great. Yet one has to remember that this similarity lies more with Jansky's idea that the source of the radiation has to do with what happens in space and not with the stars themselves. No mention of magnetic fields, or systematic movements of electrons, was made by Jansky.

8. In fact, radio astronomers established the "Jansky" unit to measure the strength of radio sources.

9. For a complete list of Jansky's works, see Sullivan 1982, 335–38.

10. For details of construction and pictures, see Reber (1958).

11. Some apparently thought it was an atom smasher, a rocket launcher, a source for death rays, or a weather controlling device (see Kraus 1982; Sullivan 1984a, 4).

12. Reber published numerous papers at that time. For a reprinted collection of his works, see Sullivan (1982, 42–79); see also Sullivan (1984a, b).

13. There were a few optical astronomers who apparently showed some limited interest in Reber's work (e.g., Keenan, Struve) and thought it was valuable (W. Sullivan, personal communication, May 10, 1984). At the same time, however, even those who did show a meager amount of interest were not willing to commit resources (e.g., to build a radio-telescope). It seems that the most they did was to maintain somewhat weak, noncommittal contacts with Reber.

14. See Kraus (1982) and Westerhout (1972). The optical astronomers who visited Reber and Struve's visit are not well-documented incidents. While both Kraus and Westerhout mention it, it is not clear how they got this information. Reber himself wrote to me on January 8, 1984, that: "the first person from the Astronomy Department at the University of Chicago to visit me at Wheaton was Philip C. Keenan, May 1939. He was interested, but bewildered by equipment. Later, Jesse Greenstein, Gerard Kuiper and others came. Finally, over a year later, Struve came to see for himself. By that time I had automatic equipment operating."

15. Otto Struve (1897–1963) was a fascinating and important figure. He was born in Russia, a son of a family of astronomers. He graduated from the Kharkov Gymnasium with honors in 1914. Having fought against the Turks in World War I, he fought again with General Denikin against the Red Army and was expelled from the Soviet Union in 1920. After many difficulties, he arrived in the United States in 1921 and developed a remarkable career in astronomy. Among other positions, he was the director of the Astronomy Department in Berkeley, editor in chief of the *Astrophysical Journal* (1932–1947), worked in Yerkes optical observatory, and in 1959 headed the new National Radio Astronomical Observatory in Green Bank, West Virginia.

16. See Sullivan (1982, 43–44); Struve was a professor of astrophysics at the University of Chicago between 1932 and 1947 and was involved in Yerkes optical observatory. As of today, no accurate description of the incident exists by either Reber or Struve. Reber himself saw the first draft of this chapter (which did not include Sullivan's interpretation) and did not comment on the interpretations presented there. While he indicated that he would write me a detailed description of the incident, he never did. Thus, the problem of which version is the more accurate remains somewhat open. While one cannot ignore the first version, I tend to accept Sullivan's interpretation as more valid. There are several reasons for that. Sullivan's work is by far more systematic and professional. Ferris' work is aimed at a more general audience and is much more popular. Ferris certainly did not commit as many resources to his work as Sullivan; thus, while Sullivan held long, in-depth interviews with the various figures involved in the early days of radio astronomy, Ferris apparently did not.

Sullivan (personal communication, May 10, 1984) maintains that despite his extensive work he could not find any written evidence that some referees advised Struve to reject Reber's work. Furthermore, he doubts that at that time Struve sent Reber's work to be referred—since the procedure of anonymously refereeing papers had not yet been developed. It is, however, possible that Struve might have sought outside advice on a work that must have been very alien to him.

17. This took place under German occupation; see Edge and Mulkay 1976, ch. 7.

18. Ignoring certainly constitutes a form of resistance, probably a passive one. Furthermore, according to W. Sullivan (personal communication, May 10, 1984), Struve encouraged Reber to submit a formal proposal so that he would be able to continue his work. Toward the end of World War II, Reber submitted such a proposal, probably to the U.S. Navy, but this was rejected (no documentation is currently available regarding this affair). While this could, perhaps, be taken as another indication of the resistance Reber encountered, one has to remember that the U.S. Navy was probably not interested in the revolutionary scientific aspects of Reber's work.

19. Since Kuhn published his thesis in 1962, it has been subjected to rigorous and intensive examinations. Some critics point out that Kuhn's description and analysis of science's development are inaccurate and misleading. For some interesting criticisms, see Ben-David (1964); Alexander (1979); and Gutting (1980). See Harvey (1982) for clarification on the use and abuse of Kuhn's ideas, and Barnes (1982) and Cohen B. (1984) for a sympathetic view.

20. Cole, Cole, and Simon (1981) indicated that when grant applications submitted to the National Science Foundation were later reviewed by different referees the initial decisions were reversed in about 25 percent of the cases.

21. For example, *Newsday*, October 11, 1983, and interviews to the major television networks in the New York City/Long Island area.

22. Obviously, one may ask how *could* optical astronomers know, at that point in time, what radio astronomy would really mean for them. Given the technical limitations of pre-World War II equipment, it is possible that even Jansky and Reber could not go beyond what they had already accomplished. However, the fact still remains that most optical astronomers were impervious to Jansky's and Reber's works, ignored tham, and did not seriously attempt to explore the significant implications of those works, even within the given limitations. This constitutes a clear illustration of the quality, amount, and scope of resistance both Jansky and Reber encountered.

23. Jansky had similar data. It is the *combination* of these factors that seems to have helped Reber.

24. The final push to radio astronomy was given by innovations in radar technology during World War II.

25. Shapley, the previously mentioned prominent and powerful contemporary astronomer, heard about Jansky's work and asked about the cost of continuing and developing it. Jansky gave Shapley an estimate. While Shapley's answer was courteous, it was essentially negative, and Jansky did not pursue the matter any further. See Sullivan (1984a, 3–41). Also, while Struve supported (at least to some extent) Reber's work, he was apparently not willing to hire him as a staff member (Sullivan 1984b).

26. Law (1980) indicated that a similar process took place in sedimentology. Furthermore, there too the change from one method to the other was not on the background of an atmosphere of "crisis."

27. Pulsars were discovered in 1967. These stars are hypothesized to be rotating, magnetized neutron stars that emit radio pulses with a very high degree of regularity (Silk 1980, 380).

28. The central thesis of the Big Bang theory is that about 10 to 20 billion years ago, the now observable universe was very dense, so dense, in fact, that the density of matter at the moment of creation was infinite. Then there was a gigantic explosion (the Big Bang), and the universe as we know it was born. See Weinberg (1977); Silk (1980); Trefil (1983); Barrow (1983); Gribbin (1986).

29. Like many other similar criticisms, one may ask whether the introduction of radio astronomy was a *revolution* or an *evolution*. I believe it is plain enough from my argument that I feel radio astronomy actually revolutionized astronomy. Let me also and briefly point out that "evolutionists" are probably more sympathetic to the conservative view of science, that is, that science evolves gradually and slowly. "Revolutionists" are probably more sympathetic to viewing scientific progress as nongradual and as unpredictable. These two opposing views cannot be really resolved as they represent two very different symbolic-moral universes of historians, philosophers, and sociologists of science.

30. Gieryn and Hirsch (1983) challenged the idea that "marginal" scientists unexpectedly contribute major theoretical or technical innovations into science. Clearly, Jansky's and Reber's works do not support this challenge.

31. If you like, the fact that one of the first-ever publications about radio astronomy was done by Jansky in *Popular Astronomy* only serves to reinforce Lankford's argument.

32. See, for example, Bliss (1982), who showed how Macleod (and others) twisted the truth about who should have gotten the 1923 Nobel prize in physiology for the discovery and isolation of insulin. Zuckerman (1977, 170); Metz (1977); Wade (1975); and Reed (1983) described how the 1974 Nobel prize in physics was given to Anthony Hewish, while the discovery of pulsars—for which the prize was given—was actually made by his graduate student, Jocelyn Bell-Burnell. Fletcher (1982) reported on a similar problem involving Millikan's famous experiment. Finally, Sayre (1975) revealed that Rosalind Franklin was dishonestly and systematically deprived of her rightful share and recognition in the discovery of the structure of DNA, for which Watson, Crick, and Wilkins were awarded the Nobel prize in 1962.

33. Even Patinkin's work is not exactly on simultaneous multiple discoveries.

34. Reber wrote to me on June 9, 1982, after I informed him of my plans to write about the early days of radio astronomy, that: "I think Karl G. Jansky would be a much better sociological study."

Chapter Eight.

1. Based on my "The Politicization of Deviance: Resisting and Reversing Degradation and Stigmatization," which appeared in *Deviant Behavior*, 1987, 8:259–82, (published by Hemisphere Publishing Corporation).

2. Some works completed recently by Israeli political scientists point out that illegalism has been an integral part of the Israeli political scene. This, obviously, only makes drawing political moral boundaries harder (e.g., see Ehud Shprinzak's 1986 work on this particular issue).

3. In 1982, Modai, still a secretary, was again accused of mismanagement, fraud, and the like. Again he was proven innocent. Modai, however, decided to "do something" about this. He started a campaign against the Israeli police and the media. Fortunately for Modai, a state committee found most of his grievances justified. He later became minister of the treasury.

4. Mr. Ziegel was the commander of the special police unit that investigated cases involving suspicions against Israeli public officials. From 1974 until 1985, Ziegel's unit investigated thirty-one public figures (including parliament members, mayors, etc.).

5. Unless stated otherwise, most of the background and reconstruction of the Abu-hatzira case is based on *Ha'aretz* and *Davar*, two reliable Israeli Hebrew language morning papers. The English speaking reader may find parallel documents in the English language daily, *Jerusalem Post*.

6. *Mea*, October 1981; *Ha'aretz*, October 27, 1978 (report by Roman Friertes).

7. A general name for prestigious religious Jewish community leaders.

8. The reason for this move was clearly ideological. See M. Roi report in *Yediot Aharonot*, July 8, 1977.

9. A small town about fifteen kilometers east of Tel Aviv.

10. A small town in the southern part of Israel.

11. Mafdal, the National Religious Party.

12. Tami, "Tenua Le'masoret Israel" meaning the movement for the tradition of Israel.

13. That was 2.3 percent of the total votes for that election.

14. *Ha'aretz*, August 27, 1980.

15. The first Knesset (February 1949–July 1951) and the second (August 1951–1955) had a few ethnic lists, most notably the "Sepharadim" and the "United Yemenites." Both lists had five parliament members in the first Knesset (four plus one, respectively) and three in the second (two plus one, respectively). Since then, no ethnic group managed to compete successfully for the Knesset (e.g., see Eisenstadt 1968; Arian 1973; Lissak 1971). Even the famous and violent ethnic unrest at Wadi Saliv in 1959 did not generate a viable ethnic party (e.g., see Eisenstadt 1968 for a short description). In local municipal elections, however, small ethnic groups were more successful in achieving representation than in the national scene.

16. A religious community near Tel Aviv.

17. See, for example, editorials and articles in *Ha'aretz*, December 3, 1980.

18. *Ha'aretz*.

19. See *Ha'aretz*, *Ma'ariv*, *Yediot Aharonot*.

20. See *Ha'aretz*, December 30, 1980.

21. For example, the agent referred to Abu-hatzira as a "Frank Parch," which is a slanderous expression aimed generally against Sephardic Jews.

22. See report in *Ha'aretz*, April 25, 1982.

23. I remember watching that particular program. Being an Ashkenasic Jew myself, I could not help being puzzled and amazed, perhaps even somewhat frightened and angry, at the opinions expressed then. Retrospectively, I think that this was the point when I began to examine the possibility of applying sociological investigation to the Abu-hatzira affair.

24. In the 1984 elections, Tami was not very successful and won only one seat in the Knesset. This, I think, had very little to do with what happened to Abu-hatzira. Tami's decline had a few reasons. First, Abu-hatzira tried to broaden Tami's electoral base, which made his followers very unhappy. Second, Tami did not project an image of a vibrant, lively, and active party. Actually, key members claimed in interviews with the media that Tami was really structureless. This complaint was reinforced when Tami's prestigious secretary-general, Binyamin Ben-Eliezer, quit the party. In other words, Tami did not deliver many of its preelection promises. Third, a very strong element in Abu-hatzira's success was a religious factor. To a very large extent this factor was neutralized when a new Baba Sally emerged and when a new religious party, Shas, emerged in the 1984 election and won four seats in the Knesset. Shas geared itself explicitly to the same population of Sephardic, religious Jews, from where Abu-hatzira drew his electoral strength. Shas, however, was more successful than Abu-hatzira; it has clearly become identified as a religious Sephardic party. No doubt, it owes much of its success of the breakthrough achieved previously by Abu-hatzira.

25. Edith Zartal, "King Abu-hatzira," *Yediot Aharonot*, the ''7 Days'' supplement, August 1983.

26. Not all inhabitants of Abu-hatzira's symbolic-moral universe were involved in nihilation to the same extent. Some claimed that there were good Ashkenasic Jews that should not be deviantized. There are a few thin indications that perhaps Abu-hatzira himself wanted to have a few token Ashkenasic Jews in his party. His motivation was probably to widen the possible appeal of his symbolic-moral universe not only to other Sephardic Jews but to some Ashkenasic Jews as well.

27. As an educated guess, I am more than willing to accept this account as valid. It is quite possible that some members of the Mafdal party felt that Abu-hatzira was creating a competitive power center within the party. An informal control mechanism failed, criminalization remained. One has to remember that the Israeli police did not just "fall" on Abu-hatzira: (1) someone must have tipped them and (2) the minister of police then was a major political figure from the Mafdal party.

28. See chapter four.

Chapter Nine.

1. See footnote 2, chapter one.

Bibliography

Adoni, Hanna, and Mane, Sherill (1984). "Media and the Social Construction of Reality. Toward an Integration of Theory and Research." *Communication Research*, II (#3):323–40.

Agassi, Joseph (1975). *Science in Flux*. Dordrecht: D. Reidel.

Alexander, Jeffrey C. (1979). "Paradigm Revision and 'Parsonianism.'" *Canadian Journal of Sociology* 4 (#4):343–58.

Alexander, J. C. (1982). *Theoretical Logic in Sociology*, Vol. One. Berkeley: University of California Press.

———, ed. (1985). *Neofunctionalism*. London: Sage Publications.

———. (1986). "Why Neofunctionalism: Two Responses to Page." *ASA Footnotes*, January, p. 5.

———, Giesen, B.; Munch, R.; and Smelser N., eds. (1987). *The Micro-Macro Link*. Berkeley: University of California Press.

Alexander, Yonah, and Kilmarx, Robert A., ed. (1979). *Political Terrorism and Business*. New York: Praeger.

Anderson, Patrick (1981). *High in America. The True Story Behind NORML and the Politics of Marijuana*. New York: The Viking Press.

Aran, Gideon (1985). *The Land of Bread Between Politics and Religion: The Movement to Stop the Withdrawal in Sinai*. Jerusalem: Jerusalem Institute for Israel Studies (Hebrew).

———. (1987). *From Religious Zionism to Zionist Religion. The Origin and Culture of Gush Emunim: A Messianic Movement in Modern Israel*. Ph.D. dissertation, Department of Sociology, Hebrew University (Hebrew).

Arian, Alan (1973). *The Choosing People*. Cleveland: The Press of Case Western Reserve University.

Ashley, Richard (1972). *Heroin: The Myths and the Facts*. New York: St. Martin's Press.

Astrachan, Anthony (1985). "When Is Right Wrong, and Vice Versa?" *Science Digest* 93 (#11):77–78.

Atkins, Burton M., and Glick, Henry R., ed. (1972). *Prisons, Protest and Politics*. Englewood Cliffs, N.J.: Prentice Hall, Inc.

Auld, John (1973). "Drug Use: The Mystification of Accounts." In *Contemporary Social Problems in Britain*, edited by Roy Bailey and Jock Young. Lexington, MA. Saxon House, Lexington Books.

Austin, G. A. (1978). *Perspectives on the History of Psychoactive Substance Use*. Washington, D.C.: National Institute on Drug Abuse (Research Issue No. 24).

_____, and Lettieri, D. J., eds. (1976). *Drugs and Crime*. Rockville, MD: National Institute on Drug Abuse.

Bachelard, Gaston (1985). *The New Scientific Spirit*. Boston: Beacon Press.

Bailey, R. (1973). "Housing: Alienation and Beyond." In *Politics and Deviance*, edited by I. Taylor and L. Taylor. Baltimore: Penguin Books.

Bakalar, James B., and Grinspoon, Lester (1984). *Drug Control in a Free Society*. New York: Cambridge University Press.

Banfield, Edward G. (1961). *Political Influence*. New York: The Free Press.

Barber, B. (1961). "Resistance by Scientists to Scientific Discovery." *Science* 134 (#3479), September 1:596–602.

Barlow, Hugh D. (1984). *Introduction to Criminology*. 3rd ed. Boston: Little, Brown and Company.

Barnea, Zippora (1978). *A Multidimensional Model of Young People's Readiness to Use Drugs*. Tel Aviv, unpublished M.A. thesis, Institute of Criminology. Tel Aviv University (Hebrew).

Barnes, B. (1977). "On the Perception of Scientific Beliefs." In *Sociology of Science*, edited by B. Barnes. England: Penguin Books.

_____. (1982). *T. S. Kuhn and Social Science*. New York: Columbia University Press.

Barrow, John D. (1983). *The Left Hand of Creation: The Origin and Evolution of the Expanding Universe*. New York: Basic Books.

Bart, P. B. (1968). "Social Structure and Vocabularies of Discomfort: What Happened to Female Hysteria?" *Journal of Health and Social Behavior* 9 (#2):188–93.

Beauchamp, Dan E. (1980). *Beyond Alcoholism: Alcohol and Public Health Policy*. Philadelphia: Temple University Press.

Bechtel, Kenneth H., and Pearson, Willie, Jr. (1985). "Deviant Scientists and Scientific Deviance." *Deviant Behavior* 6(#3):237–52.

Becker, Howard S. (1953). "Becoming a Marijuana User." *American Journal of Sociology* 59:235–42.

_____. (1963). *Outsiders*. New York: The Free Press.

_____. (1967). "Whose Side Are We On?" *Social Problems* 14 (#3):239–47.

Becker, Jillian (1977). *Hitler's Children*. Philadelphia and New York: J. B. Lippincott Co.

Becker, Theodore L., ed. (1971). *Political Trials*. Indianapolis and New York: The Bobbs-Merrill Co., Inc.

Beirne, Piers, and Quinney, Richard, eds. (1982). *Marxism and Law*. New York: John Wiley and Sons.

Bellah, Robert N. (1968). "Civil Religion in America." In *Religion in America*, edited by William G. Mcloughlin and Robert N. Bellah. Boston: Houghton Mifflin.

Ben-David, Joseph (1964). "Scientific Growth: A Sociological View." *Minerva* 2:455–76.

————. (1960). "Roles and Innovations in Medicine." *American Journal of Sociology.* 65:557–68.

————. (1977). "Organization, Social Control and Cognitive Change in Science." In *Culture and Its Creators: Essays in Honor of Edward Shils,* edited by J. Ben-David and T. Clark. Chicago: University of Chicago Press.

Ben-Yehuda, Nachman (1979). *Drug Abuse in Israel—A Survey.* Jerusalem, Interministerial Committee on Drug Abuse, Ministry of Social Affairs (Hebrew).

————. (1980). "The European Witch Craze of the 14th to 17th Centuries: A Sociologist's Perspective." *American Journal of Sociology 86,* (#1):1–31.

————. (1981). "Success and Failure in Rehabilitation: The Case of Methadone Maintenance." *American Journal of Community Psychology 9* (#1):83–107.

Ben-Yehuda, N. (1982). "Private Practice, Competition and Methadone Maintenance," *The International Journal of the Addictions,* 17 (#2):329–41.

————. (1984). "A Clinical Sociology Approach to Treatment of Deviants: The Case of Drug Addicts." *Drug and Alcohol Dependence* 13:267–82.

————. (1985). *Deviance and Moral Boundaries: Witchcraft, the Occult, Science Fiction, Deviant Sciences and Scientists.* Chicago: The University of Chicago Press.

————. (1986a). "Deviance in Science." *The British Journal of Criminology* 26 (#1):1–27.

————. (1986b). "Therapy as a Form of Social Control: A Clinical Sociology Approach for Treating Drug Addicts." *In Planning for Treatment,* edited by S. Einstein. Sandoz Monograph Series, U.S.A.

————. (1987). "Common Elements in Structure in Magic, Witchcraft and Analytically Oriented Psychoterapy." *Quarterly Journal of Ideology* 11 (#2):75–88.

————. (1989). "The Prevalence of Drug Abuse in Israel—Is It Expanding or Is It Static? A Sociological Hypothesis." Forthcoming in *Delinquency and Social Deviance* (Hebrew).

_____. (forthcoming): *Political Assassinations by Jews in the Land of Secular Miracles: A Rhetorical Device for Justice.*

_____, and Einstein, Stanley (1984). "Human Garbage and Physical Garbage: A Sociological Case Example of Institutional Violence." *The International Journal of the Addictions* 19 (#1):1–23.

Berger, Peter L., and Luckmann, Thomas M. (1966). *The Social Construction of Reality.* Baltimore: Penguin Books.

Bergesen, Albert J. (1977). "Political Witch Hunts: The Sacred and the Subversive in Cross National Perspective." *American Sociological Review* 42:220–33.

_____. (1978). "A Durkheimian Theory of 'Witch Hunts' with the Chinese Cultural Revolution of 1966–69 as an Example." *Journal for the Scientific Study of Religion* 17 (#1):10–29.

_____. (1984). "Social Control and Corporate Organization: A Durkheimian Perspective." In *Toward a General Theory of Social Control.* vol. 2., edited by D. Black. New York: Academic Press, Inc.

Berlet, C. (1981). "War on Drugs," *High Times* 69:49–51, 76–77.

Bernstein, Devorah (1979). "The Black Panthers: Conflict and Protest in Israeli Society." *Megamot* 9:69–81 (Hebrew).

Best, J. (1979). "Economic Interests and the Vindication of Deviance: Tobacco in Seventeenth Century Europe." *The Sociological Quarterly* 20 (#2): 171–82.

Beyleveld, Deryck, and Wiles, Paul (1975). "Man and Method in David Matza's 'Becoming Deviant.'" *British Journal of Criminology* 15 (#2):111–27.

Biernacki, Patrick (1986). *Pathways from Heroin Addiction: Recovery Without Treatment.* Philadelphia: Temple University Press.

Black, Donald, ed. (1984). *Toward a General Theory of Social Control.* 2 vols. New York: Academic Press, Inc.

Bliss, M. (1982). *The Discovery of Insulin.* Chicago, University of Chicago Press.

Blum, Alan F. (1970). "The Sociology of Mental Illness." In *Deviance and Respectability,* edited by J. Douglas. New York: Basic Books.

_____, and McHugh, Peter (1971). "The Social Ascription of Motives." *American Sociological Review* 36 (February):98–109.

Blumberg, A. S. (1975). "Drug Control: Agenda for Repression." In *Drug Abuse Control*, edited by R. L. Rachin and E. H. Czajkoski. Lexington, MA: Lexington Books.

Blumer, Herbert (1969). *Symbolic Interactionism*. Englewood Cliffs, NJ: Prentice Hall, Inc.

Boles, Jacqueline and Lyn Myers (1988). "Chain Letters: Players and Their Accounts," *Deviant Behavior*, 9 (#3):241–57.

Bonacich, Edna (1972). "A Theory of Ethnic Antagonism: The Split Labor Market." *American Sociological Review* 37:547–59.

Bonn, R. L. (1984). *Criminology*. New York: McGraw-Hill Book Co.

Bonnie, R. J., and Whitebread, C. H. (1974). *The Marijuana Conviction*. Charlottesville: University Press of Virginia.

Bourdieu, Pierre (1975). "The Specificity of the Scientific Field and the Social Conditions of the Progress of Reason." *Social Science Information* 14(#6):19–47.

Box, Steven (1981). *Deviance, Reality and Society*. New York: Holt Reinhart and Winston.

_____. (1983). *Power, Crime and Mystification*. London: Tavistock Publications.

Braithwaite, John (1985). "White Collar Crime." In *Annual Review of Sociology*, vol. II, edited by R. H. Turner and J. F. Short. California, Annual Reviews Inc.

_____. (1989). *Crime, Shame and Reintegration*. New York: Cambridge University Press.

Brannigan, Augustine (1981). *The Social Basis of Scientific Discoveries*. Cambridge: Cambridge University Press.

_____. (1986). "Crimes from Comics: Social and Political Determinants of Reform of the Victoria Obscenity Law 1938-1954. *The Australian and New Zealand Journal of Criminology* 19(#1):23–42.

Brecher, Edward M, and the Editors of Consumer Reports (1972). *Licit and Illicit Drugs*. Boston: Little, Brown and Co.

Brissett, Dennis, and Edgly, Charles (1975). *Life as Theatre: A Dramaturgical Sourcebook*. Chicago: Aldine Publishing.

Bromley, David G., and Shupe, A. D. (1980). "Financing the New Religions: A Resource Mobilization Approach." *Journal for the Scientific Study of Religion* 19 (#3):227–39.

Bromley, David G., Shupe, Anson D. and Ventimiglia, J. C. (1979). "Atrocity Tales: The Unification Church, and the Social Construction of Evil," *Journal of Communication* 29 (#3):42–53.

Brook, R. C. and Whitehead, P. C. (1980). *Drug Free Therapeutic Community*. New York: Human Science Press.

Bruce, Steve, and Wallis, Roy (1983). "Accounting for Action: Defending the Common Sense Heresy." *Sociology* 17 (#1):97–111.

Brush, S. G. (1974). "Should the History of Science Be Rated X?" *Science* 83 (#4130):1164–72.

Burkof, Haim (1981). *Use of Drugs and Alcohol Among Youth in Ramat Hasharon — An Epidemiological Survey*. Jerusalem: An Interim Report No. 1. The Interministerial Committee on Drug Abuse, Ministry of Social Affairs (Hebrew).

Burton, Frank and Carlen, Pat (1979). *Official Discourse: On Discourse Analysis, Government Publications, Ideology and the State*. London: Routledge and Kegan Paul.

Byrne, Noel T. (1976). "Emile Durkheim as Symbolic Interactionist." *Sociological Symposium* 16:25–45.

Cantril, Hadley (1940). *The Invasion from Mars*. Princeton, NJ: Princeton University Press.

Caplan, R. B. (1969). *Psychiatry and the Community in Nineteenth Century America*. New York: Basic Books.

Carlen, Pat, and Collison, Mike, eds. (1980). *Radical Issues in Criminology*. Totowa, NJ: Barnes and Noble Books.

Chambers, Carl D.; Inciardi, James A.; Siegal, Harvey A. (1975). *Chemical Coping: A Report on Legal Drug Use in the United States*. New York: Spectrum Publications, Inc.

Chambliss, W. J. (1978). *On the Take: From Petty Crooks to Presidents*. Bloomington, IN: Indiana University Press.

Chauncey, Robert L. (1980). "New Careers for Moral Entrepreneurs: Teenage Drinking." *Journal of Drug Issues* 10:45–70.

Christenson, Ron (1986). *Political Trials: Gordian Knots in the Law*. New Brunswick, NJ: Transaction Books.

Christie, Nils (1984). *Suitable Enemies*. Paper given at the Howar League Second Annual Conference. "The Individual and the State: The Impact of Criminal Justice." Oxford, September 10.

―――, and Bruun, Kettil (1985). *Den Gode Fiende*. Oslo, Norway: Universitetsforlaget As. (Norwegian).

Chubin, Daryl E. (1985). "Misconduct in Research: An Issue of Science Policy and Practice." *Minerva* 23(#2):175–202.

Clarke, James W. (1982). *American Assassins: The Darker Side of Politics*. Princeton, NJ: Princeton University Press.

Cleaver, Eldridge (1968). *Soul on Ice*. New York: Dell Publishing Co., Inc. A Delta Book.

Clinard, Marshall B. (1952). *The Black Market: A Study of White Collar Crime*. New York: Holt, Rinehart and Winston.

Clinard, Marshall B. (1957). *Sociology of Deviant Behavior*. New York: Holt, Rinehart and Winston, Inc. (see the 1974 edition).

―――. (1983). *Corporate Ethics and Crime*. Beverly Hills, CA: Sage Publications.

―――, and Yeager, Peter C. (1980). *Corporate Crime*. New York: The Free Press.

Clutterbuck, Richard (1973). *Protest and the Urban Guerrilla*. New York: Abelard-Schuman.

Cohen, Albert (1966). *Deviance and Control*. Englewood Cliffs, NJ: Prentice Hall.

Cohen, Bernard I. (1984). *Revolutions in Science*. Cambridge, MA: Belknap Press/Harvard University Press.

Cohen, Erik (1972). "The Black Panthers and Israeli Society." *Jewish Journal of Sociology* 14 (#1):93–109.

———. (1983). "Ethnicity and Legitimation in Contemporary Israel." *Jerusalem Quarterly* 28:111–24.

———, ed. (1987). "The Evacuation of Yamit Region." A Special issue of the *Journal of Applied Behavioral Science*.

———, and Ben-Arie, Eyal (1985). *Hard Choices: The Sociological Analysis of Value Incommensurability*. Unpublished paper, Department of Sociology, Hebrew University, Jerusalem.

———, and Ben-Yehuda, Nachman (1987). "Counter Cultural Movements and Totalitarian Democrary." *Sociological Inquiry* 57 (#4):372–93.

———; Ben-Yehuda, Nachman; and Aviad, Janet (1987). "Recentering the World: The Quest for 'Elective' Centers in a Secularized Universe." *The Sociological Review* 35, 320–46.

Cohen, Gerald Allan (1978). *Karl Marx's Theory of History: A Defence*. Princeton, NJ: Princeton University Press.

Cohen, Ronald L., ed. (1986). *Justice: Views from the Social Sciences*. New York: Plenum Press.

Cohen, Stanley (1972). *Folk Devils and Moral Panics*. London: MacGibbon and Kee (see 1980 U.S. edition by St. Martin's Press).

———. (1974). "Criminology and the Sociology of Deviance in Britain." In *Deviance and Social Control*, edited by P. Rock and M. McIntosh. London: Tavistock Publications.

———, ed. (1981). *Images of Deviance*. Middlesex: Penguin Books.

———. (1985). *Visions of Social Control*. Cambridge: Polity Press.

———. (1986a). "Bandits, Rebels or Criminals: African History and Western Criminology." *Africa: Journal of the International African Institute*. 56 (#4):468–83.

————. (1986b). *Against Criminology.* New Brunswick, NJ: Transaction Books.

————, and Scull, Andrew, eds. (1983). *Social Control and the State.* Oxford: Martin Robertson.

Cole, Steven (1970). "Professional Standing and the Reception of Scientific Discoveries." *American Journal of Sociology* 76:286–306.

————; Cole, Jonathan R.; and Simon, G. A. (1981). "Chance and Consensus in Peer Review." *Science* 214:881–86.

Coleman, James W. (1985). *The Criminal Elite: The Sociology of White Collar Crime.* New York: St. Martin's Press, Inc.

Coleman, John A. (1970). "Civil Religion." *Sociological Analysis* 31 (#2):67–77.

Collins, Randall (1986). "Is 1980s Sociology in the Doldrums?" *American Journal of Sociology* 91 (#6):1336–55.

Conklin, J. E. (1977). *Illegal But Not Criminal.* Englewood Ciffs, NJ: Prentice Hall, Inc.

Conklin, John E. (1986). *Criminology,* 2nd ed. New York: MacMillan Publishing Company.

Conrad, Peter, and Schneider, Joseph W. (1980). *Deviance and Medicalization.* St. Louis: The C. V. Mosby Co.

Cook, Robert M. (1968). "The Police," *The Bulletin of the American Independent Movement,* 3 (#6):1–6.

Cook, Shirley J. (1970). "Social Background of Narcotics Legislation." *Addictions* 17:14–29.

Coser, Lewis A. (1962). "Some Functions of Deviant Behavior and Normative Flexibility." *American Journal of Sociology* 68 (#2):172–81.

Courtwright, D. T. (1982). *Dark Paradise: Opiate Addiction in America Before 1940.* Cambridge, MA: Harvard University Press.

Covington, Jeanette (1984). "Insulation from Labeling." *Criminology* 22 (#4):619–43.

Crane, D. (1967). "The Gatekeepers of Science: Some Factors Affecting the Selection of Articles for Scientific Journals." *American Sociologist* 2:195–201.

Crenshaw, Martha, ed. (1983). *Terrorism, Legitimacy and Power.* Middletown, CT: Wesleyan University Press.

Cressey, Donald R. (1953). *Other People's Money: The Social Psychology of Embezzlement.* Belmont, CA: Wadsworth Publishing Co.

———. (1962). "Role Theory, Differential Association and Compulsive Crimes." In *Human Behavior and Social Processes,* edited by A. M. Rose. Boston: Houghton Mifflin.

Crittenden, Kathleen S. (1983). "Sociological Aspects of Attribution." In *Annual Review of Sociology,* edited by Ralph H. Turner and James F. Short. Palo Alto, CA: Annual Reviews Inc.

Cromer, Gerald (1986). " 'Secularization Is the Root of All Evil'—The Response of Ultra-Orthodox Judaism to Social Deviance." In *Proceedings of the 9th World Congress on Jewish Studies* (August 1985), 2nd Division, 3rd Volume, Jerusalem: World Association for Jewish Studies.

Crotty, William J., ed. (1971). *Assassinations and the Political Order.* New York: Harper and Row, A Torchbook Library edition.

Cullen, Frances T. (1983). *Rethinking Crime and Deviance Theory.* Totowa, NJ: Rowman and Allanheld.

Cumming, E., and Cumming, J. (1957). *Closed Ranks: An Experiment in Mental Health Education.* Cambridge, MA: Harvard University Press.

Cusky, W. A.; Berger, L. H.; and Richardson, A. H. (1978). "The Effects of Marijuana Decriminalization on Drug Use Patterns: A Literature Review and Research Critique." *Contemporary Drug Problems.* Winter: 491–532.

Darley, J. M., and Zanna, M. P. (1982). "Making Moral Judgements." *American Scientist* 70 (#5):515–21.

Davies, Paul (1983). *God and the New Physics.* New York: Simon and Schuster.

Davis, F. J., and Stivers, Richard, eds. (1975). *The Collective Definition of Deviance*. New York: The Free Press.

Davis, J. (1952). "Crime News in Colorado Newspapers." *American Journal of Sociology* 54:325–30.

Davis, Kingsley (1938). "Mental Hygiene and the Class Structure." *Psychiatry* 1:55–56.

Davis, Nanette J. (1975). *Sociological Constructions of Deviance: Perspectives and Issues in the Field*. Dubuque, IA: W. C. Brown Co., Publishers.

_____, and Anderson, Bo (1983). *Social Control: The Production of Deviance and the Modern State*. New York: Irvington Publishers Inc.

Decriminalization of Marijuana and the Maine Criminal Justice System, The. (1979). Maine: Office of Alcoholism and Drug Abuse Prevention.

DeFleur, Louis B. (1976). "Biasing Influence on Drug Arrest Records: Implications for Deviance Research." *American Sociological Review* 40:88–103.

Delong, James V. (1972). "Treatment and Rehabilitation." In *Dealing with Drug Abuse. A Report to the Ford Foundation*. The Drug Abuse Survey Project. New York: Praeger Publications.

Denisoff, Serge R., and McCaghy, Charles H., eds. (1973). *Deviance Conflict and Criminality*. Chicago: Rand McNally and Co.

Dickson, Donald T. (1968). "Bureaucracy and Morality: An Organizational Perspective on a Moral Crusade." *Social Problems* 16:143–56.

_____. (1975). "Narcotics and Marijuana: Two Case Studies of Bureaucratic Growth and Survival." In *Drug Abuse Control*, edited by R. L. Rachin and E. H. Czajkosh. Lexington, MA: Lexington Books.

Dietz, Mary Lorentz (1983). *Killing for Profit: The Social Organization of Felony Homicide*. Chicago: Nelson-Hall.

Dingle, A. E. (1980). *The Campaign for Prohibition in Victorian England*. New Brunswick, NJ: Rutgers University Press.

Ditton, Jason (1977). "Alibis and Aliases: Some Notes on the 'Motives' of Fiddling Bread Salesmen." *Sociology* 4:233–55.

Dodge, David L. (1985). "The Over-Negativised Conceptualization of Deviance: A Programmatic Exploration." *Deviant Behavior* 6:17–37.

Dolby, R. G. A. (1979). "Reflections on Deviant Science." In *On the Margins of Science: The Social Construction of Rejected Knowledge*, edited by Roy Wallis. England: University of Keele Press.

Dole, Vincent P., and Nyswander, Mary E. (1967). "Heroin Addiction—A Metabolic Disease." *Archives of Internal Medicine* 120:19–24.

_____, and Nyswander, Mary E. (1968). "Successful Treatment of 750 Criminal Addicts." *Journal of the American Medical Association* 206:2708–11.

Dominelli, Lena (1986). "The Power of the Powerless: Prostitution and the Reinforcement of Submissive Femininity." *The Sociological Review* 34:65–92.

Dotter, Daniel L., and Roebuck, Julian B. (1988). "The Labeling Approach Re-Examined: Interactionism and the Components of Deviance." *Deviant Behavior* 9:19–32.

Douglas, Jack (1967). *The Social Meaning of Suicide*. Princeton, NJ: Princeton University Press.

_____. (1970a). "Deviance and Order in a Pluralistic Society." In *Theoretical Sociology: Perspectives and Development*, edited by J. C. McKinney and E. A. Tiryakian. New York: Appleton-Century-Crofts.

_____, ed. (1970b). *Deviance and Respectability*. New York: Basic Books.

_____. (1971). *American Social Order: Social Rules in a Pluralistic Society*. New York: The Free Press.

_____. (1977). "Shame and Deceit in Creative Deviance." In *Deviance and Social Change*, edited by Edward Sagarin. California: Sage.

_____, and Johnson, John M., eds. (1977). *Official Deviance*. Philadelphia: J. B. Lippincott Co.

_____, and Frances Waksler (1982). *The Sociology of Deviance: An Introduction*. Boston: Little, Brown and Co.

Douglas, Mary (1966). *Purity and Danger*. London: Routledge and Kegan Paul.

Douglas, M. (1986). *How Institutions Think*. Syracuse: Syracuse University Press.

Downes, David (1977). "The Drug Addict as a Folk Devil." In *Drugs and Politics*, edited by P. Rock. New Brunswick, NJ: Transaction Books.

Dumont, M. P. (1973). "The Junkie as a Political Enemy." *American Journal of Orthopsychiatry* 43 (#4):533–40.

Durkheim, Emile (1933 , 1964). *The Division of Labor in Society*. New York: The Free Press (published originally in French in 1893).

_____. (1938). *The Rules of Sociological Method*. New York: The Free Press (published originally in French in 1895).

_____. (1951). *Suicide*. New York: The Free Press (published originally in French in 1897).

_____. (1973). *On Morality and Society*. Chicago: University of Chicago Press.

Duster, Troy (1970). *The Legislation of Morality*. New York: The Free Press.

Duvall, Henrietta J., Locke, B. Z. and Brill, L. (1963). "Follow Up Study of Narcotic Drug Addicts Five Years After Hospitalization." *Public Health Reports* 78 (#3):185–93.

Edelhertz , Herbert (1970). *The Nature, Impact and Prosecution of White Collar Crime*. U.S. Department of Justice, Law Enforcement Assistance Administration.

Edge, David O., and Mulkay, Michael J. (1976). *Astronomy Transformed: The Emergence of Radio Astronomy in Britain*. New York: John Wiley and Sons.

Eisenstadt, Mimi (1984). *The Israeli Treatment of "Deviant Behavior" in Schools as a "Social Problem."* Jerusalem, unpublished M.A. thesis. Institute of Criminology, Hebrew University (Hebrew).

Eisenstadt, Samuel N. (1968). *Israeli Society*. New York: Basic Books.

Eldridge, W. G. (1971). *Narcotics and the Law*. Chicago: University of Chicago Press.

Elkana, Yehuda (1970). "The Conservation of Energy: A Case of Simultaneous Discovery?" *Archives Internationales d'Histoire des Sciences* (January–June):31–60, 90–91.

EL-Roy, Ruth (1981). *Punitive Policy of the State of Israel Towards First Offense of Possessing and Using Drugs.* Headquarters unit on drug abuse, the Interministerial Committee on Drug Abuse. Ministry of Labour and Social Affairs, Jerusalem (Hebrew).

Enquist, V., and Coles, F. (1970). " 'Political' Criminals in America: O'Hare (1923): Cantine and Raines (1950)." *Issues in Criminology* 5 (#2):209–20.

Epstein, J. E. (1977). *Agency of Fear.* New York: G. P. Putnam's Sons.

Erikson, Kai T. (1962). "Notes on the Sociology of Deviance." *Social Problems* 9:307–14.

――――. (1966). *Wayward Puritans.* New York: Wiley.

Ermann, David M., and Lundman, Richard J. (1978). *Corporate and Governmental Deviance.* New York: Oxford University Press.

――――, and Lundman, Richard J. (1982). *Corporate Deviance.* New York: Holt, Rinehard and Winston.

Evaluation of the Decriminalization of Marijuana in Maine, An (1978). State of Maine, Department of Human Services, Office of Alcoholism and Drug Abuse Prevention.

Evans-Pritchard, E. E. (1929). "Witchcraft (Mangu) Amongst the Azande." In *Sudan Notes and Records,* vol. 12. Quoted from the abridged form in *Witchcraft and Sorcery,* edited by Max Marwick. (1970). Penguin Books.

Faia, Michael A. (1986). *Dynamic Functionalism: Strategy and Tactics.* London: Cambridge University Press.

Fairchild, Erika S. (1977). "Politicization of the Criminal Offender." *Criminology* 15 (#3):287–318.

――――, and Webb, Vincent J. (1985). *The Politics of Crime and Criminal Justice.* Beverly Hills, CA: Sage Publications.

Farrell, Ronald A., and Swigert, Victoria L. (1982). *Deviance and Social Control.* Glenview, IL: Scott, Foresman and Co.

Fauconnier, Gilles (1981). "Social Ritual and Relative Truth in Natural Language." In *Advances in Social Theory and Methodology: Towards an Integration of Micro- and Macro-Sociologies*, edited by K. Knorr-Cetina and A. Cicourel. Boston: Routledge and Kegan Paul.

Feldman, H. E.; Agar, M. H.; and Beschner, G. M. eds. (1981). *Angel Dust: An Ethnographic Study of PCP Users*. Lexington: Lexington Press.

Ferris, Timothy (1977). *The Red Limit. The Search for the Edge of the Universe*. New York: Bantam Edition (1979).

Feyerabend, P. (1975). *Against Method*. London: Verso.

Fiddle, Seymour (1967). *Portraits from a Shooting Gallery*. New York: Harper & Row.

Finestone, Harold (1964). "Cats, Kicks and Color." In *The Other Side*, edited by H. Becker. New York: The Free Press.

Fireside, Harvey (1979). *Soviet Psychoprisons*. New York: W. W. Norton.

First Report of the Impact of California's New Marijuana Laws, A. (January 1977). Health and Welfare Agency, State Office of Narcotics and Drug Abuse.

Fishburne, P. M.; Abelson, H. I.; Cisin, I. (1979). *National Survey on Drug Abuse: Main Findings 1979*. Rackville, MD: National Institute on Drug Abuse.

Fishman, Mark (1978). "Crime Waves as Ideology." *Social Problems* 25:531–43.

Fletcher, H. (1982). "My Work with Millikin on the Oil-Drop Experiment." *Physics Today* 35:43–47.

Ford, Franklin (1985). *Political Murder*. Cambridge, MA: Harvard University Press.

Forster, Peter G. (1986). "Functionalism and the Devlin-Hart Controversy." *The British Journal of Sociology* 37 (#1):74–87.

Foucault, Michel (1977). *Discipline and Punish: The Birth of the Prison*, trans. Alan Sheridan. New York: Pantheon Books.

———. (1980). *Power/Knowledge*. New York: Pantheon Books.

Frank, Jerome D. (1961). *Persuasion and Healing*. New York: Schocken.

Frank, Nancy (1985). *Crimes Against Health and Safety*. New York: Harrow and Heston.

Frankel, E. (1976). "Corpuscular Optics and the Wave Theory of Light: The Science and Politics of a Revolution in Physics." *Social Studies of Science* 6:141–84.

Frazier, Charles E. (1976). *Theoretical Approaches to Deviance*. Columbus, OH: Charles E. Merrill Publishing Co.

Freedman, Lawrence Z., and Alexander, Yonah, ed. (1983). *Perspectives on Terrorism*. Wilmington, DE: Scholarly Resources Inc.

Frenkel, Henry (1979). "The Reception and Acceptance of Continental Drift Theory as a Rational Episode in the History of Science." In *The Reception of Unconventional Science*, edited by S. H. Mouskopf. AAAS Selected Symposium 25. New York: Westview Press.

Friedman, Leon (1983). "War Crimes." In *Encyclopedia of Crime and Justice*, edited by Sanford H. Kadish, vol. 4, New York: The Free Press.

Fuhrman, Ellsworth R., and Oehler, K. (1986). "Discourse Analysis and Reflexivity." *Social Studies of Science* 16 (#2):293–307.

Fuller, John G. (1984). *The Day We Bombed Utah*. New York: New American Library.

Gallagher, Bernard J. (1980). *The Sociology of Mental Illness*. Englewood Cliffs, NJ: Prentice Hall, Inc.

Galliher, John F., and Cross, John R. (1983). *Moral Legislation Without Morality*. New Brunswick, NJ: Rutgers University Press.

_____, and McCartney, J. L. (1977). *Criminology: Power, Crime and Criminal Law*. Homewood, IL: The Dorsey Press.

_____, and Walker, A. (1973). "The Puzzle of the Social Origins of the Marijuana Tax Act of 1937." *Social Problems* 34:367–76.

Gans, Herbert (1972). "The Positive Function of Poverty." *American Journal of Sociology* 78:275–89.

Gardner, Martin (1983). "Margaret Mead and the Paranormal." *The Skeptical Inquirer,* 8 (#1):13–16.

Garfinkel, Harold (1950). "Conditions of Successful Degradation Ceremonies." *American Journal of Sociology* 61:420–24.

———. (1967). *Studies in Ethnomethodology.* Englewood Cliffs, NJ: Prentice Hall, Inc.

Gartner, Allan, and Riessman, Frank, eds. (1984). *The Self-Help Revolution.* New York: Human Sciences Press, Inc.

Geertz, Clifford (1964). "Ideology as a Cultural System." In *Ideology and Discontent,* edited by D. Apter. New York: The Free Press.

———. (1973). *The Interpretation of Cultures.* New York: Basic Books.

Geis, Gilbert, and Stotland, Ezra, eds. (1980). *White Collar Crime.* Beverly Hills, CA: Sage Publications.

Gibbons, Don C., and Jones, Joseph F. (1975). *The Study of Deviance: Perspectives and Problems.* Englewood Cliffs, NJ: Prentice Hall, Inc.

Gibbs, Jack P. (1985). "Social Control." In *The Social Science Encyclopedia,* edited by Adam Kuper and Jessica Kuper. London: Routledge and Kegan Paul.

Giddings, Franklin H. (1898). "Introduction." In Proal Louis (1898): *Political Crime.* Reprinted in 1973. Montclair, NJ: Patterson Smith.

Gieryn, T. F. (1983). "Boundary Work and the Demarcation of Science from Non-Science: Strains and Interests in Professional Ideologies of Scientists." *American Sociological Review* 48 (#6):781–95.

———, and Hirsch, R. F. (1983). "Marginality and Innovation in Science." *Social Studies of Science* 13 (#1):87–106.

Geis, Gilbert and Stotland, Ezra, eds. (1980). *White Collar Crime.* Beverly Hills, CA: Sage Publications.

Gilbert, Nigel G., and Peter Abell, eds. (1983). *Accounts and Action. Survey Conferences on Sociological Theory and Method.* Hampshire, England: Gower.

Gilbert, Nigel G., and Mulkay, Michael (1984). *Opening Pandora's Box. A Sociological Analysis of Scientists' Discourse.* New York: Cambridge University Press.

Ginat, Joseph (1984). "The Role of Mediator: With Special Reference to Blood Disputes." In *Israel Studies in Criminology,* vol. 7, edited by S. G. Shoham. New York: Sheridan House Inc.

Goffman, Erving (1959). *The Presentation of Self in Everyday Life.* New York: Doubleday Anchor Books.

Goffman, Erving (1961). *Asylums.* Garden City, NY: Doubleday and Company, Inc.

_____. (1963). *Stigma.* Englewood Cliffs, NJ: Prentice Hall, Inc.

_____. (1974). *Frame Analysis: An Essay on the Organization of Experience.* New York: Harper & Row.

Goldberg, Peter (1980). "The Federal Government's Response to Illicit Drugs, 1969–1978." In *The Facts About Drug Abuse.* New York: The Free Press.

Gonzales, Laurence (1982). "The War on Drugs: A Special Report." *Playboy,* April, 135–216.

_____. (1984). "Cocaine: A Special Report." *Playboy* (September) 31 (#9):112–14.

Goode, Erich (1972). *Drugs in American Society.* New York: Alfred A. Knopf.

_____. (1978). *Deviant Behavior: The Interactionist Approach.* Englewood Cliffs, NJ: Prentice Hall, Inc.

_____. (1984a). *Deviant Behavior.* 2nd ed. Englewood Cliffs, NJ: Prentice Hall, Inc.

_____. (1984b). *Drugs in American Society.* 2nd ed. New York: Alfred A. Knopf.

_____. (1988). *Sociology.* 2nd ed. Englewood Cliffs, NJ: Prentice Hall, Inc.

_____. (1989). *Drugs in American Society.* 3rd ed. New York: Alfred A. Knopf.

———, and Preissler, Joanne (1983). "The Fat Admirer." *Deviant Behavior* 4:175–202.

Goodell, Charles (1973). *Political Prisoners in America.* New York: Random House.

Goodstein, Judith R. (1984). "Atoms, Molecules, and Linus Pauling." *Social Research* 51 (#3):691–708.

Gould, Leroy; Walker, Andrew L.; Crane, E. Lansing; and Lidz, Charles W. (1974). *Connections, Notes from the Heroin World.* New Haven, CT: Yale University Press.

Gould, Stephen J. (1977). *Ever Since Darwin.* New York: W. W. Norton and Co.

Gouldner, Alvin (1970). *The Coming Crisis of Western Sociology.* New York: Basic Books.

Graven, D. B. (1977). "Experimental Heroin Users: An Epidemiologic and Psychosocial Approach." *American Journal of Drug and Alcohol Abuse* 4 (#3):365–75.

Greenberg, David, ed. (1981). *Crime and Capitalism.* Palo Alto, CA: Mayfield Publishing Company.

Greene, Mott T. (1984). "Alfred Wegener." *Social Research* 51 (#3):739–61.

Greene, Penelope J.; Durch, Jane S.; Horwitz, Wendy; and Hooper, Valwyn S. (1985). "Policies for Responding to Allegations of Fraud in Research." *Minerva* 23 (#3):203–15.

Gribbin, John (1986). *In Search of the Big Bang.* New York: Bantam Books.

Grim, Patrick, ed. (1982). *Philosophy of Science and the Occult.* New York: State University of New York Press.

Grinspoon, Lester, and Hedbloom, P. (1975). *The Speed Culture.* Cambridge, MA: Harvard University Press.

Grove, J. W. (1985). "Rationality at Risk: Science Against Pseudoscience." *Minerva* 23 (#2):216–40.

Gusfield, Joseph R. (1963). *Symbolic Crusade: Status, Politics and the American Temperance Movement.* Chicago: University of Illinois Press.

———. (1981). *The Culture of Public Problems: Drinking-Driving and the Symbolic Order.* Chicago: The University of Chicago Press.

Gutting, G., ed. (1980). *Paradigms and Revolutions: Applications and Appraisals of Thomas Kuhn's Philosophy of Science.* Notre Dame, IN: University of Notre Dame Press.

Haar, Jeremy (1976). "In Pursuit of Happiness: An Evaluation of the Constitutional Right to Private Use of Marijuana." *Contemporary Drug Problems* 5 (#2):161–85.

Hacker, Frederick J. (1976). *Crusaders, Criminals, Crazies. Terror and Terrorism in Our Time.* New York: W. W. Norton and Co., Inc.

Haddock, F. T. (1958). "Introduction to Radio Astronomy." *Proceedings of the Institute of Radio Engineers* (January) 46 (#1):3–12.

Hagan, Frank E. (1987). *Espionage as Political Crime?: A Typology of Spies,* paper presented at the American Society of Criminology Meeting, Montreal, P.Q., Canada, November.

Hagan, John (1977). *The Disreputable Pleasures.* Toronto: McGraw Hill, Ryrson Ltd.

———. (1985). *Modern Criminology.* New York: McGraw-Hill Book Co.

Hajnal, J. (1965). "European Marriage Patterns in Perspective." In *Populations in History,* edited by D. V. Glass, and D. E. C. Eversley. London: Edward Arnold Ltd.

Hall, Stuart; Critcher, Chas; Jefferson, Tony; Clarke, John; and Roberts, Brian (1978). *Policing the Crisis. Mugging, the State, and Law and Order.* London: The Macmillan Press Ltd.

Halleck, Seymour L. (1971). *Psychiatry and the Dilemmas of Crime.* Berkeley: University of California Press.

Hanen, M. P.; Osler, M. J.; and Weyant, R. G., eds. (1980). *Science, Pseudo-Science and Society.* Canada, Waterloo, Ontario: Wilfrid Laurier University Press.

Hardiker, Pauline, and Webb, David (1979). "Explaining Deviant Behavior: The Social Context of Action and Infraction Accounts in the Probation Service." *Sociology* 13 (#1):1–17.

Har-Paz, Haim, and Hadad, Moshe (1976). "Drug Use." In *Studies, Employment and Leisure Time Activity Among Young People*. Tel Aviv: A survey published by the Department of Research and Statistics of Tel Aviv Municipality (Hebrew).

Harris, Anthony R. (1977). "Sex and Theories of Deviance: Toward a Functional Theory of Deviant Type-scripts." *American Sociological Review* 42:3–16.

Harvey, L. (1982). "The Use and Abuse of Kuhnian Paradigms in the Sociology of Knowledge." *Sociology* 16 (#1):85–101.

Haskell, M. R., and Yablonsky, L. (1983). *Criminology: Crime and Criminality*. Boston: Houghton Mifflin Co.

Havens, Murray; Leiden, Carl; and Schmitt, Karl (1970). *The Politics of Assassination*. Englewood Cliffs, NJ: Prentice Hall, Inc.

Heidenheimer, Arnold J., ed. (1970). *Political Corruption*. New Brunswick, NJ: Transaction Books.

Helmer, John (1975). *Drugs and Minority Oppression*. New York: Continuum Press.

Henry, Stuart (1976). "Fencing with Accounts: The Language of Moral Bridging." *British Journal of Law and Society* 3 (#1):91–100.

Hepworth, Mike, and Turner, Bryan S. (1974). "Confessing to Murder: Critical Notes on the Sociology of Motivation." *British Journal of Law and Society* 1 (#1):31–49.

———, and Turner, Bryan S. (1984). *Confession. Studies in Deviance and Religion*. London: Rouledge and Kegan Paul.

Herzog, Hanna (1986). *Political Ethnicity—The Image and the Reality*. Tel Aviv: Yad Tabenkin, The Institute for the Investigation of the Zionist and Pioneer Movement in the Eastern Countries. Hakibbutz Hameuchad. (Hebrew)

Hewitt, J. P. (1976). *Self and Society*. Boston: Allyn and Bacon, Inc.

Hewstone, Miles, ed. (1984). *Attribution Theory: Social and Functional Extensions*. Oxford: Basil Blackwell.

Hey, J. S. (1973). *The Evolution of Radio Astronomy.* New York: Science History Publications.

Higgins, A. C. (1983). "The Games of Science: Science Watching." In *The Dark Side of Science,* edited by B. K. Kilbourne and M. T. Kilbourne, vol. 1, part 2. San Francisco: Pacific Division, AAAS.

Hills, Stuart L. (1980). *Demystifying Social Deviance.* New York: McGraw Hill Book Co.

_____, ed. (1987). *Corporate Violence: Injury and Death for Profit.* Totowa, NJ: Rowman and Littlefield.

Himmelstein, Jerome L. (1983). *The Strange Career of Marijuana. Politics and Ideology of Drug Control in America.* Westport, CT: Greenwood Press.

Hines, Terence (1988). *Pseudoscience and the Paranormal.* New York: Prometheus Books.

Hirschi, Travis (1969). *Causes of Delinquency.* Berkeley, Los Angeles, and London: University of California Press.

_____, and Gottferedson, Michael (1987). "Causes of White Collar Crime." *Criminology* 25 (#4):949–74.

Hochstedler, Ellen (1984). *Corporations as Criminals.* London: Sage Publications.

Hoffman, Abbie, and Silver, Jonathan (1987). *Steal This Urine Test: Fighting Drug Hysteria in America.* Baltimore: Penguin Books.

Hollingshead, A. B., and Redlich, F. C. (1958). *Social Class and Mental Illness.* New York: John Wiley and Sons, Inc.

Homans, George C. (1961). *Social Behavior: Its Elementary Forms.* Rev. ed. New York: Harcourt Brace Javanovich.

Horowitz, Dan, and Lissak, Moshe (1989). *Trouble in Utopia: The Overburdened Polity of Israel.* Albany: State University of New York Press. (forthcoming).

Horowitz, I. L. (1977). "The Politics of Drugs." In *Drugs and Politics,* edited by Paul Rock. New Brunswick, NJ: Transaction Books.

_____, and Leibovitz, M. (1968). "Social Deviance and Political Marginality: Towards a Redefinition of the Relation Between Sociology and Politics." *Social Problems* 15 (#3):280–97.

Horowitz, Tami, and Amir, Menachem (1981). *Coping Patterns of the Educational System with the Problem of Violence.* Research Report No. 219, Publication No. 602. Jerusalem: The Szold Institute (Hebrew).

Horwitz, Allan V. (1984). "Therapy and Social Solidarity." In *Toward a General Theory of Social Control,* edited by Donald Black, vol. 1. New York: Academic Press.

Howe, Richard Herbert (1978). "Max Weber's Elective Affinities: Sociology Within the Bounds of Pure Reason," *American Journal of Sociology* 84 (#2):366–85.

Huaco, George (1986). "Ideology and General Theory: The Case of Sociological Functionalism." *Comparative Studies in Society and History* 28 (#1):34–54.

Hughes, H. M., ed. (1961). *The Fantastic Lodge.* Greenwich, CT: Fawcett Publications.

Hughes, Pennethorne (1952). *Witchcraft.* Baltimore: Penguin Books.

Hunter, Richard and Ida Macalpine, eds. (1963). *Three Hundred Years of Psychiatry 1535 — 1860.* London: Oxford University Press.

Hunt, Halsey G., and Odoroff, Maurice E. (1962). "Follow Up Study of Narcotic Addicts after Hospitalization." *Public Health Reports* 77:41–54.

Hyams, Edward (1974). *Terrorists and Terrorism.* New York: St. Martin's Press.

Ingraham, Barton L. (1979). *Political Crime in Europe.* Berkeley: University of California Press.

_____, and Tokoro, K. (1969). "Political Crime in the United States and Japan: A Comparative Study." *Issues in Criminology* 4 (#2):145–70.

Inverarity, James (1980). "Theories of the Political Creation of Deviance: Legacies of Conflict Theory, Marx and Durkheim." In *A Political Analysis of Deviance,* edited by Pat Lauderdale. Minneapolis: University of Minnesota Press.

_____. (1987). *Durkheim's Theory of Sanctions and Solidarity: A Defense*. Unpublished paper. Bellingham, Washington: Department of Sociology, Western Washington University.

_____, Lauderdale, Pat; and Feld, B. (1983). "Sanctions and Solidarity: The Contribution of Emile Durkheim." In *Law and Society*. Boston: Little, Brown and Co.

Jaffe, Jerome H. (1975). "Drug Addiction and Drug Abuse." In *The Pharmacological Basis of Therapeutics*, edited by L. S. Goodman and A. Gilman. Fifth ed. New York: Macmillan Publishing Co.

Jansky, C. M. (1958). "The Discovery and Identification by Karl Guthe Jansky of Electromagnetic Radiation of Extraterrestrial Origin in the Radio Spectrum." *Proceedings of the Institute of Radio Engineers* (January) 46 (#1):13–15.

Jansky, K. C. (1932). "Directional Studies of Atmospherics at High Frequencies," *Proceedings of the Institute of Radio Engineers* 20:1920–1932.

_____. (1935). "A Note on the Source of Interstellar Interference." *Proceedings of the Institute of Radio Engineers* 23:1158–63.

Javitz, Rachel, and Shuval, Judith T. (1982). "Vulnerability to Drugs Among Israeli Adolescents." *Israel Journal of Psychiatry* 19 (#2):97–119.

Jayyusi, Lena (1984). *Categorization and Moral Order*. Boston: Routledge and Kegan Paul.

Jensen, Eric L.; Jurg, Gerber; and Babcock, Ginna M. (1987). *Drugs as Politics: The Construction of a Social Problem*. Paper presented at the annual meeting of the Society for the Study of Social Problems, Chicago, August.

Jensen, Gary F. (1988). "Functional Research on Deviance: A Critical Analysis and Guide for the Future." *Deviant Behavior* 5:1–17.

Johnson, Bruce D. (1975). "Righteousness Before Revenue: The Forgotten Moral Crusade Against the Indo-China Opium Trade." *Journal of Drug Issues* 5:304–26.

Johnson, D. M. (1945). "The 'Phantom Anesthetist' of Matoon: A Field Study of Mass Hysteria." *Journal of Abnormal and Social Psychology* 40:175–86.

Johnson, Doyle P. (1981). "Integration and Social Order in Society: The Functional Approach." In *Sociological Theory*. New York: John Wiley and Sons.

Johnston, L. D. (1980). *Marijuana Use and the Effects of Marijuana Decriminalization*. Testimony before the Subcommittee on Criminal Justice, Judiciary Committee, U.S. Senate. January 16, Washington, D.C.

_____; Bachman, J. G.; and O'Malley, P. M. (1981). *Student Drug Use, Attitudes and Beliefs*. Rockville, MD: National Institute on Drug Abuse.

_____; Bachman, J. G.; and O'Malley, P. M. (1984). *Highlights from Drugs and American High School Students 1975–1983*. Rockville, MD: National Institute on Drug Abuse.

_____; O'Malley, P. M.; and Bachman, J. G. (1986). *Drug Use Among American High School Students, College Students, and Other Young Adults. National Trends Through 1985*. Rockville, MD: National Institute on Drug Abuse.

Jones, Anthony T. (1981). "Durkheim, Deviance and Development: Opportunities Lost and Regained." *Social Forces* 59 (#4):1009–24.

Judson, Horace F. (1979). *The Eighth Day of Creation*. New York: Simon and Schuster.

Kandel, Denise B. and Adler, Israel (1981). *The Epidemiology of Adolescent Drug Users in Israel and in France*. New York: Department of Psychiatry and School of Public Health, Columbia University.

_____, Adler, Israel, and Sudit, Myriam (1981). "The Epidemiology of Adolescent Drug Use in France and Israel." *American Journal of Public Health* 71:256–65.

Kaplan, John (1983). *The Hardest Drug: Heroin and Public Policy*. Chicago: The University of Chicago Press.

Karp, D. A., and Yoels, W. C. (1979). *Symbols, Selves and Society*. New York: J. B. Lippincott Co.

Kearney, H. F. (1971). *Science and Change 1500–1700*. London: Weidenfeld and Nicholson.

Keller, Evelyn F. (1983). *A Feeling for the Organism. The Life and Work of Barbara McClintock*. New York: W. H. Freeman and Co.

King, D. (1981). "Hyppocrites: Antidrug Cult Linked to Mob Cronies." *High Times* 76 (December):19–31.

King, Rufus (1972). *The Drug Hang Up*. Springfield, IL: Charles C. Thomas.

Kirchheimer, Otto (1961). *Political Justice*. Princeton, NJ: Princeton University Press.

Kirkham, James F.; Levy, Sheldon G.; and Crotty, William J. (1970). *Assassination and Political Violence*. New York: Praeger Publishers.

Kitsuse, John I. (1962). "Societal Reaction to Deviant Behavior." *Social Problems* 9 (#3):247–56.

———, and Spector, Malcolm (1975). "Social Problems and Deviance: Some Parallel Issues." *Social Problems* 22 (#5):584–94.

Kitzinger, Celia (1987). *The Social Construction of Lesbianism*. London: Sage Books.

Klapp, Orrin E. (1969). *Collective Search for Identity*. New York: Holt, Rinehart and Winston, Inc.

Klein, R. (1981). *Wounded Man, Broken Promises: How the Veterans Administration Betrays Yesterday's Heroes*. New York: Macmillan.

Klerman, G. L. (1970). "Drugs and Social Values." *The International Journal of the Addictions* 5 (#2):313–19.

Knoepler, Seth (1986). "Open Forum: Still More on Neofunctionalism." *Footnotes*, (October) 14 (#7):12.

Knorr-Cetina, K; and Cicourel, A., eds. (1981). *Advances in Social Theory and Methodology: Towards an Integration of Micro- and Macro-Sociologies*. Boston: Routledge and Kegan Paul.

Koch, H. (1970). *The Panic Broadcast: Portrait of an Event*. Boston: Little, Brown and Co.

Kohn, Alexander (1986). *False Prophets*. New York: Basil Blackwell.

Kooistra, Paul G. (1985). "What Is Political Crime." *Criminal Justice Abstracts* 17 (#1):100–15.

Kramer, J. C. (1976). "From Demon to Ally—How Mythology Has, and May Yet, Alter National Drug Policy." *Journal of Drug Issues* 6 (#4):390–406.

Kraus, J. (1966). *Radio Astronomy.* New York: McGraw Hill.

———. (1981). "The First Fifty Years of Radio Astronomy, Part I: Karl Jansky and His Discovery of Radio Waves from Our Galaxy." *Cosmic Search* 3 (#4), Serial 12:8–13.

———. (1982). "The First Fifty Years of Radio Astronomy, Part II: Grote Reber and the First Radio Maps of the Sky." *Cosmic Search* 4 (#1), Serial 13:14–18.

Krisberg, Barry (1975). *Crime and Privilege.* Englewood Cliffs, NJ: Prentice Hall, Inc.

Kuhn, T. S. (1962). *The Structure of Scientific Revolutions.* Chicago: The University of Chicago Press.

Kupperman, Robert H., and Trent, Darrell M., eds. (1979). *Terrorism, Threat, Reality, Response.* Stanford, CA: Stanford University, Hoover Institution Press.

Lankford, J. (1981). "Amateurs and Astrophysics: A Neglected Aspect in the Development of a Scientific Specialty." *Social Studies of Science* 11:275–303.

Laor, Nathaniel (1984). "The Autonomy of the Mentally Ill: A Case Study in Individualistic Ethics." *Philosophy of the Social Sciences* 14:289–302.

Laqueur, Walter (1977). *Terrorism.* Boston: Little, Brown and Co.

Larner, Jeremy, and Tefferteller, Ralph, eds. (1964). *The Addict in the Street.* New York: Grove Press.

Lasch, Christopher (1979). *The Culture of Narcissism.* New York: Warner Books.

Latour, Bruno, and Woolgar, Steve (1979). *Laboratory Life.* Beverly Hills: Sage Publications.

Laudan, Larry (1983). "The Demise of the Demarcation Problem." In *The Demarcation Between Science and Pseudo Science*, edited by R. Lauden. Blacksburgh, VA: Polytechnic Institute and State University.

Lauderdale, Pat (1976). "Deviance and Moral Boundaries." *American Sociological Review* 41:660–64.

_____, ed. (1980). *A Political Analysis of Deviance*. Minneapolis: University of Minnesota Press.

Law, J. (1980). "Fragmentation and Investment in Sedimentology." *Social Studies of Science* 10 (#1):1–22.

Law, John (1986). "On Power and Its Tactics: A View from the Sociology of Science." *The Sociological Review* 34 (#1):1–38.

Lemert, Edwin M. (1983). "Deviance." In *Encyclopedia of Crime and Justice*, edited by Sanford H. Kadish, vol. 2, New York: The Free Press.

Levi, Ken (1981). "Becoming a Hit Man: Neutralization in a Very Deviant Career." *Urban Life* 10 (#1):47–63.

Levi, Shlomit (1982). *Use of Drugs and Medications in Israel*. Jerusalem: Israel Institute for Applied Social Research. Publication No. 52/865/H. (Hebrew).

Levi-Strauss, Claude (1963). *Structural Anthropology*. New York: Basic Books.

Lewin, R. (1983). "A Naturalist of the Genome." *Science* 222 (#4622):402–05.

Liazos, Alexander (1972). "The Poverty of the Sociology of Deviance: Nuts, Sluts and Perverts." *Social Problems* 20 (#1):103–20.

Lidz, Charles W., and Walker, Andrew L. (1980). *Heroin Deviance and Morality*. Beverly Hills: Sage Publications.

Liebman, Charles S., and Don-Yehiya, Eliezer (1983). *Civil Religion in Israel*. Berkeley: University of California Press.

Lissak, Moshe (1971). "Continuity and Change in the Voting Patterns of Oriental Jews." In *The 1969 Israel Election*, edited by A. Arian. Jerusalem: The Academic Press.

Liu, Binyan (1983). *People or Monsters?* edited by Perry Link. Bloomington: Indiana University Press.

Lodge, Juliet, ed. (1981). *Terrorism: A Challenge to the State.* Oxford: Martin Robertson.

Lofland, John (1969). *Deviance and Identity.* Englewood Cliffs, NJ: Prentice Hall, Inc.

Lowinger, Paul (1977). "The Solution to Narcotic Addiction in the People's Republic of China." *American Journal of Drug and Alcohol Abuse* 4 (#2):165–78.

Luban, David (1987). "The Legacies of Nuremberg," *Social Research* 54 (#4):779–829.

Lyman, S. M., and Scott, M. B. (1970). *A Sociology of the Absurd.* New York: Appleton-Century-Crofts.

MacAndrew, Craig (1969). "On the Notion That Certain Persons Who Are Given to Frequent Drunkenness Suffer from a Disease Called Alcoholism." In *Changing Perspectives in Mental Illness,* edited by S. C. Plog and R. B. Edgerton. New York: Holt, Rinehart and Winston.

McAulay, Robert (1978). "Velikovsky and the Infrastructure of Science: The Metaphysics of a Close Encounter." *Theory and Society* 6 (#3):313–42.

McCaghy, C. H. (1968). "Drinking and Deviance Disavowal: The Case of Child Molesters." *Social Problems* 16 (#1):43–49.

———. (1985). *Deviant Behavior.* New York: Macmillan.

McClenon, James (1984). *Deviant Science. The Case of Parapsychology.* Philadelphia: University of Pennsylvania Press.

McGlothin, W. H.; Anglin, M. P.; and Wilson, D. B. (1978). "Narcotic Addiction and Crime." *Criminology* 16 (#3):293–315.

Manis, J. G., and Meltzer, B. N., eds. (1972). *Symbolic Interaction.* Boston: Allyn and Bacon, Inc.

Mann, Peggy (1985). *Marijuana Alert.* New York: McGraw-Hill Book Company.

Marijuana: A Study of State Policies and Penalties. (March 1977). Prepared by Peat, Marwick, Mitchell and Co. for the National Governors' Conference, Washington, D.C.

Marshall, G. (1981). "Accounting for Deviance." *International Journal of Sociology and Social Policy* 1:17–45.

Matza, David (1964). *Delinquency and Drift.* New York: John Wiley and Sons.

――――. (1969). *Becoming Deviant.* Englewood Cliffs, NJ: Prentice Hall, Inc.

Mauskopf, Seymour H., ed. (1979). *The Reception of Unconventional Science.* AAAS Selected Symposium 25. New York: Westview Press.

Mauskopf, Seymour H. (1989). "Marginal Science," forthcoming in *Companion to the History of Modern Science,* edited by G. N. Cantor, J. R. R. Christie, M. S. J. Hodges, and R. C. Olby.

Maxwell, Milton A. (1984). *The Alcoholics Anonymous Experience.* New York: McGraw-Hill Book Company.

Medalia, N. Z., and Larsen, O. N. (1958). "Diffusion and Belief in a Collective Delusion: The Seattle Windshield Pitting Epidemic." *American Sociological Review* 23:180–86.

Meltzer, B. N.; Petras, J. W.; and Reynolds, L. T. (1975). *Symbolic Interactionism.* London: Routledge and Kegan Paul.

Mendelsohn, Everett, Weingrt, Peter, and Whitley, Richard, eds. (1977). *The Social Production of Scientific Knowledge.* Boston: D. Reidel Publishing Co.

Menzies, Robert J. (1980). "Law, Politics and Madness: On the Pathologization of Deviance." *Canadian Criminology Forum* 2 (#2):11–28.

Merton, Robert K. (1968). *Social Theory and Social Structure* (enlarged edition). New York: Free Press.

――――. (1973). *The Sociology of Science.* Chicago: The University of Chicago Press.

Messeri, Peter (1988). "Age Differences in the Reception of New Scientific Theories: The Case of Plate Tectonics Theory." *Social Studies of Science* 18 (#1):91–112.

Messinger, S. L. (1962). "Life as a Theatre: Some Notes on the Dramaturgic Approach to Social Reality." *Sociometry* 25:98–110.

Metz, William D. (1977). "Astrophysics: Discovery and the Ubiquity of Black Holes." *Science* (January 21) 195 (#4275):276–77.

Michalowski, Raymond J. (1985). *Order, Law, and Crime: An Introduction to Criminology.* New York: Random House.

Mickolus, Edward F. (1980). *Transnational Terrorism. A Chronology of Events, 1968–1979.* London: Aldwych Press.

Miller, Judith D.; Cisin, Ira H.; Gardner-Keaton, Hilary; Harrell, Adele V.; Wirtz, Philip W.; Abelson, Herbert I.; and Fishburne, Patricia M. (1983). *National Survey on Drug Abuse: Main Findings 1982.* Rockville, MD: National Institute on Drug Abuse.

Miller, W. B. (1973). "Ideology and Criminal Justice Policy: Some Current Issues." *Journal of Criminal Law and Criminology* 64:141–62.

Mills, C. W. (1940). "Situated Actions and Vocabularies of Motives." *American Sociological Review* 5:904–13.

———. (1943). "The Professional Ideology of Social Pathologists." *American Journal of Sociology* 49:165–80.

Minor, W. W. (1975). "Political Crime, Political Justice and Political Prisoners." *Criminology* 12 (#4):385–98.

———. (1981). "Techniques of Neutralization: A Reconceptualization and Empirical Examination." *Journal of Research in Crime and Delinquency* 18 (#2).

Mitchell, D.; Mitchell, C.; and Ofshe, R. (1982). *The Light on Synanon.* New York: Putnam.

Mizruchi, E. H. (1983). *Regulating Society.* New York: The Free Press.

Monter, William E. (1980). "French and Italian Witchcraft." *History Today* 30:31–35.

Morgan, Patricia L. (1978). "The Legislation of Drug Laws: Economic Crisis and Social Control." *Journal of Drug Issues* 8 (#1):53–62.

Morgan, Wayne H. (1974). *Yesterday's Addicts*. Norman: University of Oklahoma Press.

_____. (1981). *Drugs in America: A Social History 1800–1980*. New York: Syracuse University Press.

Mulkay, M. J. (1972a). *The Social Process of Innovation. A Study in the Sociology of Science*. London: Macmillan.

_____. (1972b). "Conformity and Innovation in Science." In *The Sociology of Science*, edited by P. Halmos. Keele, Staffordshire: University of Keele.

Musto, David (1973). *The American Disease*. New Haven: Yale University Press.

Nation's Toughest Drug Law: Evaluating the New York Experience, The (1977). Final Report of the Joint Committee on the New York Drug Law Evaluation. Published by the Drug Abuse Council, Washington, D.C.

Nelkin, Dorothy (1973). *Methadone Maintenance: A Technological Fix*. New York: George Braziller.

Nettler, Gwynn (1972). *Explaining Crime*. New York: McGraw-Hill Book Co.

_____. (1982). *Killing One Another*. Cincinnati, OH: Anderson Publishing Co.

Newman, R. G. (1977). *Methadone Treatment in Narcotic Addiction*. New York: Academic Press.

Norbeck, Edward (1961). *Religion in Primitive Society*. New York: Harper and Row.

Norland, Stephen, and Wright, Joseph (1984). "Bureaucratic Legitimacy and the Drug Menace: Notes on the Marijuana Tax Act." *Deviant Behavior* 5:239–54.

Nowotny, Helga, and Rose, Hilary, eds. (1979). *Counter-Movements in the Sciences*. Boston: D. Reidel Publishing Co.

Nurco, David N.; Shaffer, John W.; Ball, John C.; and Kinlock, Timothy W. (1984). "Trends in the Commission of Crime among Narcotic Addicts over Successive Periods of Addiction and Nonaddiction." *American Journal of Drug and Alcohol Abuse* 10 (#4):481–89.

Nye, Ivan F. (1958). *Family Relationships and Delinquent Behavior*. New York: John Wiley.

Nye, Robert A. (1984). *Crime, Madness and Politics in Modern France*. Princeton: Princeton University Press.

O'Donnell, John A. (1964). "A Follow-up of Narcotic Addicts." *American Journal of Orthopsychiatry* 34:948–55.

Ofshe, Richard (1976). "Synanon: The People Business." In *The New Religious Consciousness*, edited by C. Y. Glock and R. N. Bellah. Berkeley: University of California Press.

Orcutt, James D. (1975). "Deviance as a Situated Phenomenon: Variations in the Social Interpretation of Marijuana and Alcohol Use." *Social Problems* 22 (#3):346–56.

———. (1983). *Analyzing Deviance*. Homewood, IL: The Dorsey Press.

Packer, H. (1962). "Offenses Against the State." *Annals of the American Academy of Political and Social Science* 339:77–110.

Packer, H. L. (1968). *The Limits of Criminal Sanction*. Stanford: Stanford University Press.

Page, C. W. (1985). "On Neofunctionalism." *ASA Footnotes*, October, p. 10.

Pallone, Nathaniel J. (1986). *On the Social Utility of Psychopathology: A Deviant Majority and Its Keepers*. New Brunswick, NJ: Transaction Books.

Parrinder, Geoffrey (1958). *Witchcraft*. Middlesex: Penguin Books.

Parsons, Talcott (1951). *The Social System*. New York: The Free Press.

———. (1971). *The System of Modern Societies*. Englewood Cliffs, NJ: Prentice Hall, Inc.

Patinkin, Dan (1983). "Multiple Discoveries and the Central Message." *American Journal of Sociology* 89 (#2):306–23.

Pearce, Frank (1976). *Crimes of the Powerful*. London: Pluto.

Peled, Tziona (1971). *Attitudes of Youth in School Towards Drugs: Selective Findings from the Study on Values, Plans and Youth Behavior.* Jerusalem: The Institute for Applied Social Research (Hebrew)

――――, and Schimmerling, Haviva (1972). "The Drug Culture Among Youth of Israel: The Case of High School Students." In *Israel Studies in Criminology,* vol. 2, edited by S. Shoham. Jerusalem: Jerusalem Academic Press.

Perspective on "Get Tough" Drug Laws, A (1973). Washington, D.C.: The Drug Abuse Council.

Pfohl, Stephen J. (1985). *Images of Deviance and Social Control. A Sociological History.* New York: McGraw-Hill Book CO.

Pfuhl, E. H. (1986). *The Deviance Process.* Belmont, CA: Wadworth.

Piven, Frances Fox (1981). "Deviant Behaviour and the Re-Making of the World." *Social Problems* 28:489–508.

Planck, Max (1950). *Scientific Autobiography and Other Papers.* (Translated by Frank Gaynor). London: Williams and Norgate.

Platt, J. J., and Labate, C. (1976). *Heroin Addiction.* New York: Wiley.

Polanyi, M. (1967). "The Growth of Science in Society." *Minerva* 5 (#4):533–45.

Pope, Harrison, Jr. (1971). *Voices from the Drug Culture.* Boston: Beacon Press.

Potter, Jonathan, and Wetherell, Margaret (1987). *Discourse and Social Psychology.* London: Sage Books.

Powell, D. H. (1973). "A Pilot Study of Occasional Heroin Users." *Archives of General Psychiatry* 28:586–94.

Proal, Louis (1898). *Political Crime.* A 1973 Reprinted Edition. Montclair, NJ: Patterson Smith.

Punch, Maurice (1985). *Conduct Unbecoming: The Social Construction of Police Deviance and Control.* London and New York: Tavistock Publications.

Quinney, Richard (1964). "The Study of White Collar Crime: Toward a Re-Orientation in Theory and Research," *Journal of Criminal Law, Criminology and Police Science,* 55:208–14.

Quinney, Richard, and Wildeman, J. (1977). *The Problem of Crime*. New York: Harper and Row.

Rahav, Giora; Teichman, Meir; and Barnea, Zippora (1985). *Drugs and Alcohol Among Adolescents*. First scientific report. Tel Aviv: Institute of Criminology, Tel Aviv University (Hebrew).

Rapoport, David C. (1971). *Assassination and Terrorism*. Toronto: Canadian Publishing Corporation.

Ray, Oakley S. (1978). *Drugs, Society and Human Behavior*. 2nd ed. St. Louis: The C. V. Mosby Co.

Reasons, Charles E. (1974). "The Politics of Drugs: An Inquiry in the Sociology of Social Problems." *The Sociological Quarterly* 15:381–404.

Reasons, C. E. (1974a). *The Criminologist: Crime and the Criminal*. Pacific Palisades, California: Goodyear.

Reber, Grote (1942). "Cosmic Static." *Proceedings of the Institute of Radio Engineers* (August), 30:367–78.

──────. (1958). "Early Radio Astronomy at Wheaton, Illinois." *Proceedings of the Institute of Radio Engineers* 6 (#1):15–23.

──────. (1983). *Radio Astronomy Between Jansky and Reber*. Lecture delivered at the Jansky Memorial Conference, National Radio Astronomy Observatory, Green Bank, West Virginia. May.

Reckless, Walter C. (1967). *The Crime Problem*. 4th ed. Englewood Cliffs, NJ: Prentice Hall, Inc.

Reed, G. (1983). "The Discovery of Pulsars." *Astronomy* 11 (#12):24–28.

Reid, Sue Titus (1982). *Crime and Criminology*. 3rd ed. New York: Holt, Rinehart and Winston.

Reiss, Albert J., Jr. (1951). "Delinquency as the Failure of Personal and Social Controls." *American Sociological Review* 16:196–207.

Richard, L. G., and Blevens, L. B., eds. (1977). *The Epidemiology of Drug Abuse*. Rockville, MD: National Institute on Drug Abuse. (Research Monograph 10).

Rittenhouse, J. D., ed. (1977). *The Epidemiology of Heroin and Other Narcotics.* Rockville, MD: The Institute on Drug Abuse. (Research Monograph 16).

Ritzer, George (1983). *Sociological Theory.* New York: Alfred A. Knopf.

———. (1986). "Neofunctionalism: Long on Rhetoric, Short (as yet) on Substance." *Footnotes* (April), 14 (#4):9.

Robbins, R. H. (1959). *The Encyclopedia of Witchcraft and Demonology.* New York: Crown Publishers, Inc.

Roberts, Keith A. (1984). *Religion in Sociological Perspective.* Homewood, IL: The Dorsey Press.

Robins, Lee N. (1973). *The Vietnam Drug User Returns.* Washington, D.C., Special Action Office for Drug Abuse Prevention.

Rock, Paul (1973a). "Phenomenalism and Essentialism in the Sociology of Deviancy." *Sociology* 7:17–29.

———. (1973b). *Deviant Behavior.* London: Hutchinson University Library.

———. (1974). "The Sociology of Deviance and Conceptions of Moral Order." *British Journal of Criminology* 14 (#2):139–49.

———. (1977). "Introduction." In *Drugs and Politics.* New Brunswick, NJ: Transaction Books.

———. (1985). "Deviance." In *The Social Science Encyclopedia*, edited by Adam Kuper and Jessica Kuper. London: Routledge and Kegan Paul.

Roebuck, J., and Weeber, S. C. (1978). *Political Crime in the United States.* New York: Praeger Publishers.

Rosenberg, Howard L. (1980). *Atomic Soldiers.* Boston: Beacon Press.

Rosenhan, D. C. (1973). "On Being Sane in Insane Places." *Science* 179:250–58.

Ross, E. A. (1907). "The Criminaloid." *The Atlantic Monthly* 99:44–50. Reprinted in Geis, Gilbert and Meier, Robert F. (1977). *White Collar Crime.* New York: The Free Press.

Rothman, David J. (1971). *The Discovery of the Asylum*. Boston: Little, Brown and Co.

Rubington, Earl, and Weinberg, Martin S., eds. (1971). *The Study of Social Problems*. New York: Oxford University Press.

――――, and Weinberg, Martin S., eds. (1978). *Deviance: The Interactionist Perspective*. New York: Macmillan Publishing Co.

Rubinstein, Amnon (1975). *Law Enforcement in a Permissive Society*. Jerusalem: Shocken Books (Hebrew).

Rudwick, Martin J. S. (1985). *The Great Devonian Controversy*. Chicago: The University of Chicago Press.

Sagarin, Edward (1969). *Odd Man In: Societies of Deviants in America*. Chicago: Quadrangle Books.

――――. (1973). "Introduction" to the Reprint Edition in Proal, L.: *Political Crime*. New York: Patterson Smith.

――――. (1985). "Positive Deviance: An Oxymoron." *Deviant Behavior* 6 (#2):169–81.

――――, and Kelly, Robert J. (1986). "Political Deviance and the Assumption of Responsibility." *Deviant Behavior* 7:217–42.

Salinger, M. Lawrence (1986). *Truth or Consequences: Fraud in Scientific Research*. Atlanta, GA: Paper Presented at the Meeting of the American Society of Criminology, (September 30).

Saper, A. A. (1974). "The Making of Policy Through Myth, Fantasy and Historical Accident: The Making of America's Narcotic Laws." *British Journal of the Addictions* 61:183–93.

Sarbin, Theodore R. (1969). "The Scientific Status of the Mental Illness Metaphor." In *Changing Perspectives in Mental Illness*, edited by S. C. Plog and R. B. Edgerton. New York: Holt, Rinehart and Winston.

Sarbin, T. R., and Mancuse, J. C. (1980). *Schizophrenia: Medical Diagnosis or Moral Verdict?* New York: Pergamon Press.

Sayre, A. (1975). *Rosalind Franklin and DNA*. New York: W. W. Norton and Co.

Schafer, Stephen (1974). *The Political Criminal*. New York: The Free Press.

Scharf, Peter, and Binder, Arnold (1983). *The Badge and the Bullet: Police Use of Deadly Force*. New York: Praeger.

Scheff, T. (1966). *Being Mentally Ill: A Sociological Theory*. Chicago: Aldine.

Scheff, T. (1986). "Micro-Linguistics and Social Structure: A Theory of Social Action." *Sociological Theory* 4 (#1):71–83.

Scher, Jordan (1966). "Patterns and Profiles of Addiction and Drug Abuse." *Archives of General Psychiatry* 15:267–71.

Schlussel, Y. R. (1983). *Structural Determinants of Resistance to Innovation: Peer Review, Disciplinary Paradigms and Formal Organizations*. Paper presented at the annual meeting of the New York Sociological Association, Potsdam, NY.

Schmid, Alex P., and Jongman, A. J. (1987). *Political Terrorism*. New Brunswick, NJ: Transaction Books.

Schmookler, J. (1966). *Invention and Economic Growth*. Cambridge: Harvard University Press.

Schneider, Joseph W. (1985). "Social Problems: The Constructionist View." *Annual Review of Sociology* 11:209–29.

Schur, Edwin M. (1969). *Our Criminal Society*. New York: Spectrum Books.

———. (1971). *Labeling Deviant Behavior*. New York: Harper and Row.

———. (1979). *Interpreting Deviance*. New York: Harper and Row.

———. (1980). *The Politics of Deviance*. Englewood Cliffs, NJ: Prentice Hall, Inc.

Scott, J. M. (1969). *The White Poppy*. New York: Harper and Row.

Scott, Marvin B., and Lyman, Stanford M. (1968a). "Accounts." *American Sociological Review* 33 (February):46–62.

———, and Lyman, Stanford M. (1968b). "Accounts, Deviance and Social Order." In *Deviance and Respectability*, edited by J. D. Douglas. New York: Basic Books.

Scott, Robert A. (1972). "A Proposed Framework for Analyzing Deviance as a Property of Social Order." In *Theoretical Perspectives on Deviance*, edited by R. A. Scott and J. D. Douglas. New York: Basic Books.

Scull, Andrew (1984). "Competing Perspectives on Deviance." *Deviant Behaviour* 5:275–89.

Shane, C. P. (1958). "Radio Astronomy in 1890: A Proposed Experiment." *Publication of the Astronomical Society of the Pacific* 70:301–03.

Shanks, Hershel (1986). "Archeology as Politics." *Commentary* 82 (#2):50–53.

Shapiro, Rhonda J.; Lauderdale, Pat; and Lauderdale, Michael (1985). *The Changing Forms of Deviance: Salem Witchcraft*. Paper presented at the 80th annual meeting of the ASA, Washington, D.C.

Sharrock, W. W., and Watson, D. R. (1984). "What's the Point of 'Rescuing Motives'?" *The British Journal of Sociology* 35 (#3):435–51.

Sherman, L. (1978). *Scandal and Reform: Controlling Police Corruption*. Berkeley: University of California Press.

Shils, Edward (1970). *Selected Essays by Edward Shils*. Student Edition. Department of Sociology, University of Chicago.

Shklar, Judith N. (1986). *LEGALISM. Law, Morals, and Political Trials*. Cambridge: Harvard University Press.

Shoham, Giora S.; Geva, Nili; Kliger, P.; and Chai, T. (1974). "Drug Abuse Among Israeli Youth: Epidemiological Pilot Study." *U.N. Bulletin on Narcotics* 20 (#2):9–28.

_____; Rahav, Giora; Esformer, Y.; Blau, Joanna; Kaplinsky, Nava; Markovsky, R.; and Wolf, B. (1979). "Differential Patterns of Drug Involvement Among Israeli Youth." *U.N. Bulletin on Narcotics* 30 (#4):17–34.

_____; Rahav, Giora; Esformes, Y.; Blau, Joanna; Kaplinsky, Nava; Markovsky, R.; and Wolf, B. (1981). "Polar Types of Reported Drug Involvement Among Israeli Youth." *The International Journal of the Addictions* 16 (#7):1161–67.

Shprinzak, Ehud (1980). *Fundamentalism, Terrorism and Democracy: The Case of Gush Emunim Underground*. Washington D.C., The Wilson Center, Smithsonian Institution Building, Occasional paper No. 4.

Shprinzak, Ehud (1986). *Every Man Whatsoever Is Right In His Own Eyes. Illegalism In Israeli Society.* Tel Aviv: Sifriat Poalim (Hebrew).

Siegler, Miriam, and Osmond, Humphrey (1974). *Models of Madness, Models of Medicine.* New York: Macmillan Publishing Co., Inc.

Silk, Joseph (1980). *The Big Bang.* San Francisco: W. H. Freeman and Co.

Simon, David R., and Eitzen, Stanley D. (1982). *Elite Deviance.* Boston: Allyn and Bacon, Inc.

Single, E. W. (1981). "The Impact of Marijuana Decriminalization." In *Research Advances in Alcohol and Drug Problems,* vol. 6, edited by Y. Israel; F. B. Glaser; H. Malant; R. E. Popham; W. Schmidt; and R. G. Smart. New York: Plenum.

Smith, J., and Fried, W. (1974). *The Use of the American Prison: Political Theory and Penal Practice.* Lexington, MA: D. C. Heath.

Smith, R. J. (1982). "Scientists Implicated in Atom Test Deception." *Science* (November 5) 218:545–47.

Smith, Robert W. (1982). *The Expanding Universe.* London: Cambridge University Press.

Smith, Roger (1981). *Trial by Medicine: Insanity and Responsibility in Victorian Trials.* Edinburgh: Edinburgh University Press.

Smith, Ronald W., and Preston, Frederick W. (1984). "Vocabularies of Motives for Gambling Behavior." *Sociological Perspectives* 27 (#3):325–48.

Snyder, C. R.; Higgins, R. L.; Stucky, R. J. (1983). *Excuses, Masquerades in Search of Grace.* New York: John Wiley and Sons.

Spector, Malcolm, and Kitsuse, John I. (1977). *Constructing Social Problems.* Menlo Park, CA: Cummings Publishing Company.

Srole, Leo; Langner, Thomas S.; Michael, Stanley T.; Kirkpatrick, Price; Opler, Marvin H.; and Rennie, Thomas A.C. (1962). *Mental Health in the Metropolis.* New York: McGraw-Hill Book Co.

Stark, Rodney, and Bainbridge, William S. (1985). *The Future of Religion.* Berkeley: University of California Press.

Stahl, Sidney M., and Lebedun, Morty (1974), "Mystery Gas: An Analysis of Mass Hysteria." *Journal of Health and Social Behavior* 15:44–50.

Stohl, Michael, ed. (1983). *The Politics of Terrorism*. New York: Marcel Dekker.

Stone, G. P., and Farberman, H. A. (1967). "On the Edge of Rapproachment: Was Durkheim Moving Toward the Perspective of Symbolic Interaction?" *Sociological Quarterly* 8:149–64.

Stone, I. F. (1988). "Was There a Witch Hunt in Ancient Athens?" *The New York Review of Books*, January 21, 34 (#21&22):37–41.

Stover, Eric, and Nightingale, Elana O., eds. (1985). *The Breaking of Bodies and Minds: Torture, Psychiatric Abuse, and the Health Professions*. New York: W. H. Freeman.

Struve, O. (1962). *The Universe*. Cambridge: MIT Press.

_____, and Zebergs, V. (1962). *Astronomy of the Twentieth Century*. New York: MacMillan.

Suchar, C. S. (1978). *Social Deviance: Perspectives and Prospects*. New York: Holt, Rinehart and Winston.

Sullivan, W. (1964). *We Are Not Alone*. New York: Signet Books.

Sullivan, W. T. (1982). *Classics in Radio Astronomy*. Dordrecht, Holland: D. Reidel.

_____. (1984a). *Early Years of Radio Astronomy*. London: Cambridge University Press.

_____. (1984b). *Grote Reber: Science in Your Backyard*. First draft. Seattle, WA: Department of Astronomy, September 11, 1984.

Summers, Ian, and Kagan, Dan (1984). *Mute Evidence*. New York: Bantam Books.

Sutherland, E. H. (1940). "White Collar Criminality." *American Sociological Review* 5:132–39.

Sykes, G. M. (1978). *Criminology*. New York, Harcourt Brace Jovanovich.

———, and Matza, D. (1957). "Techniques of Neutralization: A Theory of Delinquency." *American Sociological Review* 22, 664–70.

Szasz, T. S. (1961). *The Myth of Mental Illness*. New York: Harper and Row.

———. (1975). *Ceremonial Chemistry: The Ritual Persecution of Drug Addicts and Pushers*. New York: Doubleday Books.

Tappan, Paul (1947). "Who Is the Criminal?" *American Sociological Review* 12 (February):96–102.

Taylor, B. (1976). "Motives for Guilt-Free Pedestry: Some Literary Considerations." *The Sociological Review* 24 (#1):97–114.

Taylor, I.; Walton, P.; and Young, J. (1973). *The New Criminology: For a Social Theory of Deviance*. London: Routledge and Kegan Paul.

Taylor, Lauri (1972). "The Significance and Interpretation of Replies to Motivational Questions: The Case of Sex Offenders." *Sociology* 6:23–40.

———. (1979). "Vocabularies, Rhetorics and Grammer: Problems in the Sociology of Motivation." In *Deviant Interpretations*, edited by David Downs and Paul Rock. New York: Barnes and Noble.

———, and Walton, P. (1971). "Industrial Sabotage: Motives and Meanings." In *Images of Deviance*, edited by S. Cohen. Harmondsworth, England: Penguin Books.

Teal, D. (1971). *The Gay Militants*. New York: Stein and Day Publishers.

Terry, Charles E., and Pellens, Mildred (1970). *The Opium Problem*. Reprint ed. Montclair, NJ: Patterson Smith.

Terry, Robert M., and Steffensmeier, Darrell J. (1988). "Conceptual and Theoretical Issues in the Study of Deviance." *Deviant Behavior* 9:55–76.

Thio, A. (1988). *Deviant Behavior*, 3rd ed. New York: Harper and Row.

Thomas, W. L., and Thomas, D. S. (1928). *The Child in America*. New York: Alfred A. Knopf.

Thornberry, T. P., and Farnworth, M. (1982). "Social Correlates of Criminal Involvement: Further Evidence on the Relationship Between Social

Status and Criminal Behavior." *American Sociological Review* 47 (#4):505–18.

Torrey, Fuller E. (1972). *The Mind Game*. New York: Emerson Hall Publishers.

Trebach, Arnold S. (1982). *The Heroin Solution*. New Haven: Yale University Press.

Trefil, James S. (1983). *The Moment of Creation*. New York: Charles Scribner's Sons.

Trevor Roper, H. R. (1967). *The European Witch-Craze of the Sixteenth and Seventeenth Centuries and Other Essays*. New York: Harper Torchbooks.

Truzzi, Marcello (1979). "On the Reception of Unconventional Scientific Claims." In *The Reception of Unconventional Science*, edited by S. H. Mauskopf. AAAS Selected Symposium 25. New York: Westview Press.

Turk, Austin T. (1975). *Political Criminality and Political Policing*. New York: MSS Modular Publishers.

———. (1979). "Analyzing Official Deviance: For Nonpartisan Conflict Analysis." *Criminology* 16 (#4):459–76.

———. (1982). *Political Criminality*. Beverly Hills: Sage Publications.

Turner, Jonathan H. (1986). *The Structure of the Sociological Theory*. 4th ed. Chicago: Dorsey Press.

———, and Maryanski, Alexandra (1979). *Functionalism*. Menlo Park, CA: The Benjamin/Cummings Publishing Co.

———, and Maryanski, Alexandra R. (1988). "Is 'Neofunctionalism' Really Functional?" *Sociological Theory* 6 (#1):110–21.

Turner, Victor (1977a). "Process, Systems and Symbols: A New Anthropological Synthesis." *Daedalus* 106 (#3):61–80.

———. (1977b). "Variations on a Theme of Liminality." In *Secular Ritual*, edited by S. F. Moore and B. G. Myerhoff. Assen/Amsterdam, The Netherlands: Van Gorcum.

Vaillant, George E. (1966). "A Twelve Year Follow-up of New York Narcotic Addicts: The Relation of Treatment to Outcome." *American Journal of Psychiatry* 122:727–37.

Vaughan, T. R., and Sjoberg, Gideon (1970). "The Social Construction of Legal Doctrine: The Case of Adolf Eichmann." In *Deviance and Respectability*, edited by J. D. Douglas. New York: Basic Books.

Wade, N. (1975). "Discovery of Pulsars: A Graduate Student's Story." *Science* 189 (#4200):358–64.

Wakefield, Dan, ed. (1963). *The Addict*. Greenwich, CT: Fawcett Publications.

Waldorf, Dan; Orlick, M.; and Reinarman, C. (1974). *The Shreveport Clinic, 1919–1923*. Washington, D.C.: The Drug Abuse Council, Inc.

Wallace, A. F. C. (1966). *Religion: An Anthropological View*. New York: Random House.

Wallis, Roy, ed. (1979). *On the Margins of Science: The Social Construction of Rejected Knowledge*. England: University of Keele Press.

Wallis, Roy (1984). *The Elementary Forms of the New Religious Life*. London: Routledge and Kegan Paul.

_____, and Bruce, Steve (1983). "Rescuing Motives." *The British Journal of Sociology* 34 (#1):61–71.

Wallwork, E. (1972). *Durkheim: Morality and Milieu*. Cambridge: Harvard University Press.

Walzer, Michael (1987). *Interpretations and Social Criticism*. Cambridge: Harvard University Press.

Wardlaw, Grant (1982). *Political Terrorism*. New York: Cambridge University Press.

Warner, Stephen R. (1986). "More on the Neofunctionalism Debate." *Footnotes* (April) 14 (#4):9.

Watson, Frances M. (1976). *Political Terrorism: The Threat and the Response*. Washington and New York: Robert B. Luce Co., Inc.

Weber, Max (1947). *The Theory of Social and Economic Organization.* Translated by A. M. Henderson and Talcott Parsons, edited by Talcott Parsons. New York: Oxford University Press.

Weber, Max (1968). *Economy and Society.* New York: Benminster.

Weinberg, Steven (1977). *The First Three Minutes: A Modern View of the Origin of the Universe.* New York: Basic Books.

Weisman, Richard (1984). *Witchcraft, Magic and Religion in 17th Century Massachusetts.* Amherst: The University of Massachusetts Press.

Wellford, Charles (1975). "Labelling Theory and Criminology: An Assessment." *Social Problems* 22 (#3):332–45.

Westerhout, G. (1972). "The Early History of Radio Astronomy." *Annals of the New York Academy of Sciences* 100:202–12.

Westermarck, Edward A. (1926). *Ritual and Belief in Morocco.* London: Macmillan.

Wheeler, Stanton (1960). "Sex Offenders: A Sociological Critique." *Law and Contemporary Problems* 25:258–78.

————; Weisburd, D.; and Bode, N. (1982). "Sentencing the White Collar Offender: Rhetoric and Reality." *American Sociological Review* 47 (#5):641–59.

Whitehead, A. N. (1917). *The Organization of Thought: Educational and Scientific.* Westport, CT: The Greenwood Press. A 1974 Edition.

Wickman, Peter, and Dailey, Timothy, eds. (1982). *White-Collar and Economic Crime: Multidisciplinary and Cross-National Perspectives.* Lexington, MA: Lexington Books.

Wiener, Carolyn L. (1981). *The Politics of Alcoholism.* New Brunswick, NJ: Transaction Books.

Wiley, Norbert (1988). "The Micro-Macro Problem in Social Theory," *Sociological Theory* 6:254–61.

Wilkins, Leslie T. (1964). *Social Deviance: Social Policy, Action and Research.* Englewood Cliffs, NJ: Prentice Hall, Inc.

Wilkinson, Doris Y. (1976). *Social Structure and Assassination Behavior. The Sociology of Political Murder.* Cambridge, MA: Schenkman Publishing Company.

Wilmarth, S. S., and Goldstein, A. (1974). *Therapeutic Effectiveness of Methadone Maintenance.* Geneva: World Health Organization.

Wilson, Bryan, ed. (1981). *The Social Impact of New Religious Movements.* New York: The Rose of Sharon Press, Inc.

Winick, Charles (1962). "Maturing Out of Narcotic Addiction." *Bulletin on Narcotics* 14 (#1):1-9.

Wolanski, Ami (1981). *National Survey on the Progress of Youth — 1980.* Jerusalem: Ministry of Education, Youth Branch (Hebrew).

_____, and Kfir, David (1982). *Characteristics, Functions and Treatment of Disconnected Youth and Those in Street Groups. Data from the Second National Survey of the Units for Progress of Youth — 1981.* Jerusalem: Ministry of Education, Youth Branch (Hebrew).

Woolgar, Steve (1986). "On the Alleged Distribution Between Discourse and Praxis." *Social Studies of Science* 16 (#2):309-17.

_____, and Pawluch, Dorothy (1985). "How Shall We Move Beyond Constructivism." *Social Problems* 33 (#2):159-62.

Wright, Charles, and Hilbert, R. E. (1980). "Value Implications of the Functional Theory of Deviance." *Social Problems* 28:205-19.

Wright, E. D. (1973). *The Politics of Punishment.* New York: Harper and Row.

Wynne, Brian (1967). "C. G. Barkla and the J Phenomenon: A Case Study in the Treatment of Deviance in Science." *Social Studies of Science* 6:307-47.

_____. (1979). "Between Orthodoxy and Oblivion: The Normalization of Deviance in Science." In *On the Margins of Science*, edited by R. Wallis. Keele, Staffordshire: University of Keele.

Yablonsky, L. (1965). *Synanon: The Tunnel Back.* Baltimore: Penguin Books.

Young, Jock (1971). *The Drugtakers. The Social Meaning of Drug Use.* London: MacGibbon and Kee Ltd.

Zilboorg, Gregory and Henry, George W. (1941). *A History of Medical Psychology*. New York: W. W. Norton and Company, Inc.

Zinberg, Norman E. (1979). "Nonaddictive Opiate Use." In *Handbook on Drug Abuse*, edited by R. I. Dupont; A. Goldstein; and J. O'Donnell. Washington, D.C.: National Institute on Drug Abuse.

Zuckerman, Harriet (1977). "Deviant Behaviour and Social Control in Science." In *Deviance and Social Change*, edited by E. Sagarino. Beverly Hills and London, Sage Publications.

———, and Merton, R. (1971). "Patterns of Evaluation in Science: Institutionalization, Structure and Function of the Referee System." *Minerva* 9 (January):66–100.

Zurcher, Louis A. Jr.; Kirkpatrick, George R.; Cushing, Robert G.; and Bowman, Charles K. (1971). "The Anti-Pornography Campaign: A Symbolic Crusade." *Social Problems* 19 (#2):217–38.

———, and Kirkpatrick, George R. (1976). *Citizens for Decency: Anti-Pornography Crusades as Status Defense*. Austin: University of Texas Press.

Index

Abell, P., 22
Abelson, H. I., 167
Abortion, 36, 51, 111
Absolutist, 7, 267
Absurd (ities), 202, 262
Abu-hatzira, Aharon, accusations of,
242; as a silent hero, 233; as a
"suasive image", 248; defaming of,
236; and defense, 237;
deviantization and criminalization
of, 241–248; first investigation of,
227; first trial of, 227, 236–237;
historical background, 227–229;
interrogation of, 234–235; and
lawyers, 235; minister of labour
and social affairs, 228; minister of
religion, 227, as Moroccan prince,
242, 248; parliamentary immunity
of, 227, 234–235; personal
background, 225–227; prison
sentence of, 228–229, 241; second
trial of, 237–239; testimony of,
236–237; use of ethnicity, 231–233;
use of religion, 230–231. See also
Criminalization, Deviantization,
Reverse, Stigma, Deviance and
politics.
Accounts, 19, 22–23, 27, 30. See also
motivational accounting systems;
vocabularies of motives.
Addictive personality, 162
Addicts, 160; former, 69; 165–166; of
the 1950s and 1960s, 157; to heroin,
75, 105, 157, 166; women, 146.
Adiv, Udi, 272
Adler, Israel, 104
Admor, 226, 230

Adolescents, and prevalence of drug
use, 103–104, 167–169; and
religion, 112
Agassi, Joseph, 200–201
Agranat committee, 82
Alcohol, 25, 61, 69, 112, 120, 141,
145, 160, 171
Alexander, Jeffrey, 262
Aliases and Alibis, 29
Alienation, 112
Alienists, 70
Al Sam, 124
Altered states of consciousness, 150
Amateur (s), 192, 204, 214
American Medical Association
(AMA), 164
American Philosophical Society, 203
American Psychiatric Association
(APA), 88
Amin, Idi, 25
Amir, Menachem, 126–127
Amnesty (International), 91
Amphetamines, 154
Anarchy, 82
Ancient Astronaut Hypothesis, 202
Anderson, B., 42
Anderson, P., 122, 154
Anomalies, 198, 201
Anomie, 21
Antenna, 186, 189
Anthropology, 195
Anti-Opium Society (British), 142
Anti-Semitism, 79
Aran, Gideon, 76, 269n.2
Arbel, Baruch, 225
Archaeology, 77, 224; and politics in
Israel, 181

333

Ariel, Zvi, 106
Argentina, 91
Ashkenasi discrimination, 239
Ashkenazi, 238
Ashley, R., 122, 144
Assassinations, 8, 71–72, 79, 84, 90
Astrology, 196
Astronomers, 191; Dutch, 192;
  Optical, 187, 197, 207, 209–212,
  215–216, 277, 279; Radio, 210. *See*
  Astronomy; Radio
Astronomy, 209, 213–214. *See also*
  Astronomers; Radio;
  Astrophysicists
Astrophysical journal, 190–192, 197
Astrophysicists, 209, 211, 214
Athens, 36
Atom smasher, 277
Atrocity tales, 98, 114
Attribution (theories), 19–20
Autonomous polity, 273
Authority, 49, 51, 247
Aviad, Janet, 55, 58
Azande, 26

Baba Sally, 226, 230
Bacteriology, 207–208, 213
Bad apples (theory), 79
Bakalar, J.B., 156
Bandit, 36
Bank robbery, 245
Baraka, 226, 230, 237
Barber, B., 200
Barnea, Zippora, 104
Bar Illan University, 226
Bart, P.B., 28
Bartky, Walter, 208
Basques, 90
Baudelaire, 150
Becker, Howard S., 17, 39, 48, 50–51,
  99–100, 114, 151, 156, 194, 221
Becker, Theodore, 88
Beer Hall Putsch, 245
Begin, Menachem, 75, 117, 228, 234,
  245

Bell Telephone, 186–187, 209,
  215–217
Ben-David, Joseph, 197, 207, 213,
  219, 279
Ben-Yehuda, Nachman, 29, 55, 58,
  114, 123–124, 255, 261
Berger, Peter, 5, 55, 123, 243
Bergesen, Albert J., 73, 90, 127
Berlin, 105
Best, J., 141
Biernacki, P., 162
Big Bang: 84, 213; characterization
  of, 280
Black: magic, 214; Muslims, 91;
  Panthers, 78, 269n.3
Blevens, L.B., 167
Blood revenge, 8
Blum, A.F., 22
Blumberg, A.S., 158
Bnei-Brak, 234
Bode, N., 83
Boles, J., 36
Bombing, 71, 245
Bonacich, E., 119
Bonn, R.L., 47
Bonnie, R.J. 137
Boomerang effect, 246
Boundaries, moral, 54–55, 58, 68, 83,
  98, 118, 123, 137, 145, 153, 233,
  243; of science, 196; of symbolic-
  moral universes, 6, 54, 250
Bourdieu, P., 181
Box, Steven, 10, 47
Braithwaite, J., 65
Brandeis, Louis, 82
Brandt, Willie, 247
Brannigan, A., 114, 204
Brecher, E.M., 137
Bribery, 71, 84, 224
Britain, 90–91, 142, 193
British, Anti-Opium movement,
  142–143; Parliament, 141; Press
  145
Bromley, D.G., 10, 98
Bruce, S., 22
Bruno, Giordano, 36, 74

Brush, S.G., 197, 199
Bruun, K., 126, 273, 158
Bryant, Anita, 121
Burg, Joseph, 224, 234
Burgess, Ernest, 80
Burglary, 7
Burkoff, Chaim, 104

California, 119, 144
Cannabis, 17. *See also* Hashish;
    Marijuana
Cantril, H., 130
Cartwright, S., 7
Cattle mutilation, 130
Center, 3, 57, 65, 72, 79, 194; and
    challenges, 60; competing, 57–8;
    definition of, 56. *See also* Collective
    conscience; Elective centers;
    Periphery; Societal community
Central message, 214–217, 219
Certified knowledge, 181, 193–195
Chauncey, R.L., 120
Chain letters, 30
Challenge(s), 3, 35, 54, 59–61, 72–74,
    204
Chambers, C.D., 25
Chambliss, W.J., 43–44
Chappequidic, 242, 247
Charisma, 49
Che Guevara, 74
Check forger, 5
Chemical coping, 25
Chicago, 38, 85, 146, 188, 274
China, 90, 119, 144–145
Christenson, R., 88
Christian F., (German movie), 105
Christie, N., 126, 158, 273
Cigarettes, 160, 171
Cisin, I.H., 167
City of David, 77
Civil, disobedience, 25; liberties,
    137; religion, 175, 275; rights, 150;
    war (in U.S.), 143
Class: economic, 260; lower, 71, 138,
    145–147, 162, 176; middle, 71, 111,

146–147, 162; working, 144; upper,
    71
Cocaine, 168
Coercion, 49
Cohen, Albert, 10
Cohen, Erik, 55, 58, 76, 233
Cohen, R.L., 83
Cohen, Stanley, 38, 43, 98, 100, 103,
    114, 121
Cohen, Victoria Ostrovsky, 237
Cole, Robert, 165
Cole, S., 200, 213
Coleman, J., 83
Collective conscience, 53, 57, 74,
    125, 269; definition of, 56. *See also*
    Center; Collective conscience;
    Societal community
Comas enfermes, 26
Confessions, 26, 28, 42
Conflict, among interest groups,
    259–260; among symbolic-moral
    universe, 35; Marxist, 42–44, 259;
    non-Marxist, 3, 42, 259–260; 263;
    theory, 40, 42–44
Congress (U.S.), 85, 161
Conklin, J., 80, 82, 117
Con man, 5
Conrad, P., 7, 23–25, 47, 87, 122,
    144–145
Conscientious objectors, 71
Conservation of energy (law of), 214
Conspiracy, 107–108, 111, 126, 128,
    237, 244
Consumer fraud, 45
Continental drift, 196
Contract, and Durkheim, 57
Control. *See* Social Control
Convictional criminal, 78
Cook, R.M., 85
Cool cat, 147
Corporate crime, 79
Corpuscular system, 201
Corruption, 80, 84, 111, 124, 224,
    250
Coser, L., 11–12, 74
Cosmic static, 189

Counter-revolutionary, delusions, 24; paranoia, 88
Court, 227, 238; as a theater, 237
Courtwright, D.T., 138, 143
Covington, J., 75, 166
Crack, 121, 168, 171
Creative deviance, 11–12
Creativity, 150
Cressey, D., 27
Crime, 38, 111; against governments, 60; by governments, 60, 72; and deviance, 47; and drugs, 161; political, 46–47, 60: street, 139, 161; types of, 71–73, 77; universal, 45; violent, 71; waves, 119–120, 130
Criminal, career, 161; elite, 83; trial, 88, 238, 243
Criminalize(ation), 24, 47, 59–60, 86, 88, 222, 229, 259
Criminology, British, 40, 42; Classical school in, 38; Marxist, 43; New, 43–44, 92; positivist, 38; radical, 44
Cromer, Gerald, 272
Cross, J.R., 114, 120, 262
Cullen, F.T., 261
Cultures, 3, 5, 9, 97, 136, 178, 248; in Israel and the U.S., 137, 174–176, 179; pluralistic, 176; and science, 181, 204; and symbolic-moral universes, 58, 253; pluralistic, 176
Cumming, E. and J., 86

Däniken, E., 202, 205
Darwin, Charles, 199
Davis, Angela, 93, 247
Davis, F.J., 66
Davis, K., 86–87
Davis, N., 42, 73
Death rays, 277
Decriminalize(ation), 51, 125, 139, 162, 165, 173, 268n.7, 274
Definition of a situation, 16
DeFleur, L., 85, 270, 274

Degradation (ceremonies), 27, 65, 221, 242, 258
Delayed recognition, 200, 213
Demand reduction, 139, 166, 168, 172–173, 177
Demonstrations, 77, 90
Depression, 217
Designer Drugs, 168, 171
Detoxification, 147
Deviance, and crime, 47, 260; and dirt, 166; a new conceptualization of, 58; definition of, 3, 59; and respectability, 84, 241; as a conflict, 48; collective definition of, 66; definition of, 4, 6, 253; functions of, 10, 55, 124; in science, 182. See science, deviance in; "hard," 7; medicalization of, 23–24, 268n.7; and motivational accounting systems, 27–31, 254; normalizing of, 67; political, 3, 13, 35, 40, 47, 53–54, 65, 74: classes of, 72–73, 256; political elements in regular, 12–13, 35, 65, 222; and politics, 12, 35, 42, 44, 53, 59–60, 73, 221, 255: positive, 10, 11; problems in sociology of, 5; purifying and cleansing from, 166; reactions to, 11; relative conceptualization of, 3, 5–14, 39–40, 47, 60, 223, 254–255; social construction of, 6, 11; "soft," 7; theories of, 5, 10. See also Crime; Deviantization; Reverse; Stigma
Deviantize(ation), 4, 7, 12, 24, 48, 55–56, 59–61, 66, 84, 86, 88, 98, 114, 120–121, 182, 205, 218, 221–222, 242–243, 254–255, 258–259. See also Crime; Deviance; Elite; Reverse
Deviant Science, definition of, 182, 201; reactions to, 205; vs. science, 201, 219; and scientists, 205
Diagram, 53–54
Dickson, D.T., 114, 118, 120, 151
Discourse, 20, 268nn.6,8

Discovery, 209, 213–214, 216–217
Distributive justice, 83
Ditton, J., 29
DNA, 280
Dodge, D.L., 10, 11
Dolby, R.G.A., 193, 201–202, 219
Dole, V., 159
Dominelli, L., 67
Dope dealers, 117
Dotter, D.L., 39, 99, 221, 255, 260
Douglas, Jack, 11–12, 53, 57, 61, 84, 202, 241, 255, 269
Douglas, M., 23
Downes, D., 157
Draft evasion, 71, 79
Dramaturgical approach, 202
Drapetomania, 7
Drift, 22
Druckman, Chaim (Rabbi), 113
Drug(s), charges, 170; and crime, 161; crisis, 85; culture, 157; damages from, 155; dirty, 172; education, 161–165, 174; encyclopedia of, 154; existential, 157; festival 107–109; free lifestyle from, 159; free society from, 156; habit, 162; legislation, 119–120, 165–166; maturing out from, 161; menace, 109, 122, 124, 161; as plague, 164; raids, 117; types of, 148; users, 5; war on, 124, 139, 158, 161. *See also* Designer drugs; Drug Abuse; Drug Use
Drug abuse, 4, 36, 53, 86, 102, 205, 260; and controversies, 152; demography, 146–149; history of, 140–146; in Israel, 103, 110–111; and morality, 151–152; patterns of, 141; and political struggle, 151–153; prevalence of, 126, 166, 168–169: in Israel, 169–171: in U.S.A., 167–169; professionals, 118, 165; social policy, 135, 138–140, 164, 173, 176, 257; theories of, 172; treatment, 158–160; among youth, 104, 111

Drug addicts: 29; 61; 67; 75;
Chinese, 69
Drugcraft, 157
Drug Enforcement Agency (DEA), 276
Drug use, 97, 138; anti, 51; leisure time, 24, 71; sociological nature of, 140–166
DSM III, 267
Duels, 9
Dumont, M.P., 122, 126, 152
DuPont, Robert, 153
Durkheim, Emile, 10–11, 15, 21, 31, 41, 53, 56–57, 74, 125, 195, 267–268
Duster, Troy, 52, 57, 118, 122, 137, 145–146

Easy enemy, 126, 158
Eban, Abba, 224
Edge, David O., 192, 215
Edison, Thomas, 154, 185
Egypt, 75–76, 124, 163
Eichmann, Adolf, 73
Einstein, Albert, 183, 190
Einstein, Stanley, 29, 270n.9
Eitzen, S., 82
Eldridge, Cleaver, 93, 245
Eldridge, W.G., 158
Election(s), 229, 239, 241
Elective affinity, 25
Elective center, 55, 58–59
Electoral assets, 244
Electronics vs. Optics (in Astronomy), 210, 213
Elite, adolescents, 11; Ashkenasi, 233–234; deviance, 80, 82; high schools, 111; scientific, 193–194
Elkana, Yehuda, 214
Ellsberg, Daniel, 82
Epstein, J.E., 85
Erikson, Kai, 39, 125, 127, 221, 261
Essentialism, 5
Ethnic, antagonism, 119; conflict, 231–233, 237; disputes, 248; fire, 238; tensions, 239; language, 237; party, 231, 246; pluralism, 137;

statements, 236
Ethnomethodology, 39, 116, 183, 198, 202
Etzel, 245
Euthanasia, 8
Evans-Pritchard, E.E., 26
Eve, 35
Evolution vs. Revolution, 200, 280
Existential: approach, 39; drugs, 157
Exploitation, 45

Fabrication, 127, 182, 273
Faked euphoria, 163
False advertisement, 71
Falsification, 182
Farrell, R.A., 10
Fauconnier, G., 31
Federal Bureau of Narcotics and Dangerous Drugs (BNDD), 120, 139, 151, 274
Feldman, H.E., 161
Feyerabend, P., 200–201
Fiddle, S., 157
Finestone, H., 146–147
Fishburne, P.M., 167
Fishman, Mark, 114, 120, 127, 130
Folk devils, 126, 157–158
Ford, Model-T, 186
Foreign currency, 224
Foucault, M., 48, 91, 152
France, 23–24
Frank, J., 69–70
Frankel, E., 201
Fraud, 182, 197; medical, 71
Free-free transition, 190, 192
Freud, Sigmund, 154, 195, 202
Friis, Harald T., 217
Fullert, J.G., 81
Fu-Manchu, 144–145
Functional equivalent, 102, 261
Functionalism, criticism of, 260–263; and deviance, 260; in sociology, 260; logic of consequences and causes in, 263; new interest in,

260; and tautology, 261. See also Neofunctionalism
Functions, manifest and latent, 262. See also Functionalism; Neofunctionalism

Galaxy, map of, 210; radio, 184; structure of, 192
Gale, H.G., 208
Galileo, 36, 74
Galliher, J.F., 114, 120, 138, 262
Gambling, 24, 29, 67, 120
Gang of four, 90
Gans, H., 262
Gardner, Martin, 206
Garfinkel, H., 27, 65, 202, 221
Garofalo, 47
Gas tanks, 238
Gay liberation, 59, 74
Geertz, C., 122, 249, 273n.9
Genetics, 199
Genocide, 8, 79
Ghetto, 146
Giddings, F.H., 60, 79
Gieryn, T.F., 204
Gilbert, N.G., 22, 23
Gladstone, William, 273
Goffman, E., 5, 29, 65, 202, 221, 244
Golan, Mati, 236
Goldberg, P., 139
Golden Triangle, 172
Goode, E., 9, 39, 99–100, 122, 137, 152, 156, 164, 221, 259
Gottlieb, Israel, 234, 236
Gould, L., 158
Gould, S.J., 199
Gouldner, A., 59, 81
Government, 80, 111, 124, 126, 128, 138; deviance and crime of, 79, 81: reasons for, 82
Graven, D.B., 162
Green, David, 112–113
Greenberg, D., 43
Grinspoon, L., 148, 156
Gusfield, J.R., 17, 66, 100, 121–122,

124, 142, 261
Gush Emunim, 76, 269n.2

Hadad, M., 104
Hagan, J., 43, 51, 146, 268
Hall, S., 119
Hall, Wesley, 163–164
Halleck, S.L., 87
Hanen, M.P., 202
Hara kiri, 8
Hare Krishna, 10, 59
Hardiker, P., 29
Har-Paz, H., 104
Harris, A.R., 10
Harvard, 165, 209
Hashish, 104, 109, 112, 137; and
  high schools, 108; users of, 124,
  163. *See also* Marijuana; Drug(s)
Haskell, M.R., 47
Hearst, Patricia, 46, 89
Hebrew University, 77, 224
Hedonism, 51, 125, 165
Hegelian, 259
Helfer, Amnon, 106
Helmer, J., 121, 152
Hepworth, M., 28, 42
Heretical groups, 243
Heroes, 74–75
Heroin, 111, 137, 139, 145–147, 159,
  161, 163, 166, 172, 273;
  experimental use of, 162
Hertz, Heinrich, 185
Hey, J.S., 185, 276
Hierarchy of credibility, 59, 116, 123,
  128, 153, 165, 183, 193, 241, 243,
  248, 275
High school, 104, 106, 111, 171
High Times, 154–155
Hills, S., 51, 58, 121, 125, 255
Himmelstein, J.L., 138, 158
Hirschi, T., 22
Hitler, Adolph, 25, 74, 238, 245
Hit man, 29
Hoax, 212
Hobbesian, 259

Ho Chi Minh, 92
Hoffa, Jimmy, 245
Hoffman, A., 158
Hollingshead, A.B., 87
Homans, Caspar, G., 83
Homicide, 7
Homosexuality, 7, 17, 24, 29, 36, 51,
  53, 56, 67–68, 121, 205, 260
Hood, Robin, 222
Horowitz, I.L., 48, 120, 153
Horowitz, T., 126–127
Housing, 74
Hughes, H.M., 157
Hypodermic needle, 143

Iceberg theory, 74
Identity, 19, 24, 27, 255; collective
  search for, 52, 67, 153; deviant, 52,
  241; of radio astronomy, 209
Ideology, 27, 42, 49, 51, 222,
  231–233, 250; conservative, 149,
  164; definition of, 122, 249,
  273n.9; and drug use, 149–158,
  164–165, 175; functions of, 122;
  and reversal of deviantization, 248,
  250; confrontation of, 151; of
  witchcraft, 26
Illinois, 188; Institute of Technology,
  188
Imperialism, 45, 92
Inciardi, J.A., 25
Indian Hemp Commission, 273
Individualism, 21, 150, 175, 176
Industrial saboteurs, 28
Ingraham, B.L., 40, 45, 60, 73
Inquisition, 26, 75, 123
Institutional violence, 29–30, 80,
  270n.9
Insulin, 280
Intent, 23, 30–31, 45–46
Interactional conflict, 260
Interministerial committee (in
  Israel), 127, 147: report of, 147
Interpretative analysis, 6, 118, 255,
  269

Invasion from Mars, 130, 271
Inverarity, J., 40, 267
IRA, 90–91, 245
Israel, 4, 29, 36, 56, 76, 90–91, 100,
    103, 111, 113, 125, 136, 162,
    169–172, 174, 178, 223, 239, 257
Israeli, army, 174; borders, 174–176;
    courts, 274; commandos, 270;
    ethos, 125; government, 102;
    judge, 175; media, 169; minister of
    welfare, 78; ministry of education,
    106–110, 112, 117; parties, 86;
    police, 84, 102, 104, 109, 116, 126,
    170, 224, 234; political figures, 224,
    247; political system, 223;
    president of, 238; prime minister,
    245; public, 101, 108; social
    structure, 223; supreme court, 104;
    supreme court president of, 238;
    system of education, 126;
    television, 104, 273; youth, 127
Italy, 90

Jaffe, J., 137
James, William, 150
Jansky, K.G., 184, 186–188, 197, 207,
    209–211, 213, 215–217, 219, 277,
    280
Javitz, R., 104
Jerusalem, 77–78, 116, 226–227, 237
Jesus, 74, 89
Jews, Ashkenasi, 232, 244, 246;
    Moroccan, 230–232, 241, 246; of
    North African descent, 226;
    Orthodox, 77, 123; Secular, 123;
    Sephardic, 228, 230, 232, 234–235,
    237, 244, 246, 269; traditional, 230
Joan of Arc, 36–37, 74, 89
Johnson, B.D., 114, 119
Johnson, D.M., 130
Johnson, L.B., 139
Johnston, L.D., 167–168
J-Phenomenon, 201
Judge, 81, 175–176, 227, 237–238
Jumping genes, 199

Junkie, 152, 161–162
Justice, 85; and injustice, 83; and
    misjustice, 85; political, 83

Kandel, D., 104
Kaplan, J., 156
Karti, Yehezkel, 110, 116
Kearney, H.F., 197
Kennedy, J.F., 139
Kennedy, Robert, 245
Kennedy, Ted, 242, 247
Keynes, 214
Kibbutz, 112–113
Kidnapings, 245
Killer drunk, 124
King, D., 155
King, R., 137
Kirkpatrick, G.R., 114, 121
Kitsuse, J.I., 51, 56, 99
Klapp, O., 52
Klein, R., 81
Kleptomania, and motivational
    accounting systems, 27
Klerman, G.L., 122, 151
Knesset, 102, 105, 109, 116–117, 228,
    234, 239, 241, 281
Knowledge claims, 205
Kooistra, P.G., 40, 44, 46–47
Koch, H., 130
Kramer, J.C., 122, 150, 158, 190
Kraus, J., 187, 189, 277
Krisberg, B., 43, 93, 271
Kuhn, T., 196–198, 212, 279;
    criticisms of, 279
Ku Klux Klan, 245

Labeling, 7, 39, 99–100, 194, 242, 255
Langer, R.M., 209
Lankford, J., 214
Larner, J., 157
LaRouche, Lyndon, 155
Larsen, N.Z., 130
Latour, B., 204
Laudan, L., 200–201

Lauderdale, P., 11, 41, 45, 125, 267
Law, contempt for, 82; criminal, 58, 125; and drugs, 84, 107, 119, 125, 137, 147–148, 158; enforcement, 172; restrictive, 151; sociology of, 51, 259
Law, J., 181
Leadership, 233
Leary, Timothy, 150
Lebanon, 113, 170, 172
Lebedun, M., 131
Legalization, 165–166
Legal–rational authority, 49
Lenin, V.I., 74
Levi, K., 29
Levi, S., 169
Levi-Strauss, C., 70, 250
Liazos, A., 30, 80–81, 84
Liberal, 107, 109, 110–111, 127
Lidz, C.W., 85, 121, 133, 152, 261–262
Liebovitz, M., 48, 120
Likud, 105–106
Liminality, 16
Lofland, J., 48, 120, 202
Loyalty, 57
Luckmann, T., 5, 55, 123, 243
Lyman, S.M., 19, 116, 202
Lynching, 8

Ma'arach, 105
MacAndrew, C., 25
McAulay, R., 203
McCaghy, C., 27, 260, 270
McCarthy, 90, 99
McClenon, J., 182, 202
McClintock, Barbara, 199
McHugh, P., 22
Macmillan publishing company, 203
Madness, 87
Mafdal, 227–228, 230, 234–236, 281, 283
Mancuse, J.C., 87
Manic reformism, 24
Manila, 276

Mann, P., 153, 164–165
Manson, Charles, 25
Margalit, Dan, 235
Marijuana, 7, 17–18, 51, 119–120, 125, 137–138, 145, 150, 153, 156, 160–161, 164–165. *See also* Cannabis
Marriage, 68, 120
Marshall, G., 29
Martyr, 239
Marx, Karl, 74, 152, 202. *See also* Conflict, Marxist
Marziano Saadia, 235
Masochistic personality, 88
Mass hysteria, 131
Masturbation, 24
Matza, David, 20–21, 93, 221, 242, 268
Mauskopf, S., 196, 202, 207
Maxwell, J., 185, 195
Mead, Margaret, 206
Meaning: abstract and Situated, 61
Medalia, O.N., 130
Media, aggressive role of, 247; electronic and printed, 112, 232; role in moral panics, 103, 107, 114, 118, 169, 271
Melting pot, 231
Mental illness, 24, 88, 163, 202, 205; and political abuse, 86–88
Menzies, R.J., 87
Merton, R.K., 193, 195, 206, 214, 262
Methadone, as a technological fix, 149; maintenance, 29; nature of 149; patients, 160; programs, 149, 160; treatment, 159
Mexican immigrants, 119
Miami, 121
Michalowski, R.J., 47
Micro-Macro link, 4–5, 13–31, 59, 222, 254
Middle East, 173
Milky Way, 276–277, 186–187, 189, 217
Miller, J.D., 167
Mills, C.R., 3, 5, 18, 27, 76

Minor, W.W., 45
Minority, 147, 150
Misinformation, 138, 159–160
Mizruchi, E.H., 48–49
Modai, I., 224, 281
Monter, W., 26
Moonies, 10, 59
Moral, agents, 17, 54; conflicts, 115; costume, 115; crisis, 99; crusade(rs), 51, 52–55, 98, 115, 120–121, 144; entrepreneurs, 51, 54–55, 65, 97–101, 114–115, 120, 137–138, 141, 152, 158; dangers, 141; degeneration, 118; deterioration, 111; language of, 59; legislation, 100; norms, 193; organization of society, 151; order, 3; position, 165; revolution, 133, 151, 153; stratification, 52–53, 59, 183, 248; superiority, 55; treatment, 70. See also Boundaries; Moral Panics; Morality
Morality, 3, 6, 35, 39, 41, 49, 50–56, 97, 253; characterization of, 50, 125; conventional, 22, 50, 72, 146; debates, 52; negotiated, 50, 53, 58; new type of, 153. See also Ideology; Moral; Moral panics
Moral panics, 4, 52, 97–101, 113–114, 116, 120, 122, 169, 257, 261; alternative explanations for, 115, 118; and collective behavior, 128–130; and fabrication, exaggeration and amplification 127, 273; and functions of deviance, 124; and mass delusions, 129–130; and social movements, 128–130; and social problems, 128–129; and sociology, 128–131; and threats, 114; at peak, 108–113; background for, 103–105; content of, 103, 120–126; definition of, 98; development of, 107–108; end of, 113; interest perspective, 100, 114, 118–120;

main themes of, 111–113; messages of, 126; moral perspective, 100, 114, 128; timing of, 103, 115–120. See also Moral; Media, role in moral panics; Morality
Moral struggle, and demography, 146–149; and drug education, 162–165; and motivational accounting systems, 156–158; and treatment and myth, 158–162; in drugs, 150–153
Morgan, P., 118, 122
Morgan, W.H., 137, 139, 143–144, 146
Morocco, 225–226, 228
Morphine, 137, 146, 273; maintenance, 147
Motivational accounting systems, 4–5, 14–31, 259; and cases of deviance, 27–30; definition of, 18; and deviance, 27–31, 254; generalized, 23, 42, 70, 124–125, 135, 233; and intent, 23, 30–31, 45–46; medical, 23; and morality, 49; by police, 106; and symbolic-moral universes, 55; and prisons, 92; and techniques of neutralization, 20. See also Accounts; Vocabularies of motives
Mugging, 119
Mulkay, M., 23, 192, 215
Multiple discoveries, 214–217
Murder, 7–8, 28
Murderers, 9, 166
Musicians, 153
Musto, D., 119–120, 138, 143, 145–146
Myers, L., 30
Mystery gas, 131
Myth, 124, 152, 158, 160

Namir, Ora, 105–106, 109, 116–118
Narcotics Bureau, 120
National Commission on Marijuana

and Drug Abuse, 139
National Institute on Alcohol Abuse
   and Alcoholism, 120
National Organization for Reform of
   Marijuana Laws (NORML), 154
National Science Foundation, 279
Natural history, 68, 136, 223
Natural selection, 172
Nature, 188
Navy, U.S., 190, 278
Nazi, 24, 238
NBC, 277
Nelkin, D., 149
Neofunctionalism, 3, 259, 261;
   characterization of, 262–263. *See
   also* Functionalism
Nettler, G., 41, 44
Neutralization, and control theory,
   21–22; of government crime, 82;
   and social control, 20; techniques
   of, 20, 93, 242, 267n.3
Neutralize, accusations, 240, 242;
   deviance, 70, 222; political
   criticism, 69; stigma, 66, 70
Neutron stars, 279
Nevada, 120
New York, 120, 155, 159, 172, 235
NIDA (National Institute on Drug
   Abuse), 153, 167
Nihilation, of symbolic universe,
   282, 243
Nixon, Richard, 85, 139, 161, 242,
   247
Nobel prize, in chemistry, 37; for
   discovery of DNA, 280; in
   medicine, 199; for peace, 37; in
   physics, 280; in physiology, 280
Norbeck, E., 41–42, 70
Normative flexibility, 11–12
Norway, 137
Nuclear bombs, 81
Nuns, 26
Nuremberg, 73
Nye, R.A., 23
Nyswander, M., 159

Objective, 61
Objectivity, 194
Observatory, Harvard college, 209.
   See also Yerkes observatory
Office of Drug Abuse Law
   Enforcement (ODALE), 85–86
Opiates, 138, 143, 146–147, 160, 163
Opium, 119, 142–145
Orcutt, J.D., 6–7, 255, 259–260
Osler, M.J., 202

Packer, V., 158
Palestine, 36, 226, 245
Pallone, N.J. 70, 75, 166
Paradigm, 197–198, 203–204, 212
Paraphilic rapism, 88
Parapsychology, 202, 258
Parents, 109, 111–112, 155
Parsons, T., 57, 198
Patinkin, D., 214–217, 219
Pauling, Linus, 37
Pawluch, D., 7, 255
PCP, 150, 161
Peled, T., 104
Pentagon papers, 82
Penzias, Arno, 213
Periphery, 3, 59–60, 72, 79
Pfohl, S.J., 10, 261–262
Phantom anesthetist, 130
Phenomenalism, 5, 253
Phenomenology, 39, 116, 183, 202
Phlogiston, 196, 198
Phoenix house, 165
Physical review, 209
Physicists, 209, 216
Physics, 208
Pilgrim America, 7
Piven, F., 5, 61, 253, 261
Planck, Max, 186, 189, 199
Plate tectonics, 196
Plato, 195
Plausible, 201, 262
PLO, 90, 113, 245
Poets, 29, 153

Polanyi, M., 197, 200
Police, corruption, 84, 270;
delegitimization of, 230, 244;
ideology, 172; in riot control, 84;
interests of, 116–117; Israeli, 56,
105, 107, 126–127, 170, 224;
military, 225; solution for drug
use, 107, 172; violence, 72
Political, crime. See Crime, political;
criminals, 45, 74–75, 269. See
Deviance, political; deviant, 61;
dissidents, 40, 88, 90–91; enemy,
152; justice, 83; prisoners, 90–93;
trials, 88–90, 238, 242
Politicize(ation), 254; of deviance,
245–248, 250; of prisons, 90–93,
245, 271
Politics and deviance. See Deviance,
politics
Pollution, 72
Polydrug abuse, 149
Pope, H., 157
Popular astronomy, 188, 197, 215,
280
Pornography, 7, 66; anti-, 66, 121
Positive exposure, 236
Positivism, 7, 38, 195
Poverty, 262
Powell, D.H., 162
Power, 39, 42, 54, 58, 62, 93, 253; of
blacks, 74; contests, 99;
distribution of, 35, 48; illegitimate,
49; legitimate, 49; legitimization
of, 3–4, 13, 49; negotiations, 58; of
reds, 74; and science, 181; and
treatment, 70
Powerful, 10, 47, 259, 268n.7
Powerless, 10, 47, 147, 153, 268n.7
Premenstrual dysphoric disorder, 88
Preston, F.W., 29
Prettyman commission, 139
Prisons. See politicization, of prisons
Privileges, 43
Proal, L., 47, 79
Probation officers, 29

Proceedings of the Institute of Radio
Engineers, 187–188, 192
Professional deviance, 79
Profiteering, 45
Prohibition, 17, 51, 66, 120–121, 125,
260
Prostitution, 24, 36, 53, 67–68, 111,
120, 145, 166, 260
Psychiatric fascism, 87
Psychiatry, 24, 28, 70, 86, 88, 163,
165
Psychoanalysis, 198, 207–208, 213
Ptolemaic worldview, 36, 196
Publications, 190
Publicity, 78
Pulsars, explanation of, 279; Nobel
prize for discovery of, 280
Purify, 166
Pushers, 159
Puzzle, 3, 201, 212
Pyromania, 27

Quantum physics, 183, 195
Quasars, 184
Quinney, R., 43–44, 269

Rabbits, 78
Rabi, I.I., 208
Rabin, Itzhak and Lea, 223
Racism, 45, 73, 79, 92
Radiation, black-body, 189;
extraterrestrial, 190; microwave,
185, 213
Radio, astronomy, 4, 184, 187, 207,
209–210, 212–213, 216–217, 258,
279, 280; engineers, 188–189, 191,
208, 210, 211, 216; extraterrestrial
emissions, 187, 216; galaxies, 184;
maps, 189, 210, 217; survey, 189;
telescope, 186, 188, 190, 211, 216;
waves, 185, 217. See also
Electronics vs. Optics;
Astronomers

Rahav, G., 104
Railroad, Southern Pacific, 144;
 transcontinental, 144–145
Rape, 88, 92
Rationality, 204
Ray, O.S., 146
RCA, 276
Reagan, Nancy, 164, 168
Reagan, Ronald, 168
Reasons, C., 138
Reber, G., 184, 188–193, 207–211,
 213, 215–217, 219, 280
Rechtman, Samuel, 224
Red brigades, 90, 245
Redlich, F.C., 87
Referees, 191, 199
Relativity, 198
Religion, and Abu-hatzira, 230–231;
 civil, 175, 275; and drug use,
 112–113; new movements, 59; and
 social control, 41–42
Retrospective interpretation, 11
Reverse, of deviantization and
 stigmatization, 222, 240–248, 258.
 See also Deviant; Deviantization;
 Stigma
Review, 199
Revitalization rituals, 90
Revlon, 224
Revolution, French, 73; ghetto, 74; in
 science, 198, 207; vs. evolution,
 200, 280
Richard, L.G., 167
Riot, 238
Rittenhouse, J.D., 167
Robins, L., 162
Rock, P., 4–5, 49–51, 53, 58, 153, 241,
 253
Rocket launcher, 277
Roebuck, J.B., 39, 71–72, 82, 99, 221,
 255, 260
Rohmer, Sax, 144
Role hybridization, 207, 219
Roman empire, 75
Rosenberg, H.L., 81

Rosenhan, D., 86
Rosenthal, Mitch, 165
Rothman, D., 91
Routine (in radio astronomy), 210,
 217

Sabag, Amos, 104–105, 126–127
Sacrifices, 9
Sadat, A., 75
Sagarin, E., 46, 67, 72, 267n.2
Salem, 26
Saint, 237, 239
Saper, A.A., 152
Sarbin, T.R., 87
Scandals, 223
Schafer, S., 5, 45, 47, 50, 74, 78
Scher, J., 161
Science, as a belief system, 196–197,
 201; challenges to, 204; and
 conservatism, 181, 198; and
 controversies in, 196, 202–203;
 crisis in, 198; demarcation of, 204;
 deviant, 4, 52, 197, 203–206, 211,
 214; definition of, 193, 201;
 deviance in, 182; disciplines of,
 181, 194; esoteric, 207; fringe, 206;
 gatekeepers of, 199; history of,
 197–198; and innovations,
 182–183, 194, 201, 204; marginal,
 206; natural, 195, 202; and
 nonscience, 201, 204, 207; normal,
 198, 201; normative structure of,
 193; orthodox, 4, 182, 193, 198,
 204; processes in, 194; pseudo,
 201, 204, 207; and power, 181; and
 resistance to change, 199–201;
 revolution in, 198, 207, 212; social,
 195; social construction of, 206;
 socialization into, 181; and
 symbolic-moral universes, 181,
 217–218; unconventional, 196, 204,
 206, 209
Schizophrenia, 87
Schmookler, J., 214

Schneider, J.W., 7, 23–25, 47, 87, 122, 144–146
Schur, E.M., 11, 39, 43, 48–49, 56, 60, 65, 67, 81–82, 98–100, 120, 221
Scientific community, 192, 208, 216–217
Scientists, 127–128
Scientology, 59
Scott, J.M., 273
Scott, M.B., 19, 116, 202
Scott, R.A., 55, 166
Scull, A., 5, 61, 253, 261
Sedimentology, 279
Self-defense, 8
Self-help, groups, 61, 67
Sensation seeking, 112
Sex offenders, 28
Sexism, 45
Sexual behavior, 68
Sexual offenses, 27
Sexual promiscuity, 111, 125
Shabac, 270
Shafir, Herzl, 224
Shame, 29, 59, 65, 84, 114, 121, 182
Shamir, Aharon, 111
Shanks, H., 181
Shapely, H., 203, 279
Shas, 282
Shils, E., 56
Shklar, J.N., 88
Shoham, G., 104
Shupe, A.D., 10, 98
Shuval, J., 104
Siberia, 75
Siegel, H.A., 25
Silver, J., 158
Simon, D.R., 82
Six Day War, 103, 124, 163
Skeptical Inquirer, 206
Slaves, 7, 79, 143, 146
Slum, 138, 176
Smith, R.W., 29, 81
Social, disorganization, 38; order. See Societies; pathology, 24, 38, 162; problems, 51, 56, 99. See also, Social control
Social control, 20–22, 171–172, 254;

and amplification of deviance, 100; external and internal, 21, 41, 268n.2; and medicine, 24; and political trials, 89; and politics, 41; and politics in Israel, 247; and religion, 41–42; and the state, 41, 268n.3; and therapy, 68–70; theory of, 40–42, 268n.2; and witchcraft, 26–27
Social policy. See Drug abuse, social policy
Societal community, 57. See also Center; Collective Conscience
Societal reaction, 39, 99, 137
Societies, complex, 6, 50–51, 53, 57–58, 62, 89, 125; mechanistic image of, 260–262; pluralistic, 6, 50, 52, 54, 89, 125; simple, 54, 57–58
Society for the Suppression of the Opium Trade (British), 142
Sociology, 4, 195; of absurd, 202; mainstream, 3–4, 6, 61, 253; structural functional, 183
Socrates, 36, 74, 89, 222
Solar systems, 203
Soldiers, 8; Egyptians, 124; Israeli, 113; U.S., 162
Solidarity, mechanic, 175, 275; organic, 57
Solzhenytsin, A., 271
Son of Sam, 25
South Africa, 91; and ANC, 90
Southern Asia, 172
Soviet Union, 75, 88, 90–91
Spector, M., 51, 56, 99
Speculative history, 202
Speedball, 148
Spiritualism, 203
Spy, 46, 71, 79, 247
Srole, L., 86
Stagner, Gordon, 276
Stahl, S.M., 131
Stalin, J.V., 74
Statistical hypothesis testing, 198
Steffensmeier, D.J., 5, 14, 253–254
Stepping stone (theory), 160

Stigma, 70; contests, 48, 55, 61; 120.
See also Stigmatization
Stigmatization, 29, 59, 65, 76, 112, 124, 152, 201, 205, 242, 258
Stivers, I., 66
Struve, Otto, 191, 206, 210, 278
Stuart, H., 29
Students, 150, 153, 164
Suasive image, 122, 248, 250
Subculture, 240, 269
Subjective, 7, 61, 259
Subterranean convergence, 21–22
Suchar, C.S., 7
Sudit, M., 104
Suicide, 8, 21, 202
Sullivan W.T., 185, 188–192, 209, 216–217, 278
Supply reduction, 139, 166, 168, 172, 177
Supreme court, in Israel, 228, 237–238; in the U.S., 81
Survival, 151
Swigert, V., 10
Swindling, 9
Swinging, 68
Sykes, G., 20, 47, 91–93, 242
Symbolic crusade, 100
Symbolic interaction, 3, 259, 263; definition of, 16
Symbolic-moral universes, 3, 5; alternative, 149; antagonistic, 245; clash of, 108, 118; compete, 203; conflict between, 123, 232; and conservatism, 164; and cultures, 58, 253; definition of, 55; and deviance, 77; and science, 181, 217–218; and type of society, 58; of Moroccan Jews, 233; and motivational accounting systems, 55, 59; negotiate, 118; oppose, 151, 203; of radio astronomy, 217
Szasz, T., 123, 126, 157

Tami, 228, 231, 237, 239–240, 281–282
Tappan, P., 80
Tax evasion, 71, 79

Taylor, I., 29, 43–44
Taylor, L., 29, 44
Teacher(s), 126
Tefferteller, R., 157
Teichman, M., 104
Tel Aviv, 104, 108, 224, 228, 238; police of, 106, 108
Temperance, movement, 66; union, 121
Teresa of Avila, 26
Terrorism, 75, 79, 83–84, 90, 245
Terry, R.M., 5, 14, 253–254
Tesla, Nikola, 185
Theft, 7, 9, 71, 245
Therapeutic community, 61, 69, 159–160
Therapeutic tyranny, 24, 87
Therapy, 68–70, 88
Thermal agitation, 187, 190, 277
Thio, Alex, 7, 47, 81–82
Thomas and Thomas, 16
Threat, amount of, 74; and drug abuse, 151; perceived, 55; potential, 48, 52, 120–121; symbolic, 74; to values, 114, 146
Thunderstorms, 186
Tobacco, 141
Tokoro, K., 73
Torrey, F.E., 70, 87
Toynbee, A., 202
Traditional authority, 49. See also Authority; Charisma; Legal rational
Traitor, 57
Transcendental meditation, 59
Transposition, 199
Trebach, A.S., 122, 156
Trevor-Roper, H.R., 27
Trivializing, 3, 253
Truzzi, M., 193, 197, 204
Turgiman, Avraham, 108, 110
Turk, A., 47–48, 269
Turner, B.S., 28, 42
Turner, Carlton, 164
Turner, N., 36
Turner, V., 16

Ufology, 196, 202–203, 205, 258
Undercover agent, 236
United Nations, 37, 91
United States of America, 4, 17, 37, 51, 71, 81–82, 85, 90, 99, 119–121, 136, 145, 162–163, 168, 172, 178, 193, 212, 257
United Yemenites (a party), 281
Universe maintenance, 55, 243
University of Chicago, 156, 190, 192, 210, 216, 277, 278
University of Wisconsin, 186
Urban Guerrilla, 46
Utopia, alcohol free, 272; analytical (Marxist) perspective of, 260

Valium, 24
Value conflict, 38, 42
Value incommensurability, 269
Vandalism, 126
Velikovsky, 202–203, 205
Verne, Jules, 154
Veteran Administration, 81
Victimless crimes, 168
Vietnam, 40, 81, 162
Vilification, 59, 65, 114, 121, 182
Vocabulary of motives, 17–18, 23, 26–27, 58–59; and therapy, 69. See also Accounts; Motivational accounting systems
Vold, 80
Voluntary, 7
Volunteers, 102
von Baer, Karl Ernst, 199

Wailing Wall, 237
Wakefield, D., 157
Waksler, F., 7, 255
Waldorf, D., 138
Walker, A.L., 85, 121, 133, 138, 152, 261–262
Wallace, A.F.C., 90
Wallis, R., 22, 201
Wallwork, E., 56
Walton, P., 29, 43
War crimes, 73, 79, 90
Washington, G., 36

Watergate, 81, 83, 242, 247
Wave length, 276
Weather control, 277
Webb, D., 29
Weber, M., 25, 49, 230, 250
Weeber, S.C., 39, 71–72, 82
Weisburd, D., 83
Weisman, R., 261
Welles, Orson, 130, 271
Wellford, C., 7
Westerhout, G., 186
Westermarck, E.A., 226
Weyant, R.G., 202
Wheaton, 188, 191
Wheeler, S., 68, 83
Whitebread, C.H., 138
White collar crime, 79, 81, 83
White paper on Drug Abuse, 139
Wilson, Robert, 213
Winick, C., 161
Witch-, craft, 25–27, 123, 130; craze, 26, 99, 157, 261; hunts, 90; trials, 89. See Drugcraft
Woody, Allan, 270
Woolgar, S., 7, 204, 255
Wright brothers, 186
Wynne, B., 201

Yablonski, L., 47
Yadin, Yigal, 224
Yadlin, A., 225
Yamit, 76
Yerkes observatory, 192–199, 210
Yom Kippur War, 247
Young, Andrew, 91
Young, J., 43, 102, 122, 150
Youth in distress (in Israel), 272

Zeitgeist, 239–240
Ziegel, B., 234, 281
Zionism, 155, 231–232
Zinberg, N.E., 162
Zola, Emil, 154
Zuckerman, H., 193
Zurcher, L.A., 66, 114, 121